D1562758

Swift Viewing

The Popular Life of Subliminal Influence

Swift
Viewing

CHARLES R. ACLAND

Duke University Press   Durham and London   2012

© 2011 Duke University Press

All rights reserved.

Printed in the United States of America on acid-free paper ∞

Designed by Heather Hensley

Typeset in Scala by Tseng Information Systems, Inc.

Library of Congress Cataloging-in-Publication Data appear
on the last printed page of this book.

For
Haidee,
Lillian Ava,
and
Stella Lucy

In the whole field of mass communication, the "hidden meaning" is not truly unconscious at all, but represents a layer which is neither quite admitted nor quite repressed—the sphere of innuendo, the winking of an eye and "you know what I mean."

THEODOR ADORNO, 1953

. . . an excess of speed turns into repose.

ROLAND BARTHES, 1957

Contents

List of Illustrations   xi

Acknowledgments   xiii

PROLOGUE Black Magic on Mars   1

ONE Subliminal Communication as Vernacular Media Critique   13

TWO Mind, Media, and Remote Control   43

THREE The Swift View   65

FOUR Mind-Probing Admen   91

FIVE Crossing the Popular Threshold   111

SIX The Hidden and the Overload   133

SEVEN From Mass Brainwashing to Rapid Mass Learning   165

EIGHT Textual Strategies for Media Saturation   193

NINE Critical Reasoning in a Cluttered Age   227

Notes   239

Bibliography   267

Index   291

Illustrations

"Black Magic on Mars!"   8

Orson Welles calls for Superman's help   10

Another hoax?   10

Bush campaign ad   15

Subliminal charm, *Vogue*   22

Wilson Bryan Key at Concordia University   37

Honoré Daumier, "The Hypnotist"   49

Without physical contact, the hypnotist implants behavior
    and belief   56

Bridging distance of beauty and mortality with hypnosis   62

Gravity tachistoscope   67

Headrest for tachistoscopic test   71

Advertisement for Keystone tachistoscope   83

Advertisement for EDL tachistoscope and controlled reader   83

Keystone Tachistoslides   85

Keystone catalogue   85

James M. Vicary   93

Graphic clutter to represent branding environment   97

James Vicary moderating a public discussion   100

Experiment adapting Univac computer to readership survey   101

Happy or angry?   109

Subliminal Projections Company, Inc.   112

Stock certificate for Subliminal Projections Company, Inc.   112

Shopper surveillance   117

The movie producer William S. Edwards with Hal Becker and
     Robert Corrigan of Precon Co.   119

Audience waving fingers to see subliminal message at Precon
     demonstration   119

Poster for *My World Dies Screaming*   121

Newspaper ad for *My World Dies Screaming*   121

Publicity effort to illustrate Psychorama   123

Gerald Mohr in trailer for *Date with Death*   123

Vicary explaining the work of Subliminal Projections Company   129

Back cover of *Beat, Beat, Beat*   135

Graphic play with embedded messages of "drink!" and "Coca Cola!"   136

Carl Rose, image for *New York Times Magazine*   138

George Price, illustration for *Consumer Reports*   140

Jack Cole, "The Subliminal Pitch"   141

Stan Freberg's commercial for Butter-Nut Coffee   145

Audiovisual pamphlet, promising special access to the world and
     speed of instruction through technological means   178

Individuality under attack: *Invasion of the Body Snatchers*   195

Title credit, *Date with Death*   212

Precon credit, opening of *Date with Death*   212

Unadvertised single frame flash of breasts, *Date with Death*   213

Cover, *Gent*   215

"New Wave in Titillation," *Gent*   215

Mad Alley's subliminal kicks in art films   215

Bursts of seemingly random images as social commentary in
     The Monitors   219

Paul (Peter Fonda) tripping on the absurdities of billboard
     advertising in *The Trip*   222

Graphic play and clutter: Marshall McLuhan, *Counterblast*   225

Information explosion as typographical clutter: newspaper ad
     for *Fortune*   233

Acknowledgments

Conversations with and commentary from the following people helped me steer clear of dead ends, redirect toward productive avenues, and clarify the destination: Blaine Allan, Darin Barney, Bart Beaty, Jenny Burman, Garnet Butchart, Bill Buxton, Barri Cohen, Scott Curtis, Jeff Derksen, Kevin Dowler, Zoë Druick, Mark Fenster, Murray Forman, Sandra Gabriele, Monika Kin Gagnon, Lisa Gitelman, Ron Greene, Lee Grieveson, Larry Grossberg, Bill Hannigan, Carrie Hannigan, James Hay, Jenny Horne, Jonathan Kahana, Peter Lester, Scott Toguri McFarlane, Lisa Parks, Dana Polan, Elana Razlogova, Corālia Reid, Gregory Reid, Carrie Rentschler, Gil Rodman, Joseph Rosen, Vanessa Schwartz, Jeff Sconce, Johanne Sloane, Eric Smoodin, Matt Soar, Rae Staseson, Jonathan Sterne, Joanne Stober, Jeremy Stolow, Will Straw, Tess Takahashi, Greg Waller, Darren Wershler, Greg Wise, Peter van Wyck, and Mike Zryd.

In addition to sharing generously his limitless knowledge of the culture of the 1950s, Keir Keightley kept his keen eyes open for useful material and sent me regular "sub spottings" over the years, some of which were true gems. I extend my fullest gratitude for his support.

No one had more impact on this book than Haidee Wasson, who read drafts, brainstormed ideas, and offered consistently enthusiastic, if exactly critical, commentary. Her influence is on every page in one way or another, and for all that she contributed I cannot thank her enough.

Research assistance came from Gerda Cammaer, Peter Conlin,

Donna de Ville, David Fiore, Antonia Hernández, Zach Melzer, Rachel Miles, Fabiana da Camara Pereira, Nikki Porter, and Mike Schulz. Heather McDougall expertly took care of the final formatting.

At Duke University Press I enjoyed the care and attention of Ken Wissoker, Fred Kameny, Jade Brooks, and Mandy Earley.

This book benefited from questions and suggestions that followed presentations at the University of Minnesota (Minneapolis), the Conjunctures Working Group (Montreal), the University of Massachusetts (Amherst), the Society for Cinema and Media Studies Conference (Chicago), and the Ryerson University Media History Conference (Toronto).

Securing image permissions can be a minefield of legal uncertainty across which one can find insurmountable financial barriers. The following individuals and organizations deserve special appreciation for their assistance, and for waiving fees to support scholarly knowledge production: DC Comics, Eric McLuhan, Michael McLuhan, Margaret Parker, Stephen Perretta (Magna Publishing), and Wendy Wintman (*Consumer Reports*).

Financial support came from the Concordia University Research Chair Fund and the Social Sciences and Humanities Research Council of Canada's Standard Research Grant program.

Chapter 3 appeared as "The Swift View: Tachistoscopes and the Residual Modern," in *Residual Media*, edited by Charles R. Acland, Minneapolis: University of Minnesota Press, 2007.

Prologue BLACK MAGIC ON MARS

The star persona of Orson Welles had many facets: whiz kid auteur, arbiter of middlebrow taste, charismatic actor, bon vivant raconteur, and tabloid darling. He was also a symbol of media deception, a status augmented by his interest in magic. Already famous for his innovative stagecraft and recognizable as the mysterious baritone radio voice of "The Shadow," he captured national attention, and found an enduring place in the history of media effects, with the Mercury Theater's radio broadcast on 30 October 1938 of H. G. Wells's classic *The War of the Worlds*, rewritten by Howard Koch as an on-the-spot radio documentary. Welles was able to bamboozle reportedly thousands into believing that an invasion of aliens, and the destruction of cities along the eastern coast of the United States, was real. Accounts of people telephoning loved ones, dashing for safety, crashing automobiles, and praying madly helped contemporary commentators see the response as a genuine mass panic. In their scholarly account of the incident, *The Invasion from Mars: A Study in the Psychology of Panic* (1940), Hadley Cantril, with Hazel Gaudet and Herta Herzog, described "a panic of national proportions," terrorizing people from "Maine to California."[1]

The broadcast came at a time of rising attention to ideas about media influence, especially on the part of scholars. Before the establishment of a lasting institutional presence for the study of mass communication after the Second World War, media research appeared in any number of disciplines, including psychology, sociology, and political science. The movement toward consolidation of this research into a single discipline was evident in the late 1930s, as interdisciplinary research programs worked toward a formalization of what mass media research might be. Especially influential in this endeavor was the work of the Rockefeller Foundation, which invested in research and cultural programs that included live theater, film, broadcasting, libraries, microphotography, and museums. Among the enterprises that the foundation supported was the Princeton Radio Research Project (PRRP). Beginning in 1937 the project undertook cooperative research ventures with business in order to understand listeners' activity. The Viennese labor and statistics scholar Paul Lazarsfeld, who arrived in the United States in 1933, was the director of the PRRP, which included as associate directors Frank Stanton, director of research at CBS (later to become its president), and the Princeton psychology professor Hadley Cantril.[2]

With these rumblings of research activity Welles's momentous Halloween broadcast was timely, arriving as a new social science configuration was beginning to be institutionalized. On the night of the broadcast Stanton, working coincidentally at the network that carried the Mercury Theater's weekly radio play series, received a late-night telephone call from Lazarsfeld, who described early reports of panic incited by the show. As Stanton tells it, the two knew instinctively that the broadcast provided a golden opportunity to study an unusual media effect.[3] They composed a survey and interview questions, and set out to gather as much information as possible on the thinking of the audiences. Fortuitously, while the Welles broadcast originated from New York City and was carried by ninety-two stations, the setting of the radio play was New Jersey.[4] As Cantril put it, "Since it happened that the study was conducted from Princeton, the interviews were almost all made in the northern New Jersey area for reasons of supervision, convenience and economy. Fortunately the first Martian machine landed only a few miles from the source of the investigation."[5] Thus a fledgling research project was near the site of the most intense hysteria. The Mercury Theater broadcast was a star-making media phenomenon for Welles, the researchers at the PRRP, and the upstart academic discipline of communication studies.

Cantril's study involved a combination of research methods, including comparison with CBS's own survey, as well as Herta Herzog's detailed descriptions of individual subjects. The researchers attempted to itemize and weigh the panic's precipitating factors, including personality traits, income, religious convictions, and education. Cantril deemed these factors "causal," which he admitted did not fit traditional behaviorist definitions of the term.[6] Cantril discussed the historical context of totalitarianism and low degrees of economic security elsewhere in the world, particularly emphasizing that the crisis in Europe was the main news story in the fall of 1938, which made invasion topical and deadly serious. More generally, the researchers reasoned, the rapidity of twentieth-century scientific discovery had been mystifying to most and appeared to come from "a universe of discourse completely foreign to the perplexed layman."[7] Many technologies seemed otherworldly to people, and "the telephone, the airplane, poison gas, the radio, the camera are but specific manifestations of a baffling power."[8] In this, Cantril felt, there resided a potential fatalism concerning the state of the world and one's ability to do anything about it—a general sentiment and assessment of contemporary society shared, interestingly enough, by another member of the PRRP, Theodor Adorno. The study pointed to some determining features of suggestibility, though it concluded that there was no single cause of the panic. Those most frightened did appear to share a lack of criticality about the broadcast. Avoiding laying blame at the feet of media corporations, and appropriately acknowledging the complexity of mass panics, the study's summation stated, "It is not the radio, the movies, the press or 'propaganda' which, in themselves, really create wars and panics. It is the discrepancy between the whole superstructure of economic, social, and political practices and beliefs, and the basic and derived needs of individuals that creates wars, panics or mass movements of any kind."[9] With this explanation Cantril fell neatly on the side of trusting the protective and restorative powers of education and reason, citing the irrationality of lynch mobs as a dangerous counterexample.[10] Arming people with the critical abilities necessary for rationality was the pressing project for mass democratic society, not to mention for the new field of mass communication research.

It is curious that such a careful and expansive analysis was prevented by its liberal presumptions from investigating the sentiment at the root of the broadcast panic. Why was belief in, and concern about, new technologies of travel and communication (not to mention species!) understood as a mark of irrationality and gullibility? In the late 1930s spacecraft would not reach the Red Planet for several decades, but they would

eventually get there and elsewhere. Only a few decades earlier a significant bestseller and curiosity in the field of psychology was Théodore
Flournoy's *From India to the Planet Mars*, which recounted in detail a person's recovered memories of past lives and space travel, and in so doing
was taken as a document of the complexities of the unconscious mind.[11]
The authenticity of the material may have been questionable, but the
book is an example of the power that parapsychological ideas had long
held for lay and expert audiences alike.

The reasonableness of expecting the unexpected, and the unimaginable, was lost on Cantril and his co-authors. Quite directly, Cantril pro-
nounced the escapist popular pleasures of movies, pulp stories, gaudy
décor, and religious fanaticism to be signs of psychological deficiency.[12]
This conclusion is all the more questionable if one considers how loosely
the authors used the term "panic." To measure the extent of the panicked
response, a survey performed six weeks after the original broadcast asked
respondents whether they had found the broadcast frightening: 28 percent said they had thought the drama was a news report, and 70 percent
of those people claimed to have been frightened or disturbed by what
they heard. This translates into 1.2 million of the estimated audience
of 6 million. Cantril went further, presuming that the true number was
higher because people would likely have been embarrassed to admit to an
interviewer that they had been frightened.[13] Given the structure of Cantril's analysis, it is impossible to separate fright from panic among his
respondents, or to identify the relation between the two. Moreover, his
survey included the question "How do you account for the fact that many
people became frightened and hysterical during the broadcast?"[14] Thus
Cantril's research presumed panic rather than documenting whether
panic is the most accurate term for what happened.

Further and most obviously, the broadcast coincided with Halloween,
an occasion that welcomes mischief and mayhem, which should lead us
to wonder if people were willfully seeking out terrors. At what point is
a listener who is scared by a Halloween broadcast contributing to a so-
called national panic? Is being frightened by a ghost story really evidence
of gullibility or psychological deficiency? In his work on nineteenth-
century magic shows, Simon During argues that one characteristic of
the modern era is the organization of different forms of understanding
for entertainment and for scientific truth: "consumers of modern culture
learn to accept one set of propositions in relation to the domain of fiction,

and another in relation to the everyday world."[15] The ability to accept unbelievable events in fiction that one would not accept in life speaks of an attentive and agile mind; it is a modern condition of being able to temporarily give oneself over to impossible and improbable things. And yet, as During notes, believing too much or being too much taken with the illusion can mark someone as childish or irrational, in contrast to the ironic disposition of someone fully rational. Might a similar split have been in operation on that October evening in 1938? The logic of Cantril's study conflated belief in the veracity of the drama with real panic. A telling problem was that Cantril's interview questions did not allow for the possibility that listeners might have been aware that they were listening to a play and yet were frightened at the same time.[16] The methodological and conceptual limits of the survey tell us something of a deeply ingrained view of mass audiences as lacking the ability to tell the difference between representational fiction and actuality. People were presumed to be easily manipulated, anti-liberal, and irrational.

Interestingly, from the material that Cantril and his colleagues provide in their study, it is apparent that there was some degree of critical involvement by the listeners, though it may not have been developed and applied appropriately. People may have been recognizing the codes of a news broadcast, reasoning that there could have been technologies and scientific achievements not yet publicized, that invading armies were real prospects, and that the first reports of a sudden invasion would be only partially reliable. Indeed, some respondents said that they had understood the broadcast as a report of an invasion by earthly enemies, having missed or not heard the "Martian" part.[17] Soon enough, global war was to begin and killing machines were about to be released that at this point were just the province of the imagination. If a comparable event had occurred during the nuclear anxiety of the late 1940s or the space race of the late 1950s, and some people had mistakenly assumed that their annihilation was nigh, would we have come to the same quick agreement about the irrationality of the masses?

Even with their nuanced conclusions, Cantril and his colleagues were echoing a stable idea about the innate feebleness of the modern mass mind. At least since Gustave Le Bon's *The Crowd* (1895), mass populations have been understood as fearsomely irrational and antidemocratic entities.[18] Significantly, this idea was not the purview of élites and ivory tower thinkers alone. As Jeffrey Sconce puts it, the "War of the Worlds" broadcast has become "a familiar chapter in the popular memory of American media and stands even today as a common reference point for critics who wish to invoke a parable of the media's awesome power over its audiences."[19] This famous production circulates ideas about the workings of masses, minds, and media, and the notion that psychological deficiencies were revealed in the panic continues to be a dominant popular understanding. This story of mass panic, in condensed and varying forms, has been retold with great frequency, with each retelling reinscribing the certainty of mass irrationalism sparked by popular culture. In Frank Morgan's comedy vehicle *Hullabaloo* (Edwin L. Marin, 1940), an old vaudevillian performer causes a national panic with a fictional on-the-spot news radio broadcast, "Battle of the Planets." Kenneth Fearing's novel *Clark Gifford's Body* (1942) depicts a revolution in the United States during which the first step is to capture the radio stations. Describing the necessity of this tactic, the title character explains, "You may remember certain historical political broadcasts, so-called panic broadcasts with the most amazing results."[20] When the voice of God first interrupts regular radio broadcasting in the film *The Next Voice You Hear . . .* (William A. Wellman, 1950), one of the explanations is that it might be a hoax, or, as one character says, "maybe it's one of those Orson Welles things."

Beyond the prominent place that the Mercury Theater's performance occupied as a sociological puzzle in the history of mass communications research, the tale of the panic took on a life of its own and, as Sconce observes, circulated as an idea about media influence. Here is one additional example. Over a period of two years beginning in 1947, Orson Welles was filming *Black Magic* (Gregory Ratoff, 1949), an Italian–United States coproduction based on the novel *Memories of a Physician* (1850), by Alexandre Dumas, *père*. The novel introduces an enduring character, the evil hypnotist Cagliostro, whom Welles plays in *Black Magic*. The film was a big-budget period piece, and it was rife with production troubles that saw Welles act as an uncredited director. Overdue and over budget, the film nonetheless had unusually elaborate publicity. For instance, the distributor, United Artists, paid the athlete Shirley May to swim across the English Channel with "Black Magic" "well displayed across her ample bosom," as one report put it. Though she didn't quite make it to France, the ship following her was rechristened *Black Magic*.[21] This stunt coincided with the film opening on four hundred screens across the United States.[22]

One particularly curious promotional tie-in for this film saw Orson Welles and Superman team up to battle a Martian invasion in the comic book *Superman #62* (1950). "Black Magic on Mars" opens with a besieged, swashbuckling Welles in period costume, sword in one hand and radio microphone in the other, yelling, "Watch out, Earth! The Martians are coming." Eggheaded Martians in military uniforms threaten Welles with ray-guns. Superman, strangely drawn to appear smaller than Welles, arrives to save him by blocking a ray-gun's blast. The opening expository panel explains that Welles unearths a plot to invade the Earth, but when he tries to alert his home planet, "the world laughed, for this was the second time that Orson was crying wolf." Only Superman believes him and comes to the rescue of Welles, the Earth, and *Black Magic* (though even Superman couldn't protect the movie from becoming a monumental box office dud).

After this opening full-page illustration, the comic's narrative begins with Welles and an opponent dueling on a rooftop. Welles loses the battle and falls to a cobblestone street below. Out of frame, someone yells "Cut!," revealing that we are on a movie set and that Welles is fine. This is the final scene in *"Black Magic,* starring Orson Welles as the sinister magician, Cagliostro." There is a ball that evening, and everyone is told to remain in costume, so the incongruous dress remains for the entire story. Welles and his co-star Nancy Guild take a drive into the Alps, reminding us of their casting: "I enjoyed playing the villainous Cagliostro!" "And I enjoyed playing Marie Antoinette!" These first panels are vaguely documentary in design. They mirror other behind-the-scenes promotional texts, like on-set shorts, presenting the work involved with movie making. But whatever naturalism had been developed to this point evaporates when Welles and Guild come upon a rocket ship, which an inquisitive Welles immediately enters. Nearby, unbeknown to our movie stars, is a crowd gathered to watch the launch of the first rocket to Mars. Welles hears the countdown, but it's too late and he is trapped inside. In outer space he looks back at a receding Earth and says, "When I fooled the world with my Martian invasion broadcast—I never dreamed *I* would invade Mars myself!"

Stepping out of the ship onto Martian soil, Welles is greeted by English-speaking, Nazi-attired midgets with a "Hail, Welles!" They explain that they have studied Earthlings with their version of television and got to know quite a bit about Orson. He is brought to the leader, the

"Black Magic on Mars!," *Superman* #62, 1950, DC Comics, all rights reserved.

Great Martler (get it? Martian Hitler), who reveals his plan for universal conquest, starting with Earth because of its uranium. Martler then offers Welles a job as propaganda minister on Earth. Rebellious as ever, and still holding his sword from the film shoot, Welles forces the dictator into the Martian broadcasting studio. He sends out a message to Superman that is distributed to other Earth-bound television viewers: "This is Orson Welles, broadcasting from Mars." Listeners at the *Daily Planet* scoff, "It's another hoax!" and "Whom does Orson think he's kidding?" Only Clark Kent knows that he must investigate. Now as Superman, he editorializes: "That hoax of Orson's, years ago, about a Martian invasion, sure backfired!" A panel shows domestic listeners commenting that the warning about a Martian attack is the funniest show in ages, "better than Bob Hope." Apparently the gullible listeners of the 1930s have become the skeptics of the early 1950s.

Superman arrives on Mars, and Martler, still recruiting, immediately offers him a job, but the attack on Earth has already begun. The Man of Steel chases down the invading rockets but finds that many are mirages. There are too many for him to hunt through to find the real rockets before they reach their destination. Meanwhile Welles performs stock magic tricks to dazzle and confuse the Martians, throwing flames and making a rabbit appear. Superman uses the gravitational pull of one of Mars's moons to trap the invading forces, and Earth is saved from the Martian invasion. In perhaps the most bizarre moment in this odd tale, Superman operates a television camera while Welles, having learned a few words of Martian, holds up the unconscious Martler to broadcast a ventriloquized message of peace to Mars: "There must be no more war. We will stay on our own planet!" One Martian viewer comments, "Great news! Now we can go home to our families! I never did want to fight anyway!" It seems that we share gullibility about the media with other planets and species. And it seems that tricks with broadcasting integrity are still a successful part of Welles's repertoire.

Back home, Superman returns the original rocket to the scientists, who are happy to receive the data from Mars. Welles appears as planned at the costume ball. Nancy Guild asks him, "Tell me, Orson, was your broadcast this time another hoax . . . a publicity stunt . . . or the truth?" "Ask Superman!," he replies. And in the final panel, a news story written by Clark Kent titled "Orson Welles Really on Mars!" is in the trashcan,

Orson Welles calls for Superman's help, "Black Magic on Mars!," *Superman* #62, 1950, DC Comics, all rights reserved.

Another hoax?, "Black Magic on Mars!," *Superman* #62, 1950, DC Comics, all rights reserved.

his editor bellowing out of frame, "This is a newspaper—not a science-fiction magazine! Get down to 10th and Western and cover that fire."

This crazy little fantasy, light in tone, relies upon background knowledge of Welles's notorious career and of the character he plays in his forthcoming movie. The comic character is an amalgam of movie star illusionist and movie character mesmerist. This hybrid creature appeared elsewhere, beyond the world of comic book fancy. For instance, the review of *Black Magic* in the *LA Times* voiced these themes yet again, declaring, "Orson Welles Pulls Mass Hypnosis Act on Us All."[23] Here we confront a startling figuration for the cultural producer: the artist as a deceiver, manipulator, and liar. The idea that the "War of the Worlds" was a hoax, as the Superman story states, is intriguing. It presupposes that the panic broadcast was an "untruth" constituting a betrayal of trust rather than a scary story misinterpreted by an audience that had misplaced its critical abilities. This, even though all that the Mercury Theater was entrusted with was the telling of a rousing science fiction tale. Welles seems to have been confused with the leading character in his most famous film, the tragic and unscrupulous newspaper magnate Charles Foster Kane, who creates a singing sensation of his shrill-toned wife with ridiculously lavish front-page praise and invents a war by reporting a fabricated incident as reality ("You provide the prose poem, I'll provide the war"). *Citizen Kane* (1941) is in many ways a story of media fallibility, following the calculated efforts of Kane to shape public opinion and the doomed enterprise to report on the "real" Kane that frames the entire film.

The narrative of the comic "Black Magic on Mars" plays with media manipulation and illusion by alternately concealing and revealing it to the reader at several points: the expository page invites the reader to remember the famous "hoax"; the first three panels situate the story in eighteenth-century France, only to be exposed as a movie set; the Nazi Martians have a ministry of propaganda, for which the master manipulator Welles would apparently be the ideal director; Welles makes a truthful but fruitless warning to Earth—though only Americans are shown—meaning that the members of the diegetic audience see themselves as being able to break through the falsehoods of broadcasting, while the comic reader, following the logic of the fantastical tale, knows that they are being dangerously smug; the Martians create illusionary rockets to confound Superman; Welles's prestidigitation confuses his alien foes, who turn out to be "superstitious savages"; the deceptive broadcast by

Superman and Welles to the Martian people is media manipulation for peace; the editor of the *Daily Planet* kills Kent's story of the invasion, thus hiding the truth from the public; and Welles, his co-star, and his new movie are swept into Superman's universe, his character's anachronistic costume reminding readers of the promotional specificity of the *Black Magic* tie-in. The comic's joke operates at multiple levels of meaning and encourages a process of judgment about various kinds of media manipulation: reference to an actual "hoax," images of naïve audiences, illusions used as weapons, tactically productive instances of media deception, and story selection by a newspaper editor.

In this elaborate representational play we see that Welles's 1938 broadcast is a recognizable reference for the very concept of media manipulation, even in this most popular of forms, the comic book. This is the starting point for the present study: the powerful and lasting way in which popular ideas about media effects circulate and are used to negotiate and understand the role of media in our lives. This book examines popular ideas about media, in particular the idea that certain kinds of media texts can have an immediate and shockingly effective impact on what is thought to be a roundly uncritical public. In a somewhat contradictory way, a thinking mass public imagines an "unthinking" one. Welles's production has been incorporated into a chronology of popular understandings of media effects and irrational masses. But there are other historical moments in that chronology, ones that reside as quiet influences upon our understanding of contemporary media technology and its users. This book is about one of those moments.

Subliminal Communication as Vernacular Media Critique

As news events, presidential elections in the United States are unusual creatures. Resources and funds flood the proceedings over a lengthy period, shaping coverage of the extensive primary process and the presidential race proper. Control of the presentation of the candidate and party underlies every decision. The orchestration of image and platform enlists experts in population profiling, spin doctoring, speechwriting, event planning, media consulting, and commercial producing. Managing the release of information to the media, the actions and appearances of the candidate, and the impressions made upon those most likely to cast a vote are tasks confronting any election team.

Nothing ever goes exactly as planned. Campaigns seek to capture media and public attention, and doing so results in high visibility for the statements made and the responses given by candidates and their representatives. Consequently, even the smallest verbal slip, inexpertly located phrase, or unthinking gesture can produce headlines and talk-show topics. Just as presidential election campaigns strive toward careful coordination, the attention they receive from the numerous print, broadcast, and Internet news agencies makes unpredictable developments ever more likely.

The election of 2000 made a generous deposit in the bank of unforeseen complications and challenges. The razor-close tallies in Florida, the subsequent recounts and stories of tampering, and the interventions of the Supreme Court were the culmination of months of news oddities. The CBS news anchor Dan Rather rambled all through election night, treating the audience to bewildering aphorisms like "If a frog had side pockets, he'd carry a handgun" and "This race is tight like a too-small bathing suit on a too-long ride home." Media outlets jumped to call races that later required embarrassing retractions, prompting Rather to blurt out, "We've lived by the crystal ball, we're eating so much broken glass." Not letting a tragic plane crash hamper his campaign, the deceased Democratic candidate Mel Carnahan remained on the ballot in Missouri and won, beating the incumbent John Ashcroft for a Senate seat. Ralph Nader's presence on the presidential ballot assured that at least some media attention turned his way, if only to try to discredit his run by portraying him as an idealistic buffoon. George W. Bush's malapropisms became legendary. While deepening a popular mistrust of the democratic process, the elections left behind new phrases that are now stuck in the popular lexicon, "fuzzy math" and "hanging chads" among them. And one of the strangest twists was Al Gore's accusation that the Republican Party was using subliminal suggestion in its advertisements.

In a slick television spot on Bush's plan for affordable prescription medicine, we see the candidate meeting with, speaking to, and shaking hands with senior citizens. The music hits a dramatic "duh-dum" punctuation as the commercial introduces Al Gore's competing "big government plan." Gore is not shown in contact with people but as a distant talking head on a television monitor, thus reiterating visually a theme running through the campaign—that Gore lacked warmth. Where the words "affordable R_x plan" and "the Bush plan" appear steady and clear as they accompany images of Bush, the flashing and unsteady phrases "interfere with doctors" and "bureaucrats decide," against a black background, graphically represent Gore's proposals. Momentarily, only parts of these words are visible, so that for a fraction of a second one reads only individual letters rather than whole words, including, most notoriously, the letters "rats" before the word "bureaucrats" appears.

Democrats challenged the Republican ad, declaring that imperceptible, embedded messages were sneaky and unfair. With them Bush's campaign was attempting to manipulate voters without their awareness, so the claim went, and some members of Gore's campaign distributed information on subliminal communication to support their accusation.

Bush campaign ad attacking Gore's prescription drug plan, 2000. Author's collection.

A minor flurry of media reports followed over the next few days, offering denials from Bush, no comment from Gore, assessments of media experts, and historical backdrop to the concerns about subliminal messages. The ad's producer, Alex Castellanos, maintained that the appearance of "rats" for 1/30 of a second was purely accidental, though he admitted that once it was brought to his attention he did not pull the spot. Many found his claim of ignorance implausible. Castellanos had previously been the target of comparable accusations. An ad that he prepared for Senator Jesse Helms in 1990 presented a white job applicant being informed that although he had superior qualifications for a job for which he had applied, he had lost out to a minority candidate because of a "racial quota." Augmenting the race baiting, a strange blemish appears on the letter read by the frustrated job seeker, a marking that resembles a black hand. Kathleen Hall Jamieson described this visual tactic as a form of negative campaigning intended to elicit a visceral response.[1]

The "rats" spot ran 4,400 times over two weeks in sixteen states, and the Republican campaign spent approximately $2.6 million on it.[2] When asked about the accusations on a tarmac in Florida, Bush replied, "Conspiracy theories abound in American politics. I don't think we need to be subliminable [sic] about the differences between our views on prescription drugs."[3] Bush feigned naivety, saying that he did not know what subliminal suggestion was, let alone know how to use it for campaign purposes. As if to emphasize the point, Bush mispronounced the word "subliminal" repeatedly. Whether deliberate or not, his verbal blunder was met with wide ridicule. How could he not know what the term is or even how to pronounce it? Was he as intellectually underdeveloped as had been suspected, or was he insincere in his protestations? The talk-show host David Letterman ridiculed Bush, saying that the mispronunciation made him wonder, "Gosh, do you think this guy is 'electimable'?"[4]

For a short time Bush's "subliminable" was homologous to Dan Quayle's "potatoe."

The Republicans pulled the ad, insisting that they had always planned to do so and that the controversy played no part in their decision. Bush and his representatives dismissed the affair as a ridiculous effort to distract from the real issues. The Federal Communications Commission (FCC) took the ad seriously, and investigated 217 stations that had aired it to decide whether they had willfully participated in deceptive broadcasting. Several months later the FCC concluded that no penalties were in order.[5] Playful responses followed as well. To an admiring Letterman, his guest Geena Davis, a Democrat, bawdily described her sheer dress as a subliminal ad for Bush.

Whether an accident or an effort to deceive, this incident is not unique. There were similar charges by Andrés Manuel López Obrador against the right-wing candidate Felipe Calderón in the Mexican presidential elections of 2006, in which the color scheme for a popular soft drink and its publicity mirrored those of Calderón's party. Opponents saw the similarity as a sneaky way to circumvent campaign spending limits by a corporate supporter of Calderón.[6] Similar suspicions in 2008 that John McCain's and Barack Obama's campaigns had planted hidden messages in their spots were rampant on the Internet, with occasional, temporary appearance in the mainstream press. Both MSNBC and ABC reported on McCain's "subliminal" attempts to link Obama with terrorism, Islam, and hypersexuality. Here the accusations referred to design choices rather than fleeting images: the messages were entirely visible, but their use was seen as unethical because they appeared as innuendo. The concern was not just the unfair ideas, but some sense that the subtlety of their appearance had an unrecognized effect upon the viewing audience, and ultimately upon voters.

The public understanding of the "subliminal" may range from the exact to the fictional, but it is undoubtedly part of popular language. Survey research published in 1983 found that 81 percent of respondents claimed to have some knowledge of subliminal advertising, of whom 81 percent believed that subliminal suggestion was being used by advertisers and 44 percent believed that it had some effect on buying behavior.[7] Surveys in 1994 demonstrated that approximately 75 percent of the population in the United States believed that advertising companies used subliminal advertising, that they did so to influence consumer behavior, and that the technique worked.[8] The gap between the questionable scientific validity of subliminal influence and the popular response to it is often captured in psychology textbooks. For example, one definition of subliminal advertising notes that it "has been received with much excitement but as yet little empirical support."[9]

Subliminal suggestion has a particularly strong association with sexuality. In his history of sex in advertising, Tom Reichert writes, "When I mention my research, many people I speak with say, 'Oh, yeah. You're researching naked people in ice cubes.'"[10] For their part, advertisers have long complained about the tenaciousness of the concept because it gives a tainted impression of their business. In light of the debate that swirled around the initial revelation of their existence—to be discussed at length in coming chapters—subliminal techniques deserve a place in the history of advertising, and the last thirty years of advertising scholarship have obliged. Stuart Ewen devoted a page and a half to a specific illustration of subliminal advertising in *All Consuming Images*.[11] Bryon Reeves and Clifford Nass included a short chapter on the topic in *The Media Equation*.[12] James Twitchell offered a mocking take on subliminal advertising, though he nonetheless concluded that "the real work of advertising *is* subliminal. But not in the sense of messages slid below the surface, but subliminal in the sense that we aren't aware of what commercial speech is saying."[13] In a book on composition, iconicity, and the indexicality of magazine advertising, Paul Messaris included a dozen pages on the debate and research on the persuasiveness of subliminal elements, taking a relatively neutral position on the issue. His section on subliminal advertising continued with a discussion of the connotations of gender, social status, and youthfulness.[14] Max Sutherland's mainstay text on the relationship between the unconscious and advertising presented itself as a practical and reasonable exploration of the topic, unlike other works that see advertisers as possessing "witch-doctor-like powers."[15] Sutherland represented many frustrated advertisers and advertising researchers when he wrote, "I hate the term 'subliminal.' There has been so much nonsense talked about so-called 'subliminal advertising' that there is always the risk that when I talk about it, I will fuel the uninformed hype."[16] He explained that a better term for the phenomenon was "shallow mental processing," implying that the audience was barely attentive to stimuli and that the advertising was therefore very ineffective.[17] An editorial in the *Journal of Advertising Research* complained of the persistent allegations: they were a problem not because "they make advertising into more than it is, though they do, but because they make ad recipients less than they really are. It is as great a sin for a critic of advertising to depict the consumer as an unthinking pawn as it is for a creative to treat his or her audience condescendingly."[18] The author called upon critics and advertisers alike to "melt the ice cubes of doubt and suspicion" on the topic.[19]

Little melting has occurred. On an anecdotal and personal level, teachers of media and cultural studies know that the idea of subliminal influences enjoys popularity among students, a popularity that curiously exists side by side with the view that the media have little or no impact upon an individual's thinking. Teachers regularly confront and attempt to manage the pedagogical frustration associated with these contradictory beliefs. On the very final day of a very bright undergraduate's education, in the very last class, after years of being introduced to the intricacies of representation and cultural practice, the student might well say, "But of course they use subliminal messages to get us to buy things." After an obligatory moment of self-loathing — "What have I done wrong?" — I am usually tempted to respond firmly that the student's assumption is unfounded and that there are more pressing forces for us to consider in the organization of power and culture. Truthfully, this is not a very satisfying response. In the end we still have to confront the appeal and longevity of the concept. For present purposes, the veracity and strength of a "subliminal" effect is a different and, I would venture, secondary concern. The empirical evidence of its reappearance in multiple situations, and its relatively elastic application, suggests that subliminality resonates as a common explanation for certain kinds of quotidian media experiences.

And what is supposed? Well, many things. Literally and traditionally, the term "subliminal" refers to something below (sub) the threshold (limin) of awareness or consciousness. But for many, it does not just describe this realm. Colloquially it implies that something can happen to us without awareness, unconsciously, and thus, as it is popularly used, the word harbors a thesis about effect and causality. For psychology, the subliminal marks a distance between perception and sensation, hypothesizing that some sensations may not be perceived but can nonetheless find their way into our minds. You may not see, feel, hear, smell, or taste something, but that external phenomenon might still register unconsciously and you may be able to respond to it. You may, in essence, discriminate without being aware of what you are discriminating about.

In the nineteenth century comparable theses about the traffic between awareness and unawareness proposed that there is some realm below our waking, conscious state, which for some theorists becomes a self below the self. As will be covered in chapter 2, the term "subliminal" was first used to refer to this newly discovered unconscious. Under certain conditions of hypnosis, itself a new term in the nineteenth century, it was believed that access to this self below the self could be gained. And exploration of this new continent—and the metaphors of colonialism were often astonishingly plain—involved, as with other forms of conquest, not only knowing but exploiting and manipulating. In other words, as we will see, influence and control are embedded in the history of the empirical and theoretical investigations of the limits of sensation and perception. This history subsumes the history of technological apparatuses designed to verify, measure, and ultimately manipulate that zone between sensation and perception, in particular the apparatus known as the tachistoscope, which flashes images and text at extremely high and variable speeds. The history of the tachistoscope is dealt with in chapter 3.

According to the psychological literature, while extremely limited subliminal effects have been shown in laboratory settings, their more general significance continues to be a matter of contest. Certainly evidence of the persuasive power of subliminal stimuli is scant if not nil. Some psychologists claim to have found evidence that subliminal influence is a form of priming, or readying people for behavior and belief, rather than direct influence, while others indicate that the findings in this area are contradictory, unconvincing, or inconclusive. Psychological research has been able to chart the variability of the perceptual threshold, and has on occasion shown slight affective relationships attributed to subliminal stimuli. This effect is only evident when stimuli are close to the sensation threshold, that is, close to a recognized point at which people normally see, hear, or feel. The further from this threshold one goes, the weaker the chances of charting any form of sub-threshold perception, a result which leads some to consider that the supposed effect, when observed, is in fact *not* subliminal to some particularly fast-sensing subjects. In addition, there has been no consistent demonstration of a causal relationship between stimuli and behavior. In the rare study that has recorded subliminal perception, the research methods have been challenged, or the effect was not reproducible, moving the explanation for whatever effect was shown away from the subliminal command.[20] For example, one of the most frequently cited studies demonstrated a rise in thirst levels among samples subjected to subliminal flashes of "Coke" and "drink Coke."[21] This finding was drawn into question when a replication of the experiment did not show any such results, leading the authors to conclude that the first experiment had resulted in a type 1 statistical error, or "false positive."[22]

Even as the first public debates about subliminal communication were taking root in the late 1950s, psychologists and social critics knew that for the most part there was "no subliminal perception mechanism known to science that can effectively coerce human action against the conscious, deliberate will of the people."[23] One researcher argued in 1960 that measuring subliminal perception varied depending on the recording procedures, from multiple choice to open response, and was led to conclude that evidence of subliminal perception was nothing more than a methodological quirk.[24] Despite this, in a comprehensive review of the psychological experiments in subliminal perception from the late 1940s to the early 1960s, William Bevan remarked upon a shift in focus from efforts to establish its existence, along with perceptual defense mechanisms, toward efforts to measure its effects upon behavior.[25] Others have attempted to provide definitional boundaries, with "subception" meaning automatic, reflex-like discrimination, and "subliminal perception" meaning discrimination without awareness, implying some sort of unconscious assessment. W. J. Rees argued that the phenomenon labeled "subliminal perception" was not perception at all, but an "epiperceptual" event.[26] Norman Dixon drew a distinction between "unconscious perception," in which one is simply unaware of an existing stimulus—like that dripping faucet that one doesn't hear after a few minutes—and "subliminal perception," in which the stimulus is below a threshold of sensation.[27]

With such variations in the definition of subliminal perception, it is not surprising that psychological research should have failed to show instances of the phenomenon, however mild, without challenge and contrary evidence. But this lack of agreement among researchers has done little to forestall an array of references to the subliminal in nonscientific realms. Popular references to the subliminal display an imaginative breadth and a porous definition. Often subliminality connotes sexual magnetism, as though subliminal influences work like a form of erotic hypnosis, encouraging libidinal activity without awareness of the trigger. For instance, in the heat of the first warnings about subliminal communication, only two months after the concept drew popular attention, *Vogue* in November 1957 presented a "subliminal" dress, "'tapping out its message to the subconscious,'" implying that the garment transmitted secret sexual signals.[28] Subliminal as an adjective can describe the cluttered product of advertisers who squeeze full and enticing impressions into limited ad space, or the compositional busyness of certain design styles, such as the jumbled typography of *Wired* magazine and Zone Books, or any number of unreadable creations by the designer Bruce Mau. Even among advertisers, whom one might assume to be particularly versed in what subliminal advertising is—if only to refute it—the term is unstable. Attempts to capture the frequency of subliminal messages among advertisers consistently show that it is rare.[29] And when survey subjects report knowing of the technique being used, they tend to refer to subtleties in design, color, and layout.[30]

The subliminal message can be a secret nod between producers and fans, rather like the "Easter eggs" buried in video games that open up new images and information once discovered. There are supplementary materials embedded in works for those who care to seek them out, as with the opening sequence of *The Simpsons*, where you can see how much baby Maggie costs, after being scanned at the supermarket checkout, only if you freeze the frame. It can figure as the mischief of bored designers and animators who slyly insert, for instance, a frame of Jessica Rabbit naked in *Who Framed Roger Rabbit* (Robert Zemeckis, 1988), a frame of Mickey Mouse for a tiger's face in Disney's *Aladdin* (Ron Clements and John Musker, 1992), or the detailed phallus as a castle turret on the videotape cover of *The Little Mermaid* (Ron Clements and John Musker, 1989).

The word "subliminal" has referred to the rapid shock-edits used to establish an unsettling tone in film, as with the flashes of male nudity and the Brad Pitt character in *Fight Club* (David Fincher, 1999) and the much-mimicked jerky snippets of text in the credit sequence for *Se7en* (David Fincher, 1995). Many ads parody this shock-edit style. For example, the "Sub-lymon-al" commercial for Sprite (2006) presented rapid, unevenly edited, technologically enhanced brainwashing scenes to connote ironically unconscious desires for a thirst-quenching product, ending with a split-second shot of the command "Obey." Some directors have used the flash-edit to evoke a vaguely "retro" sensibility, as in the music video for *Last Night* (2001) by the Strokes, in which the "live" television appearance of the band, the glaring electric crispness of videotape, and rapid inserts make the video seem to have been shot in the 1970s.

Subliminal charm, *Vogue*, November 1957, Condé Nast Archive, © Condé Nast Publications.

Subliminal suggestion is a topic that arouses the suspicions of the conspiratorially minded, such as those who spread rumors about messages bursting from the Microsoft clouds that used to appear when a computer booted up. Or it can accompany quasi-religious revelations, such as claims that the smoke from the second plane crashing into the Twin Towers contained the image of the face of Satan and a thumbs-up gesture. The studio experiments conducted by the Beatles in the mid-1960s sparked what would become outrageous accusations in the 1970s and

1980s of the powerful influence of "back-masking" in music, prompting worries that hidden commands could compel people to violent extremes. Additionally, a good deal of the pseudo-psychology self-help industry relies on people's belief in subliminal powers. The annual amount spent on video and audio material that employed subliminal methods to treat habits from smoking to overeating, and that promised life improvements like inner peace and fabulous sex, was estimated at $50 million in 1990.[31] The presence of this material on the Web, on eBay, and in bookstores has expanded this industry greatly over the last two decades.

Subliminal techniques of political and marketing manipulation have regularly appeared in popular narratives for decades. The film *Fight Club* makes the insertion of pornographic subliminals into films part of the rascally ways of Brad Pitt's character. *The Ring* (Gore Verbinski, 2002) makes unseen messages on a videotape both the source of the murderous proceedings and the resolution. The original source novel spends time explaining the subliminal messages embedded in the tape and how they work.[32] *Josie and the Pussycats* (Harry Elfont and Deborah Kaplan, 2001), *Subliminal Seduction* (Andrew Stevens, 1996), *Looker* (Michael Crichton, 1981), and *Serenity* (Joss Whedon, 2005) all use subliminal control as part of their denouements. In *Agency* (George Kaczender, 1980) Lee Majors plays an advertising writer who battles the evils of commercial mind control. A new owner of his company, played by Robert Mitchum, is using subliminal messages in television spots to influence an election. While the film actually focuses on office intrigue, as the takeover of the company leads to the mass firing of employees, Saul Rubinek's character has the opportunity to record his concerns about the influence of advertising on society. In this film the subliminal technique becomes the filmmaker's pretext for engaging in the flash-editing of some parody ads for fictional products. In many of the films treating the hidden influences of corporations, the social concern translates into stylistic flourish.

In fact genre fiction, especially horror and science fiction, is fond of subliminal themes as a narrative device. Dean Koontz, an author whose work regularly depicts brainwashing and mind manipulation of various sorts, focused on subliminal suggestion in *Night Chills*.[33] In it latter-day Nazis are planning a takeover of Kuwait in order to disrupt oil markets, and have their sights set on achieving complete social domination through a mix of drugs and subliminal influences. As the head villain Salsbury declares, "We will simply contaminate our enemies' water supplies with the drug, then inundate them, through their own media—television, radio, motion pictures, newspapers, and magazines—with a continuing series of carefully structured subliminals that will convince them to see things our way."[34] Though this mind control will give the Nazis access to a veritable army of assassins, along the way Koontz devotes considerable attention to gruesome episodes in which subliminals are used to control women for humiliation and rape. Not all novelistic uses revel in such sadism. Theodore Roszak's *Flicker* offers a phantasmagoric history of motion pictures as a grand conspiracy dating back to the Middle Ages, told as a scholarly hunt to track down the mesmerizing films of an enigmatic B-movie director, Max Castle, whose filmic tricks involve a variety of effective subliminal images and scenes.[35] Tom Robbins in *Still Life with Woodpecker* gives us the world inside a package of Camel cigarettes, a story that resonates with rumors of embedded images in the product's packaging. In the novel Leigh-Cheri studies the package to find a woman and a lion hidden in the drawing of the camel—this a message from the redhead of Argon.[36]

Episodic television has deployed subliminal influences so regularly that it is practically a cliché for the format. *The Family Guy* and *The Simpsons* have both had episodes on subliminal advertising. Four decades earlier the Green Hornet contended with the same influence in the fashion industry in a two-part episode, "Beautiful Dreamers," in 1966. The detective Columbo trapped a murderous advertising researcher and author of books on subliminal advertising, played by Robert Culp, when he deduced that subliminal influences assisted in the crime, in *Double Exposure* (Richard Quine, 1973), and CHiPs contended with subliminal messages in rock music in the episode "Rock Devil Rock" (1982). In the 1980s the sweep of the series *Max Headroom*, known for its titular postmodern avatar, ran to the revelation that the oppressive world of the near future was maintained by nearly imperceptible advertisements called "blipverts" that could make people explode.

The season première of *Saturday Night Live*, on 11 October 1988, introduced a new recurring character, Kevin Nealon's Subliminal Man. The scene is set in an advertising office, at which Mr. Maloney (Nealon) arrives late to hear his boss say, "Your subliminal advertising campaign was due yesterday." While making excuses, Maloney says under his breath, "your fault," "Mets tickets," "company car," "promotion," and "vacation." To the secretary he mutters, "hot sex," "Four Seasons," and "push-up bra."

The humor and absurdity of the skit lies in the paradox that this "subliminal" technique is quite obvious and audible to all, and that it works miraculously, with all characters giving Maloney whatever he wants. The audience finds itself aligned with Subliminal Man; we hear the commands but are not affected by them. The joke is not simply about manipulation, but about effortless manipulation. It's a lazy person's idea of how to get ahead in the world.

The term "subliminal" can appear in scholarly and literary writing as a shorthand way to characterize what might not be immediately apparent, from ideology to subtext. For example, Robert Stam, Robert Burgoyne, and Sandy Flitterman-Lewis described one goal of deconstruction in film analysis as exposing "the subliminal ideological influences of the cinematic apparatus and of the dominant cinema."[37] Characterizing the methods of what he calls "multiperspectival cultural studies," Douglas Kellner asserts that "one needs to draw on a spectrum of critical methods, as some are better to grasp class, others to conceptualize gender and sexuality, and yet others to articulate race, myth and symbol, subliminal and latent dimensions of culture and so on."[38] David Bordwell refers to screenwriting manuals that describe visual motifs reiterating character as a form of "subliminal communication."[39] Even writings about product placement in film and television often borrow the term, among which Mark Crispin Miller's research has had an agenda-setting influence.[40]

Overall, subliminal influences occupy a place in the storehouse of things that are known of the contemporary world. The range of uses, definitions, and appearances presented above shows both play and worry about the concept. And it is fascinating that much of what is characterized as subliminal is not subliminal in the strictest meaning of the term. Instead, in popular usage the term refers to the unknown, the imperceptible, the almost imperceptible, the subtle, the quick, the backgrounded, or simply the connotative. In compiling these usages my intention is not to police the term, but to provide evidence of its malleability and its handiness for reflexive critics of commercial culture, serious commentators, satirists, and designers alike. In the end, and partly because of all the fun and fantasy evident in its usage, I maintain that the popular sense of subliminal suggestion represents a nexus of concerns that include the nature of language and signs, the concept of the unconscious, the tugs between subject and agency, and the daily experience of media culture in late capitalism.

The idea of subliminal perception and influence has migrated from experimental psychology to become part of the popular lexicon. William James wrote in *Varieties of Religious Experience* (1902), "If the grace of God operates, it probably operates through the subliminal door, then."[41] By this James proposed that divine influence could only be exerted without awareness, without perception, deep in the unconscious mind. This made forms of religiosity, for James, signs of something else altogether, most likely a response to concrete conditions in one's life. By way of comparison, in *Bedazzled* (Stanley Donen, 1967), Peter Cook as the Devil says to Dudley Moore, "God doesn't like to work subliminally; he prefers the soft-sell." The quip implies that God prefers to influence in a gentle rather than manipulative fashion, echoing the concept of free will even as the line compares God to a huckster. Something had happened to this term, moving from a way to refer to the unconscious in James to an advertising technique in Cook and Moore. Further, the reference in *Bedazzled* is a marker of the term's popular recognition, indicating that a contemporary film audience of the mid-1960s was presumed to be familiar enough with the meaning and connotations of the term to be in on the joke.

Indeed, the multiple and competing definitions of "subliminal"—as something that influences, something that one doesn't notice, something that one sort of notices, and something that one can notice but likely doesn't think about—may be taken as one indication of the concept's import. This popular familiarity is historically specific, for until late 1957 the subliminal was exclusively the purview of psychology, psychotherapy, and psychical research. Since then, however, there has been a lasting connection between subliminal effects, advertising, and popular media. The years leading to this historical pivot point of 1957, and the subsequent years into the mid-1960s, will be examined in chapters 4–7. Following the subliminal thesis into popular cultural texts, chapter 8 treats the place of media mind control in fictional narrative and the related rise of an aesthetic of flash-editing among filmmakers in the 1950s and 1960s.

Since the late 1950s several controversies have reinvigorated the circulation and evaluation of the term "subliminal," of which Gore's accusation against Bush and worries about back-masking in music are just two examples. Nevertheless, to see only panics would be to overlook the ordinariness of the term. In fact there is little if any panic, despite the beliefs about the use and effectiveness of subliminal techniques that appear to be held. We find ourselves closer to Kevin Nealon's banal cynic than to Koontz's Nazi sadist Salsbury in these matters. Nevertheless, the subliminal has folkloric status. It has occupied a prominent and lasting place in popular culture for the last five decades, with no sign of that run abating. The word's meaning is not stable, and even its core premise is not agreed upon. Some of its implications are variously seen as obvious and as controversial, as commonsense and nonsense. As a contentious set of ideas about critique and insight, the "subliminal thesis" recommends that one must pay very close attention to the demands and influences lodged in our media environment. In this respect the thesis is reflexive and is not far from the beliefs of current advocates of "media literacy." Appended to, and supporting, the subliminal thesis are numerous stories and testimonies, some recent and some half-remembered from previously told tales. Uttering the word triggers this vaguely apprehended chain of ideas, evidence, and events. The term has a life, a career, and a trajectory. Put simply, it appears that the debate about subliminal influences is one that we keep wanting to have.

When I say "we" I don't mean media scholars, who have generally left this phenomenon aside. Indeed, the emergence of communication studies involved pushing aside totalizing models of how the media influence people, of which the subliminal thesis is an extreme case, to make room for limited-effects models. To be sure, Paul Lazarsfeld and Robert Merton described a narcotizing dysfunction of media, and Daniel Lerner helped formalize terms for the psychological warfare programs of the postwar period, called "sykewar."[42] But the core research contribution of this first generation of mass communication scholars was to introduce the inherently reasonable personal influence, two-step flow model, in which the impact of media messages is contingent upon a range of local factors. When introduced in the 1940s this so-called dominant paradigm rested upon a hypothesis that the media have at best limited effects upon people, who instead turn to their immediate social networks and contacts to verify what they see, hear, and read.

But outside the academy, massive-effect models of media influence continue to thrive. From the budding high school media critic to the sci-fi fan, young audiences in particular are taken with narratives of the awesome power of media messages. Subliminality is notable as a popular explanation for the operations of media, mind, technology, and representation. Other, comparable terms related to popular media include "virtual reality," "social media," "copycat crime," "media addiction," and "lowest common denominator." Highly visible concepts such as these fuel an experience of sharing among people. They perform what might be thought of as a form of *cultural work*, by organizing, limiting, circulating, and directing ideas about phenomena. They shunt free-floating experiences toward explanations. They link random observations with what are understood to be common values and beliefs. This cultural work effectively anchors aspects of social life that otherwise might seem unintelligible and even chaotic.

These concepts are nodal points; they are sites of meeting and condensation at which the culture recognizes issues, gives them attention, and tenders a convenient synthesis of elaborate and ambiguous circumstances. Identifying core idiomatic expressions indicates both preoccupations and manners of comprehensibility. These expressions are vehicles that capture attention and shape it. Particularly vibrant concepts can be thought of as *command metaphors*, insomuch as they not only bear rich connotative veins that typify and characterize an era but also guide and mold thinking. Conversely, command metaphors steer our conceptual life away from other characterizations and accounts. They may begin as nomenclature, yet through use and over time they become modes of announcing particular explanatory frameworks. While all symbolic units and forms may hold the potential to be command metaphors, only a select few become recognizable shorthand terms for a place and time, and become topics of debate, anxiety, fun, and investigation. Cultural authorities weigh in on them, concerned citizen groups form to demand action on them, public representatives stake out political territory and assess what resources are to be put in service of them, and popular audiences come to some sort of understanding about them.[43]

Analytically, the prominence of command metaphors offers a point of entry to shared concepts and concerns. Though the metaphors are not uniformly salient across a population, one finds evidence of their context-specific life in newspaper and magazine editorials, feature articles, thrillers, satirical movies, speculative science fiction, situation comedies, legislative hearings, scholarly surveys, patent applications, business records, nonfiction bestsellers, retrospective characterizations of an era, talk-show appearances, interviews, lawsuits, websites, and computer games. Core expressions can uncover cultural obsessions and their organizational structure. They link up—articulate—strings of associations, arrays of suppositions, chronologies, and judgments of value that are constitutive of how we understand a phenomenon. Command metaphors are the frontline of an elaborate apparatus of discourse—talk and expression—that produces understandings of the world and through which decisions are taken and institutional initiatives launched. With command metaphors we are able to chart what people are thinking about, but also what they are thinking with, to paraphrase the economic historian and communication theorist Harold Innis.

The deviance amplification of moral panics does not capture what I want to call command metaphors. Though there may be relatively bracketed periods of intense anxiety, and such periods may serve to introduce and disseminate what will become new and recognizable explanations for a phenomenon, lasting concepts also exist in less fraught, and more everyday, situations. Command metaphors have multiple operations and valences, and are pulled provisionally into various political agendas. Their application in the service of right-wing social programs is simply not as cleanly delineated as it is described for moral panics. Angela McRobbie has suggested provocatively that we have moved into a phase of endless moral panics, to a postmodern circuit of perpetual social anxiety spurred on by a saturation of images, and that such panics are now part of the everyday institutional workings of journalism.[44] This assessment intuitively matches a sensibility of the last few decades that has involved both a rising social anxiety and a moralistic assessment of its root causes and solutions. Yet it is disadvantageous to lose the specificity of the term "moral panic," which helps us designate periods of intensification. For the present case, though there may be an ongoing worry or suspicion about subliminal manipulation, or for that matter about copycat crimes and addiction to video games or social media, these ideas have also been incorporated into less alarmist sites in myriad ways. Without any sustained widespread panic about it, the subliminal thesis resides in the popular lexicon as a latent explanatory energy, as the embers of anxiety ready to be stoked into a flame periodically, and as a familiar bogus thesis available for comic or dramatic application. Having said that, this is not a causal, idealist, or constructivist cognitive model in which the word brings the thinking and the world into being. On the contrary, the term is a vessel for a range of conditions of popular alertness and attentiveness. The lasting power of the subliminal and its status as a myth of media effects means that it has a kind of adhesive component; it is good at attaching itself to situations. Malcolm Gladwell has called this feature the stickiness factor, which is the degree to which ideas are memorable and salient to people, and likely to spread further among larger populations.[45]

What does the term harbor? What meanings and ideas has it bundled and introduced into popular idiom? What cultural work has it done? As a preliminary claim, concepts like the subliminal thesis do not magically appear. A confluence of historical circumstances is needed to launch, authorize, and sustain the popular life of an idea. And for the subliminal thesis, this launch involved the movement of ideas from the generally cloistered world of scholarly and scientific research into popular knowledge. Of course, the apprehension of a field as vast as something that we call popular culture is no idle pursuit. Media theory and cultural criticism examine the nature of social life in light of the complexities of mediation, that is, the wonderful and frustrating fact that something is always in the way every time we communicate, whether that something is language, technology, or distance. A subfield focuses directly upon the most pervasive and quotidian dimensions of our communication universe found in popular culture. So enmeshed are we in the world of signs and culture that it can be a challenge to think outside our representational net. We inhabit a world of things and works not of our own making, and an astonishing number of these items travel great distances very quickly to find us in our streets, offices, schools, cars, and living rooms. Regardless of the varying circumstances of media abundance, in the final moment decisions must be made. Family, market, politics, business, leisure, and education all demand an organization of priorities and preferences, even under conditions of extreme austerity or rhetorical impossibility. The choices made during the course of daily life may be emotionally, rationally, or socially motivated, or may only be a chimera of choice. They may be determined by restrictions of resources or efficiency; decisions may result from scarcity, time sensitivity, financial constraints, and limited options. From the inconsequential quandary to the life-altering dilemma, everyday life requires us to make up our minds, to come to an agreement or not, and to follow a path, however haphazardly or irrationally, even if for but a short distance.

One consequence of the entwinement of media culture with quotidian existence is that an escalating number of those dilemmas, both petty and considerable, involve our cultural life. What television program to watch, where to place the computer, where to see a specific film, what book to read, what magazine to throw out, which newspaper subscription to discontinue, where to find traffic updates, to whom to send e-mails and texts, what website to bookmark, what CD to burn, what program to record, what app to download, what DVD to purchase—the list extends infinitely as our reliance upon media technology becomes a central organizing feature of home and work. These are decisions about hardware, software, and social networks. They are decisions made for others, in particular children, in which case competing generationally defined ethical and aesthetic universes may collide. But this is not just a matter of consumer choice. These decisions are determining features of participation in public life. At root are core issues for a politics of the everyday: what source does one trust, what manner of affiliation does one take up, and what energy does one direct toward knowable goals. The choices extend to the way we think about the media in our midst, and how we assess, reject, celebrate, or critique the media, technologies, and texts with which we engage.

Put differently, given the sheer abundance of media, from telephone to television and from print to pay-per-view, a range of ways of talking about them and our relation to them has developed. Few people today are without opinions and arguments concerning advertising, the Internet, social media, television, music, and movies. Regardless of their scholarly legitimacy, these ideas harbor elaborate conceptual frameworks and beliefs. We fortify ourselves with modes of critique, building up strategies of evaluation, justification, restriction, and interpretation. Opinions and arguments, whether specific to a text or to a technology, abound. They may be fleeting and unelaborated; they may spring from unexamined presumptions; and they may not be consistent with previous stances. Nonetheless, they are evaluative discourses that are expressive and critical. The everyday interpretative process is a form of intellectual labor; the work of speaking and of argument construction includes sifting through reigning ideas and situating oneself within the often unacknowledged grains of commonsense. This informal intellectual labor helps to construct and circulate senses of the real and of truth. The Italian Marxist Antonio Gramsci wrote in the 1930s that though all are intellectuals, "not all men have in society the function of intellectuals," drawing the analogy that frying an egg or sewing a tear in clothing from time to time does not make one a cook or a tailor.[46] To be blunt, we are all media critics, though only a few of us are paid as such.

Any teacher of media or popular forms can attest to the extraordinary range of understandings that students of any age bring to a classroom. More often than not, students confront their instructor with a dizzying cornucopia of knowledge about media, including detailed experiential data, elaborate hierarchies of value, and works running from the immediately recognizable to the obscure. One of the frustrating challenges facing teachers of media and popular culture is that the wildly escalating number of works at their fingertips makes it physically and financially impossible to keep up entirely. Believe me, I've tried. Students accrue their own pockets of attention and commitment that surpass anything a single soul could ever totally command. Now, it is unfortunately true that many instructors fail to acknowledge the deep experience and expertise of students, or that many proceed to disabuse their students of internalized knowledge, believing that knowledge to be mistaken or in some way inappropriate. Often students' assortment of expertise will go unrecognized as such, and will be actively debased, with the sincere intention of leading students to a better, more effective, and more socially productive critical framework. I would hazard that the result is at best a bifurcated critical apparatus, such that students learn what mode of critique is appropriate for the classroom, all the while continuing to live through and build upon existing cultural commitments and connoisseurship—becoming highbrows in the classroom, lowbrows in life. At worst, students depart with an all-too-familiar anti-intellectualism after witnessing the chasm between "true" critical analysis and their own experience.

It is more respectful, efficient, and advantageous pedagogically to take seriously whatever understandings are already in play. What explanatory frameworks have currency for a population and for an affinity group? In what ideas have people invested themselves and their intellect? At a basic level, this is the raw material with which one works as a teacher, community organizer, or political activist. Meeting people where they already live, and stretching one's own hierarchy of value accordingly, opens up a whole new terrain of understanding, and potentially of action. Taking popular culture as well as its fans and audiences seriously is not a project of celebration or apology. It does not mean that critical standards must be set in reserve or lowered to accommodate all. Taking the popular in its entirety seriously means that the work of the cultural critic is not the work of moralizing or prescribing. It is the work of engagement.

I present this argument because I have become convinced that some of the fundamental lessons of cultural studies have been forgotten. Though I hesitate to advocate a return to an earlier era, as though the last fifty years of cultural analysis had not happened, I do think that some reminders are in order. The anti-disciplinarity of cultural studies has led to some compromises, and the invigoration that the field has enjoyed from multidisciplinary *frottage* has been matched with a process of thinning out its critique. For many, cultural studies has become the Oakland of the academy—no there there—and the voices decrying its irrelevance have been rising in volume.

One of the basic lessons of cultural studies concerns the everyday lived nature of cultural life, which cannot be reduced to brute economic explanations nor textualist acrobatics. The caricature, especially in the United States, has been that cultural studies is about locating and championing resistance. And to be sure, there is a substantial number of uncritical analyses of empowering leisure. However, the attacks—some justified, others merely ideological screeds—have often missed the root contribution being made, or declared that the root lesson does not need restating. What is that lesson? It is that structures and understandings of the world reside in part in the most proximate and ordinary forms of cultural life. Many critics have tossed out this insight, resulting in the parallel return of clever, closed textual play and crude economic determinism posing as forms of cultural studies.

This book endeavors to examine the historical circumstances and ramifications of a slice of ordinary culture. It is a study of *vernacular cultural critique*, that is, a popular and common language of interpretation and analysis. The mere existence of vernacular critique, however, tells us little, and the task at hand is not to justify its explanatory function, as though there were no role for additional educational and critical agendas. Studying a popular idiom should not be mistaken for an argument of nonintervention, leading toward an irresponsible mass autodidactism. Let us bear in mind that language—popular and specialized—operates by arresting further steps in critical analysis, placing barriers on evidence and logic, as much as it facilitates expression. Such towering figures as Raymond Williams, Stuart Hall, Pierre Bourdieu, and Michel Foucault differently remind us that ideas structure views of the world, organizing people into hierarchical cohorts, and leaving other ideas and people aside. This is no place for *laissez-faire* pedagogy.

Gramsci has inspired much writing on commonsense, not all of which puts to good use his insight that the popular realm of sense is not a unified category. There are many "commonsenses," and they spike in currency and impact among certain populations and at certain times, and even so, there are likely to be counter-positions as well. Commonsense tends not to be a realm of agreement, let alone consensus, but rather of agreement to the terms of debate. Some have misread Gramsci's concept of hegemony as a leveling out of struggle, as the totalizing win of ideological forces, rather than more accurately as a space organizing the conflicting views of the world and the populations represented by those views. The coexistence of multiple ways in which sense is made means that the validity and authority of explanations are neither equal nor stable. Some explanations of phenomena are seen as more complete and more convincing than others, only to be unseated by subsequent explanations. But not all earlier understandings that previously enjoyed high credibility vanish once the newer view appears. Raymond Williams wrote of "practical consciousness" as a form of thought that is of "a present kind, in a living and interrelating continuity," as distinct from "official consciousness" and "false consciousness."[47] Capturing the lived dimension of thought, and its organization into intelligible patterns, "practical consciousness" builds distinctive understandings of the world, allowing us to live with and negotiate the historical moment in which we find ourselves. For our immediate purposes, a particular vernacular cultural critique, one that focuses on media, represents an effort to wrestle with bewildering and troubling circumstances. This effort may not necessarily be taken up as the only or best approach to those circumstances, but it is present even as a popular process of comprehension-seeking continues.

The arrangement of discourses producing the concept of the "subliminal" is historically specific. What groundwork prepared the way for the initial appearance of the term, and what fueled its continuing consideration by popular critics, novelists, editorialists, and filmmakers? A documentary impulse animates this book: the process of collecting, collating, and stocktaking to amass an archive of uses and appearances of this vernacular media critique. Accordingly, this historical record includes newspaper articles, books, book reviews, editorials, magazine cartoons, television shows, motion pictures, comics, short stories, and popular novels. Archival research on educational equipment manufacturers, advertising agencies, media producers, and legislative committees supplements these popular sources. The portrait is an approximation, not a magic mirror offering telepathically direct access to distant circumstances. Yet a panoply of instances, encompassing the serious and the ridiculous, the credible and the unbelievable, allows me to document the currency and longevity of the subliminal thesis.

As distant as the accusation of subliminal media influence may be currently from scholarly criticism, it was not always so. At various times the accusation has had glancing encounters with legitimacy, and there are still academically acceptable analyses that reiterate claims to reveal secret, hidden, but powerful meanings, especially found in some forms of structuralist ideological critique. The steps between Judith Williamson's widely respected semiotic *Decoding Advertising* (1978), Doris-Louise Haineault's and Jean-Yves Roy's psychoanalytic analysis *Unconscious for Sale* (1984), the feminist "exposé" of advertising *Killing Us Softly* (Margaret Lazarus and Renner Wunderlich, 1979), and presumptions of subliminal manipulation are few and short. More directly, in the 1970s it was not unheard of to find Vance Packard's *The Hidden Persuaders* or, though much more rarely, Wilson Bryan Key's *Subliminal Seduction* on course syllabi. Even in the 1980s the first-generation communication researcher Orrin Klapp placed Key and the persistently respectable political economist Herbert Schiller side by side as examples of critics of advertisers.[48] As kooky as Key's work is, I continue to be impressed by the range of people—students and scholars, designers and lay people—who know his work, and can reproduce, however imprecisely, his illustrations of orgies embedded in ice cubes, phantom phalluses peeking through *Playboy* centerfolds, and obscenities scratched into Ritz crackers and the arms of babies. We can find today other authors making deliberate and calculated attempts to replicate Key's pseudo-psychological muckraking style on the same topic.[49] For many his work is *the* defining voice on hidden manipulative messages, a voice that is seen by turns as authoritative, radical, and nonsensical.

Key was a professor in the mass communication and journalism department at the University of Western Ontario when he wrote his most famous work, *Subliminal Seduction*, in the early 1970s. In it he tested his ideas about subliminal messages on students. As Jack Haberstroh tells it, "On the first day of class he would have his students lie on the grass and stare at the clouds. And then reveal to Dr. Key the creatures they saw in the clouds. Properly 'prepared,' on the next day of class they stared at magazine advertisements. And the creatures that lurked in the artwork."[50] This anecdote reveals much about Key's assumptions. For him, finding a shading or shape that resembles something else is the same as discovering its psychological impact and the suspect intent of a creator. The problems with Key's logic only compound from there, beginning with the incredible conviction that hidden and embedded messages were more powerful and direct than manifest ones. And of course, there are no controls or limits to the messages he discovers. When asked to stare at an image and find something in particular (creatures or phalluses) in whatever imaginative fashion we wish, we should not be surprised by what comes into view.

In an effort to prop up a weak set of propositions, Key rooted himself in loosely configured versions of critical theory and psychology. He opened *Subliminal Seduction* with epigraphs from Marshall McLuhan, Herbert Marcuse, and Norman Dixon. The book's mix of psychology and semiotics provided shaky ground for what amounts to a physiological argument for the working of symbols. Key juxtaposed James Vicary's marketing "tests"—which I discuss in full in the coming chapters—Rudolf Arnheim's theories of perception, Carl Jung's work on archetypes, Wilder Penfield's neurology, and numerous uncited psychological experiments with vaguely Proppian readings of the patriarchal structure of *The Mod Squad*, the comic strip *Peanuts*, the Boston Bruins, the White House, and the Beatles (before *Sgt. Pepper*, he qualified). The book notably contained numerous examples, many with accompanying illustrations, from magazines and advertisements that purportedly reached the unconscious through imperceptible, embedded words and icons. Not solely an argument about popular culture, Key's book extended his ideas to reveal the hidden influences of the fine arts, a direction that he pursued in *Subliminal Ad-ventures in Erotic Art*.[51]

Subliminal Seduction was a portrait of conspiratorial efforts to manipulate and control the mass population on the part of industry and government. The book's subtitle made clear the author's intent to expose a hidden agenda of advertisers: *Ad Media's Manipulation of a Not-So-Innocent America*. Their efforts, Key maintained, consisted of accessing the unconscious, that rich trove of desires, fantasies, and taboos, transforming people into a hypnotic state of suggestibility. Hypnosis metaphorically described techniques of manipulation, frailties of consciousness, normal functioning of the mind, and conditions of media consumption. At times Key claimed that the human mind was naturally primed for hypnotic

Wilson Bryan Key
at Concordia University,
Montreal, 1976. Author's
collection.

intervention, and at other times he saw the effects of the contemporary media environment as especially hypnosis-inducing. He summarized: "Media has the proven, completely established ability to program human behavior much in the same way as hypnosis."[52] The border between hypnotic suggestibility and individual will disappears, leaving a characterization of mass society as always already splayed open to a puppetmaster's command.

For its radically interdisciplinary spirit, the book has no figure looming more prominently over it than the Canadian media luminary Marshall McLuhan. In a book that is spotty at best in its source noting, Key directly cited McLuhan more than any other author, and he acknowledged the influence of McLuhan's seminars at the University of Toronto, which Key attended at roughly the time when *Subliminal Seduction* was germinating.[53] For Key, a quote from McLuhan provided a succinct warrant for the study: "advertising is a subliminal pill designed to massage the unconscious."[54] Elsewhere Key asserted, erroneously, that McLuhan had never directly discussed the subconscious or the subliminal, and claimed immodestly that McLuhan expressed embarrassment to Key for not having thought of the topic first.[55] More accurately, Key acknowledged that "Subliminal or unconscious perception, and its effects upon cultural value systems and behavior, was the central focus for much of McLuhan's writing."[56] Indeed, as will be discussed in later chapters, McLuhan was one of the first media scholars to incorporate the subliminal thesis into his research, doing so over an extended period and thus influencing major currents in media criticism. After the enviable book sales of *Subliminal Seduction*, McLuhan retrospectively described the subject of his first book, *The Mechanical Bride: The Folklore of Industrial Man* (1951), as "the subliminal effects of advertising."[57]

McLuhan shared Key's concern about the powerful influence of the world of commerce. As he put it in the opening lines of *The Mechanical Bride*, "Ours is the first age in which many thousands of the best-trained individual minds have made it a full-time business to get inside the collective public mind. To get inside in order to manipulate, exploit, control is the object now."[58] The book is an epigrammatic, modular study of the sea of images and commodity appeals in which people live. McLuhan targeted speed and clutter as primary conditions that challenge the senses and the mind, leading most drastically to a trivialization and banalization of death. He asserted that the problem with George Orwell's *1984* was that the author had mistakenly situated it in the future rather than the present.[59] Diagnosing the hazards of a mechanized society, automatism, desensitization, and the confused gender roles of the contemporary culture, McLuhan paid attention to unconscious forms of manipulation. With the Nazi death camps haunting its pages, *The Mechanical Bride* implicated the advertising industry in the problem of speed and clutter. As McLuhan saw it, the agencies "give spatial form to hidden impulses . . . breaking through into the *Alice in Wonderland* territory behind the looking glass which is the world of subrational impulse and appetites."[60]

One might see *The Mechanical Bride* as a young literature professor's attempt to get a grasp on the shifting ground of contemporary popular culture, a ground that seemed increasingly incomprehensible to the learned contributors to legitimate culture who focused primarily on the unified and unifying elements of literary works. McLuhan saw art as the best indicator of the concerns of the day, and advertisements as the best and most prominent form of collage. Taking cues from Mallarmé and the Symbolists, McLuhan thought that newspapers were an especially powerful form of collage. *The Mechanical Bride* gave prominence to full-page reproductions of the ads being examined, and each essay included two or three slogan-like provocative statements in bold and bullet format. Tellingly, in the book's preface, McLuhan announced the critical strategy that would invigorate his writing for years to come, recommending an embrace of textual chaos. Launching his career-long approach, McLuhan recounted the Edgar Allan Poe story "A Descent into the Maelstrom," in which a drowning sailor saves himself by accepting and participating with a whirlpool rather than fighting it. Not only does he survive, but the sailor finds amusement. McLuhan, in the end, sought a similar engagement with popular media, a view that immediately earned him status as an iconoclast.[61]

Twenty-five years later, still digging to reveal the technological ground hidden below the spark and flash of media content, and still diving into the sea of cultural abundance, McLuhan thought Key's work important enough to write a foreword to *Subliminal Seduction*, comparing it obliquely—and frankly, astonishingly—to Foucault's *The Archeology of Knowledge*.[62] In a letter to a long-time colleague and psychology professor, D. Carleton Williams, he called Key "a man of very much integrity and courage," expressing the belief that the mass media made "everybody much more vulnerable to the subliminal world."[63] McLuhan's foreword described the totalizing environment of advertising, which he called "striptease for a world of abundance."[64] Environments that did not draw attention to themselves worked "mostly subliminally,"[65] thus shifting the definition of the term in Key's book away from the psychological and toward the metaphoric. McLuhan's essay asserted that the "clamorous and simultaneous" world post-Sputnik had changed the place of the subliminal, here meaning the imperceptible more than the unconscious.[66] In a classic McLuhanesque argument, complete with an imaginative allusion to Harold Innis, McLuhan wrote that new electronic technology was weakening restrictive monopolies of knowledge, opening general access to ideas and information that had been available only to a few expert eyes, a claim that one hears applied to the Internet today. This weakening, according to McLuhan, created a clot of information, too abundant to systematize and study, as we moved from the visual-sequential-mechanical world to the aural-simultaneous-electric one: "Even the future is not what it used to be. For at electric speeds it is necessary to anticipate the future in order to live in the present, and vice versa."[67] As a result, those who tried to detect the meanings and operations of the new environment were elevated in stature, an argument which can only have been a sly reference to McLuhan himself, though it reads as flattery of Key. McLuhan wrote that the era of the instant and "total information environment" was "an age of investigation and of espionage" and "the age of the hunter."[68] As he examined the foundational struggle between unconscious desires and rational social order, McLuhan saw links with Freud, while reiterating the connection to Poe's cooperative sailor. As with Key, "It is the role Freud himself played as diver into the dirty unhygienic depth beneath the dewy Romantic sentiment. At the extreme point, Freud the diver got a signal: 'Surface at once. Ship is sinking.' When he came up for air he wrote about 'Civilization and its Discontents.'"[69]

After expressing doubt about the effectiveness or even the seriousness of "subliminal graffiti,"[70] McLuhan continued with a word of support for Key's attention to the highly sexual nature of contemporary life: "Thanks to color photography, and then to color TV, the magnetic city has become a single erogenous zone."[71] The foreword ended with a cryptic recommendation and one-liner that could just as easily be targeting Key himself as a wider critical audience: "Let's tighten up the slack sentimentality of this goo with something gutsy and grim. As Zeus said to Narcissus: 'Watch yourself.'"[72] McLuhan's foreword bears all the stylistic attributes of the author at his best—the pithy wordplay, the jokes, and the lively tone. Regardless of the shaky status of his historical and scientific claims, the essay holds pleasures that the entirety of Key's book does not. But it would be a mistake to glance over the function of its appearance, that is, the bestowal of legitimacy on the core ideas and aims of Key's project.

While McLuhan's introductory essay no doubt helped to sell a few copies, Key's work never had real credibility among media scholars. He had courted such recognition earlier in his career, and as an assistant professor of journalism at Boston University he had published work on translation techniques.[73] But widely taken to be a charlatan, he lost his university position soon after the appearance of *Subliminal Seduction*. Key included a bitter chronicle of the University of Western Ontario's firing of him in his follow-up volume, *Media Sexploitation*.[74] He also claimed to be a victim of subliminal influence, confessing that the cover of his first book, unbeknown to him, contained a hidden message (though he did not belittle his own writing by making this manipulation responsible for the impressive sales figures). Never bowing to what he saw as a conspiratorial scholarly establishment, he continued his heretical accusations of the advertising establishment in *The Clam-Plate Orgy: And Other Subliminals the Media Use to Manipulate Your Behavior* (1980) and *The Age of Manipulation: The Con in Confidence, the Sin in Sincere* (1989).[75]

Key's works were not always denounced, nor ignored, and his books did garner some degree of critical attention. Despite the pulp nonfiction status of *Subliminal Seduction*, one scholarly periodical, the *Journal of Communication*, opted to review it. In the review James W. Tankard Jr. remarked upon the truck that many media critics had with the book and cited Vance Packard as a point of origin for revelations about sexual imagery in advertising.[76] But Tankard was unconvinced by Key's sweeping, unsubstantiated claims about embedded sexual words and imagery, asking, "What *research*?"[77] More favorable notice appeared from the artist Robert Baldwin, who wrote a positive review of Key's *Subliminal Seduction* and Norman Dixon's *Subliminal Perception* in the art journal *Leonardo*.[78] Baldwin had already discussed the relation between Key's and Dixon's ideas and his own art in an earlier issue of the same journal, mapping an aesthetic argument about perception and kinetic art.[79]

It is important to acknowledge the role that works by Key and others like him have had in the intellectual life of many who have gone on to more sophisticated treatments. His books helped circulate broadly the subliminal thesis from the mid-1970s onward. *Subliminal Seduction*, now a mainstay of garage sales and flea markets everywhere, has over the years provided a palatable entry point for media criticality for many teenagers, offering an extreme initial vision of a world that deserves to be treated with suspicion. It is an appealing aspect, or at least an intriguingly erotic one, that a libidinal charge can be discovered in the blandest corners of daily life—orgies in ice cubes, vulgar language on soda cans, and genitalia in cigarette ads. Who would deny that from time to happy time, we live part of our lives in such a universe . . . or at least hope to do so?

Regardless of its dubious nature, the subliminal thesis harbors a history of ideas about minds, media, and influence. In its strongest iteration the subliminal thesis claims, or at least worries, that the things of which we are not aware are more influential than those we can detect, that below consciousness is a wild and impressionable creature that can be reached through messages that we cannot perceive. In this way, as it moves from empirical psychology toward a popular Freudianism, the subliminal thesis is a vernacular understanding of the unconscious and its relation to media and representation. The idea of subliminal messages, in a weaker form, encourages us to be mindful of the inherently meaningful world of images and sounds. On this level, asking if subliminal messages exist is rather like asking if there is connotation, if there is an affective dimension to representation, if there is something we can call innuendo or even the suggestive, to which one must of course respond in the affirmative. Broadly, this vernacular critique in both its stronger and weaker images of influence feeds suspicions that there is more going on than meets the eye or conscious mind. Representation, according to the rationale of the subliminal thesis, is doing very specific work, work with intention, by interested parties, and at your expense. Thus it betrays a cynicism about representation and is at some basic level a call to critical thinking, even as it closes off analysis, in many cases, by reducing the complexities of the mind to a presumed, but undocumented, motor activity.

However illegitimate and plainly misleading the strong thesis of subliminal influence may be, it is not a fabrication. Subliminal influence is no phantasm that wormed its way into an already weak mass mind. The thesis can be traced and located in concrete historical events. In its multiple and elastic forms it lives outside a stable institutional setting. Rumor seems to amplify its effect, making it seem that much more like an underground critique. Its imprecision and its uncertain origins, at least as most understand it, give the subliminal thesis credibility as something that one just knows and that unspecified powers apparently want to keep secret, the impression of which is the smoking gun confirming that imperceptible messages must be effective manipulators.

The subliminal thesis is a form of *practical consciousness about false consciousness*. With it we are in the presence of a vaguely oxymoronic unauthorized commonsense—a dubious obvious. As the Enlightenment arts patron Madame du Deffand responded when asked if she believed in ghosts, "No, but I'm frightened by them." This book will argue that the subliminal thesis is a way of seeing media change, and that it is a way to recognize and pose questions about the bewildering pace of cultural upheaval. Though it is not a point of origin, after the fall of 1957 we witness a surge forward of what we soon began to call "the information age," as well as a settlement of the ground upon which this age would operate and expand. This vernacular media critique was one effort to negotiate and understand what it meant to live in that new age. It is, I contend, part of a historically specific language that captures the mystery, skepticism, and wonder of the new media age, an age that we continue to imagine we inhabit and hope to understand in full eventually. To present some of the longstanding, residual features inherent in the subliminal thesis, the next chapter traces the historical links between modernity, commercial culture, and mass influence through the discovery of a hidden battleground of the will and a weapon with which to attack it: the unconscious and hypnotism.

Mind, Media, and Remote Control

CHAPTER TWO

As creatures of categorization, we expect all facets of our lives to be saddled with labels and typified with nomenclature. Eras and epochs are no exception. While the twentieth century can easily accommodate several sweeping descriptors—the age of America, of identity, of genocide, and so on—it can also be identified with the powerful reach of a set of racy ideas associated with the mind of a single person: Sigmund Freud. His influential corpus includes diagrams of the layers of personality and desire, insights into the gender and sexual impulses of children as determining features in their relations with the world, analytic methods of dream interpretation and free association, and extraordinary studies of kinship and family as historical conditions limiting the development of our selves and our societies. The reach of his theories and concepts extends beyond psychoanalysis into therapy, self-help, political manifesto, modern art, developmental psychology, and marketing research. Most tellingly, as a consequence of this influence there is an everyday understanding that a self below the self exists, along with some sort of motor force that propels us, often without our awareness. However used, misused, and abused, a set of ideas and conditions we describe as Freudian circulates widely. In this way, psychoanalytic concepts have a life apart from psychoanalysis. The twentieth may have been the Freudian century, but more accurately it encompassed the popularization of Freudian thought.

Freud's powerful influence upon our understanding of the unconscious is such that many continue to claim the very idea of the unconscious to have been his exclusively. I can easily excuse such assertions when they surface in everyday discourse. I am struck, though, by the frequency with which I hear from advanced students of science, culture, and psychoanalysis—by which I mean from people who should know better—that Freud "invented" the unconscious. Influences may be acknowledged with rote reference to Jean-Martin Charcot and Friedrich Nietzsche, but the substantiality of Freud's innovations is so much taken for granted as to amount to a view that the unconscious sprang from his brain alone. I can remember being taught as much in the university survey course in psychology that I took in the early 1980s, and judging from the views that persist, the curriculum has not been much revised on this count.

Wherever one marks the initial point of consolidation of Freud's thinking, after which his original contributions soar—his work on hysteria in the 1890s or the publication of *The Interpretation of Dreams* in 1900—it is indisputable that the questions he posed and the manner in which he attempted to explore them were fully a part of the European historical and intellectual context in which Freud worked and lived. He studied hypnotism as a diagnostic method, as did others of his generation, including Pierre Janet, Alfred Binet, and Gilles de la Tourette, at Salpêtrière Hospital in Paris, and the development of Freud's ideas benefited from his collaboration and correspondence with Josef Breuer in the 1880s. Some have even argued that his eventual rejection of hypnotism had more to do with his iconoclasm than with deficiencies in the method.[1] As Henri Ellenberger comprehensively if idiosyncratically documented, the concept of the unconscious had a long and tangled past, with key philosophical turning points that included Arthur Schopenhauer's *The World as Will and Representation* (1819), Carl Gustave Carus's *Psyche* (1846), Eduard von Hartmann's *Philosophy of the Unconscious* (1869).[2] Even earlier we find Leibniz and his "petits perceptions."[3] Moreover, Freud's influence was far from immediate and took several decades to be felt, especially across the Atlantic in the United States. As Eric Caplan notes, "Prior to 1910 there are virtually no references to his work in American medical periodicals and none whatsoever in popular cultural sources."[4] In contrast, the decidedly non-Freudian Hugo Münsterberg was a frequent contributor to popular United States periodicals, and his book *Psychology and Industrial Efficiency* was one of the top ten nonfiction bestsellers of 1913.[5]

But Ellenberger went further than chronicling pre-Freudian ideas about the unconscious, arguing that the early period of dynamic psychiatry, which proposed the active and ongoing formation of selves as whole and complete, was a persistent influence upon later stages. He wrote, "Common opinion states that the first dynamic psychiatry disappeared around 1900 to be replaced by wholly new systems of dynamic psychiatry. But a careful scrutiny of facts reveals that there was no sudden revolution but, on the contrary, a gradual transition from the one to the others, and that the new dynamic psychiatries took over far more from the first than has been realized. The cultural influence of the first dynamic psychiatry has been extremely persistent and still pervades contemporary life to an unsuspected degree."[6] In this effort to temper the view of Freud's radical break with his predecessors, Ellenberger reminded us of the multiple intellectual and institutional contributors to what we came to designate casually as Freudianism.

The end of the nineteenth century witnessed an energetic ferment of theories and proposals in Europe concerning the workings of the mind. As Ellenberger put it, "the philosophical concept of the unconscious, as taught by Schopenhauer and Von Hartmann, was extremely popular, and most contemporary philosophers admitted the existence of an unconscious mental life."[7] There was a profusion of terms attempting to characterize the newly theorized realm, including Pierre Janet's subconscious and Frederic W. H. Myers's subliminal self.[8] Accordingly, when Myers explained hypnosis he characterized it as "a fuller control over subliminal 'plasticity.'"[9] Myers's terminology had its moment of prominence. For instance, Norman Pearson wrote a periodical essay in 1916 on "Sub-human consciousness" without using the term "unconscious" but stating, "Now the subliminal conscious is a well-established psychological entity, and can properly be described as an abnormal consciousness. It is concerned with a realm which to the ordinary or supraliminal consciousness is closed."[10] When the *New York Times Magazine* did a feature called "Dethroning the Will" in 1922, it placed Freud, Jung, the philosopher Henri Bergson, and the self-help progenitor Emile Coué side by side, taking as established that Myers's "subliminal self" and James's "transmarginal mind" were part of the "new psychology."[11] In other words, there was a surface commensurability between different terms describing the prospects of a nether region of the mind.

The uncertain boundaries of the self below the self, and its powers to control or be controlled, motivated Myers to found the Society for Psychical Research in England in 1882. The organization attracted far-flung and diverse luminaries, including William James, whose nascent pragmatism questioned the usefulness of "consciousness" as a unified entity apart from the outside world, while challenging the very idea of "unconscious judgment."[12] James took to task the neo-Kantians who advanced the notion that knowing and experience involved separate states. Investigating the subliminal, James reasoned, was a way of skirting the misplaced concreteness and homogeneity of the human functions evident in the new experimental psychology. His empiricism led him to characterize knowing as "pure experience," and to describe concepts such as non-perceptual experiences.[13] In favorably quoting Myers on subliminal consciousness, James wrote, "Each of us is in reality an abiding psychical entity far more extensive than he knows—an individuality which can never express itself completely through any corporeal manifestation. The Self manifests through the organism; but there is always some part of the Self unmanifested; and always, as it seems, some power of organic expression in abeyance or reserve."[14] This supplementary realm accounted for growth, expansion, and influence as some unrealized facet that awaits exploitation. For support James noted evidence of successes in treating "drunkenness and sexual vice" with hypnotism and "suggestive therapeutics." With James there was, fundamentally, intense traffic between the inside and the outside, such that these were not two locations like points on a map but inseparable and interdependent elements of the Self.

The possibility of a sub-self provoked some to imagine an unhinged battle with the exterior public face of oneself, rather than a unified entity as we see in James. This dichotomous proposal found its way into contemporaneous literature. For example, Frank Tweedy's "The Subliminal Brute" (1918) told a slight tale of suburban domestic anxiety in which a lunch-induced daytime nightmare (from Welsh rarebit, no less) terrifies a husband about the well-being of his family. The brute of the title was his own hidden self, revealed when he slept.[15] The best-known version of the double-self was of course Robert Louis Stevenson's novella *The Strange Case of Dr. Jekyll and Mr. Hyde* (1886). The scientific basis for the double-self motif emerged from Pierre Janet, a particularly under-credited figure despite his introduction and elaboration of such key concepts as the subconscious, split self and double consciousness, trauma, dissociation, and catharsis, as well as the ethical and holistic treatment of patients.[16] Janet, for his part, felt that Freud had never acknowledged his indebtedness to these and other ideas. A source of significant resentment for Janet, Freud even refused to respond to his letters or to meet Janet, publicly or otherwise. On one occasion in 1913 Janet faced a hostile reception from a panel debate on psychoanalysis, with Carl Jung and Ernest Jones appearing as Freud's proxies and defenders, depicting Janet and his ideas as being without influence upon Freud and Freudianism. Janet had a high ethical regard for his patients, and his will required the burning of his lifetime's accumulation of five thousand detailed case files, an act that no doubt stunted the record of his influence and reputation.[17]

Of all his innovations, Pierre Janet's first widely acknowledged accomplishment—his first big splash at the young age of twenty-two—involved an extensive study of a subject called Léonie B., who was the first fully documented multiple personality. In 1885, noting that she could fall into a hypnotic state with remarkable ease, Janet created conditions under which he and others could elicit this response and have her carry out tasks suggested "mentally." The rapport with Léonie was so acute, he found, that a hypnotic state could be induced, and that she could execute commands like offering water to those present, opening an umbrella, and locking the doors of the house, even though the hypnotizer was not physically present with her.[18] The most stunning series of demonstrations for visiting doctors, including Myers, came in 1886 in Le Havre, during which Janet and his collaborator were able to hypnotize Léonie B. at a distance of one kilometer, with no visual or auditory contact of any kind, and to command her to sleepwalk around various obstacles.[19] So easily hypnotized was she that while flipping through an album of photographs, Léonie fell into a cataleptic state merely upon seeing the image of a doctor who had hypnotized her earlier.[20]

Previously, mesmeric states had typically involved touching, passes of the hand, and "magnetized" props like tubs of water or iron filings. According to Anton Mesmer's own propositions about animal magnetism, as represented in *Mémoire sur la découverte du magnétisme animal* (1779), the phenomenon was "action . . . exerted at a distance without the need for any intermediate object" and was reflected, intensified, and communicated by light and sound.[21] One of Mesmer's heirs, the Marquis de Puységur, could provoke more passive, trancelike states, which he named "somnambulism." One of the legacies of this work has been the supposition of special skills on the part of the mesmerist, concentrating in a central charismatic person the power to create trances and guide somnambulists.

Mesmerism and its variants were discredited as unscientific and fraudulent, though they continued to be the province of quack healers, spiritualists, and entertainers throughout the nineteenth century, having what John Durham Peters describes as a "subterranean influence on literature and thought."[22] It was only in the mid-nineteenth century that comparable conditions and processes were given consideration among scholarly practitioners, now under the term coined by James Braid in the early 1840s for intense visual and mental fixation—hypnotism. At the moment of Janet's debut an abundance of doctors studied telepathy and examined the long-distance effects of drugs and toxins.[23] But there were scant reports of long-distance magnetism. In this context the leading figures of the day received Janet's findings as a breakthrough. For some, a previously uncharted passage between minds was being revealed with his extraordinary spectacle of long-range command. His hypnotizing and manipulating Léonie B. from a distance was more than the clairvoyant claiming to see at a distance; it presented the possibility of remote influence.

Janet himself was skeptical. He expressed "astonishment and regret" about the all-too-casual tendency to cite his early demonstrations as proof of telepathic control.[24] In *L'automatisme psychologique* (1889) he described the special rapport that developed between subject and hypnotist, rather like a passion or addiction. The patient could begin to depend upon the experience of entering a hypnotic state, and could wish to please the hypnotist by doing so commendably. Freud would later elaborate this important observation, especially in his work on crowds and groups, in which he described the relationship between patient and analyst, or between masses and leaders, as rather like that of love.[25] Janet furthermore took note of Léonie B.'s lifetime experience of being hypnotized. Ellenberger described her as a student rather than a patient.[26] Indeed, she was a veritable living archive of past therapeutic practices for Janet, able to instruct on the techniques and results of earlier magnetizers. As a consequence, Janet did not believe that he had actually communicated with her mentally at a distance or taken part in a telepathic event. Instead, Janet

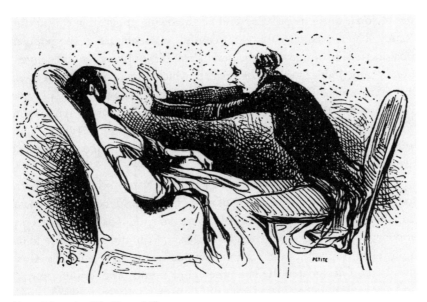

Honoré Daumier, "The Hypnotist"

drew up some lasting recommendations for research standards, which included the need to use subjects who had not been previously examined. No matter. Even as he went on to explore other aspects of the dynamic production of the self, this notion of control at a distance prospered.

Whatever the status of Janet's demonstration of long-distance hypnotic influence, comparable efforts to explore the reach of hypnotic control were undertaken. The practice of hypnosis, as developed by Hippolyte Bernheim in the 1880s at the University of Nancy, expanded to be potentially effective on all people, not just those who were products of trauma and psychological disorder, and was redefined as primarily a form of suggestion. For Bernheim the root of the therapeutic potential of hypnosis rested in these two precepts, regardless of the subject and of whether the suggestion came from an authority figure or from oneself.[27] In an early demonstration of somnambulistic manipulation, Bernheim reported instructing a hypnotized man that he had been insulted by an imaginary figure, that the paper knife in the subject's hand was a real blade, and that the subject should stab the offending party. The patient did so, violently.[28] Such demonstrations were in direct conflict with the view advanced by Charcot and his colleagues at Salpêtrière Hospital, who saw hypnosis as a diagnostic and investigative method, not effective on the majority of the population and not involving suggestion.[29] Still, the Nancy school was particularly successful in its seizure of the popular imagination. Its proposal of the generalizability of hypnosis and suggestion became fodder for legal defense, in which doubt could be cast upon intent, as well as for fictional renditions. Two of the most popular were Bram Stoker's *Dracula* (1897), which imbued the famous vampire count with the powers of hypnosis, and George du Maurier's *Trilby* (1894), which introduced the maniacal opera lover, hypnotist, and opportunist Svengali.

The popularization of Bernheim's and the Nancy school's approach to hypnotism led to the securing of a link between suggestion and mass populations. With the possibility of the entrancement of ordinary people supported by a respected school of research, hypnotic sleep came to be a powerful trope for the condition of modern existence generally. Gustave Le Bon designated the late nineteenth century the "era of crowds" and worried about a related retarding effect upon the forward direction of civilization. In *The Crowd: A Study of the Popular Mind* (1895) Le Bon described the emerging force of the masses as an entity that had hardly figured in the past but was a newly prominent challenge to governments of the day. Blaming the expansion of rights, universal suffrage, and workers' movements, Le Bon concluded that masses were inherently destructive. He wrote that "crowds act like those microbes which hasten the dissolution of enfeebled or dead bodies."[30] Throughout his book were assertions about the diminishing of intelligence of people and early versions of that fictional "lowest common denominator." For example, "This very fact that crowds possess in common ordinary qualities explains why they can never accomplish acts demanding a high degree of intelligence."[31] The most troubling feature, Le Bon reasoned, was that the conditions of the crowd, and its unified and homogeneous disposition, suppressed people's individual will and rationality, transforming them into virtual automatons.[32] Members of the crowd thus were vulnerable to suggestion. They found themselves in conditions that approximated those of hypnosis. Crowds consisted in people "perpetually hovering on the borderland of unconsciousness, readily yielding to all suggestions."[33] The limited intellectual capabilities of masses meant that distraction by transitory ideas and interests was easy. Le Bon took special note of the role of images, which were the simplest way to persuade masses to accept temporary thoughts.[34] He went as far as to say that "crowds being only capable of thinking in images are only to be impressed by images."[35] By implication Le Bon grasped popular entertainment, new kinds of public meeting places, and advertising as formidable forces in the manipulation of masses, specifically referring to theatrical performances as not unlike the placating function of the Roman bread and circuses.[36] For Le Bon popular audiences were primed for influence. They were half-conscious and already in a near-dream state.

Though Le Bon's tract is best understood as a synthesis of ideas from the preceding decades, its influence cannot be overestimated. Its popularity with political leaders and a wide reading public was astounding; there were twenty-six French printings by 1920, sixteen English printings by 1926, and translations into thirteen languages by 1916.[37] Susanna Barrows presents Le Bon as a point of consolidation of ideas about crowds drawn especially from Hippolyte Taine, Alfred Espinas, Gabriel Tarde, and Scipio Sighele. She places the "crowd theory" of France's Third Republic in the context of the Paris Commune and several milestones in workers' rights, including the recognition of May Day and the concept of the general strike. Barrows recounts the defenestration of a manager who was then mauled and trampled to death by a crowd of striking women workers, and shows that this incident was frequently cited as proof of the irrationality of mobs and the inherently violent potential at the heart of workers' organizations.[38] The excessive attention paid to the "bloodlust" of such popular political movements fed the impression of threat and danger described in many theories of crowds.

Moreover, the rise of hypnotism as therapeutic practice and entertainment in France after 1880 provided the epistemological groundwork enabling crowd theories to emerge. Barrows gives special credit to Gabriel Tarde as an adherent of the Nancy school for proposing a link between social interaction and somnambulism.[39] It was Tarde who in 1892, three years before Le Bon's *The Crowd*, may have been the first to compare crowd behavior to sleepwalking. The popular mind, its uncharted unconscious depths, and its relationship with the fast-paced world of industrial culture ignited concerns for the easy manipulability of the masses and hence for the impossibility of advancing civilization. The expansion of hypnotism from a restricted clinical practice to the imagined trance-readiness of vast populations is a key development in the prominence of ideas about mass manipulating messages of control. The late-nineteenth-century efforts to describe crowds were not just about elements of brains and behaviors but about the ability to influence and guide people. In effect Léonie B. was an individual prototype of modern mass subjectivity.

Wading into this territory was Hugo Münsterberg, the foremost public interpreter of psychological findings for Americans during the first decades of the twentieth century. Though the originality of his ideas is a matter of debate, Münsterberg's contributions assured that the everyday uses of psychology would be acknowledged. His appearances at celebrated trials, his articles for mass-circulation periodicals, and his popular books assisted in moving psychology out of the laboratory and into the workplace and the home. Münsterberg's work is especially interesting for its focus on the influence of commerce upon the modern mind. In his work we find a growing sense that promotional and marketing campaigns had a significant impact upon people. In "Psychology and the Market" Münsterberg contended that psychology's findings had been embraced by educators and doctors. In contrast, the world of commerce, labor, retail, and economics had yet to exploit psychology's advantages. Münsterberg provided illustrations of how certain kinds of testing could assist in job hiring, product evaluation, and advertising.[40] On this latter point, in 1909 he made one of the first direct recommendations for the place of the chronoscope, a type of tachistoscope—the topic of chapter 3—to measure in "thousandths of a second" how rapidly different advertising type can be read.[41]

Münsterberg attracted attention with his claim that there was no subconscious, arguing that the physical demonstration of automatic action (e.g. walking home without thinking of the route) showed that there was a powerful relation between memory and muscles, but not that there was some other controlling substratum of the brain.[42] This position did not steer him away from hypnosis, which he spent a good deal of time explaining in empirical terms. He was particularly influential when it came to delineating how hypnotism could be used ethically by police and in the courts. The arrest, conviction, and execution of Richard Ivens for the murder of Bessie Hollister drew responses from many psychologists, including Münsterberg and William James, who suggested that Ivens had been in a hypnotic state when he confessed and was most likely innocent of the crime. The psychologists agreed that Ivens's guilty confession was procured through suggestion, though the source of the influence could have been either Ivens himself or the police.[43] The definition of hypnosis here was broad enough to encompass a general state of lack of willfulness. Demonstrating this expanded characterization, Münsterberg explained that at its root hypnotism referred "to the experiences of absorbing attention, vivid imagination, and obedient will, and on the other side, to sleep and dreams and mental aberrations."[44]

Agreeing with some of the founding views of the researchers at the University of Nancy, Münsterberg wrote that hypnotism was to some degree possible for a broad population and could be a useful remedy for a variety of ailments; in his view anyone could hypnotize or be hypnotized. Münsterberg equally worried about the popular misunderstandings of hypnosis propagated by the newspaper, "the dime novel and, alas! the dollar-and-a-half novel."[45] Though a hypnotist could get regular subjects to respond truthfully to questions under hypnosis that they would not answer truthfully otherwise, one could not get new subjects to do so, despite the popular belief that hypnosis works like a truth serum.[46] Drawing strict lines between hypnosis and telepathy, Münsterberg reinforced the possibility that a person could be hypnotized in the absence of the physical presence of a hypnotizer save for, say, a voice on the telephone.[47] This middle ground dismisses "the hypnotic eye which fascinates at first glance and the malicious magnetism which destroys from a distance," though "the slow and persistent gaining of power of an unresisting mind is certainly possible."[48] In theory Münsterberg held out the possibility that crimes could be commanded and carried out by a hypnotized person, or through post-hypnotic suggestion. And yet he did not have evidence of heinous crimes having been committed in this fashion, and recommended caution in using the hypnotism defense in court.[49] More definitively, he wrote that stories of criminal activities conducted under hypnosis "exist in my opinion only in the imagination of amateurs."[50]

In making a case for the social factors contributing to criminality, Münsterberg provided arguments against the more racist claims that some people are born criminals. Instead, some "feeble-minded" people could be encouraged to imitate criminal behavior, and here we see Münsterberg's relation to ruling ideas about modern society, culture, and the suggestibility of mass populations. Summarizing the complexity of factors, he nonetheless argued that the psychology experiment is the best method of investigation, even if it must hold constant a multitude of influences. Still, he made clear the historical chaos confronted by the psychologist of crime, citing "the commercialism of our time or the vices of the street, the recklessness of the masses and the vulgarity of the newspapers, the frivolity of the stage and the excitement of the gambling-halls."[51] Even as Münsterberg hoped to advance the place of experimental psychology, his arguments routinely commented upon the situation of the contemporary individual. Münsterberg's work returned, at times with some urgency, to assess the conditions of modern life and the specificity of masses, including among his examples the brash, burgeoning popular amusements: "In millions of copies the vulgar newspaper pictures of crime reach the homes of the suggestible masses, and every impulse toward the forbidden is dangerously reinforced."[52]

Arguing against prohibition, Münsterberg considered the emotional well-being of the nation, the hard workday of most laborers, and the benefits of alcohol, in contrast to the other, more nefarious vices that might replace it. Münsterberg maintained that alcohol was a benign influence when compared with "vulgar rag-time music, the gambling of speculators, the sensationalism of the yellow press, the poker playing of the men and the bridge playing of the women, the mysticism and superstition of the new fancy churches, the hysterics of the baseball games, the fascination of murder cases, the noise on the Fourth of July and on the three hundred and sixty-four other days of the year, the wild chase for success—all are poison for the brain and mind."[53] All these attractions were dangerous and poisonous because they were engrossing and fascinating, and indeed the entire age was filled with "noise." Popular amusements called for an intense, focused absorption, which put mass audiences into conditions that approximate hypnotic trance, according to Münsterberg. This was especially true of film and the theater, which instilled in the audience "a state of heightened suggestibility" through the "one great and fundamental suggestion" that this "is life which we witness."[54] Though Münsterberg found ample aesthetic and psychological possibility in motion pictures, influence and suggestibility still figured as hazardous states-in-waiting among their audiences, the product of the modern commercial environment.

It was not only prominent scholars who saw all manner of influences emanating from popular media in the early twentieth century. Some speculated that the conditions of theatrical spectatorship opened the popular mind to suggestibility, to a kind of hypnotic control, and hence to the imitation of criminal acts seen on the stage.[55] One review praising the stage work of Max Reinhardt celebrated him as a mesmerist and described his abilities as those of "the experienced psychologist" and the hypnotist.[56] In 1907 the *Independent* described the possible consequences of sensational newspaper coverage of "sexual crimes" and murder trials as related to recent medical findings concerning suggestion. The article stated as fact that newspaper reports of suicides inspired imitation suicides across the country.[57] An itemization in 1917 of the unusual effects of motion pictures included the reduced accuracy of a basketball team in New Jersey (supposedly due to "the effect of the flicker on the eyes"), the spontaneous marriage of a couple in South Carolina during a screening of a romantic movie, a parson's mistaking of the musical effects during a production of *Quo Vadis* for a real lion's roar, a wounded soldier's recovery of speech after seeing a particularly humorous Billy Ritchie film, and a night watchman's discovery of a hypnotized woman in a cinema in New York who had been affected by the scenes of Svengali's influence in a film adaptation of *Trilby*.[58] Despite their variety and questionable veracity, all these anecdotes are tales of suggestion—though the basketball team's response appears to be physiological—of minds finding themselves in an open and weakened state brought on by popular film entertainment, and of control from a distance. As ideas about the unconscious and hypnosis drift into the storehouse of popular common sense, so too does an idea about the entrancing nature of modern media. One rich capsule of these concepts is the German Expressionist masterpiece *The Cabinet of Dr. Caligari* (Robert Wiene, 1920), which constructs an association between the medical and entertainment uses of hypnotism. In it a hypnotist arrives as a popular entertainer, but uses his skills to commit terrible crimes.

From Le Bon's fearsome, irrational crowd to Münsterberg's heightened suggestibility of popular audiences, the links between modernity, media, and mind provoked concern about influence from a distance. *Tel*, derived from the Greek for "far off," was used as a prefix in several new words denoting notions of expanded capabilities to bridge distance. In addition to "telepathy," John Durham Peters takes note of other neologisms: "'telesthesia' (1892), the sharing of feelings at a distance, and 'telekinesis' (1890), the movement of objects through psychic powers"[59] and "'teleplasm' (flesh at a distance)."[60] Jeffrey Sconce has shown how modern media systems assault sensibilities about distance by appearing to have a life of their own. Importantly, Sconce demonstrates that the "electronic presence" of media is a point of continuity from nineteenth-

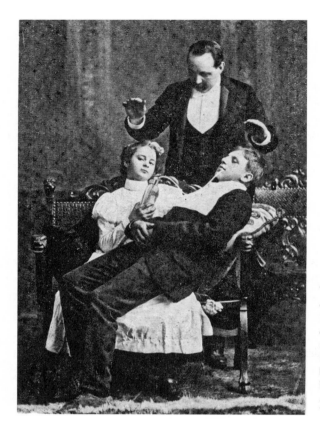

Without physical contact, the hypnotist implants behavior and belief. Here a man believes he is an infant, and the woman believes she is nursing him. From *Practical Lessons in Hypnotism*, 1900.

century occultism, through telegraphy, and on to radio and television, one that had associations with the mainstream and fringes of science as much as it did with popular culture.[61]

In this fascination with influence at a distance, we can see how a "problem" of communication hovered in the background—what mediated and distorted connections among people, and what might have reduced the distortion. In the late 1940s Joshua Gregory wrote about transmitting images between brains in exactly these terms, as perfecting communication.[62] Paradoxically, the absolute reduction of distance between two minds—a supreme condition of non-mediation—was often imagined as facilitated by some new mediating form. We see how noninterference, sensory appeal, and message fidelity tend to be the terms of the so-called improvements and advancements of one medium over another, from postal service to telegraphy to the wireless to radio to television to the

Internet. The less a medium appears to mediate, the better we assume it to be doing its job, and the closer we believe we are to the communicative ideal of Mr. Spock on *Star Trek* and his mind-meld. Whether telegraphy's annihilation of space, telepathy's transport of messages between the spirit world and our mortal coil, or Freud's passage between the latent and manifest layers of the self, distance was imagined as something that one could conquer or circumvent, potentially with the proper modern media inventions and techniques.

But technological change was not the only issue. Human minds and bodies, as analogous to electrical machines, were also available for upgrading.[63] The migration of terminology from the technological to the biological provides some proof of this. For instance, the term "wireless" was in use for about a decade before Marconi's breakthroughs, after which it became directly associated with radio communication. Until the first years of the twentieth century the word "wireless" referred to the evidence of any number of immaterial events of a presumably electric nature, including potentially those of the mind, a point that has been elaborated in the work of Peters and Sconce. Myers introduced the term "telepathy" in 1882 to signify unmediated, non-externalized communion between minds. Janet's reputed demonstration of apparent automatic somnambulism thus arrived just after the naming of "telepathy" as a specific site of inquiry and just as "wireless" was beginning to appear. Oliver Lodge, a physicist who had developed some aspects of "wireless" technology, was an early proponent of radio as a door to the mysteries of telepathy in the 1890s.[64] Decades later, in the 1940s, new research likened the modus operandi of images on the mind to that of a television receiver.[65] And why shouldn't there be parallel tracks between media and bodies, given that we are, as one author put it in an article from 1925 expounding the usefulness of radio in testing telepathic powers, "really electrical machines."[66]

Changing technological capabilities reignited dormant or low-rumbling senses of magical connections among people and minds, as though distance did not matter. For example, the founder of Christian Science, Mary Baker Eddy, described in her wildly popular book *Science and Health* (1875), "The electric telegraph is a symbol of mind speaking to mind, that in progress of time will not require wires, for Spirit destroys matter, electricity, etc. . . . Mind, like a telegraph office, holds the message conveyed to the body."[67] And we find similar metaphors deployed to capture concerns about the hazards of new technology. A cartoon in the *New York Daily Graphic* in 1877 "illustrated 'the terrors of the telephone' by showing an announcer at a telephone-like device mesmerizing masses of people listening simultaneously throughout the world."[68] In 1899, immediately in the wake of the first reports of radio, one author proclaimed, "Signor Marconi has proved to the whole world that, by the use of his apparatus, messages can be passed through space, for great distances, from brain to brain in the entire absence of any known means of physical communication between two widely separated stations."[69] In short, as Peters puts it, "telepathy was radio's doppelgänger."[70]

Alongside the vaguely spiritual and utopian shadings to both the literal and metaphoric relation between media and minds was a resolutely modern sense of efficiency. Keeping up with the pace and demands of a rapidly changing world required equally advanced modes of learning, of which speed-reading was just one practical and lasting development. Special access to the mind lay behind the claims made about sleep-learning. In 1923, years before Aldous Huxley wrote of "hypnopaedia" in *Brave New World* (1932), the U.S. Navy experimented with sleep-learning to boost the speed of sending and receiving radio code by writing it on the subconscious mind, or so it was claimed.[71] An editorial in the *New York Times* on the topic boldly raised the exciting prospect that "subconscious" could replace "automatic" as the watchword of the day.[72] Huxley's evocative description in his most famous novel became a reference point for explaining subsequently developed processes and experiments. For example, *Time* characterized Max Sherover's "cerebrograph" in 1948 as another example of Huxley's imaginary "hypnopaedia."[73] Later public demonstrations of this system took on a quietly erotic tone when the beauty-pageant winner Miss Washington learned French by using Sherover's tapes while she slept in a street-level window at the Washington offices of BOAC airlines.[74]

The common thread that I wish to accentuate is that just as new concepts of mind were taking root, innovations in media provoked new understandings of, and new ways to think about, the working of minds. Moreover, the discovery of the unconscious framed a communication problem whose central concerns were access to, contact between, and influence upon minds. In the language that linked mind and media, there was a reformulation of the experience of psychic and geographic distance, one that continued in a vigorous fashion in the popular imagination of the twentieth century. The mysteries of mind and media both elicited a sense of amazement and marvel at the novel "third" space that their interrelation implied. While today people talk of the virtual universe of cyberspace, people in the past were similarly wondering where our voices were when we spoke on the phone. As the borders were thought to be muddied between even such titanic realms as presence and absence, spirit and material, self and other, interiority and exteriority, life and death, and as the various new sciences proposed to clarify *and* complicate these distinctions, conjecture about the ostensibly moving target of the threshold that separated each pairing flourished. What were these third, in-between, liminal zones?

In the expert and popular literature from the second half of the nineteenth century onward, hypnosis was a recurrent theme, metaphor, and technique through which one gained access to liminal states. Hypnotic trances were a form of opening up. This logic reappeared predictably throughout the various self-help programs that trumpeted hypnosis as an efficient way to release energy and realize potential that already resided, dormant, in all of us. Though it pushed the boundaries of most definitions of hypnosis, in the early 1920s Emile Coué had an enormous impact with his auto-suggestion techniques, including the still-familiar "day by day in every way I'm getting better and better."

The popularity of hypnosis crossed a number of scientific, spiritual, entertainment, and medical fields. Discouragement of, and at times bans on, stage hypnotism rested on the assumption that it was possible to do irreparable harm to audience members, as hypnosis was seen to be a dangerously powerful tool. Some reasoned that with the rise of vaudeville mesmerism at the beginning of the twentieth century it was the gullible popular audiences that had to be protected, for they were liable to believe what they were seeing.[75] And tragic events supposedly precipitated by hypnosis received regular news attention. At one séance in 1923 a distraught police officer was instructed to fire a wooden stick at the audience. When it would not work, he drew his own gun and killed three.[76] Two years later two Yugoslavian girls apparently slept for months after being put under hypnosis by a vaudeville performer.[77] Incidents such as these raised the ire of cultural authorities, for now that the new and powerful realm of the unconscious had been agreed upon, and now that we appeared to have set out possible points of entry through hypnosis, concern shifted to the ethics of influence, especially as they pertained to broad populations. The longevity of Le Bon's ideas came as no surprise as imaginative examples of influence at a distance continued to accumulate and circulate.

For example, broadcasting in 1924 from the Zenith station WJAZ in Edgewater Beach, the Columbia University professor Gardner Murphy thought of a number between one and a thousand, an animal, and a food that listeners were to divine. Thousands of volunteers mailed in answers, many apparently correct.[78] Curious from my point of view is less the experiment and its results than the fact that it made the front page of the *New York Times*, which followed up with stories and editorials for several weeks. One of the newspaper's editorials was supportive, characterizing the experiment as science and not the more suspect spiritism.[79] When follow-up tests proposed transatlantic telepathy tests, the *Times* remained encouraging.[80] This scientific openness notwithstanding, the editors felt that telepathy would never "develop into a serious rival of the radio, the telegraph, or even the mails."[81] A range of opinion and skepticism is evident, and one can only guess how seriously readers took the reports and editorials. But the attention received indicates that events like this were visible and served as occasions to revisit and reinforce popular conceptions of mind, media, influence, and scientific procedure.

The significance of this brand of demonstration heightens when we observe that Murphy's performance was not unique. The hypnotist Joseph Dunninger performed long-distance hypnotism through radio in 1923, creating a sensational news story. His voice was broadcast from WHN in Ridgewood, Long Island, to his subject, Leslie B. Duncan, ten miles away. To prove the effectiveness of this command at a distance, Duncan then had a long needle thrust through the skin of his forearm without flinching, pain, or blood.[82] Dunninger "predicted a medical use of radio within a decade, asserting that painless and bloodless operations will be made possible with wireless taking the place of chloroform."[83] And rather like Janet, he added, "Only those who have served as his subjects and whose eyes he has looked into will be affected."[84] Other tests followed, including one on NBC's *Ghost Hour*, which broadcast a telepathy experiment in 1929.[85] Two decades later Dunninger repeated a radio telepathy stunt, this time with sociological legitimacy. His witness-assistants were Paul Lazarsfeld and Robert Merton, who were among the most eminent sociologists of the day. Dunninger was able to divine a passage selected by a remotely located Paul Lazarsfeld. In the studio with the telepath was

Robert Merton, who maintained telephone contact with Lazarsfeld and was thus able to confirm that the passage was the right one.[86] Note the intriguing conflation; this is not a test of telepathy per se but of radio telepathy, with telephone wires acting to guarantee the veracity of the wireless event.

As these illustrations show, worry and conjecture about suggestibility traveled across media and cultural forms. In the 1920s versions of Le Bon's crowd theory were relatively mainstream, and not located only in psychoanalysis, psychology, and sociology. Strikingly, and extending the conservative fears found in Le Bon's work, hypnotic sleep was an expression of a dwindling agency *and* of a technological dehumanization resulting from the rapid onslaught of modernity. Throughout the twentieth century, versions of this association guided the understandings of many events. In 1921 Dr. James Hendrie Lloyd wrote of "pandemic psychosis," or "functional mental disorder which tends to spread over large numbers of people," like cholera or smallpox.[87] The two central characteristics were emotion and imitation, and "automobile mania" and Zionism were cited as illustrations.[88] Lloyd typified the thinking of the day by stating that the shock of war and industrialism created the conditions for mental contagion.[89] These tales of influence and irrationality persisted after the Second World War. Spectacularly, 165 girls spontaneously fainted at a football game in 1952, presumably struck by some brand of "mass hysteria."[90] It was not uncommon, certainly through the 1950s, to understand the rise of Nazi Germany as a consequence of Hitler's successful hypnotizing of the entire nation. Not only was mass activity, like that of these varied illustrations, described with reference to actual or metaphoric hypnosis, but some saw incidents of suggestibility as a way to rank the character of populations, much as Le Bon had done. Frank Illingworth wrote in 1946 that "some races are more susceptible to hypnotism than others, the French, for example."[91]

New media often take on the concerns of previous ones, with earlier media then seeming benign as the worry transfers to the fresh location. In the 1950s experiments with televised hypnosis received popular attention, and frequent reference was made to *Trilby* as a way to frame what was occurring. In the United Kingdom some claimed to have been hypnotized by a television experiment by the BBC in 1948, leading to the banning of television hypnotism.[92] Popular media as a sourcebook for criminals occupied a resilient place in the popular imagination, and seemed

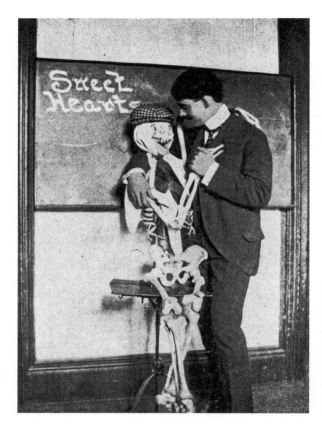

Bridging distance of beauty and mortality with hypnosis, which has led this man to believe that "he holds in his arms the beautiful object of his affection." From *Practical Lessons in Hypnotism*, 1900.

handy and feasible enough to imply influence by the mere fact of being a part of our lives. When copycat criminals confess to media inspirations, as a young killer did in 1944 when he claimed that his ideas for killing had come from a movie he had seen,[93] we appear to have gained an irrefutable insight into the delinquent mind. As Fredric Wertham put it in his classic work *Seduction of the Innocent*, "chronic stimulation, temptation and seduction by comic books . . . are contributing factors to many children's maladjustment."[94]

It would be unproductive to see these episodes as a chronology of wrong turns in the advancement of science, or to use them to confirm the gullibility of earlier generations of scholars and readers. Instead, revisiting these instances opens up our own access to the range of questions, concerns, and tentative explanations of the past. Regardless of the place that they eventually occupy in the perpetually redecorated corridors of scientific truth, through them we can chart priorities and tendencies, as well as situate in context those formulae that emerge and rise out of their historical moorings to a position of lasting impact. And tales of media-inspired manipulation and criminality continue to abound today, which shows, in the very least, a willingness by scholars and popular audiences to hold close to notions of suggestible popular audiences.

These news stories and scientific speculations make it apparent that the exploration of liminal zones and conditions bespeaks a concern with mediated influence upon human behavior, as well as an interest in how those zones might themselves be manipulated. The contact with and cartography of the human mind was equally an investment in control and in the mechanisms of how we understand the exercise of influence from a distance. Something powerful emerged in the blurring of the boundaries between material and immaterial, interiority and exteriority: *it became a popular language of media effects.* This was a low or vernacular modernism, to use Miriam Hansen's phrase, and a form of "practical consciousness" that organized how people lived and experienced the fears and promises of the modern age.[95]

A root presumption is apparent in this practical consciousness about media and mind, one that has guided so much of twentieth-century thought. It is an idea that has shaped our understanding of the role of art, politics, education, community, justice, and pleasure, and it has been at the heart of much sociology, political science, and communication studies. The idea is this: the people constitute a force to be feared and at best managed. Among the many twists and tumbles of modernity—the shock of the new, the speedy, the urban, and the loud—we find a related conceptual innovation, one that has driven much of our current media criticism: the terror of the popular. This fear may be manifested in attacks on taste, state of mind, individual rationality, or intellectual aptitude. It may appear as concerns for and about teens, women, mobs, masses, crowds, and fans. Regardless of the form it takes, responses to the changing conditions of the modern world and of new media environments frequently betray an uneasy relation with the popular, as though Le Bon were still shaping our rhetoric.

Industrially produced culture continues to unsettle our thinking, with claims that the culture shared may not be the people's culture to begin with. However, the mode of production, whether the factory or the cottage, the mechanical arm or the human hand, is only one determinant for circulation and consequence in the world. To cut short the possibilities of rapport and relation among people that may exist as a significant part of cultural life is to dismantle the foundational possibility of communion and can but be a political and intellectual dead end. I can think of no more anti-democratic and anti-progressive stance than to deny the validity of popular cultural affinities and experiences just because at some point a purchase may have been required.

Returning to some of the earlier moments in the career of the "lowest common denominator" argument, as this chapter has done, and seeing the slippage between explorations of the unconscious, hypnotic suggestion, media influence, and the modern mass subject confirms my discomfort. The democratic revolution, as Raymond Williams referred to it, of the rising demands of people for a say in their own governance brought with it a reactionary plea for social order.[96] The greater the extension of rights and the greater the influence of markets of culture, the more elaborate the rationales of division and exceptionalism. From the hierarchies boosted by various incarnations of Social Darwinism to the nostalgia for an imaginary pre-modern harmony, an epistemological apparatus has weighted down the full flourishing of a modern people's culture. Instead, robots, zombies, and somnambulists have occupied our repertoire of images of the modern mass subject. Accordingly, in popular and intellectual venues alike, the cherished autonomous individual has been replaced by an empty husk of irrational, childlike, and primitive impulses.

This chapter has presented some of the beginnings of our contemporary sense of the presumed malleable nature of the mass subject. This characterization was the discursive heritage on which the subliminal scandal of the late 1950s rested. As we will see, the scandal similarly submitted an image of the easily hijacked mass mind, and associated this with industrial culture and social upheaval.

The Swift View

S peculative, cautionary, and comic renditions of the future have left us with a collection of immediately recognizable relics, among which we find moving sidewalks, hovering vehicles, ray-guns, and soaring needlepoint buildings. Joining these identifiable motifs are machines for the acceleration of reading and learning. In the proto-hippie classic *Stranger in a Strange Land* (1961), one character reads the morning newspaper on an automatically scrolling screen at his "optimum reading speed."[1] For the sad and doomed guinea pig in the novel *Flowers for Algernon* (1966), part of his hyper-learning program involves an array of flashing television images.[2] Popular film has regularly reiterated this situation of force-fed screen images, often as a mode of mind control. Recall Alex in *A Clockwork Orange* (Stanley Kubrick, 1971), Joseph in *The Parallax View* (Alan J. Pakula, 1974), and the brainwashing scene from the teen horror flick *Disturbing Behavior* (David Nutter, 1998). These film scenes—and there are many other comparable examples—are enactments of some dominant ideas about subject positioning in film spectatorship, with the viewer's attention planted unwaveringly upon the screen and with his or her consciousness written upon by the stream of images. All these illustrations depict scenes of extreme and intense education, in the broadest sense. The conditions created by these accelerated learning machines vary from the streamlining of a quotidian activity (reading the morning paper) to the expanding anxieties about idea implantation. Reflecting this powerful strain of direct influence, as the brainwasher Dr. Yen Lo in Richard Condon's novel *The Manchurian Candidate* (1959) puts it, we have imagined the present or near-future application of a "radical technology for descent into the unconscious mind with the speed of a mineshaft elevator."[3] More generally, these renditions of "machine instruction" are representations of the uses and effects of representation.

As outrageous as these fantastic stories of screen instruction may be, we can pinpoint historical corollaries. Their authors have built upon a combination of dominant sensibilities, experimental programs, and actual technologies. One key source for these imaginings, versions of which can be identified in the fictional illustrations above, is an underacknowledged and highly influential apparatus called a tachistoscope. Literally meaning "a swift view," a tachistoscope can be put to multiple uses, though it originally measured the speed with which visual stimulus is recognized. According to the science historian Ruth Benschop, A. W. Volkmann first proposed a horizontally sliding instrument in the late 1850s as a way to reduce contaminating stimuli from a visual perception test, that is, to assure reactions could be traced to a specific exposure.[4] Wilhelm Wundt in Leipzig in the 1870s and James M. Cattell in Germany in the 1880s (subsequently at Columbia University in the 1890s) both figure in the formation of the young field of psychology and in the development of the tachistoscope. Cattell's "fall tachistoscope" was prototypical for future devices; he redesigned it as a miniature guillotine, with a mechanism that used gravity to move a screen downward. The screen had a small opening that passed by a stationary field on which icons could appear. The contents of the field would be visible for an extremely short but calculable amount of time, one that could be lengthened by increasing the size of the passing window, or shortened by decreasing the size. To assure that one was measuring rapid visual perception, everything else—the head, body, eyelids, eye movement, pupil dilation—had to be held constant as surely as possible. Thus the tachistoscope's brief stimulus appeared in an otherwise uninterrupted field of vision, which allowed for accurate measurement of responses. Other devices incorporated measures to capture the subject's speed of responses. Cattell had subjects place a telegraph key between their lips; when dropped, the key would break an electrical circuit and provide a record of split-second timing. In

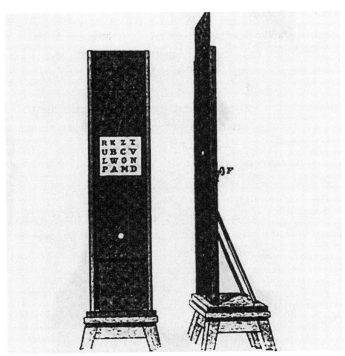

Gravity tachistoscope, ca. 1880. From *Experimental Psychology and Pedagogy*, 1909.

theory, a broken circuit signaled visual perception. From the 1880s onward psychologists used "swift viewing" instruments to measure and test an assortment of visual tasks—reaction time, attention, recognition, and retention, among others. For instance, Cattell adapted his device to include studies of reading.[5]

The little cultural analysis that has been done on this technology has exclusively dealt with its place in the field of psychology. Especially noteworthy is Benschop's research. She uses Wittgenstein's "family resemblances," in which differences among members are as important as similarities in defining families, to unsettle "the idea that similarities among instruments should be taken as proof of a shared fundamental or transcendental quality."[6] Benschop largely limits her research to the late nineteenth century and the early twentieth, charting the tachistoscope's movement from physiology to experimental psychology, with a discussion of the current longing that some contemporary psychological researchers have for pre-computer instruments.[7] What impresses me, however, and what I focus on here, is that as we move into the twentieth century the tachistoscopic function—the swift view—extends to unpredictable locations, away from the psychology lab and toward schools, reading courses, military training, and advertising. One of the tachistoscope's contributions was to reorient reading from the page to the screen. With this movement the technological interface of the screen, projected or otherwise, connoted an efficient and optimizing function. The tachistoscope's initial substitution of the screen for the page, an exchange that would come to define a contemporary information era, signaled the new, improved, and up-to-date. Put differently, hyper-reading, whether of prose or advertisements, was a pursuit well tailored to the conditions of modern cultural acceleration.

I find the malleability of the tachistoscope intriguing, for it is not a single laboratory instrument but one that designates a set of ideas, impulses, and metaphors, or what Mark Seltzer calls "cultural logistics."[8] These logistics are not rigid and essential but establish an empirical and durable material dimension for a loose band of priorities, organizing the resources of sundry individuals, disciplines, and institutions, and subsequently offering us a point of access to what is valued. With each iteration of the tachistoscopic idea we have yet another instance of what I think of as a *residual modern*, that is, the persistence of certain modern priorities, sensibilities, and materials. Many technologies and media have assisted in our grasping of foundational qualities of modernity; Benjamin's essay "The Work of Art in the Age of Its Technological Reproducibility" is easily and deservedly an ever-present point of reference for this claim.[9] My intention is not to throw one more "forgotten" technology into a collective critical potlatch, proffering one more object lesson for what went wrong with advanced capitalism. Although much work has treated motion pictures as having a special relationship with modernity, I contend that attention to the tachistoscope draws out two elemental aspects of contemporary visual media: a fascination with the rapid arrival and departure of texts, and an epistemological tension between perceptual fragmentation and synthesis. The tachistoscopic idea carries with it a curiosity about the effects of the often imperceptible replacement of images, one followed by another. And as the tachistoscope moves out of the realm of psychological experimentation, it is rather like an everyday science of exploring the liminal zones of consciousness, becoming a quotidian perception test that may no longer be associated with the device specifically.

This everyday science became part of a popular understanding of the unconscious and a vernacular critique of media ubiquity, and had a formative impact upon ideas about subliminal communication in the late 1950s. Indeed, the revelations in 1957 about modern media and unconscious processes are so powerful that the tachistoscope is occasionally said, incorrectly, to have been invented at that time, with the marketer James Vicary credited, just as incorrectly, as the inventor. *The People's Almanac*, for instance, discusses the device largely as related to the subliminal scare of the late 1950s.[10] So this genealogy of the trajectory of the tachistoscope—as it moved from the laboratory to the classroom—and of the tachistoscopic idea helps us understand how the ground was tilled for the subliminal controversy.

The tachistoscope was in fact several different technologies employing diverse mechanical principles for a wide array of experiments and purposes. Through most of its early years no commercial manufacturer supplied tachistoscopes, and many of the modifications and improvements pertained to the demands and interests of individual experimental contexts. Many of the gadgets were makeshift, using materials available in typical laboratories and classrooms of the time, which made assembling the devices simpler. Distortion and changes in brightness had to be minimized, as they would cause the eye to move and the pupil to change size. The use of camera-like shutter systems, with apertures that revealed fields evenly and quickly, was one eventual option, though even this was not as fast as needed for some experiments. Raymond Dodge's tachistoscope of the early 1900s employed a mirror and gelatin film to eliminate the noisiness and distraction of the dropping screen, appropriating techniques used by stage illusionists.[11] Whipple's and Schumann's tachistoscopes both employed a rotating disk and an adjustable window. Some machines were intended to expose actual objects rather than representations or characters.[12] Continuing the demand for more accurate, soundless, and motionless laboratory instruments, the modified Gulliksen tachistoscope borrowed from the mechanics of one built by Samuel Renshaw and I. L. Hampton.[13] New innovations to tachistoscopes were launched in the 1930s,[14] some tailored to measure reading reactions[15] and others, taking cues from Dodge, drawing on stage magic to expose large fields of actual objects.[16] During these first decades tachistoscopes were primarily apparatuses for testing individual subjects; sometimes the devices were boxes into which someone peered. Dozens of versions continued to appear through the 1930s, with flash projection beginning to be an equal competitor. Projection tachistoscopes aided classroom demonstrations for psychology students. E. O. Lewis and C. W. Valentine used a projection tachistoscope at the beginning of the twentieth century to explore spatial illusions.[17] In 1931 Harold Schlosberg and Sidney Newhall both introduced similar devices, specifically for classroom use; Newhall's was a magic lantern or opaque projector ingeniously converted into a tachistoscope by means of a rotating disk placed in front of the lens.[18]

The tachistoscope is still a staple of psychology labs today, although now a computer software program typically serves the tachistoscopic function by producing flashing images. In its early years it captured a lasting investment in the quantification of essential human functions, as well as in the inspection of the tiniest, most fleeting manifestations of behavior. The study of reaction time, attention, reflex, recognition, and so on involved operationalizing procedures and making one phenomenon observable by holding all the others constant. In addition to satisfying the usual standards of experimental methods—measurability, generalizability, and reproducibility—it was important to isolate function and observation. One studied vision as separate from hearing as separate from touch, reflex as separate from identification, icons as separate from words, depth as separate from color, source as separate from pitch. The continuous range of human sense perception was broken into its component parts. The subject's body underwent a radical partitioning, one that matched a division of empirical experimental labor and that presumably corresponded to a universal human form. The brain was understood to coordinate the incoming information into composite portraits, but the point of access, and hence the focus of quantitative measurement, was the pick-up device (eye, ear, skin, tongue, nose).

Because of the way it accumulated data, the tachistoscope required an immobile subject. Friedrich Kittler says that the body was "chained" in place,[19] but this is misleading, as the subject was more likely to have had a cushioned headrest and been expected to lean into it.[20] Still, it is correct to say that the research subject, or more accurately the research eye, waited expectantly for the infinitesimal flash that was to be reported upon. Jonathan Crary has investigated how tachistoscopic experiments produced and studied "a fragmentation of vision perhaps even more thorough than anything in early forms of cinema and high-speed photography."[21] Crary has written about "attention" as a special problem of late-nineteenth-century modernity, doing so by investigating the role

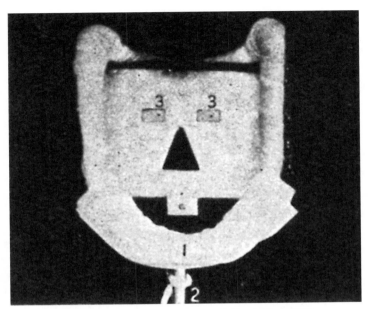

Headrest for tachistoscopic test, ca. 1930. From *Children's Sleep*, 1933.

that the new field of psychology played in settling an epistemology of perception: "Attention as an object of knowledge involved the recognition that perception was essentially temporal and unstable but was also, if studied resolutely enough, capable of management and relative stabilization (as the example of the tachistoscope demonstrated)."[22] The work to which quantitative research is put explains the managing and stabilizing impulse of which Crary writes. His historical narrative focuses upon the nascent stimulus-and-response, behaviorist strain of experimental psychology. And he elaborates the paradox of modern sensory synthesis, which is the experience of perpetually reoriented perception and its consequences for a fragmented and reconstituted self.

Crary's wide-ranging and subtle work notwithstanding, it seems to me that fragmentation and rationalization have been placed at the front of our understandings of modernity; one need not read too deeply in postmodernist critiques to stumble across them. This emphasis has come at the expense of a fuller consideration of synthesis, that is, the blending of sensory stimuli into a perceptual unity. To the emphasis on the functionalist, behaviorist strain of experimental psychology that helped produce this rationalized view of the human sensorium, we need to add that there were other contemporaneous and competing frameworks. At precisely the same time that the first psychology labs were being built in the second half of the nineteenth century, William James proposed the experiential continuity of a stream of consciousness; the paths between physical and metaphysical worlds proposed by psychical research had not yet entirely waned in legitimacy; and Pierre Janet documented the "tension" existing in the synthesis of the dynamic production of the self.[23] True enough, despite these contemporaneous frameworks, the rising dominance of experimental psychology strove to section psychological traits into fundamental elements. The point is that this rise does not describe the entirety of the field. Moreover, even tachistoscopes were put to uses that revealed findings other than the fragmented human form. They were just as influential in exploring the perceptual linkages and continuities across sequences of exposed fields.

Particularly pioneering was Max Wertheimer, who in the early twentieth century advanced ideas about the interrelationship of sensation and the perceptual formation of wholeness, while remaining inside a controlled experimental context. Considered the founder of Gestalt psychology, Wertheimer was led to this approach by the tachistoscope, his first instrument of experimentation, which he used to show the perception of movement between two still-exposed fields. In this instance in 1910, the tachistoscope was replicating an effect that Wertheimer had noticed in a stroboscope, a spinning, proto-cinematic toy then a century old.[24] Other debates raged: Carr Harvey, who completed a survey of tachistoscopy in 1912, challenged Wundt's conclusion that there was no judgment in the briefest of perceptual events, which he described as reflexive or automatic.[25] Harvey pointed out that focus on isolated exposures failed to account for what happened among exposures. Others ignore Wundt's insights even today, as when Kittler mistakenly reads the tachistoscope for its reduction of perception to reflex: "Tachistoscopes measure automatic responses, not synthetic judgments."[26] My point is not to validate one assessment rather than the other, but to indicate that a century ago psychologists debated the extent to which the instrument measured both. As demonstrated by their role in Gestalt psychology and the debates that ensued, it is accurate to say that tachistoscopes assisted in investigating *a tension between fragmentation and assemblage*, a tension that defines the modern sensory and perceptual subject. In short, assessments about fragmented and reflexive humans tell but half the tale of the epistemological battles engulfing the modern subject. The other half is the instrument's particular role in understanding the synthetic and combinatory function of human senses.

The apogee of this synthetic quality is evident in the analogy between tachistoscopes and motion pictures, that other late-nineteenth-century medium. Both initially facilitated individual viewing and only later incorporated projection technologies for communal viewing. This parallel is not lost on Crary, who has noted that the tachistoscope's quick flashes of fields "certainly prefigure the effects of high-speed montage in cinema, where perceptual thresholds are approached and the question of subliminal images becomes important."[27] Crary comments on the tension between cinema's impulses to pull apart and to stitch together: "Cinema . . . is a contradictory form of synthetic unity in which rupture is also part of an unbroken flow of time, in which disjunction and continuity must be thought together. Cinema is the dream of the fusion, of the functional integrity of a world where time and space were being uncoiled into a manifold of proliferating itineraries, durations, and velocities. As numerous critics have suggested, film became a validation of the authenticity of the perceptual disorientations that increasingly constituted social and subjective experience."[28] Kittler similarly wrote, "Chopping or cutting in the real, fusion or flow in the imaginary—the entire research history of cinema revolves only around this paradox."[29] He was direct in pronouncing the relation between the tachistoscope and the cinema: "The tachistoscope of the physiologists of reading was the twin of the movie projector, with the side effect of typographically optimizing the typewriter."[30] However, Kittler soon flipped this assertion: "The film projector's twin thus functions in an opposite manner. The projector, in the unconscious of the movie house, presents a continuum of the imaginary, generated through a sequence of single images so precisely chopped up by and then fed through the projector's mechanism that the illusion of seamless unity is produced. With the tachistoscope, in the darkened laboratory of the alphabetical elite, a cut-up image assaults as a cut in order to establish out of the torment and mistaken readings of victims the physiologically optimal forms of letters and script."[31] Kittler's claims here rest on a highly selective understanding of the uses to which the tachistoscope was put, and oddly reduce the diversity of experimental psychologists to an "alphabetical elite." As a result, despite the variety of applications of the device, this comparison led Kittler to conclude that the program of reading promoted by the tachistoscope became noticeable differentials of material type, rather than reading per se.

Crary recalls Eadweard Muybridge's sequential photographs, seeing a similar operation in the isolation of visual fields and the sequential arrangement of those fields, although the tachistoscope's sequences were not necessarily consecutive.[32] I wish to draw special attention to this sequential aspect, the pattern of one image or text being replaced by another. In its pre-digital form, film is an arranged series of still images that move at a constant rate, separated by imperceptible black fields. The tachistoscope is an arrangement of a still, black field, interrupted by nearly imperceptible images exposed at a variable rate. One instrument from the 1920s used to assess memory, the bradyscope, illustrates further this mechanical affinity between film and tachistoscopy. The bradyscope's innovation was its ability to flash its images or text at a constant rate, a feature that would develop into reading pacers.[33] Where the traditional tachistoscope was premised upon a certain element of surprise, with flashes of light appearing randomly and suddenly, the bradyscope offered a way to measure the changes over time with ongoing exposures appearing at a steady rate, just as a metronome strikes beats. Although not designed to do this, a bradyscope hypothetically set to twenty-four flashes a second would transform its functions into that of a standard film projector. Thus at a slow frequency the bradyscope is a reading pacer, at a faster one it produces a tachistoscopic flicker, and at an even faster one, reaching what is called a fusion frequency, we have motion pictures.[34] *The primary feature differentiating these devices is the speed of arrival and departure of frames and fields.* I take time to establish these cognate elements because the ample and convincing claims about film's relationship to the modern fragmentation and elasticity of time and space (because of, for example, its variable point of view and its editing) neglect what examining the tachistoscope illuminates: the speed of screen sequencing. The tachistoscope and film share the high-speed mechanical replacement of images and text occupying a visual field. Even the relatively slow reading pacers were designed to increase eventually, not slow down, reading speed.

As Benschop puts it, Cattell specifically used visual cues to measure other brain functions, or "how fast we think," as he said.[35] As one might imagine, the speeds of perceptual and "thinking" functions vary among people, as well as with practice, and appear to be a range rather than some absolute. The mounting number of trials in reading produced statistical evidence for standards of performance, that is, what constituted the normal, the exceptional, and the substandard. Charting how the brain learns, along with the other interests of experimental psychology, fashioned new ways to define, calculate, predict, and depict the sensory world of humans, knowledge that could be, and was, deployed in the service of maximum mechanical and cognitive efficiency (for example, of labor). Where uncovering expected or normal rates of knowledge acquisition was a preoccupation, curiosity about improvements in reaction time followed. As growing attention was paid to differentials, new questions were asked: how could the performance of the slower subjects be accelerated? Moreover what, if any, was the role of the tachistoscope in measuring but also in facilitating the improvement in response time? With these queries we witness an extraordinary transposition: a measurement apparatus is understood as the agent of change. Intriguingly, although the point has been left out of the existing histories, the tachistoscope became both a diagnostic and a therapeutic instrument in the service of improving rates of response. As Crary reminds us, this turn toward behaviorist experiments as offering base measures of individual performance, with a special relation between human perception and mechanical devices, was already evident in Cattell's work of the 1890s,[36] although this was not systematized into training regimes until much later.[37]

After decades of laboratory use, the tachistoscope was reconstructed, manufactured, and marketed as a device of instructional technology in the first decades of the twentieth century. Its tabulation of times was refashioned as the tabulation of scores, and the very process of being hit repeatedly with flashing type became a form of classroom lesson. Not all agreed on the tachistoscope's educational effectiveness, and some attributed variations in results to the mere repetition of actions, the focusing of attention, or innate perceptual capacity. Nevertheless, the move from lab to classroom is significant because it indicates the transportability of the "swift view" idea, and because this linkage gradually emerged during the initial rumblings of a discourse of educational technology. This classroom connection would never have developed without the budding field of visual, and later audiovisual, education. Just as machine-assisted reading instruction was beginning to establish its pedagogical paradigm, psychological research understood silent reading to be among the speediest of all human processes.[38] The relationship between behaviorist inquiry and modern mass education framed the question of learning as one of technological mediation.

The widespread turn to such instrumental instruction can be traced to an unlikely and innovative source. Catherine Aiken, a teacher in Pennsylvania in the 1890s, found a way to accelerate learning and heighten concentration through what she called "exercises in mind-training."[39] Her popular books proposed a separation of content from the "muscles" of perception and understanding, and addressed the particularly modern threat of boredom. Students were put through a routine of brain exercises that echoed other rising forms of physical culture at the time. "Muscular Christianity" for Aiken could be reworked as a brand of mental calisthenics. Her first improvised prop was a rotating blackboard, which she would spin so that the girls in her class could see the material for but a brief instant. Arguably, this is the fount from which later permutations of flashcards and tachistoscopic training emerged. Indeed, where psychologists endeavored to test Aiken's claims, a tachistoscope was used rather than the spinning blackboard.[40]

The classroom tachistoscope had the design advantage of repetitive, sequential presentation of material, so that one was not only learning about a subject but being drilled on it. Teaching through a mechanized screen, as opposed to the page, was something done to an entire class and at the same time. These first educational devices would have been seen as souped-up magic lanterns, essentially a technology adaptable to any subject content. Explorations of possible uses in industrial training are also evident by the end of the 1920s. Industrial applications tested, for instance, the reading rates of executives at Johnson & Johnson and the eye-mind coordination of telephone operators.[41] W. Hische determined that the speed of sequential presentation of material greatly affected how people retained and understood lessons, with too slow a pace leading to boredom. He indicated that this observation had implications for repetitive factory work.[42]

Tachistoscopes were especially useful in teaching and improving the core skill of reading, and were regularly employed to study reading and reading disabilities in the first decade of the twentieth century.[43] One did not just read; ideally one read efficiently, quickly. Kittler put the first attempt to measure reading speed at 1803,[44] but most histories begin with Émile Javal in 1878 and his attention to the movement of the eye and the discovery of its saccadic, or jumpy, motion. Some psychologists agreed that reading was a perceptual activity, hence one that could be developed by altering perceptual skills.[45] The tachistoscope helped by disciplining the eye, training it to move in a regimented fashion, to take in more with each fixation of the eye's journey across the page, not to rest too long with each fixation, and not to wander without purpose.[46] Moreover, these activities would have a measure for their change. Improvements could be documented and averaged, expectations could be set, and "problems" could be identified. E. Grund, in Germany, conducted an experiment using tachistoscopes to assess reading skills, charting how children learn to see whole words rather than parts,[47] extending research by W. Stein from the previous year.[48] Tachistoscopic training was literally a form of discipline in some tests. For instance, one study divided a group of African American students into "trouble-makers" and "non-trouble-makers," and measured the effects on reading skills of teaching with tachistoscopes.[49] Other research employed tachistoscopes to show that accelerated reading first required correcting perceptual difficulties,[50] and to argue that the tachistoscope might be used to diagnose reading problems.[51] Not coincidentally, reading troubles like dyslexia were officially recognized in the 1930s, part of the consolidation of new understandings of the operations of the brain and mass education.

Tachistoscopes had competition early on from other eye-training devices. Motion picture series were developed that sought to capitalize upon findings about perceptual skills and reading. Harvard, Iowa, and Purdue all had programs of 16mm film that taught controlled reading by projecting a filmed, even-paced scroll of text, on which a class would be tested afterward. But this approach suffered in that the films did not offer flexibility in teaching and required the class to move at the pace set by the projector, with some teachers preferring instead 35mm filmstrips. The tachistoscope's variability in presentational speed made it the more felicitous technology, although it was best used to teach reduced eye movement and reflexive recognition, rather than assimilation of material. Other basic instructional devices to teach reading in the early 1950s included controlled reading devices, which promoted left-to-right continuity, and accelerators. The latter were pacers, some of which had light bars moving smoothly down the page of a book. Some were marketed to homes as well as schools. Many aids could be either handheld for individual use or projected for group instruction, with some instruments combining these functions.

Earl Taylor set a path-breaking course as a reading technology innovator and entrepreneur. His book *Controlled Reading* (1937) elaborated experiments in eye movement and training exercises for visual improvement.[52] He had developed, in conjunction with his brothers James Y. and Carl C. Taylor, a three-field tachistoscope called a Metronoscope in 1931 and a device that could record eye movement called an Ophthalmograph. With the Metronoscope each field would appear in sequence from left to right, working to condition the eye to move efficiently when reading. This device, the first introduced to schools in the United States, was distributed by American Optical Company (which later became Educational Development Laboratories, or EDL), marking an initial reworking of the tachistoscope as a manufactured teaching tool.

In this reworking few were as influential as Samuel Renshaw, professor of experimental psychology at Ohio State University. This enigmatic figure has appeared tangentially in the history of several fields, including film studies and education theory, though his influence has often gone unacknowledged. He was the main author of perhaps the most notorious of the Payne Fund studies in the 1930s, in which his team documented the effects of motion pictures upon children's sleep. One aspect of this work, conducted by students under his direction, used a tachistoscopic device to study the effect of visual flicker upon a child's eyes.[53] From 1939 to 1962 Renshaw wrote the entirety of a monthly bulletin, successively called *Psychology of Vision, Demonstrations in Psychological Optics*, and finally *Visual Psychology*.[54] Renshaw began offering a 120-hour program in 1942 to train Navy pilots to recognize aircraft and ships. Using a tachistoscope, he documented precisely the rate at which he could accelerate pilots' abilities to see and identify planes and ships. When Renshaw reported his findings he noted that one class continued to improve its response rate and accuracy through seventy sessions, and he claimed that the rate for some was at a level ordinarily reserved for geniuses.[55] After taking his course, men distinguished planes in 1/75 of a second and ships in one second.[56] Renshaw inferred that what the tachistoscope did was enlarge the subject's field of vision, training the eye to take in more at once.

Pilots identifying and reacting automatically, and attaining this machine-like reflex through a controlled stroboscopic device, captured public imagination. These were the newest, most technologically advanced methods of instruction, methods that outshone the quaint, humanistic educational models of the past. Here technologized humans produced through technologized programs fit with a sensibility about how modern mass education was to be pursued. The Renshaw Recognition System received as much individual fame as any of the other significant educational programs of the Second World War. For his training regime Renshaw received a Distinguished Public Service Award from the U.S. Navy in 1955, and the National Air and Space Museum exhibited material from the program.[57] *Science Digest* drew attention to Renshaw's innovation in speed-learning.[58] *Time* reported, on the occasion of his commendation, Renshaw's intention to speed up "sluggish readers" among the civilian population.[59] To this end he helped to develop and market his own device, the individually operated Stereo-Optical Tachitron, for which he wrote the manual.[60]

Buoyed by Renshaw's program, these swift-viewing instruments appeared to be the freshest offerings of a technologized age, and promised to alleviate the postwar glut of students to teach and information to impart.[61] Just as Renshaw was receiving attention for his military training work, Melcer and Brown documented improvements on reading and intelligence tests for children after tachistoscopic training in 1945.[62] The U.S. Air Force sponsored tachistoscopic research in the area of target recognition,[63] and the Navy funded hand-eye coordination tests that used a version of the tachistoscope.[64] In 1953 Henry Smith and Theodore Tate found that students trained with a tachistoscope and an accelerator improved their reading speed, though with some loss in comprehension. Their test subjects appeared to increase speed more significantly with projected rather than printed material. They also had an inflated impression of their own improvement.[65] Even into the 1960s research tested the effectiveness of tachistoscopes for training, generally finding that reading could be sped up, and fixations could be reduced, though errors would also increase.[66]

Commercial uses went beyond the educational market. Tachistoscopes were long used to test advertisements, and they continue to be used in this way.[67] Advertising studies in the 1930s charted which length of an advertisement was most likely to promote accurate recall, and how quickly men and women could distinguish a magazine page as having either editorial or advertising content.[68] In a key text, the authors presented the psychological objectives of advertising as capturing and holding attention, and maintaining an impression. The primary challenge was "the presence of counterattractions."[69] The authors included a study of ways to grab attention through psychological triggers in advertising graphics. And among the techniques used to test the effectiveness of ads, including consumer surveys, panel interviews, Nielsen ratings, and cameras that tracked eye movement, were tachistoscopes, recommended for measuring the legibility of advertisements in brief durations.[70] Experiments paired tachistoscopes with other instruments. For example, the psychogalvanometer lie detector reduced the wily element of subject reporting of tachistoscopically flashed word association.[71] In the 1960s Seymour Smith used a tachistoscope and survey questions for a cross-media comparison of advertising, studying film, print, brochures, publicity, phone, mail, trade shows, and internal business communication.[72] Speed in commercial appeals remains an objective for marketers, who continue to test product packaging using tachistoscopes, flashing the design, color, and copy at subjects to chart the most easily recognizable ones.[73] So widespread was the interest in qualities of "swift viewing" training and testing that in 1964 a psychologist declared, "More than any other psychological apparatus, the tachistoscope . . . has earned its place in commercial research."[74]

Tachistoscopes for groups also became more varied in function, and were often adaptable to other projection uses.[75] Low-cost projection tachistoscopes were developed specifically for classroom instruction at the same time.[76] Even as late as the 1970s new versions were being introduced, for instance one that resembled a slide projector.[77] Studies examined the varying applicability for different learners, from college students to clerical workers.[78] In the 1950s flash film for driving education combined filmstrips and a tachistoscope to surprise students with a driving decision.[79] During that decade *Educational Screen* published several articles on tachistoscopic teaching.[80] Postwar mass-marketed devices for educational use included the Perceptoscope from Perceptual Development Laboratories, which developed and marketed its projection tachistoscope along with reading instruction guides in 1957. The Speed-I-O-Scope, from the Society for Visual Education (sve), appeared in the early 1950s. The Taylor family's firm edl introduced the Tach-X Tachistoscope in 1953, after a trademark battle over their unsuccessful attempt to use the name Time-X.

TACHISTOSCOPES FOR GROUP USE

— EDL Tach-X, Educational Development Laboratories
— Keystone Standard Tachistoscope, Keystone View Company
— Rheem-Califone Percepta-matic, Carleton Films
— T-ap All Purpose Tachistoscope Attachment (changes projectors into tachistoscopes), Lafayette Instrument Co.
— SVE Speed-I-O-Scope, Society for Visual Education, Inc.

TACHISTOSCOPES FOR INDIVIDUAL USE

— Electro-Tach, Lafayette Instrument Co.
— Tachist-O-Viewer and Tachist-O-Flasher, Learning Through Seeing, Inc.
— AVR Eye-Span Trainer, Audio-Visual Research
— Phrase Flasher, Reading Laboratories, Inc.

READING PACERS

— Shadowscope, Psychotechnics, Inc.
— Prep-Pacer, Reading Laboratories, Inc.
— AVR Reading Rateometer, Audio-Visual Research
— SRA Reading Accelerator, Science Research Associates
— Reader Pacer, Genco Educational Aids

FILMS OR FILMSTRIPS

— Controlled Reader, Controlled Reader Jr., EDL
— Tachomatic 500 Reading Projector, Psychotechnics, Inc.
— Craig Reader, Craig Research, Inc.[81]

The Keystone View Company, whose name had been made with stereoscopes and stereoscopic views, experimented with school uses in 1938, and it began to market its Flashmeter in 1944, a device with a top speed of 1/100 of a second.[82] Keystone actively produced manuals of instructions by educational psychologists with clear lesson plans for teachers to follow for tachistoscopic training, beginning in 1949.[83] These were whole teaching programs, entire course curricula, for subjects ranging from vocabulary to math. In effect the Keystone View Company was selling what we now call both hardware and software to schools. One instructional set provided a way to use the tachistoscope as a timing device for other reading activities, enabling students to assess how many words per minute they read during a particular trial.[84] Other tachisto-slides tested math skills, drilled object and geometric identification, improved vocabulary, presented picture-and-word pairs, assessed reading proficiency, and offered motivational slogans for efficient reading ("You Can Read Well," "Keep Your Mind Alert," "Don't Move Your Lips").[85] A reading program that began with the identification of shapes for young children was to train the controlled movement of the eye, a muscular preparation for the development of literacy.

Among other things, these companies successfully made the tachistoscope an indispensable tool for speed-reading, a faddish approach in the 1950s eventually supplanted by the Evelyn Wood hegemony in the 1960s. Earlier reports in popular and trade publications about speed-reading did not focus on technique or instructional aids. For example, one in the *New York Times* in 1923 referred only briefly to the possibility that movies might exercise the eyes and hence improve reading speeds, concentrating instead upon a long list of the word counts for the Bible, newspapers, and novels, and average word-per-minute scores of different levels of schooling.[86] This contrasts with articles in the postwar years that highlighted the technological aids to speedy reading, including tachistoscopes.[87] In 1953 *Fortune* reported on a full-blown "speed-reading craze," documenting the competing approaches of tachistoscopic training, reading films, and nonmechanical skimming.[88] At the time, speed-reading had become a tool for achieving career success; the captains of industry and leaders of government, it was assumed, possessed a valuable skill in their ability to scan and assimilate an abundance of material, and were seen as better armed to manage the rapidly changing information that characterized the modern world. Reports on the craze presented idolizing word-per-minute scores of famous fast readers, among them John F. Kennedy and Theodore Roosevelt, and corporations set up special speed-reading seminars for their aspiring executives.

Competing experiments questioned the actual contribution of instructional devices. One study compared tachistoscopically trained reading students who received oral direction and encouragement from their teachers with those who did not, finding that the teacher's presence greatly improved performance.[89] EDL sponsored research to measure the singular contribution to improved reading made by different learning technologies. Previous research showed that a controlled reader could reduce fixation and regressive eye movements, and could do so better

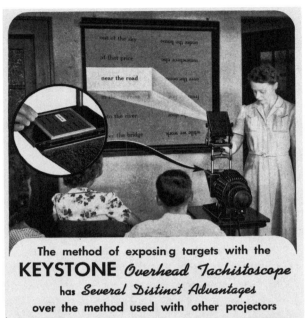

Advertisement for Keystone tachistoscope, 1946. Courtesy of Crawford County Historical Society, Meadville, Pa.

Advertisement for EDL tachistoscope and controlled reader, 1953. Courtesy of Crawford County Historical Society, Meadville, Pa.

than two brands of pacers (Shadowscope and Rateometer).[90] Even if tachistoscopy produced observable improvements, a conclusive showing that the technology itself was the *source* of changes in reading rates had not been made by any of the research, including that of Renshaw, which used Navy pilots who had an unusually high degree of education and did not compare them with a control group.[91] EDL's study of different combinations of technology demonstrated that each does indeed contribute uniquely, and that the tachistoscope was most effective in lowering the length of each fixation.[92]

The speed-reading mania continued into the 1960s. As Lawrence Galton put it, "Already, indeed, there are reports that, in some circles, no longer is the content of a book a subject for conversation; all anybody wants to know is how fast the book was read."[93] Although this report reasserted the tachistoscope's role in speed-reading, again tracing its origins to Renshaw's recognition training during the Second World War, in the 1960s Evelyn Wood's reading method, notable for its self-help tone and simple hand-skimming technique, effectively overtook the tachistoscope as the dominant speed-reading program. Stanford Taylor spoke for many of those supporting reading technologies when he admonished the Wood students for not reading everything on the page. That method, he argued, was teaching skimming and scanning, not controlled reading, which involved disciplining the eye. Even as Wood's program rose to prominence, in 1962 Keystone's client list of regular purchasers and users of its tachistoscope programs, slides, and equipment included over 2,300 schools and boards of education in the United States, and fifty abroad.[94] By the end of the 1970s Stanford Taylor, president of EDL, estimated that there were 240,000 of his company's devices in schools in the United States.[95] The extent to which any of these devices were being put to use, and not just cluttering up audiovisual closets, is another matter. At the very least, Taylor's company continues to operate today after seventy years, indicating that a sizable and lasting market for these reading technologies persists.

Most infamously, as we will investigate in the coming chapters, some advertising firms in the late 1950s experimented with using tachistoscopes to flash messages at movies, sparking a scandal about the subconscious influences of imperceptible text, and incidentally moving the term "subliminal" from psychology into the popular lexicon. The twentieth century was awash with concerns about the mass media and propaganda.

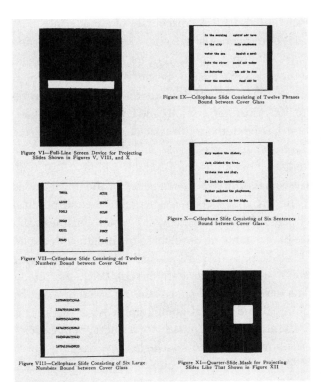

Figure VI—Full-Line Screen Device for Projecting Slides Shown in Figures V, VIII, and X

Figure VII—Cellophane Slide Consisting of Twelve Numbers Bound between Cover Glass

Figure VIII—Cellophane Slide Consisting of Six Large Numbers Bound between Cover Glass

Figure IX—Cellophane Slide Consisting of Twelve Phrases Bound between Cover Glass

Figure X—Cellophane Slide Consisting of Six Sentences Bound between Cover Glass

Figure XI—Quarter-Slide Mask for Projecting Slides Like That Shown in Figure XII

Keystone
Tachistoslides, 1954

Keystone
catalogue, 1966

A related phenomenon, springing from discourses of a modern techno-logical character, was the prevalence of extreme visions of a passive and irrational contemporary subject, as depicted in the fictional accelerated learning scenarios with which this chapter began. As seen in chapter 2, some have long surmised that certain techniques and conditions can cre-ate a special entrée to individual unconscious and collective will. Consis-tent with this claim, it has been thought that tachistoscopes have "the power to activate psychodynamic processes," and that with them "one could then subject to laboratory study the fascinating kinds of relation-ships that psychoanalysis has posited between behavior and unconscious mental processes."[96] In this view tachistoscopes replicate and produce the conditions of somnambulism. Since the 1970s dubious business ven-tures using the device have abounded, developing in tandem with the in-dustry of subliminal self-help. With quasi-evangelical zeal, the founder of Subliminal Dynamics/Brain Management, Richard Welch, took credit for inventing in 1975 a new method of speed-reading based on what he variously called subliminal and mental photography. As advertised, it offered a "Whole-Life Enhancement Course, not a photographic mem-ory course."[97] This "new method" used a tachistoscope flashing words at the impossible speed of two million per minute. Welch presented this as a missionary project to get the message out, "to help an ever overbur-dened world to find the answers for tomorrow."[98]

One should not be perplexed by this last direction. It is the realization of an underlying dream involving the necessity of meeting the demands of a speedy era. After all, Walter Benjamin long ago alerted us to our mod-ern universe of milliseconds, calling it the "optical unconscious" of pho-tography.[99] In a way we are part of a Leibnizian age, obsessed with the in-finitesimal *petite différence* that constitutes the barest minimum of event. The tachistoscope's functional operations provided concrete figures for what had been imprecise tabulations of how fast, how much, and how well people learn, not to mention how much faster and how much more. In so doing the device participated in moving part of the laboratory and the classroom into the fleeting realm of split seconds. The preoccupation with micro-manifestations of human behavior, and adjoining aspirations to accelerate those manifestations, eventually pushed responses to previ-ously improbable rates (or at least the recordability of those responses).

We might think of the subliminal as an idea of the vanishing point of speed in human recognition, decision, and action, where a type of automatic reflex or assessment in thought is said to occur. Experimental psychologists pursued this for decades before the popular subliminal controversy of the late 1950s. In 1933 O. A. Simley used a chronoscope with the intention of testing what sort of learning, if any, took place above and below consciousness, that is, between supra- and sub-liminal learning, seeking to identify the bond that might build between memory, association, and a flickering stimulus.[100] As demonstrated in this chapter, the resonant concern represented by the tachistoscope's history had an initial incarnation as an empirical project to chart the range of normal human perception. The sure draw toward improvement saw questions arise about testing the limits of that threshold, and saw the tachistoscope become an instrument for controlled experiments and a training aid. For all of the instrument's legitimate uses in reading instruction, underlying the movement from lab to classroom is a valorization of the efficient and the quick in perceptual faculties, as well as an exploration of automatic responsiveness over critical (seen as slow) reasoning. The tachistoscope, as a medium of nearly instantaneous communication, helped to imagine a short-circuiting of rhetorical ploys. The extreme incarnation of its educational objective is the mind-control trope. The wide acceptance of the *possible* manipulation of minds through subliminal means was a perfectly reasonable extension of the *actual* urgency to manage mass populations and the *actual* desire to do so efficiently, quickly, and to special advantage. The tachistoscopic idea thus circulated with a language of media manipulation even as the device offered remedies for media and textual abundance.

Friedrich Kittler argued not only that the tachistoscope was "the twin of the movie projector" but that it embodied elements of the typewriter, with flashing text striking eyes and brain. He wrote, quite plainly, "The tachistoscope is a typewriter whose type hits the retina rather than paper,"[101] by which he ostensibly linked it with the technology that was the primary focus of his study of modern notation and storage systems. The association of tachistoscope and typewriter prompted Kittler to see the processes observed and measured as "mindless," that is, as an image of direct and crisp imprinting in our skulls. When Kittler wrote, "The automatism of tachistoscopic word exposition is not designed to transport thoughts,"[102] he neglected to appraise the technology's transformation into an instructional aid. And it is this idea of "mind-writing" that carries through to the employment of the tachistoscope for subliminal influence. Such views of media influence structure the reigning under-standings of the relative immobility, concentration, and suggestibility of subjects. And these views are by no means only applicable to the tachisto-scope, once we note that they are reminiscent of claims made of the pur-portedly manipulative properties of television, popular music, and video games. Pushing further, whether in imagining the forced learning or the overpowering nature of some media, critics contemplated how the same strategies and instruments might become vehicles for the injection of ideas and the overt control of action.

This chapter has shown the sluggish historical trajectory of the tachis-toscopic idea as it moved into a series of arenas, dragging along a set of logistics about knowing and influencing the workings of the mind. As a diagnostic and therapeutic instrument, the tachistoscope helped to iden-tify and rectify extraneous action in the movement of eyes. As an experi-mental instrument, it helped to discover and measure optical and mental processes. As a teaching instrument, it helped to accelerate recognition and memory, and provided a quantifiable performance indicator. As a speed-reading instrument, it disciplined eyes to take in entire fields of in-formation rapidly. As a military instrument, it pushed target recognition into a reflex response. As a marketing instrument, it helped to streamline decisions about advertising copy and layout. The tachistoscope began as an instrument for measuring physiological functions and in subsequent generations became an instrument for measuring the achievements of students, teachers, and the curriculum. The logic of the performance in-dicator is evident in this technologizing of instructional procedure, the guiding principles being more students and content, fewer teachers and digressions, faster lesson acquisition, less expensive course delivery, and quicker course completion.

In sum, the tachistoscope reoriented reading from pages to screens, demonstrating that the ground for screen reading was well tilled long before computers appeared. Second, the tachistoscope responded to, and amplified, the consequences of the accelerated appearance and dis-appearance—arrival and departure—of images and text, an acceleration that we have come to think of as information overload. And third, it was continuous with the priorities of modernity and its emphasis on efficien-cies of production, including the construction of a synthetic subject who could handle the new image and textual abundance of a mass media era.

In light of these applications, the tachistoscopic idea is about the orientation of attention, one that carries forward other ideas about the mass mind and the culture of speed. Crary calls the tachistoscope "paradigmatic of an ideal of experimental control."[103] The claim could apply to any number of equally prevalent psychological instruments. Nevertheless, he is right to see the tachistoscope as emblematic of a trajectory of research and as instrumental in a shifting understanding of the perceptual apparatus. I would add that *it is especially paradigmatic of media control, technologized instruction, and rapid mind manipulation*. It is evidence of the view that perception is a muscle to be trained and disciplined through a careful arrangement of a technological apparatus. The tachistoscope, in its many incarnations, is a material manifestation of what we take to be quintessential modern qualities—mechanized sight, Taylorist instruction, contained and focused attention. It helped to institutionalize subject performance into perceptual and cognitive processes, becoming a procedure to chart speeds and a program to improve them. Working on eye muscles and mental faculties, efficiency and speed reigned as a goal for teachers and students, and as a measure of success of that mineshaft elevator to the brain. Speed, as investigated by commentators as varied as Paul Virilio and Stephen Kern, was especially salient. The tachistoscope designated a mental sound barrier to be smashed, this in the context of the fantastic warp speed in the contemporary universe of signs. Speed, it seems, is a modern environmental condition; the swift arrival and departure of words and images, the apparent fleeting presence of texts, necessitated acclimatization and instantaneous judgment. Moreover, identifying these conditions catalyzed speculation about our relative inadaptability to "unnatural" shocks.

Here we have a significant point: once we consider the entirety of the tachistoscopic idea, we must acknowledge that the story of modernity is not only one of fragmentation, shock, and disorientation, as we are continuously reminded, but of the language and procedures of acclimatization, orientation, and synthesis, as well as mass instruction. What is drawn out is a lasting, residual array of concerns about adaptability to the pace of textual flow, or the assembly of a survival kit for modern screen visuality. The following chapter describes one watershed moment in which a new concept was added to the contents of this survival kit, and the modern menace of semiotic abundance became an explicit focus of public attention.

Mind-Probing Admen

The summer of 1957 saw the release of a resonant critique of the fascistic undercurrents of media power, Elia Kazan's *A Face in the Crowd.* The film tells the story of Lonesome Rhodes as he takes his homespun individualist philosophy from a jail cell to national stardom, with conservative forces battling to appropriate his voice for their purposes along the way. Increasingly cynical, Rhodes is a willing participant in this political recasting. This parallels his energetic endorsement of a vitamin supplement with dubious claims to boosting libido. To depict this, the film includes an exaggerated parody of a commercial for the fictional product. *A Face in the Crowd* presents Rhodes's accumulation of political and commercial might as bound up with the manipulations of mass opinion. And it was part of a growing popular suspicion about the power of the commercial realm and the failure of public rationality.

One of the most mythologized events of media influence from that year, retold in countless variations, was the announcement of a test of subliminal messages reading "eat popcorn" and "drink Coca-Cola" at a movie theater. The test took place in the Fort Lee Theater in New Jersey, which was reportedly showing *Picnic* (Joshua Logan, 1955) at the time. Virtually every discussion of subliminal advertising since has included a rendition of this trial, though the details often amount to no more than what

I've just presented in the two previous sentences. Tales of media influence return to this event partly because its dramatic results have never been reproduced. And most significantly, it was the release of these unbelievable results that sparked the wave of public interest and anxiety about subliminal methods of influence. Before the public disclosure of the experiment, there were relatively few mentions of "subliminal" in popular venues and none in connection to advertising. Afterward, the term would find itself part of a popular lexicon about advertising, psychology, and media manipulation.

The man who conducted the experiment in New Jersey was the marketing researcher James Vicary. He claimed that over the course of six weeks he was able to increase consumption of popcorn at the theater by 57.5% and of Coke by 18.1% by flashing those simple messages for 1/3,000 of a second every five seconds and projecting them upon dark areas of the screen.[1] Even though Vicary, in 1962, admitted that these results were exaggerated,[2] and that there had been no controls against which to measure the increases, the event has remained a touchstone for awareness of subliminal advertising. The association with *Picnic* does not begin to appear in press until the spring of 1958, and it was never confirmed by Vicary, so like many details of this event its veracity is questionable. It is noteworthy, though, that this most memorable of public subliminal demonstrations is gilded as particularly American, with popcorn and Coke as props, Kim Novak and William Holden—the stars of *Picnic*—as characters, and New Jersey as the setting. These elements were tailor-made to evoke a contrasting sentiment of wholesome American sensual pleasure and suspicion about underlying manipulative forces. The small-town and Labor Day setting of *Picnic*, and the disruption caused by the unexpected presence of a handsome stranger, offer an oblique parallel to the dramatic events that unfold. In the versions that follow, James Vicary is our William Holden.[3]

The unusually large number of subjects reportedly involved—45,699 movie-goers—made this a fairly extensive trial. Even if the figure is little more than a wild estimate, which it most likely is, the procedures that would capture this remarkable number are as unethical as they are impressive. Few if any test subjects would have known that they were participating in a test, hence informed consent would not have been provided. So in this first major episode in popular comprehension of the subliminal process, the method of scientific study was itself at issue. In

James M. Vicary

subsequent public experiments this is a consistent element and may account for some of the concern provoked by the idea of hidden messages. Unconscious manipulation by advertisers was mirrored by the secret activities of researchers and experts, testing a general population without their knowledge or approval. Paranoia surfaced with the next logical question about the situation: How do we know we are not being tested now? Whether manipulated by advertisers or by researchers, the general public was conceptualized as an abstract field subjected to invisible forces of scrutiny and influence.

The respected marketing professor and consultant Stuart Rogers provided a sober assessment of this touchstone incident in *Public Opinion Quarterly* in 1993. The article, though, shifts the chronology of what happened. Rogers dated the press conference at which Vicary first released his impressive test results as after November 1957, when it was actually in September of that year. As a result, in Rogers's version this invitation to the press seems to be in response to public outcry, where it was in fact the initiation of public concern. Rogers wrote that most stories mistakenly place the tests in Grover's Mill, New Jersey, coincidentally one of the settings for Orson Welles's *The War of the Worlds*. However, I have not seen a reference to Grover's Mill in the stories about Vicary's tests except in Rogers's article. Rogers, a psychology student in 1957 at nearby Hofstra University, described driving to Fort Lee and talking to the theater manager, who denied that any test had taken place, though the manager contradicted himself by later telling *Motion Picture Daily* that there had been no effect on the audience (implying that there had indeed been some test). Rogers referred to a flurry of press releases into 1958, but without indication of how he had access to these largely unpublished documents. He described going to the U.S. Patent Office in 1969 to see if Vicary had filed an application and failing to find any such documentation, or any other applications for subliminal advertising devices.[4] This latter claim is, in the least, a result of incomplete research, because by the late 1960s not only were there many patents received for tachistoscopic devices of various kinds, but some were explicitly for marketing and promotional purposes. Rogers then estimated, without supporting evidence, that Vicary had received $4.5 million from an advertising firm for consulting fees, and then disappeared, "leaving no bank account, no clothes in his closet, and no hint as to where he might have gone," which is absolutely incorrect.[5] In keeping with his portrait of Vicary as a Barnum-like figure who took advantage of the mass of suckers, Rogers wrote a sidebar description of Wilson Bryan Key, with similarly uncited claims that Key's unscrupulous work also earned him $4.5 million.[6] Rogers also claimed that Jan David Brunvand's *The Choking Doberman* put Vicary's legendary experiment in the 1930s. But checking that and Brunvand's many other books of urban legends did not reveal any such inaccurate detail. Rogers himself dated the experiment to 1958—contradicting dates earlier in his essay—when it was in fact in 1956. I can only conclude that Rogers's article is yet another contribution to the misinformation surrounding this event.

While the absolute veracity of details can easily be exposed as shaky with the testimony of a fresh witness or the unearthing of a new account, what follows is the most complete version of Vicary's subliminal controversy that I could assemble. I rely upon industry reports, state investigative commissions, and expert assessment. But primarily I have amassed and integrated periodical features, reports, and news items from the period. This incident, after all, was a media sensation. The sheer abundance of published responses is a testament to the popular visibility of the "invisible sell." Repetition of details provides material evidence for the building of a publicly shared event. The critical commentaries and editorials show that the questions posed by subliminal messages were ones to which periodicals, legislatures, and industry organizations felt they had to respond. Positions had to be staked out and publicly declared, if only to prove the ethical mettle of the organizations concerned. Returning to this material, we find that the issue was not isolated nor shuffled off into some obscure corner of the cultural scene reserved for crackpot ideas. We find a lively ferment that extends from a single proposal for advertising research to expressions of doubt as to the democratic potential of mass society.

This ferment was not instigated automatically. Among the mitigating circumstances were Vicary's own prior activities in marketing research. In his book *Adcult USA*, James Twitchell inaccurately described Vicary as unemployed and likened him to P. T. Barnum.[7] Impressions continue to suggest that Vicary was a confidence artist and a charlatan. While the veracity of his research was sometimes questionable and he may have been a habitual liar or a bad researcher, he was also an innovator of what he later referred to as "creative marketing research," for which he advocated. As Vicary put it, "risk reduction is the goal of market research — not pure science."[8]

Before the international breakout appearance of subliminal advertising, with which he would forever be associated, James McDonald Vicary was a successful survey researcher with his own company. Born in 1915, Vicary displayed a long interest in word association and public opinion. He launched his reputation for unorthodox research methods in 1930, when as a teenage employee of the *Detroit Free Press* he conducted his own survey, with which he was able to accurately predict that the mayor of Detroit would be recalled.[9] As a business student at the University of Michigan, Ann Arbor, and head of the Bureau of Student Opinion, he received a degree of attention in 1939 for an extensive poll that tracked and ranked words with negative associations in 1939 (the three most negative terms were fascism, anti-Christ, and Sunday blue laws).[10] Graduating in 1940 and taking conscientious objector status during the Second World War, Vicary worked for Crowell-Collier Publishing and then did market research at Benton and Bowles, but he did not last long at the latter. Years afterward he explained his departure by describing his "methods [as] too advanced for the company," but it is unclear if he was discharged or asked to resign.[11] In 1945 he formed his own market research company, James M. Vicary Company, in New York. By 1957 his company had six staff employees and four hundred field researchers across the country.[12]

Vicary had such prominent clients as AT&T, *Family Circle* magazine, and B. F. Goodrich Chemical.[13] He had some success building a niche for helping businesses name their companies and products, producing detailed reports on word connotations and surveys of word associations of potential consumers. He had a hand in the renaming of Armco Steel Corporation, Colgate-Palmolive Company, Nationwide Insurance Company, Socony Mobil Oil Company (from Socony Vacuum), Sylvania Electric Products, and Underwood.[14] His research often involved hundreds of subjects and hundreds of pages of analysis.[15] In addition to supplying research for clients, Vicary regularly circulated short summaries of findings in press releases. These releases courted attention by highlighting the most sensational and surprising elements of his research, placing and keeping Vicary's name in the public eye. Among the findings that he circulated as short statements of fact: prunes had a limited market because their use as a laxative created an "emotional block"; television characters were seen as intimate household members by their domestic audience; businessmen each year spent more than five times the cost of their hats in tips to hat-check girls; the word "nationwide" was understood as "international" by a significant number of those surveyed; the word "lagered" was a poor term with which to sell beer, as many associated it with "tired" or "slow"; "standard" was seen more positively than "standardization," which suggested "regimentation"; for women, baking a cake is psychologically comparable to giving birth; and women enter a light trance while shopping in supermarkets.[16] Vicary appeared eager to circulate general psychological assertions as pithy truisms, with some apparent success. Some of these claims reappear even today as statements of fact or as examples of the rampant irrationality of the 1950s. This split in his reception is evident in literature contemporaneous with Vicary's work. For instance, Steuart Britt, in his book on the business of marketing from 1960, approvingly described the word association study that questioned the value of the word "lagered" to sell beer. Then, to illustrate the absurd side of the same approach to market research, Britt wrote,

How to Think about a Brand Name
For a New Product

Brand names that are pat . . . that are rememberable . . . that carry the right connotation . . . that are protectable, are hard indeed to come by. These rules may limit your choice, but they also may open new avenues of creative thought to a name that has just the proper "sales-flip."

BY JAMES M. VICARY

not apply to any one product; in fact many are contradictory. Their value lies not in providing final answers, but in furnishing a stimulant and perhaps a corrective to thinking. Here are 59 rules which I have heard at one time or another. Other rules may occur to the reader—probably will! —but the person with a naming problem on his hands who has considered all these criteria can feel he has taken a major step toward his ultimate objective— the selection of the *one best*

Graphic clutter to represent branding environment, image accompanying James Vicary, 1956. Courtesy of Thomas J. Dodd Research Center, University of Connecticut.

"Someone . . . apparently in all seriousness, claimed that when a woman bakes a cake she is symbolically recreating the process of giving birth!"[17]

No simple Madison Avenue huckster, Vicary participated in academic and market research publishing. In 1945 he worked at Paul Lazarsfeld's Bureau of Applied Social Research. There he advanced the use of "mass observation" techniques, comparable to those pioneered in the mid-1930s in the United Kingdom, involving diaries and essays to chart the subjective responses of survey subjects.[18] His interest in this, as with other researchers at the time, was partly driven by a sense that quantitative measures neglected the variety and unpredictability of human responses. His published research, in such respected journals as *Harvard Business Review* (1948) and *Journal of Marketing* (1956), bore a relationship to the most advanced developments in marketing research. His work as the head of a private business concern who contributed to scholarly debates could be called "administrative research," that is, research in the service of, and frequently commissioned by, existing institutions like government and corporations. However cynical his motivations may have been, Vicary was an innovator, working with the newest theories of marketing research and looking for a breakthrough in the practical application of psychological schemas to advertising and promotion. For instance, he conducted a two-year study of a factory cafeteria, concluding with the social psychology argument that the cafeteria was a site not only for food consumption but for generating a sense of job satisfaction. Furthermore, he found that as a venue shared by all employees, the cafeteria was a space of reconciliation between labor and management.[19]

In these and other published materials Vicary showed a distinct leaning toward a new area of marketing called motivational research (or motivation research, or MR), which brought psychoanalytic and psychological research to bear upon marketing problems. MR was part of a sea change in how advertisers did their work, taking unconscious drives as a root location for understanding how people acted in the marketplace. According to this approach desires, sometimes latent, were sought out and appealed to directly by marketers, a view that challenged liberal market ideals about consumers as rational decision makers and advertisers as information providers. MR used expansive interviews and interpretive methods to ascertain deep desires that drove purchasing behaviors. The most prominent figure in MR in the 1950s was Ernest Dichter, who had studied with Lazarsfeld in Vienna before coming to the United States in 1938. His Institute for Motivational Research was a lightning rod for enthusiasm and concern about the new approaches.[20] Dichter recommended conducting "depth interviews" with consumers, which was a version of the psychoanalyst's couch for market researchers on which they probed the consumer psyche for hidden drives and manifest expressions for hidden meanings. Though the two were openly combative, Dichter's ideas were inspiring to Vicary and his research concern. Extending an imagined conspiratorial connection, Stuart Rodgers suggested that the entire subliminal scare was a fabrication, and that if Dichter and Vicary had not been colluding to stir up controversy, they might as well have been doing so.[21]

Believing that one could not trust responses to survey questions like "Why did you buy that?," MR interviews used techniques often found in psychoanalysis sessions, such as word association. Vicary specifically promoted himself as an expert in "projective techniques" for analyzing interview responses. He wrote, "Especially where respondent's opinions or attitudes are secret or subconscious, these methods are capable of uncovering hidden motives. This is done by asking vague, unstructured questions as opposed to the direct and highly specific questions used in poll-type studies."[22] Vicary's article "Word Association and Opinion Research," from 1948, challenged direct and open interviewing in polls and surveys, which "still leave in obscurity the irrational and subconscious motivations which psychologists have found to govern much of our thinking."[23] Vicary's study provided evidence for the usefulness of word association tests, inspired by those developed by Carl Jung in 1905, to reveal the subtler aspects of a subject's attitudes. Tellingly, this research charted the connotative shadings of the term "advertising," with some variation on "huckster" being the most frequent response.

With reference to Gestalt psychology, Vicary elaborated on the "thought transference" that occurred among a researcher's questions, explaining the apparent tendency to answer one in relation to a previous one.[24] His interest in word association—the unconscious connections made between words—prompted him to write and self-publish an annotated bibliography on the subject in 1954.[25] A few years later, reporting findings after a year-long market analysis commissioned by *Family Circle*, for which his team interviewed 5,426 women, Vicary found that a clear majority of the respondents associated the term "season" with "spring." Though he noted that the study took place during an uncommonly warm year, 1952–53, he viewed his findings as evidence of a "psycho-seasonal trend." He concluded, "This pattern of perception . . . influences other cultural factors, becoming another index to man's sometimes baffling mass behavior."[26] Such a line takes on a knowing twist, having been written but a few months before Vicary began his New Jersey subliminal advertising trial in 1956.

By the mid-1950s Vicary had a solid reputation as a creative, experimental market researcher. His talk to the American Marketing Association (AMA) on projective techniques in 1952 was one of only three addresses featured by *Advertising Age* in its coverage of the conference. The other two were delivered by Burleigh Gardener, of Social Research, Inc., on the use of stereotypes and prejudicial images by marketers, and by Paul Lazarsfeld on the role of personal influence and opinion leaders in

James Vicary (center, wearing dark suit) moderating a public discussion, "Forming and Changing Attitudes of People," in the Roosevelt Hotel Ballroom, New York, fall 1954, featuring leading social scientists and public relations executives. Courtesy of Thomas J. Dodd Research Center, University of Connecticut.

decision making for women consumers (this being the Decatur study, famed in the field of communication studies, commissioned by Macfadden Publications).[27] The *Wall Street Journal* also singled out Vicary's talk in a report on the AMA meeting.[28] The same talk formed the basis of a radio script for *Dorothy and Dick*, broadcast on 6 January 1953 on WOR in New York, which emphasized the newness of "projective techniques": "And this whole field is so new that there aren't even any textbooks on the subject. But a man who is an expert, a New York research consultant named James M. Vicary, estimates that already two dozen marketing organizations have begun to use projectives."[29] In 1954 Vicary introduced and moderated a panel discussion on public relations and attitude change before a capacity gathering in the Grand Ballroom of the Roosevelt Hotel. Among the five social scientists and four public relations people invited to speak was the leading sociologist Dr. Bernard Berelson.[30] Vicary was also the main research consultant for an early effort at the computer tabulation of magazine readership surveys, using the UNIVAC.[31]

Experiment adapting UNIVAC computer to readership survey, with research consultant
Vicary (center), 1956. Courtesy of Thomas J. Dodd Research Center, University of Connecticut.

With activities such as these Vicary had achieved a degree of public
visibility and, in some ways, notoriety for his original and creative research methods before the subliminal sensation in the fall of 1957. An
impact audit of his company's research in June 1957 shows citation of its
work in five psychological abstracts, ten books, and fifty-five magazine
and newspaper articles.[32] For example, Edith Efron described Vicary's research in a July 1957 article in the *New York Times Magazine* on the use
of MR in the naming of products and companies.[33] A sizable portion of
the references pertained to Vicary's claim that he recorded eye-blinks of
women at supermarkets with hidden cameras, allowing him to conclude
that shoppers were in a state comparable to hypnosis. A report on motivational research in *Newsweek* in 1955 recounted this same study, including
a photograph of Vicary with the caption "blink, blink, blink."[34] Vicary was
a featured expert interview in a promotional film for the National Association of Food Chains on consumer motivation in supermarket shopping, *They're Talking about Us!* (1954). Vicary and the image of the hypnotized suburban shopper were the main illustration for a report on the NBC
radio program *People*, "Why Did You Buy That?"[35]

This research claiming the hypnotic state of female shoppers is among the most often cited of Vicary's works, though he is not always mentioned by name. It is, however, questionable for a number of reasons. Contradictions abound in the description of how the data were gathered. Sometimes the cameras are described as hidden, sometimes they are just ignored. Vicary claimed to have recorded eye-blinks at the entrance, in the food stacks, at the checkout counter, and at the exit.[36] Even if such a highly surveyed store could have been rigged up in this way in 1953, which is doubtful, one wonders about the enormous quantity of film that would have had to be produced to capture an even marginally representative sample. Furthermore, not only is there a vast associative leap between an increase in eye blinks and a trance state, but the study appears to exist only in the form of press releases and references in periodicals. There is no fuller documentation or published record, and I could find no unpublished draft of this study in the volumes of research available among the admittedly incomplete James M. Vicary Papers at the University of Connecticut. What makes this research suspicious, to my mind, is that Vicary did not advocate strongly for doing research in such a mechanized way, with a distant technological recording mechanism. His entire reputation, to this point in his career, was based on individual surveys, depth interviews, and free association between words. For these reasons I suspect that these research conclusions were a publicity-seeking embellishment of what might have been a small trial test.

Regardless of how sincere, dishonest, or naïve a researcher he might have been, Vicary was part of a new wave of mainstream marketers seeking ever more complete understandings of the workings of consumer minds in order to better reach and affect them. The techniques involved dominant forms of survey and public opinion research, nascent forms of psycho-graphics, combinations of behaviorist and Gestalt psychology, and freshly minted popular Freudian ideas. Vicary exhibited a scholarly predilection for measuring and charting the relationship between the subconscious and consumer activity.[37] The fascination with links between the unconscious and buying habits, the interest in the automatic associations made between words and actions, and attention-grabbing press releases all make Vicary's next and most infamous study, using subliminal word flashes, perfectly continuous with his research history.

Vicary's famed subliminal advertising test ran over the spring of 1956 and received no press attention in the United States. The first report appeared in the *Sunday Times* in London. The date of the publication was 10 June 1956, so it is possible that the tests were still ongoing at that moment. It is not clear how the anonymous reporter came to hear of Vicary's work. Vance Packard himself later tried to track down the source to no avail, and quoted the *Times* as saying, "Although the facts we published are well attested, the authorities in question are unwilling to come any further into the open."[38] And indeed Vicary was not mentioned by name, though the article mentioned the test location as an unnamed cinema in New Jersey, indicating that the experiment was his work. In what would become a convention for similar reports, the article began with a reference to *1984* and contained worried speculation about what had been inflicted upon an "unsuspecting American public." Even before the specifics had been listed, the theme of totalitarian manipulation surfaced. In this first account the invisible ads were said to have been for ice cream (not popcorn and soda as later stories had it), and sales to have risen by 60 percent. The article described several "sub-threshold" experiments but did not explore their implications except in a closing line: "If this method of communication were developed it could obviously have far-reaching and highly undesirable potentialities."[39] Note that the word "subliminal" was not used in this first news announcement.

In direct response to this report, BBC television conducted its own test of subliminal perception, producing telling results that later played a part in the chronology of evidence.[40] On 22 June 1956 *A Question of Science* presented a filmed ballet performance, asking viewers to contact the show if they saw a news item.[41] The message "Pirie Breaks World Record" flashed momentarily, referring to the British runner Gordon Pirie's victory in a five-kilometer race three days earlier. The reported results included 430 postcards, with 131 getting part of the message, 20 getting it exactly, and 1 dreaming about it later.[42] These figures are less impressive when one then discovers that approximately 4.5 million people were watching and that the message flashed for 1/25 of a second, which is actually above many people's perceptual threshold for eight icons.[43] It is likely that some of those people who reported accurately may have only seen "Pirie Breaks" or "World Record" and then remembered the prominent national news story about the British middle-distance runner, or made a guess.

Like a good science fiction story, subliminal advertising methods struck a chord with the public, and a growing rumble of interest followed the newspaper scoop. As one source put it, "the rumors have been wafting their devious way among the clouds of smoke in the cocktail lounges and conference rooms which are the habitat of the ad men."[44] One who heard those rumblings was Vicary, who said that the attention in the United Kingdom and the clamor that followed the BBC test prompted him to take control of the media response, though he had other business matters to take care of first.[45] Most importantly, he had to incorporate a new company to deal specifically with this new advertising method. So the much-recounted tale of the Fort Lee cinema trial does not spring into popular life until 12 September 1957, over a year after the results had been compiled, with a press conference held by Vicary.[46] Within days reports on hidden advertisements appeared in the United States, buried in *Advertisers and Agencies* and *Broadcasting/Telecasting*, but making their way to the front page of *Billboard* on 16 September 1957.[47] In these very first notices the tone is distinctly one of bemusement, winking at the reader about the absurdity of the idea of hidden advertising. *Billboard* introduced its article as follows: "An updated version of the 'Ladies Will Please Remove Their Hats' slides which once flashed between reels on movie screens may soon unleash on unsuspecting TV audiences a new brand of selling – the 'invisible' commercial."[48] The darker elements surfaced immediately too, and a reference to *1984* appeared in this same source.[49] The brief mention on the same day in *Broadcasting/Telecasting*, under the title of "Whazzat?," suggested that admen were "skeptical."[50] And confused versions of the story were already apparent. Some reports described the test as "recent" even though it was over a year old.[51]

By the third week of September a full-scale media sensation had blossomed. Sustained coverage of Vicary's test results, with feature articles, follow-up pieces, and editorials, continued for the next year, then sporadically for the next five years. Few advertising and media scandals capture the imagination as thoroughly as this one did. As such, this incident is a popular revelatory moment about media power that compares with the radio broadcast of *War of the Worlds* in 1938. As Jeffrey Sconce notes, Welles's broadcast was a point of departure for contemporaneous considerations about mass hysteria, public rationality, and the powerful role of broadcasting: "The *War of the Worlds* incident has thus become the most famous parable of the oppressive presence associated with network broadcasting, a horror story in which the monster ultimately is not the invading Martians but the invasive broadcaster."[52] There was no widespread hysteria after Vicary's press conference. If anything, there was curiosity and a desire to witness this new mysterious media form. But undeniably, the first public attention to subliminal communication was an occasion to think through other issues of the day, among them the ethics of advertising, media, social planning, behaviorism, and psychology.

What happened between the conduct of the test in 1956 and the September 1957 news event to ready the media and the public for this response? Most importantly, Vance Packard published his first book, *The Hidden Persuaders*, which soon became an extraordinary bestseller. His biographer, Daniel Horowitz, points out that until this book's appearance no popular nonfiction title specifically critiquing advertising had made any waves since Stuart Chase's *The Tragedy of Waste* in 1925.[53] The tortured ethical world of the advertising and public relations business was a major theme of fairly well-known novels and several films, including *The Hucksters* (Jack Conway, 1947), *It Should Happen to You* (George Cukor, 1954), *The Man in the Gray Flannel Suit* (Nunnally Johnson, 1956), and *Will Success Spoil Rock Hunter?* (Frank Tashlin, 1957), but no book-length exposé like Packard's had struck home. *The Hidden Persuaders* ushered into American popular consciousness not only the memorable titular phrase but a wide-ranging disquiet about new and supposedly nefarious techniques of advertisers. In particular, Packard got credit for alerting people to the use of motivational research, which he called "mass psychoanalysis." One of his main examples was the work of Ernest Dichter, the man who expanded the use of Freudianism in ads and devised a sort of psychoanalytic technique to understand potential markets. After *The Hidden Persuaders* became a popular bestseller, despite its attacks on MR, Dichter actually thanked Packard for sending a good deal of business his way.[54]

Before the book's publication there was some inkling of the changes that advertising was undergoing. Packard was not alone, nor was he the first to fire a warning shot about new marketing methods. In 1953 the *Nation* published a story about the use of psychoanalytic ideas in advertising called "Freud and the Hucksters."[55] In the following year *Saturday Review* had a substantial report by Lynda Strong under the alarming banner "They're Selling Your Unconscious."[56] This feature announced the arrival of motivational research on Madison Avenue, and included examples that Packard repeated in his book three years later. *Newsweek* augmented this attention to MR by asking: Did the consumer "know his own mind?"[57] And shortly before the release of Packard's book, an article in *Esquire* described the best typography for print advertisements as one that a reader's mind "absorbed unconsciously."[58] *The Hidden Persuaders* should be seen as a work that crystallized public awareness of the expanding role played by psychological and psychoanalytic concepts for modern marketing methods.

Packard's book contended that a paradigm shift was taking place, one that moved a blend of psychoanalysis and behaviorism into the mainstream of marketing decision making. Though the effectiveness of such procedures and the accuracy of such interpretations of consumer activity were a matter of contest, the notion that the unconscious mind might now be a battleground was sufficient to ignite a degree of alarm. "Mass psychoanalysis," Packard reasoned, was not an outrage because of the claims about the latent and manifest content of desire, about a split in the psyche, nor about the ordinariness of taboo drives, but because the use of such concepts in marketing research might provide the key to controlling minds and behavior. The psychoanalytically informed marketer was akin to the evil hypnotist, implanting impulses to make people behave in an unwelcome manner. Beyond the details of the new advertising agendas, Packard's book expressed worry about the loss of individual will. A fear of social engineering, perpetrated by a select few without our consent, pervaded the book. Its imagery of consumers becoming figurative and literal zombies echoed other critiques of modern mass society. It fell in with a long line that saw modern life, and especially the psychology of crowds, as hypnotic and somnambulistic. In this way *The Hidden Persuaders* drew more in tone and substance from the immediate prehistory of psychoanalysis than from Freudian thought. It had much in common with the general assertions of Gustave Le Bon's *The Crowd*, and kept intact the core nineteenth-century ideas about control from a distance. In this version, though, Janet's research subject Léonie B. was not a patient susceptible to hypnotic suggestion; she was an anonymous shopper.

The reviews of Packard's work were impressive, not only in number but in the level of engagement with his claims. In May 1957 *Time* did a story on MR in conjunction with publication of the book.[59] A review in the *Atlantic* in June emphasized "admen and the id."[60] Repeatedly there were punning references to Huxley, as in the *Atlantic*'s final assessment that mass psychoanalytic tinkering was "pushing us toward an unbrave new world."[61] Soon advertising executives were compelled to defend themselves as being more ethical than they appeared to be in Packard's description. At a public debate one executive viciously attacked the "malicious" Packard, and received heroic coverage in *Advertising Age*.[62] Packard faced off against the executive vice-president of Donahue and Coe, Walter Weir, in what the *New York Times* called "an oral slugging match."[63] At a debate about MR during a meeting of the AMA's New York chapter that drew the largest attendance ever recorded for an event of its kind, Weir attacked *The Hidden Persuaders* for offering "little new information," a devastating accusation to be leveled against a journalistic exposé.[64] Elmer Roper rather smartly challenged Packard on a number of points, such as his use of the oxymoronic phrase "mass psychoanalysis," and accused him of being "hypnotized with the term 'hypnosis.'"[65] The publication in the UK of *The Hidden Persuaders* in the fall of 1957 engendered shrugged shoulders and skepticism among British ad executives. Reviews scoffed at the idea that MR was anything more than a con to sell unscientific and imprecise ideas to the advertising industry, mentioning Dichter and Vicary by name. Some recommended it for comedic purposes. This skepticism did not seem to hinder the book's roaring sales.[66]

The defensiveness of the advertising industry was not representative of all responses to Packard's argument. Some commentators took heed and saw his warning as a sign of an encroaching communist conformity; such was the approach taken by the liberal Catholic periodical the *Commonweal*, which paired Packard's bestseller with William Sargant's book on brainwashing, *Battle for the Mind*.[67] The *New York Times* took Packard's book as a revelation about the brainwashing agents of motivational research. In its review A. C. Spectorsky wrote, "These are the new breed of merchandising brainwashers who wield an invisible club-like baton of applied depth psychology over the secret, silent symphony of our discontents."[68] He concluded by noting the significance of the book as "frightening, entertaining and thought-stimulating to boot."[69] Left-wing critics seized upon Packard's critique of consumer culture but failed to identify a critique of capitalism among his claims. Liberals identified with Packard's defense of the resilience of the individual mind.[70] And references to the work were plentiful, including in ads themselves.[71] With such attention sales mounted, keeping *The Hidden Persuaders* placed highly on nonfiction bestseller lists and paving the way for Packard's long career of writing bestselling "kitsch sociology," as one critic put it.[72]

In the wake of the rising notoriety of Packard's book, motivational research became an even hotter topic of debate among advertisers themselves through 1957. In June Dichter appeared on a special panel devoted to MR at the 53rd annual convention of the Advertising Federation of America. Presenting a counter-position at the event, "R. J. Williams, a professor of psychology at Columbia University, advised caution. He warned that 'MR had plunged headlong into many areas where its parents would fear to tread.'"[73] In early 1958 the *Atlantic* defended advertising's aims and denounced Packard's "absurd," "conspiratorial claims."[74] More boldly, Julia Morse, an executive at Anderson and Cairns, supported the advertising uses of MR and attacked Packard's book as cynical, in the very same week as Vicary's first "subliminal" press conference.[75]

In Packard's copiously itemized, if not always accurately rendered, examples of MR, Vicary made an appearance. In many ways Vicary was Packard's model of the new breed of scientific manipulators of the unconscious that Packard called the "depth boys."[76] Packard described him as "the most genial and ingratiating of all the major figures operating independent depth-probing firms," and as "handsome" enough to have "stepped out of a clothing ad."[77] He summarized and commented on several studies by Vicary throughout *The Hidden Persuaders*. Packard referred to Vicary's memorable technique of counting the eye-blinks of women at supermarkets.[78] Elsewhere Packard described this study as showing how women fell into a "light trance" in which the "lovely packaging" actually whispered to them, saying "buy me, buy me."[79] It was one of the illustrations regularly drawn from Packard in reviews. Take note that these references to Vicary and his research were written and published before the September press conference and before Vicary was associated publicly with subliminal advertising.

Concerning the experiment at the movie theater in New Jersey, Packard made casual mention of the report on it in the *Sunday Times*, describing what he called a "subthreshold" effect, without mentioning Vicary's involvement.[80] But that's it. Still, on the basis of that single fleeting reference in *The Hidden Persuaders*, a book in which the words "subliminal" and "subception" *did not appear*, Packard would later claim to have presaged the use of subliminal communication and to have been the first to sound the general alarm concerning a possible invasion of the mass mind through that technique.[81] This exaggerated misattribution continued, with David Halberstam referring to *The Hidden Persuaders* three and a half decades later as a book "about subliminal tactics in advertising."[82]

FIG. 1. SUPRALIMINAL STIMULUS

Happy or angry? Image upon which subliminal words flashed in experiments by Klein et al., 1957.

Mark Crispin Miller's smart introduction to the fiftieth-anniversary edition of *The Hidden Persuaders* helps fix the record on this count, though he underplays Packard's own efforts to link his exposé to the public debate on subliminal influences.[83]

Another demonstration was also part of the backdrop to the subliminal sensation of 1957. One of the scientifically legitimate illustrations of a subliminal effect had just received some public attention earlier in September, though the full research paper would not appear in a peer-reviewed venue for another two years.[84] George Klein and a team of psychologists at New York University found they could influence what subjects thought of an expressionless face by subliminally flashing with a tachistoscope either the word "happy" or the word "angry." Michael Goldstein and Richard Barthol, both at the University of California, Los Angeles, repeated a version of this experiment, adding focused and slightly out-of-focus slides. They found some influence of subliminally flashed adjectives for the "fuzzy" images, though not for the clearly defined ones.[85] When *Time* reported on Klein's study, 9 September 1957, it immediately and somewhat jokingly drew attention to the implications for marketers, titling the piece "Supersoft Sell." Concerning the commercial potential, *Time* wrote: "Chuckles one TV executive with a conscious eye on the future: 'It smacks of brainwashing, but of course it would be tempting.'"[86] The executive knew enough to remain anonymous. It is safe to say that someone in that position would not have uttered such a glib statement to a reporter less than a week after news of Vicary's experiment began to cause a stir.

Though not designed in this way, Klein's test and subsequent variations on it were basically modified versions of demonstrations of the Kuleshov effect, one of the foundational principles for theories of film editing and film acting. Kuleshov's unscientific study pointed to a cumulative effect of subsequent images, as the connotations of one image bleed into proximate ones. Klein extended this manifestation into the unconscious, where a sort of affective arithmetic was said to take place below our perceptual thresholds. Where Kuleshov validated the sequentiality of images as a way to create new meanings and sentiments, Klein pointed toward speedy connotative simultaneity. There is no greater illustration of the power and influence of visual triggers if one can demonstrate that they have an effect even if invisible! Like those who conducted the earlier Soviet demonstration, Klein too had a noteworthy if largely unrecognized impact on filmmaking, especially experimental film.

On newsstands in September 1957 was a feature article by Packard in the *Atlantic*, "The Growing Power of Admen." It contained a précis of his book and described motivational research and Dichter's leading role. Packard highlighted several examples of MR experiments, in addition to research on "subthreshold" effects. Here again the test at the movie house in New Jersey appeared: the article described increased ice cream concessions, apparently still relying upon the report in the *Sunday Times* from the previous year.[87] The article did not include Vicary's name. Nonetheless, the confluence of attention prompted the ambitious Madison Avenue researcher to stake his claim.

Crossing the Popular Threshold

With the ideas and examples of concealed messages, unconscious influence, and advertising research already in circulation, a public relations opportunity had been primed. The notoriety of *The Hidden Persuaders* and the release of research findings that seemed to back up subliminal suggestion spurred Vicary to hold a press conference on 12 September 1957.[1] He even stated that he felt rushed to do so, without being completely prepared to offer the advertising service he presented. Unambiguously, what Vicary *was* doing beyond reporting results of a year-old test was announcing the formation of a firm, Subliminal Projection Company, which was in the process of seeking patent protection for its device. The company was a venture with René Bras, the developer of the subliminal projector, and Francis C. Thayer of U.S. Productions, a producer of medical, institutional, and television films that had Ford, *Fortune* magazine, and CBS as clients.[2] Bras served as secretary-treasurer and Thayer as president of Subliminal Projection. The technological apparatus they had developed was designed, according to a press release, to expose messages at an exceptional speed without awareness or sensation on the part of those viewing them, that is, subliminally.[3]

As documented by the journalist Marya Mannes, the press conference treated some fifty reporters to a demonstration. The gathering saw a nature documentary, *Secrets of the Reef* (Murray

Subliminal Projections Company, Inc., November 1957. From left: Vicary, Francis C. Thayer, René Bras. Courtesy of Thomas J. Dodd Research Center, University of Connecticut.

Stock certificate for Subliminal Projections Company, Inc., June 1957. Courtesy of Thomas J. Dodd Research Center, University of Connecticut.

Lerner, Lloyd Ritter, Robert M. Young, 1956), in the middle of which Vicary and company flashed the message "Drink Coca-Cola" 169 times. The message flashed at different speeds, and over both light and dark spots on the screen, so that those in attendance were assured of seeing at least some of the flashes.[4] In explaining the process, Vicary used the freshly reported "happy/angry" experiment of the NYU psychologist George Klein to give his technology scientific validation.[5] Mannes commented that the "debut sent some people running to their dictionaries" to find the meaning of "subliminal." The reporters immediately questioned Vicary on the ethical dimension; as Mannes vividly described it, "the newsmen were at him like terriers."[6] In his own defense, Vicary insisted that these messages only act as reminders, and even went so far as to suggest brashly that subliminal ads might "eliminate bothersome commercials and allow more entertainment time."[7] He would later claim that the criticism of these imperceptible advertisements was "like saying a whiff of a Martini is worse than a swallow. This is simply a new band in human perception like FM. It's an innocent band."[8] But pride in the ostensible strength of the results prompted Vicary to boast that the government might well wish to regulate its use.[9]

Vicary refused to answer questions about the process on the grounds that a patent was pending, or about the New Jersey test from the previous summer. He also refused to duplicate the test for the audience. Articles appearing in the week following the press demonstration were adorned with titles like "The 'Invisible' Invader" and "'Persuaders' Get Deeply 'Hidden' Tool," helping to seal the link between Packard and Vicary. The same week saw the first public denunciations of the validity of the claims of subliminal influence. George Klein expressed skepticism and later became a vocal critic.[10] Other psychologists went on record as saying that subliminal advertising would not work as an advertising tool and that even if it did, using it would be unethical.[11] *Science News Letter* reassured readers that it was impossible to brainwash people in this way, and that psychologists thought Vicary's findings "greatly exaggerated."[12]

Some were aware that there had been precursors, questioning the novelty of what was being unveiled. Peter Rantell, at a Scottish organization called the Studio, insisted that nothing new had been demonstrated and that years of experiments had not definitively shown commercial potential.[13] The Studio had already tested a comparable technique, with the wonderful science-fiction-sounding name Strobonic Psycho-injection.[14] *Advertising Age* said that the concept of hidden messages was old hat for advertisers, but that the new direction was just "nuttiness."[15] Some thought it technically impossible to televise completely "invisible" messages, and there were doubts that it would ever be possible to do so, even though television experiments quickly proved otherwise.[16] Furthermore, it was no mystery to some that Vicary used a type of tachistoscope. The first reference to this popular knowledge was in a letter from Robert Schultz to *Variety* in October that, with the distinct tone of the unconvinced, questioned the current "hullabaloo" over what was obviously an old "flash-meter" or tachistoscope, a version of which was available at many camera stores.[17] Schultz reminded readers of training use of the technology by the United States armed forces and of speed-reading use at NBC, demonstrating familiarity with this supposedly new machine and learning concept.

In a letter to the editor, a poetic reader of *Broadcasting/Telecasting* recommended the following technique to combat subliminal influence: "The secret's in the wink / Of your eye-lash. / Just put your blink / In sync with every flash."[18] But only three weeks after the press conference, attacks and outrage became the story, with Maurice Rappoport of the Stanford Research Institute calling subliminal advertising "a virtual social H-bomb."[19] Condemnations from the advertising industry followed, with Kenyon and Eckhardt, one of the country's largest firms, declaring that the techniques were ridiculous and unethical, and that "no self-respecting advertiser would have anything to do with them; no self-respecting TV network or station would touch them."[20] In a direct reference to the popularity of Packard's criticisms of new advertising methods, the company's chairman, Edwin Cox, stated, "This poor business of ours has become something of a punching bag lately; now this subliminal idea adds credence to all this nonsense about 'hidden persuaders.'"[21] The defensive stance included a distinction between subliminal methods and the work of marginally more legitimate motivational researchers. The vice-president of the Institute for Motivational Research, Albert Shepard, declared that "the place for subliminal stimulation or hypnotic suggestion is in the experimental laboratory or in clinical therapy."[22]

The specific issue at this point was exposure to simple direct commands through subliminal messages, though MR and other efforts to understand the workings of human desire for commercial purposes were implicated as well. Soon the "subliminal thesis" encompassed subleties of design in perfectly visible messages, such as the suggestive placements of people and props in advertisements. Responses to the proposed actions of subliminal advertisers expanded beyond the root concern that advertisers were tampering with the unconscious for commercial purposes, and in so doing frequently referred to Packard, Huxley, and Orwell, as well as recent studies of brainwashing. Some, like *Science* magazine, were blasé and dismissive of the idea of subliminal influence.[23] *Business Week* saw the criticisms as "grumbling over the increasingly torrid love affair between psychology and advertising."[24] Foreseeing the condemnation to come, at the press conference in September 1957 Vicary found it necessary to fortify himself against the prospect that the suspicions toward Packard and others might be directed toward him, stating explicitly, "I'm no hidden persuader."[25]

Anger rang through the earliest commentaries; efforts to design concealed and effective means to direct human behavior were said to embody the worst and most cynical American values. Vicary and similarly inclined advertisers stood accused of exploiting and widening antidemocratic sensibilities. The first editorial on the topic in the *Nation* asserted "subliminal advertising is the most alarming and outrageous discovery since Mr. Gatling invented his gun."[26] And an outraged reader wrote to *Business Week*, "Himmler and Goebbels had, at least, the decency to commit suicide. In the absence of any such display of ethical sense on the part of James M. Vicary, I submit that said gentleman be shot out of hand."[27] In early October the *Christian Century* published a fascinatingly vitriolic editorial, "The Invisible Monster," in which the editors called for mass mobilization against subliminal techniques, which they decried as a step toward the "robotization" of people, and challenged their readers to recognize that unconscious advertising is a logical extension of the existing commercial culture. They recommended a simple solution: "Don't go to movies. Turn off TV. Buy no brands that do not display a 'No Subliminal Projection Advertising' affidavit. Refuse to discuss ways for the churches to redeem this thing for their own use . . . Plan a down payment on some sort of Walden Pond." In the end, combating the implications of subliminal advertising required "prayer and fasting. And a rage of resistance."[28] As represented here, the subliminal experimenters were symptomatic of the threat of mechanized mass society.

Ernest Dichter was especially devastating in his attacks, wanting to distance himself from the direction that Vicary was taking. He reasoned that a "gimmick" like subliminal advertising would shake the budding legitimacy of psychoanalytic methods in advertising.[29] But try as he might, the subliminal controversy was extending to Dichter and others who sought to exploit the unconscious for marketing purposes. In November, on the Sunday evening radio program *Counterpoint* on WNEW in New York, the lawyer William Kunstler interviewed Vance Packard on the topic of MR, focusing on and denouncing subliminal techniques. Particularly pressing was the rising importance of political campaigning on television. The combined "merchandising" of candidates and manipulative marketing tactics could have undue undemocratic effects on voters' decisions, Packard said. Going further, he associated several prominent social concerns, including divorce and juvenile delinquency, with the dissatisfaction and acquisitiveness inspired by ever more effective advertising. The following week, Dichter appeared on the same program to respond to these criticisms.[30] Yet as more people became aware of MR, the ethical dimensions were understood as particularly troublesome. At what point did the thorough analysis of consumer desire amount to tinkering mechanistically with individual will? When do the methods that chart and measure deep impulses and associations become technologies of control?

A feature in *Business Week* on the mainstreaming of MR offered a graphic window onto the uneasiness with this turn in marketing operations. The article responded to the annual convention of the Advertising Research Foundation, which had given prominent attention to MR in the wake of Packard's bestseller and the subliminal scare.[31] The feature opened with a cartoon drawing depicting a female shopper with a child in a supermarket reaching to take a product off the shelf. Attached to her calf, elbow, and skull are electrodes, leading to a recording device of some sort. Around this contraption are four men and one woman, all in business attire, each observing the shopper and charting her actions on film, on graphs, in notation, and in audio recording. Four wear eyeglasses, and one appears to sport dark sunglasses. One especially upright character has a distinguished goatee. They adopt a comically intense posture of secret observation. Together they create a portrait of meddlesome snoops and intellectuals, dissecting and interfering with the privacy of a person going about a mundane activity.

Even though such images of the cynical and ridiculous market researcher accrued, business for the services offered seemed to grow unaffectedly. It is difficult to assess exactly how much business the company

Shopper surveillance, image accompanying article on motivational research, *Business Week*, November 1957, by special permission, copyright © by Bloomberg L.P.

Subliminal Projection managed to drum up with its press demonstration, but it did experience a minor if temporary boom. Its executives claimed to be in negotiations with a movie chain.[32] In this respect the company's device resembled other exhibition novelties tested by theaters as they tried to reinvent their business in the 1950s in the face of industry restructuring and competition from television, including such short-lived gimmicks as Percepto and Hypno-Vision. Within weeks of their press conference in September, according to Subliminal Projection's own figures, over 250 advertisers had contacted the company for more information.[33] The extraordinary results prompted J. Walter Thompson to investigate potential applications in television spots.[34] The vice-president of CBS's Western Division, Howard S. Meighan, announced that the idea had attracted serious interest among leading ad agencies, and that the network's television station in Hollywood, KNKT, would conduct its own tests.[35] At exactly the moment in television history when conversion from sponsored programming to commercial spot advertising was taking place, Subliminal Projection asked for the considerable sum of $100,000 for the honor of having the first television usage of their hidden service, a fee that included rental of the equipment and provision of a technician. They acknowledged that this high fee was due less to its spectacular results than to the publicity that the first commercial application would garner.[36] Richard E. Forrest, who handled Subliminal Projection's marketing, reiterated the interest that the company had received from an unnamed major movie theater chain. By December negotiations with four unnamed chains of movie houses were in process.[37] And by the new year the company claimed that fifteen theaters would be testing its device, with Vicary boldly and unrealistically proclaiming "that within the year the hidden commercial will be in most out-of-doors and second-run cinemas."[38]

I suppose that even with this media attention, and with the backdrop of a nonfiction bestseller, Subliminal Projection might have been treated as an anomalous oddity and disappeared into nothing more than a curious footnote in the history of the 1950s, an extreme against which other advertising research techniques, including MR, appeared that much more reasonable. However, the appearance of another company, promoting its own subliminal advertising methods, assured that Vicary's project could not be seen as an isolated enterprise. Fearing that it had been scooped by Subliminal Projection, Precon Process and Equipment Co. of New Orleans announced its own explorations on 26 November 1957 at a meeting of the New Orleans branch of the American Marketing Association. Precon is significant because in a way it was the more successful of the two companies, though it did not receive the notoriety of Subliminal Projection. Precon's key executives were H. Brown Moore, Robert Corrigan, a former fighter pilot and psychologist at Douglas Aircraft based in Los Angeles, and Hal C. Becker, an engineer and physicist teaching experimental neurology at Tulane University. They had had a patent application submitted a year earlier under the name of Experimental Films, Inc.,[39] for a modified "magic lantern" device, reportedly in development for eight years, that they thought could be used for billboards, for entertainment, and in retailing.[40] The device measured $1\frac{1}{2} \times 2 \times 2$ feet and was intended to be used primarily in stores; since 1954 Corrigan had also been studying its possible uses in motion pictures.[41] For the AMA meeting Precon's device projected an image of a swimming pool and a bathing beauty, along with a subliminal message to drive safely.[42]

Precon, while entirely sincere about the marketing prospects for its technology, understood its novelty as well. At the moment of their first public demonstration, the company's principals were already talking to film producers about using their process in a science fiction film tentatively titled ESP, and other future film negotiations were under way.[43] They did strike a few such deals to use their technology in a couple of horror films, calling the process Psychorama, which, like their other tachisto-

The movie producer William S. Edwards with Hal Becker and Robert Corrigan of Precon Co., 1958. Photo by Bill Bridges, Time-Life Pictures, Getty Images.

Audience waving fingers to see subliminal message at Precon demonstration, 1958. Photo by Bill Bridges.

scopic processes, rapidly flashed icons and words on dark parts of the film image at suitably dramatic moments. Together with the North Carolina exhibitor Howco they completed *My World Dies Screaming* (Harold Daniels, 1958), also released as *Terror in the Haunted House*; and *Date with Death* (Harold Daniels, 1959), also released as *Blood of the Man Devil*. But for all the obvious funhouse appeal of this exhibition gimmick, the individuals who developed and marketed it were respected psychologists who would remain involved in research for several decades to come. They were also more forthcoming than Vicary about their technologies, which were profiled in *Popular Science*.[44]

Robert C. Dennis sold the story of "My World Dies Screaming" to Brevilana Productions in November 1957, and William Edward intended to write the screenplay.[45] Released a year later by Howco International and circulated on a double bill with *Lost, Lonely and Vicious* (Frank Myers, 1958),[46] *My World Dies Screaming* featured Psychorama and was the "first picture in [the] fourth dimension, the new subliminal process," as the promotional material would have it.[47] Psychorama, never hidden from audiences, was the primary selling point for the film. Kevin Heffernan's research put this process in the context of other extra-cinematic exhibition and distribution ploys from the period, exemplified by the audience hypnosis sequence in *The Hypnotic Eye* (George Blair, 1960), as well as a mini-cycle of films about hypnotism and mind control.[48] The press book for *My World Dies Screaming* contained elaborate descriptions of subliminal communication, with reference to the infamous "popcorn" test and reassurances that although advertising in films had been "banned," it remained an effective tool to heighten a film's dramatic elements. To exploit the uniqueness of Psychorama, the distributors recommended the following radio advertising copy: "What is the 4th dimension? Do you know? How much can your eye see in 1/50 of a second? What is subliminal communication? Do you know? Did you know that subliminal communication has been banned on Television? Is it true that women can perceive subliminal communication faster than men? Q: what is the fourth dimension? . . . Q: Where can I see 4th Dimension? . . . You become a part of the cast yourself."[49]

Direct references to new exhibition technologies like widescreen and stereophonic sound were not uncommon in popular films at the time. Similarly, *My World Dies Screaming* included a prologue in which the star, Gerald Mohr, explains that with subliminal communication, "Not

Poster for *My World Dies Screaming*, describing Psychorama as the fourth dimension, using subliminal communication, 1958. Author's collection.

Newspaper ad for *My World Dies Screaming*, illustrating a skull image to be flashed and promising an effect without having to wear glasses, 1958. Author's collection.

only will the picture communicate with you visually, but subconsciously through your brain."[50] An epilogue, again with Mohr, replays scenes, showing the word "death" and drawings of hearts, skulls, and snakes that had been projected subliminally.[51] In a trailer to accompany the next and last Psychorama film, *Date with Death*, Mohr, also the star of this film, describes the process in a vaguely menacing fashion, though he does so while also reassuring the audience that it is not brainwashing, that it will not make people buy something against their will, and that there is no advertising hidden in the coming feature. He shows the instrument employed and points out a lie detector used to test the device's effectiveness. He impresses the viewer with the commotion caused by Psychorama and subliminal communication, which have been written up in "thousands of newspaper articles" and been the subject of government concern. He says, "It amazes me, but it scares some people." At one point, to illustrate what Psychorama does, Mohr shows a clip of the film with the inserts flashing at a slower rate, making "blood," "kill," and a skull icon visible. Mohr then illustrates the effect of the unseen flashes by holding a teaching model of the human brain and jabbing it in the temple with a letter opener. These messages, he says, stab at the unconscious. He smiles weakly and encourages the audience to enjoy the show. These extra-diegetic, explanatory devices adhere to the necessity that magicians must make it clear to their audiences that they have witnessed a trick. After all, if people were paying for Psychorama—invisible film components—they needed to be reassured that they had actually experienced it even though they couldn't see it. Reviews focused on the novelty of Psychorama, though Vincent Canby noted the dilemma that it produced for the critic: "A reviewer of only ordinary skills is prevented by the very definition of the technique to appraise its effect. His subconscious mind may have been dazzled but then, his subconscious mind ain't talking."[52]

My World Dies Screaming is a portrait of a woman unsure of her own sanity and of the trustworthiness of her new husband. The narrative is structured in such a way as to make unconscious influence a central theme, thus doubling on the influence that Psychorama is supposedly having upon viewers. Drawing immediate associations with hypnosis, *My World Dies Screaming* begins with a swirling spiral graphic. Echoing *Rebecca* (Alfred Hitchcock, 1940), a calm woman's voice describes a house that she claims to have never seen, with a point-of-view camera

Publicity effort to illustrate Psychorama, with multiple frames and faint background appearance of a skull and the word "blood," 1958. Author's collection.

Gerald Mohr in trailer for *Date with Death*, demonstrating how Psychorama stabs at the unconscious, 1959. Author's collection.

moving forward to the front door and up a staircase until she experiences a moment of sudden terror. She has been talking in a hypnotic trance, broken by her own scream. The woman, Sheila (Cathy O'Donnell), is in a psychiatrist's office in Switzerland. Since her recent marriage she had been haunted by terrible nightmares associated with this house. With a history of mental instability—she had spent two years in a sanatorium—she has been sent by her husband, Philip (Gerald Mohr), to see this doctor.

Arriving at their new home in the United States, Sheila screams when she sees that the house in which she is to live, Philip's family home, is identical to the one in her dreams. Clearly frightened, she refuses to go to the attic and basement. In true gothic fashion, the matrimonial home provides a sinister setting, and the loving husband seems riddled with secrets and darkly uncertain desires. Sheila becomes increasingly suspicious, finding that she doesn't know her husband's real name. As a cure for her fears, he insists that she enter the attic with him. Doing so, she begins to remember that she was the only witness to the ax murder of Philip's siblings, which occurred in that very room. Sheila is revealed as the daughter of the estate's caretaker. As Philip puts it, "Your mind locked it away," to which she replies, "You had to dig it up." Thus the dreams in Switzerland had been induced by the psychiatrist at the request of Philip. Sheila is now able to identify the killer as Philip's Uncle Jonas. Significantly, the film itself reiterates the idea that the mind has a secret life, one that can be accessed with specially designed procedures and techniques. According to the film's story, induced dreams and hypnosis can recover deeply repressed memories, the associated horror being relived and re-experienced. Psychorama similarly promised to induce such dramatic results in curious fans of thriller movies.

Psychorama was just one of a number of popular efforts to test and play with the possibility of mechanical tinkering with the unconscious. Enthusiasm for the "secret sell" led several media concerns to experiment with it, even without any reliable evidence of an effect, positive or otherwise. After all, it seemed to be simple and harmless enough to turn a slide projector off and on rapidly or to whisper into a microphone. In December 1957 reports surfaced of Midwestern theater owners flashing advertisements for their concessions, when they had previously been simply placing slides for audiences to read.[53] A flurry of radio and television tests took place, mostly products of the quasi-scientific or publicity-seeking initiatives of individual broadcasters, none showing any persuasive effects. KLTI in Longview, Texas, called its process "Radio Active Iso-Spots." WTWO-TV in Bangor, Maine, flashed "Write W-TWO" rapidly, though at least one TV technician said he could see it, to no noticeable effect.[54] WAAF radio in Chicago whispered "Fresh up with Seven-up" and "Oklahoma Gas is best" under its music programming. Reportedly about three hundred people contacted the station and three-quarters of them responded affirmatively, liking the novelty of the new ads, which contrasted favorably with louder, traditional ads. The other quarter complained that the ads were deceptive and unethical. The companies in question did not pay for these plugs, but they did consent to allow their names to be used for the test. Though this radio experiment was not below the threshold of audibility, it was one of several similar efforts to capitalize upon the clamor about nearly imperceptible ads.[55] WCCO-AM in Minneapolis tried its own "phantom spots" whispered under music or dialogue, with assistance from psychologists at the University of Minnesota, promoting an appearance by President Eisenhower on one of its shows with the phrase "Hear Ike tonight."[56] For a brief moment, PS (phantom spots) described radio subliminals and SP (subliminal projections) described visual ones.[57]

Subliminal communication thus raised questions of broadcast standards in addition to ethical conundrums for advertisers. Despite the lackluster demonstrations, by October congressmen and senators were taking public stands, demanding hearings and legislation banning the process.[58] The most vocal were Senator Charles Potter of Michigan and Representative William A. Dawson of Utah, both Republicans, who pushed the chairman of the Federal Communications Commission, John C. Doerfer, to investigate.[59] Dawson encouraged Doerfer to call an immediate ban on subliminal messages on television until a regulatory position had been taken by the FCC.[60] Potter, a member of the Senate Interstate Commerce Committee and a former member of the House Committee on Un-American Activities and the Senate Permanent Subcommittee on Investigations (when Senator Joseph McCarthy was its chairman and afterward), declared that according to all available signs the FCC would institute a ban on subliminal advertising.[61] He described his worries in a constituents' newsletter: "Soon many of the viewers may find themselves wanting a drink of Glugg beer, strange, for some are teetotalers, others have a longstanding preference for Glotz ale."[62] Potter's fanciful description of the consequences of hidden commercials had more in common with comic books and science fiction than any actual evidence. Still, the satirical comic versions of the technique were taken as possibilities by many. The ultimate fear, as Potter presented it, was that "an evil genius gets exclusive rights to the process and headlocks the nations. He'll control everybody's cerebellum and we'll all become robots. I'm against it."[63] It is an odd historical moment when politicians feel it necessary to declare publicly their opposition to roboticized citizens.

Doerfer reported mistakenly that subliminal messages had already been used in some television ads, adding fuel to the growing fire in Washington.[64] The FCC and the Federal Trade Commission received letters expressing curiosity about the process and also complaints about potential brainwashing with "foreign ideologies."[65] Subsequently the FCC had to quell rising fears by issuing a statement indicating that it was looking into the matter and that there was no cause for alarm.[66] Doerfer said that with no broadcasts there was no action to take, and that it was not the FCC's job to censor programming anyway.[67] Further, he reasoned, the Communications Act of 1934 required the clear announcement of paid broadcasts, which would preclude hidden commercials.[68] As broadcasting licenses were awarded with the understanding that stations would identify paid broadcasts, which with subliminal broadcasting they would presumably not do, no broadcasters had a license for hidden advertising transmissions. The FCC saw its position as clear, with no need for more specialized policy.

Meanwhile, when the Code Review Board of the National Association of Radio and Television Broadcasters (NARTB, now the National Association of Broadcasters, or NAB) met in Beverly Hills in November 1957, it addressed subliminal advertising and televised horror film packages that had been recently sold to broadcasters. Taking some of the heat off the FCC, the board resolved not to allow subliminal ads until a thorough review of the process and its effects had been completed.[69] The NARTB prepared a memorandum on the topic, titled "Industry Implications," that stated, "While it is not yet definitely established that subliminal advertising can be effective, the possibilities are sufficiently strong to warrant the industry's taking steps to cope with . . . several implications of the problem."[70] Doubting the technical feasibility of rapid flashes on television, the memo nonetheless expressed concern about the negative "reaction of the public to having subliminal advertising thrust upon them."[71]

This position was reiterated at a meeting in New York on the topic a few weeks later between the NARTB and network executives from NBC, CBS, and ABC.[72] The president of NBC, Robert Sarnoff, unilaterally forbade subliminal ads on its radio and television stations, as did the president of CBS-TV, Merle S. Jones.[73] American Broadcasting–Paramount Theaters declared its intention to refuse subliminal technology in its facilities.[74] The full NARTB ban, amending its television code, appeared in May 1958. The association's code banned "any technique whereby an attempt is made to convey information to the listener by transmitting messages below the threshold of normal awareness."[75] Curiously, theater-owner organizations did not respond in this fashion, nor did non-network radio organizations.[76] Still holding a brave face, Vicary praised the ban, hoping that it would drive away competitors until his patent had cleared.[77]

Vicary had other worries. *Motion Picture Daily* broke the news, on 16 December, that the site of his experiment had been the Fort Lee Theater in Fort Lee, New Jersey, part of the B.S. Moss Theater Circuit. The equipment, installed in the balcony, ran throughout the six-week test period during movie screenings without a technician present. The theater manager, Marvin Rose, said he did not see any of the images, but that some people whom he had asked to look for the ads did see the odd one. More damaging, executives with the Moss Circuit reported there were no effects of the flashing ads on concession sales, let alone an increase.[78] A livid Vicary ran to the head of the theater chain, Charles Moss, to present data demonstrating that his own claims were legitimate. Moss offered the press a weak word of support, saying that the data, which had not been available to his executives nor to theater managers, showed some promise in increasing refreshment sales, but that more testing was necessary. Moss also reasoned that the problem in noticing sales effects is that a rise in demand for the advertised popcorn might lead to a decrease in chocolate sales, explaining why managers might not have noticed any specific increase.[79] *Motion Picture Daily* ran Moss's comments but did not print a retraction of the first article, only adding to the already shaky credibility of Vicary's claims, a shakiness to which he contributed with his resolute secrecy about the testing procedures.

As agencies and networks began to take public stands on the issue, the FCC called Subliminal Projection Co. and others to Washington for a demonstration. Frank Ewing, chairman of Fensholt Advertising Agency, commended the FCC on its quick response, declaring in characteristically xenophobic Cold War terms that "subliminal advertising is distinctly un-

American and its perpetrator belongs in the same class as the Russian brainwasher, the Japanese thought police, or the office snoop," a view seconded by the editors of *Advertising Age*.[80] The first scheduled presentation by Subliminal Projection had to be postponed until the New Year because of technical problems.[81] On 13 January 1958 Vicary conducted a closed-circuit television test at the WTOP studios. Described as the first public television presentation of his tachistoscope, the test was Vicary's attempt to persuade the FCC and others in attendance that subliminal communication was both serious and benign, and that contrary to what the NARTB had claimed, the technology could be adapted for television.[82] As announced, "eat popcorn" flashed at a rate of 1/20 of a second, at five-second intervals, throughout an episode of the television show *The Grey Ghost*. Toward the end of the episode, and impromptu, Vicary replaced that message with "fight polio."[83] The *New York Times* reported that "several Congressmen and members of the [FCC] showed no inclination to rush for the popcorn stand to buy. In fact, they seemed disappointed that they had not been prompted to do so."[84] Apparently Senator Potter mused, "I think I want a hot dog."[85] An unimpressed FCC commissioner, Robert E. Lee, simply didn't believe that subliminal advertising would work.[86] Though the demonstration was a technical success, people were skeptical of its effectiveness. Vicary was in the strange situation of having to argue for the validity of subliminal messages and at the same time to reassure that their effect was not great or automatic.[87]

Despite his contradictory protestations, the impression of mind control hovered in the background from the very first announcements about the technique. There was some amplification of communist paranoia during the same week of the Washington demonstrations with reports that the Soviets had perfected a subliminal audio device that "presumably could make for less painful brainwashing."[88] Just as Vicary was facing the FCC and congressmen, Precon demonstrated its product to the Los Angeles Advertising Club.[89] To waylay fears, Corrigan argued that subliminal perception involved active, if subconscious, assessment of messages, in contrast with the passivity implied by brainwashing.[90] A month later, on 13 February, Precon offered the FCC and members of the NARTB a demonstration of its product.[91] Even if the manipulative powers of subliminal advertising had not been established, many voiced support for cautionary action anyway. Congressman Dawson continued to pressure the FCC to stop these subliminal efforts, citing a need to protect the public from

Vicary explaining the work of Subliminal Projections Company to members of Congress and the FCC, Washington, January 1958. Photo by Hank Walker, Time-Life Pictures, Getty Images.

their uncertain effects.[92] And the *New York Times* added, "The idea that American audiences might become unconsciously captive at the hands of invisible advertising is as yet just a little too Alice-in-Wonderlandish to be taken seriously; but we hope the FCC is taking it seriously enough to be carefully watching this eerie development."[93]

Skittishness was the order of the day. KTLA, a television station in Los Angeles, announced that it would flash subliminal messages about fire safety and the March of Dimes.[94] KTLA struck a deal with Precon to broadcast public service announcements, and later perhaps advertisements, in return for the company's technology.[95] As an independent station owned by Paramount Pictures, it was under no obligation to adhere to the NARTB ban. However, KTLA backed out of the deal slightly more than a month later, citing the FCC's ambiguous position on the matter, as well as "heavy and negative mail response" and petitions.[96]

Even as sober assessments reassured the public that reflexive, mesmeric control was impossible, media messages were scrutinized for the slightest twitch of effect, and the most minuscule and insignificant responses drew the attention of industry and periodicals. Fears rose that one could be unknowingly enticed to perform morally or ethically objectionable acts. For example, the Methodist Temperance Board warned about subconscious appeals for alcohol consumption.[97] Occasionally, isolated individuals were willing to attribute ordinary actions to forces other than themselves upon hearing of a subliminal broadcast. Radio station KOL Seattle used its own phantom spots to ask, "How about a cup of coffee?" and to say, "Someone's at the door." Audience members called in to say they had heard the messages, indicating that they were not subliminal at all. Reportedly a non-coffee-drinker spontaneously made coffee and another person checked the front door.[98] KOL later jokingly discouraged TV consumption, whispering, "TV is a crashing bore," "Goodness, isn't TV dull?," and "Those TV westerns are all the same." They planned to say "TV gives you eye cancer" but balked.[99]

The Canadian Broadcasting Corporation (CBC) took a stand against the process, with advertising personnel concluding that it was a brand of "hypnosis" by "Big Brother."[100] But proudly declaring their position "against totalitarianism," the CBC went ahead with Subliminal Projection's first live television field test during the third week of January 1958.[101] Going to the neighboring country allowed Vicary to circumvent the NARTB ban with a national broadcast while showing that his technology would work for television as well as movie theaters. The CBC Board of Governors and the Canadian Department of Transport had granted special permission for the test.[102] Notices alerted the audience to the test during *Close-up*, though without disclosing the content of the invisible message. A straw poll of CBC technicians, managers, and advertisers the next day revealed that none could see the message.[103] As one CBC executive put it, "I felt like a beer, my wife had an urge for some cheese and the dog wanted to go outside in the middle of the program."[104] For a demonstration of this kind, imagine people sitting around their living rooms while self-monitoring their desires for any spark. Would getting the right answer indicate an intimate understanding of one's own libido, or a telepathic sensibility? Certainly audiences could claim participation in a national exploration of a novel mode of mass communication.

On the following Sunday *Close-up* revealed the message and results, thus offering a news cliffhanger for a week. "Phone now" had been the message, broadcast 352 times. The message flashes were at the unusually slow rates of one-fifth and one-half second. Even with this assistance the test failed to show the desired manipulative effect (though an advocate could protest that the message was not subliminal enough!). The show generated five hundred letters, only one of which got the message correctly, and the writer of that lone letter might have received the answer from a CBC insider. Verifying the result with telephone companies and its own switchboards, the CBC found no unusual increase in calls made across the country. Of the letters received, about half were from viewers who said they felt the impulse to eat or drink something, as though audience members were remembering Vicary's earlier cinema experiment while they squinted and watched for something to appear on their television sets.[105] In any case one cannot discount the influence of merely being a part of an experiment, a sort of special attention that on its own can compel people to seek out some (any) action. This demonstration, and many others, might have been instances of Elton Mayo's Hawthorne Effect, or the product of observer expectancy, in which a change in the subject's behavior has to do with the increased attention of the researcher and the expectations of what one is supposed to see or do, rather than the phenomena directly under investigation. Asked for a comment on the CBC results, Vicary said, "The less it seems to work, the easier to market it."[106] Again, the paradoxical logic of the invisible sell called forth claims of its *ineffectiveness* to guarantee continued interest.

Such bizarre yet, in context, reasonable logic captured the inverted world in which concerns about subliminal techniques blossomed. A "good" advertising technique was a benign one in the mind of the public. The industry had to reassure that its operations were well within the bounds of acceptable business practices, which meant that they didn't work too well or without fair possibility for individual will to exercise itself. As the general population understood it, motivational research was already pushing the limits of industry ethics. Now, subliminal advertising seemed no different from brainwashing or hypnotic suggestion; those invested in exploring its use had to construct a rhetorical distance from such analogies, even though interest in the technique arose from its unobtrusiveness and presumed effectiveness in establishing a shortcut to the consumer's mind and desires. MR proponents argued that its work was not subliminal advertising, and subliminal advertisers argued that its work was not mind control. Both groups sought ways to show they were giving but gentle taps on the subconscious.

But of course, what client would want to pay for something that didn't work well? Despite the wave of curious and amateurish applications, and some rumors of big investments, substantial contracts did not materialize and ultimately no significant accounts were won over. Prospective advertisers may have been skittish about the controversy, or uncertain about legality or effects on their reputation. Could they afford to be branded as mass manipulators? And in one of the most striking developments, it was becoming apparent that the process didn't work. In fact, most believed that it bordered on the ridiculous. Even if it did work, a solid agreement about its undesirability would have mobilized bans. *But this did not slow the trajectory of the "subliminal" and the "subliminal thesis" into vernacular language and onto the popular agenda.* This was because subliminal communication was in part a proxy for a host of other social concerns. The weight of the issue shifted from the actual operations of subliminal advertising to a broader and more cynical understanding of the advertising industry. In what might be described as a crisis of faith in the model of the good corporate citizen, advertisers found themselves confronting a growing popular distrust with the information that commercials provided. The freshly prominent "subliminal thesis" about hidden influences in popular media offered an occasion for that confrontation. It served, and at times continues to serve, as a nexus for identifying the social limits of consumerism. As advertisers overreached in their efforts to measure and exploit consumers' desires, critics coalesced around the antidemocratic undercurrents of advertisers' manipulation and deception of the public.

The Hidden and the Overload

By the late 1950s changes in the advertising industry epito-mized the ethical predicaments of the period. The industry offered a creative and quasi-bohemian environment that none-theless survived in and contributed to a consumerist good life. But it also provoked suspicions about covert manipulations of desires and actions. "The Philosophy of the Beat Generation" (1958), John Clellon Holmes's sequel to his groundbreaking article "This Is the Beat Generation" (1952), characterized the postwar years as follows: "It is the first generation in American history that has grown up with peacetime military training as a fully accepted fact of life. It is the first generation for whom the catch phrases of psychiatry have become such intellectual pabu-lum that it can dare to think they may not be the final yardstick of the human soul. It is the first generation for whom genocide, brain-washing, cybernetics, motivational research—and the re-sultant limitation of the concept of human volition which is in-herent in them—have been as familiar as its own face. It is also the first generation that has grown up since the possibility of the nuclear destruction of the world has become the final answer to all questions."[1] For Holmes, motivational research, as a "limita-tion of the concept of human volition," had the same historical status as other freshly popular terms like "brainwashing" and "cybernetic." And in a demonstration of the extreme concern that it evoked, the rise of advertisers' interest in MR illustrated the devastating inhumanity of the era along with genocide and nuclear annihilation.

Though the lasting impact and usage of the term "subliminal" could not have been predicted, its unusual prominence was already evident by the end of 1958. In his assessment of some of the voguish postwar additions to the English language, Thomas Pyles noted bureaucratic neologisms adding the suffix "-ize," as in *personalize, moisturize* and *accessorize*. Similarly "-wise" was popular, as in *healthwise* and *budgetwise*. The presence of *global* and *media* stood out for Pyles, but it was the abundance of psychoanalytic and psychological terms that seemed to offer the most historically distinctive new expressions: *guilt complex, herd complex, inferiority complex, sadism, compulsive, neurotic, psychosomatic*, and *subliminal*.[2]

These newly visible terms were indicative of larger priorities, and they were more than simply fashionable. They carried with them points of orientation for the United States of the late 1950s. Distinctive terminology is a linguistic compass, guiding us toward the magnetic north of a culture's sensibilities. As these sensibilities could reside in and influence both predictable and bizarre pockets of culture, fair attention must be devoted to their fullest range of deployment. Legitimate and authorized debate is only one arena. The more widely accepted a term or concept, the wilder one can expect the uses and appropriations to be. This was amply apparent with the term "subliminal." To be sure, at the very moment of popular recognition and public debate about subliminal communication there was a wide swath of positions on the subject, ranging from defenses of advertising research to critiques of modern alienation. And among these positions was an abiding suspicion that the technique was a hoax or at least an exaggeration; still, this did not arrest the dissemination of the idea. And despite the raucous distress about the implications of subliminal methods in media, creative uses of the term followed. It found its way into both comedic and sober works, often becoming a departure point for speculations and examinations of the operations of human consciousness and volition in mass consumer society.

After 1957 *The Hidden Persuaders* had company in every arena of commentary and expression for the challenge it posed to the work of advertisers. And the subliminal thesis was one angle on that critique, though the tone was not always entirely serious. Even in the heat of the first public introduction to the subliminal thesis, satirical and comical play was prevalent. Picking up on the currency of the term in order to comment on

CRAZY !

Come on Dad. Crawl outa that pad.
Get with it, man, as fast as you can.
We got subliminal sex.
Who knows what next?

DIG this COOL collection of HIP CARTOONS.
GET WITH the bearded BEATNIKS
and Dharma BUMS. GO, GO, GO
—way out for KICKS— at home and on the road.

IT'S
WILD
MAN
WILD!

Back cover of *Beat, Beat, Beat*, 1959.

a neurotic demand for being hip, William F. Brown's humorous illustrations of scenes from the beatnik life in *Beat, Beat, Beat* (1959) were advertised on the paperback cover with the semi-literate poetry parody "Come on Dad. Crawl outa that pad. Get with it, man, as fast as you can. We got subliminal sex. Who knows what next?"[3] A distinctly graphic element associated with the notion appeared in January 1958. An editorial in the *New Republic* dismissing the controversy over subliminal techniques included the messages "Drink!" and "Coca-Cola!" embedded throughout in italics and parentheses. The editorial joked about a demonstration of the techto ask the projectionists to slow *(Coca Cola!)* the apparatus to the point where we viewers could see the slogan. The projectionist did so, and sure enough, we were able to make out, plain as plain, the words:

SUBLIMINAL ADVERTISING IS HARMLESS

"Imbecile!" the demonstrator said *(Drink!)* and the embarrassed projectionist hastily tugged at the switch *(Coca Cola!)* once more, as we chuckled among ourselves, and then in a moment we saw another legend take shape upon the screen. *"Drink Coca Cola!"* it said. We stared at it intently, to see if it had the power to affect us to a greater degree than other forms of advertising. It did not. We find it difficult, therefore, to understand why anyone should become upset over so ridiculous a matter. Others can say what they please, but as for ourselves, we sat through the entire demonstration and have not observed the slightest alteration in our accustomed mode of life, except for a trifling matter of a constant and insatiable thirst for *(Coca Cola!)*

Graphic play with embedded messages of "drink!" and "Coca Cola!," from the *New Republic*, January 1958.

nique in which a projectionist substituted the announcement "Subliminal advertising is harmless" in place of the familiar "Drink Coca Cola," confounding flashes with hypnotic suggestion.[4] Two months later a more complete feature in *Life* documenting the issue printed "Marilyn Monroe call Herb Brean" interspersed in tiny font and block letters throughout the article (Brean was the article's author). The final page presented a glamour photograph of the star on the telephone and "Hello, Marilyn" in bold typeface.[5] Typographical play such as that employed in these illustrations brought forth the materiality of the printed page, as attention was drawn to the alternating selection of text and font. Foregrounding graphics and fonts transformed these articles about media effects into self-aware, if light in tone, statements about the form in which ideas were presented. The articles were no longer simple, transparent vehicles for the ideas on the page; the very process of communication and persuasion was the topic. And whatever alarm might be expressed in the article or elsewhere was tempered by the playfulness of the layout.

Gay Talese's feature in the *New York Times Magazine* began with an elaborate cartoon depiction of the process by Carl Rose.[6] A contemporary family of father, mother, teenage daughter, baby boy, and dog watch a western on a rather oversized television set. The father stands with a cigarette, wearing a smug expression. The mother sits with her sewing at her side, and the teenager relaxes with her shoes half off. The television fixes the family's collective attention, including that of the baby, who stands as close to the set as his playpen will allow. The lowbrow western on the television contrasts with the distinctly modern artwork, reminiscent of a Miró, displayed in the background. This scene of an ordinary suburban living room, however, has been invaded by tiny ghostly creatures. They hover around each family member and whisper shopping recommendations. The style-conscious teenager hears "Exotiquette—cosmetics with that forward look." The father hears "Philtos are the all-filter no-tobacco cigarettes!" in one ear and "Whizzee shaver—it gets *under* your skin" in the other. Two invisible gremlins tell the mother "Bubbl-x soap ditches the dirt!" and "Hurry buy Pagliacci pizza mix!" The baby is informed that "Krakkiwaks is the cereal with the new sound" and, ironically, that "Anti-sub pills will protect you from subliminal ads." From atop the television all are told, "Your dentures need Dento!," and even the dog's ear is lifted to receive the message "Yappo dog food makes yap-happy dogs!" With prominent brand names and desperate pleas, these fake consumer products make familiar claims to address human needs or to possess attributes superior to those of their competitors.

Though it is not stated explicitly, the source of these message-bearing ghosts is clearly taken to be the gigantic television set image that dominates the left side of the cartoon and not, for instance, the modern art hanging on the wall. This assumption reveals a presumably stable cultural hierarchy in which only television would stoop to such unethical depths of commercialism. As rendered here, the invisible sell is also a form of super-efficient target marketing. Devilish salespeople float through domestic space and perfectly target the prospective consumer according to criteria of gender and age. Unlike other comparable depictions, the cartoon is not an image of effect, save the rapturous staring at the TV program. It is a representation of the secret delivery of information and of advertising access to a supposedly private sanctuary. The entertainment program is thus a Trojan horse, with the commercialized media apparatus opening domestic space to small huckster soldiers.

The paradox of an invisible spot was a primary element in the humor that accompanied popular attention. *Advertising Age* used it in its running variation on the "dumb blonde" joke, featuring Gladys the beautiful receptionist. Over a water fountain, Gladys chats with another secretary:

Carl Rose, image for *New York Times Magazine*, January 1958.

"What's all this fuss about subliminal advertising? Personally, I can't see it."[7] The potential joys of the hidden commercial were explored by some. The *New Yorker* presented a cartoon of a man and a woman watching a pitchman on television in a domestic scene, with the visibly irate male viewer saying, "Any time they want to start flashing commercials I'm not conscious of, it's all right with me."[8] *Mad Magazine*'s version showed Alfred E. Newman, and his A. E. Newman look-alike date, prompted to buy and drink Coke at a movie; the on-screen characters also leave their scene to get the same refreshment. In *Mad*'s imaginative universe the movie industry flashed "Television viewing causes cancer of the eyeballs," the TV industry flashed "Movies are worse than ever," and librarians got into the act with "Buy and read *The Hidden Persuaders*."[9]

Others used these newly popular ideas about the consumer unconscious to imagine the inside workings of the advertising business. On her live comedy album *Again?* (Columbia 1958), Anna Russell's routine on the use of motivational research and subliminal techniques to sell bananas made reference to Packard and Pierre Martineau, author of *Motivation in Advertising* (1957). Russell described herself as a professor of subliminal musicology and merchandising at the Women's Schizo-Marketing School who hoped to use Freud to make the public "banana prone." The skit referred to the research that successfully made the prune "sexy," which Vicary had been involved in. As Russell put it, she needed to "prune up the banana." Indicating the currency of the issue, Mort Sahl's comic monologues on pressing topics included "evangelism, air raid drills, the Middle East, sports cars, penology, subliminal perception, civil liberties, smog."[10] And capitalizing on connotations of the subliminal as futuristic and an experience of total entrancement, the Leo Diamond Orchestra released an exotica album titled *Subliminal Sounds* (ABC Paramount 1960).

In January 1958 *Consumer Reports* included a cartoon of a man in front of a television set with his hair in curlers.[11] On a side table, beside his beer and opener, are assorted hair-care and beauty products. He explains to a blank-faced "wife," who is somewhat masculine in appearance, "I don't know what came over me. I was just sitting here watching the TV." Neither appears to be upset by the development, and neither rushes to tear the offending items from his head. The image is either one of crass and direct media effects or a lame attempt to blame television for something that the man was experimenting with anyway, having been caught in the act! Whether audiences read the cartoon in its overt or its subversive register, the concept of hidden and powerful influences motivates a satirical scene of disruption and becomes an occasion for gender play.

Subtextual subversion recedes in the face of Jack Cole's outrageous pictorial spread "The Subliminal Pitch" in the September 1958 issue of *Playboy*.[12] Cole, best known among comic book fans as the creator of Plastic Man, drew a series of colorful scenarios, all of which capture some transgressive element of subliminal influences. The first image parallels the cartoon in *Consumer Reports*: an attractive woman in a loose negligee watches TV while shaving her (presumably) imaginary beard. In other panels lovely women are guided magically into a movie house manager's office; a woman disrobes as she watches home movies of a vacation; pinch-faced censors nod approvingly at a pornographic film; a woman

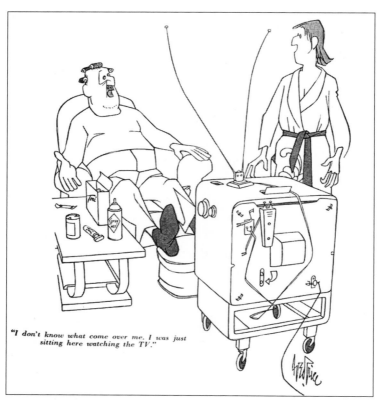

"I don't know what come over me. I was just sitting here watching the TV."

George Price, illustration for *Consumer Reports*, January 1958. Copyright Consumers Union of United States, Inc., Yonkers, N.Y., reprinted with permission.

chows down head first in a doggie bowl, with a man waiting his turn, while a forlorn puppy looks on with a quizzical expression; and children drink beer with bacchanalian glee while watching television.

Some of these images are fantasies of control, whether in seduction or business, in which people's will can be manipulated mechanically by others. And many represent men mesmerizing women, reiterating a thematic line seen in countless hypnosis tales. Equally prominent is the invitation to a carnivalesque social universe: children acting like adults, men acting like women, women acting like men, prudes acting like libertines, and people acting like animals. In the idea of mind control from a distance is a dream of social inversion. The lack of human volition corresponds to a license to role-play, most frequently with gender and sexuality. The premise of the subliminal thesis is that the hidden commercial caused the action, not some individual decision, hence absolving the

actor of responsibility for the consequences. Moreover these are images of media consumption, and virtually every instance depicts characters situated before a television set or in a cinema. The fantasies of controlling, and being controlled by, others through invisible messages is here also a fantasy about media effects.

NBC's *Steve Allen Show* aired a humorous take on the technique on 9 March 1958. An announcer comments on rising interest in the "hidden commercial," deeming it worthy of "The Allen Report to the Nation." Steve Allen appears on stage, sitting on a stool next to a card on a stand that reads "subliminal advertising." In a mock educational tone Allen explains the idea, using a blown-up image of film frames, one of which contains the phrase "smoke cigars." He points to the word "subliminal," which he breaks down as follows: "Sub actually means under or below as in submarine which means under water. The rest of the word liminal simply refers to the limits of the brain. So subliminal means more or less

. . . water on the brain, something like that, Chinese water torture, something in that area." Continuing the investigative report as a remote interview, Allen introduces the founder of the American Subliminal Company, a mustachioed G. G. Tishman, who, seated in his office, insists on being addressed as "colonel." Asked to explain the meaning of "subliminal," Tishman stumbles comically over the word, calling it "sublinial, uh, sublimim, Sal Mineo, subinial, we're concerned with a subli-animal . . ." Allen tries to help, asking what Tishman is working on at the moment. Tishman replies, "A new name for this process."

Tishman declares that tests have been taking place across the country with "a sublimindale message" of "smoke cigars" embedded in films. Sales have soared, but the problem is that the sponsor was . . . a cigarette company. Tishman leads viewers to his laboratory next door, presenting the inventor, Fred Guber, played in a white lab coat by a fumbling Don Knotts. The colonel enters and yells, "Tenhut!," startling the nervous inventor, and reiterating the suggestion of either a military presence behind the research or a boyish desire to play soldier on Tishman's part. Beginning to explain it, Guber also trips on the word: "sublimi, the subli, the silipad . . ." Tishman ventures with "subillygoat?" As the skit continues, the company president keeps trying to say the word: "subliminander?" "Sublimininim?"

Allen asks Guber how he came up with the idea of subliminal advertising. Guber responds that it was his nagging wife who pestered him to invent a new kind of advertising, and now she doesn't bother him any more. "Since subliminal advertising, huh?," Allen prompts. "No, since I divorced her." Guber proposes a demonstration. He presents a brief film clip of two men fighting and asks the colonel if he got the message and if it has made him feel like doing anything. The colonel says yes, and proceeds to beat up Guber. Whatever the hidden command may have been, the humor lies in the fact that the colonel responds automatically to the supraliminal content, mimicking the fight scene he has witnessed in what amounts to an exaggerated copycat media effect.

Cutting back to our host, Allen suggests that TV commercial actors could be put out of work if subliminal techniques are a success. He introduces Miss Betty Eyesore, who appears on the set of a commercial. Asked to comment, she says she is not worried. She went to a demonstration of subliminal advertising by a tobacco company and it simply didn't work. As Allen says goodbye, she reaches for a cigar and begins puffing madly.

This conventionally unfeminine act plays as a sly, perhaps suggestive gender reversal.

A nervous scientist and a delusional, autocratic CEO capture the bluster and ineffectiveness of authority figures in this skit. Accentuating this ineffectiveness is their inarticulateness concerning the very process they have created. Not only can they not explain it—and even Steve Allen's introduction lapses into dismissive nonsense when defining the term—but Tishman, Guber, and later Betty Eyesore can't even pronounce it. The primary source of humor for the first half of the skit is a populist anti-intellectualism: the commanding characters of researcher and entrepreneur are more bumbling and less intellectually developed than the viewing audience. This skit was broadcast a little more than a month after Vicary's and Corrigan's demonstrations for congressmen and the FCC, at which Congressman Potter expressed his desire for a hotdog—a line that would not have been out of place in Steve Allen's rendition.

Another humorous element in the skit plays with the possibility that the subliminal process actually works, and one can see that the comic possibilities of people under the command of others is immeasurable. With the slightest of suggestions, Allen's characters exhibit extreme swings in behavior. A boss attacks an employee and an actress devours a cigar after detecting corresponding messages to do so, whether subconsciously or not. The idea of subliminal commands is funny because it is ridiculous and because it was the product of supposedly smart people.

Beyond the skit's absurdities, "hidden" commercials already had a place in broadcasting media. Just before the announcer introduces "The Allen Report to the Nation," the show's sponsor, Timex, has its spot. A few moments later, when Allen throws to the G. G. Tishman character, what we see prominently displayed on Tishman's wrist is, of course, a Timex watch. This is not the blink of a tachistoscope or the single frame of film, but an unannounced reiteration of a sponsor's product, perfectly visible and absolutely unacknowledged. While extreme and automatic responses to media commands was laughable, an increasingly saturated advertising environment was indisputably in development.

Some advertising directly addressed the hidden commercial through spoofs. The writer and director Stan Freberg, of Freberg/Fine Arts Production Statement, created an animated TV spot for Butter-Nut Coffee, called "Subliminal," in 1959. A little cartoon man begins, somewhat nervously, by saying, "Um, ladies and gentlemen, this commercial is going to use sublim . . . sublim." As if to help him, there follows a quick flash of "subliminal advertising," after which he is able to say the phrase, suggesting that there may have been a degree of undetected influence. He continues, "That means you will never see or hear the name of the product. Oh, it'll be there on the screen all right, but the naked eye cannot detect it. This way you can sit back, relax and enjoy . . . *me* as I tell you this, heh-heh, rather funny story. You see it seems these three men decided to take a trip and . . ." As the pitchman tells his story, fireworks and fanfare drown out his words. Bright flashes of "Instant Butter-Nut Coffee" appear behind him. He continues his tale, unaware of the distractions or the fact that we cannot hear what he is saying. "The second guy goes back to the dry cleaner's . . ." More fireworks and music obscure his monologue, and this time the phrase "Butter-Nut Buy it Today" appears. We hear the next portion of the little man's story as he continues without apparent knowledge of the show taking place behind his back: "So he opens the little door and goes opsy dopsy dopsy." Again interrupting, intense music accompanies copy reading, "It took 5 years to make and it's worth it. Delicious Instant Butter-Nut Coffee." The exhausted pitchman concludes the tale, chuckling, "So the third guy says, 'Yeh but ya better bring back the hangers.'" The super-soft sell is inverted to become a loud, brash, and crass plea, drowning out the comic tale. The hard sell tramples over the nervous, diminutive, subliminal salesman.

In late 1958 Chevrolet promoted its newest automobile with a song-and-dance number that sold the product "the subliminal way." As Pat Boone and Dinah Shore dance up and down a multi-tiered set to a jaunty tune, they sing, "Hey, have you heard about the crazy new way, To send a message today, It flashes on a screen too quick to see, But still you get it subliminally." A perceptible flash of the new car appears, after which Boone says, "See it?," then reprises the tune. The ridiculousness of invisible ads becomes a teasing peek at a new product.

A drive-in advertising spot for refreshments similarly plays on the audience's understanding of subliminal communication. It presents a silhouetted boy and girl in the foreground watching a movie of a Sherlock Holmes–like character. Images of a hamburger flash, interrupting the mystery. The spectating characters wonder what they saw and comment upon their growing hunger. As the hamburger's appearances recur and lengthen, taking over the Holmes story, our characters rise to visit the snack bar. A simple narrative, but to get the joke you need to know

Stan Freberg's
commercial for
Butter-Nut Coffee,
1959. Author's
collection.

something about claims that flashing images exercise direct influence on behavior. The result is nothing like the assertions of Vicary and others. Instead we see a weird montage: mystery story, hamburger, mystery story, hamburger, and so on. These lead to a depiction of direct effect, with the silhouetted audience members going to the snack bar. Most importantly, the images in these parodic ads are not truly subliminal; they suggest the subliminal through rapid edits. They are in fact perfectly perceptible, though fleeting, which marks an aesthetic transition evident in the Butter-Nut and Chevrolet spots as well: given that it is impossible to present something unperceivable, aesthetically *the visible flash comes to signify the invisible flash of the subliminal.*

For some in the advertising industry, the subliminal controversy was no laughing matter. They felt increasingly targeted by critics like Packard, who challenged the pervasiveness of advertisements and new advertising methods. Throughout 1958 several state governments sifted through the contradictory evidence in efforts to establish a legislative position on the matter, pressured by constituents who worried about the infringement upon human self-determination that the very idea of hidden influences represented. The New York State Senate voted to pass a bill banning subliminal sales pitches, with Thomas C. Desmond (Republican, Newburgh) as its sponsor.[13] The bill originated from active teenagers associated with the YMCA who had lobbied the state to take this action.[14] Accordingly, the State of New York planned to amend civil rights law to protect against subliminal techniques at motion picture theaters. The bill prohibited any projection "designed or intended to communicate any idea or message to the subconscious or unconscious minds of the audience, unless, at least thirty minutes prior thereto, the identical idea or message in its entirety is audibly and visibly transmitted to and projected . . . to convey the same to the conscious minds."[15] Curiously, the bill maintained the right to use the technique as long as fair notice was given to patrons. In any case, it failed to get through the State Assembly and never became law. The California State Senate, for its part, voted to ask Congress to ban subliminal television ads.[16] And Congressman James C. Wright Jr., Democrat of Texas, introduced a bill on 9 January 1959 to make subliminal advertising illegal, specifically targeting devices used to "indoctrinate the public by means of making an impression on the subconscious mind wherein the viewing audience would not reasonably be fully aware of the employment of said device."[17] Proposed penalties were fines up to $5,000 and revocation of the station's broadcasting license. This bill too went no further.[18]

A similar fate befell proposed legislation in New Jersey.[19] One member of the New Jersey Assembly, Mildred Barry Hughes, introduced a resolution to form a study committee. With Hughes as chairwoman, the New Jersey Senate committee on subliminal projection included none other than Vladimir Zworykin, television pioneer and at the time a professor at Princeton.[20] The resolution expressed worry that "subconscious motivation is beyond the control of reason," posing a "grave danger of the misuse of such a device to influence the thinking of our citizens."[21] The commission consulted with several psychologists, including George Klein and Donald Spence, and with representatives from Precon. The commissioners described fears of "Big Brother" who could "determine elections, convert the United States to communism."[22] Even while subliminal commercials died as a news sensation, and psychologists authoritatively challenged the claims of massive subliminal effects, enough people remained uncertain about the ads to prompt the New Jersey legislature to respond. Effectiveness was somewhat of a side issue. The legislators acknowledged that "subliminal influence is not one on which concrete evidence can be obtained, for and against, and from this evidence find the answer. So much is a matter of conjecture that, in almost every sense, personal opinion is an important factor in the determination of one's views on the subject."[23] Should this not have closed down the need to continue the commission's work? Apparently not. The core claim about strong subliminal influence was a sufficient entreaty to further public debate and study. From the fall of 1957 through 1959 a comparable rhetorical slippage occurred regularly in news reports, editorials, and parodies of subliminal communication: subliminal techniques were handled as though their effects were substantial and unavoidable. Typically, references to the techniques appeared as speculative "what-if" discussions. Still, of all the "what-ifs" imaginable, this "what-if" was especially evocative and compelled legislative bodies to join in.

Initially limited to considering only visual uses of subliminal suggestion, the New Jersey commission narrowed its own scope further to consider only film, reasoning that television regulation was the domain of the FCC. The members consulted with psychologists, advertisers, and technology developers and found themselves awash in information, making completion of their work in the assigned six months impossible. Hughes introduced another resolution (no. 6, 1959) that allowed the commission to continue its work beyond the first deadline. The commission met with representatives of the Subliminal Projection Co. on 7 January 1959 for a discussion that the report described as "disappointing" without additional explanation, though it implied that Vicary and his colleagues did not agree to demonstrate their device.[24] On 8 April 1959 a public hearing involved psychologists, theater owners, concerned citizens, and Robert Corrigan of Precon. The commission noted, without further detail, that "subliminal projection has been used widely in several motion pictures being shown throughout the State of New Jersey."[25] Indicating that the process used was Precon's, these films must have been *My World Dies Screaming* and *Date with Death*. These were fairly obscure, independently distributed films with limited circulation, which call into question the commission's claim of widespread use of subliminal projection in theaters, unless it was taking into account anecdotes about theater managers who flicked advertising slides off and on.

A submission from Melvin L. De Fleur of Indiana University described his experiments in closed-circuit and television broadcasts of subliminal messages, finding a slightly greater-than-chance effect with the former and absolutely none with the latter. In a carefully reasoned analysis De Fleur indicated that the usual "mental calluses" people develop with respect to advertising could be a factor as much as some infinite openness to suggestibility. He made a point of referring to the dominant paradigm of communications research—a model of limited effects and personal influence—that contradicted claims about strong and immediate effects producing media copycat behavior. Most tellingly, De Fleur advanced the claim that subliminal advertising was a cultural norm and had been for ages, insomuch as ads have saturated the media world, were evident in every form of printed and broadcast media, and were far too numerous to process perceptually or mentally.[26] For De Fleur, sensory saturation had naturalized the particularity of the hidden message, a view that was turning critical attention to a general condition of "overload." In their published writings De Fleur and his co-author concluded that the persuasive impact of subliminal messages upon behavior was insignificant.[27] A submission by Israel Goldiamond, professor of psychology at Southern Illinois University, joked that subliminal ads might be championed as a remedy for "obnoxious" television commercials, recalling the remark by the man in the cartoon in the *New Yorker*. Again, referring to the lively debate around subliminal influence, Goldiamond charted how the concept contradicted some of the most basic findings of psychology, as well as common sense.[28]

The commission's summation reasserted the lack of evidence that subliminals had any effect, despite weak evidence of some form of perception without awareness. Citing caution concerning the as-yet untapped mysteries of the mind, the commission nonetheless recommended "legislative recognition of the technique in the protection of the public right of privacy."[29] Here the commission was referring to the freedom from being pestered without choice by commercial appeals, conscious or not. Still charmed by the notion, the commission members tried to subdue what they repeatedly called the emotional and hysterical response to subliminal communication and turned to its potential educational and therapeutic uses.[30] Protecting privacy and quelling public fears required acknowledging that subliminal influence was a possibility, despite evidence to the contrary.[31] The commission proposed a statute to prohibit the unannounced use of subliminal messages in public places.[32] Again, this proposal was careful to protect corporate freedom, proposing regulation rather than outright prohibition.

Legislators were not alone in the pursuit, however fruitless, of limits on certain practices of subliminal influence while disregarding the information on their desks. Overall the advertising industry was peculiarly uncertain in its response, and many spoke of the possibility of a backlash of negative press for those who struck a devil's bargain with hidden messages. Still, there were ample, and speedily accumulating, indications that segments of the advertising business continued to salivate at the possibility that some subconscious mechanisms could be uncovered and exploited. The tantalizing possibility of an extreme method found its supporters and attracted attention in the trade press. The results of psychological experiments at Stanford University showing subliminal associations between images and words appeared in *Advertising Age* in 1958.[33] The same spring an editorial in the *Wall Street Journal* wondered about the possibly benign process of subliminal advertising being no different from any other acceptable form of MR, and suggested that it could lead to a welcome decrease in commercial interruptions.[34] The participants at the Western Radio and Television Conference in San Francisco witnessed a subliminal ad for Coca-Cola, flashed three hundred times during a half-hour film interview with Frank Lloyd Wright. Some expressed desires for chewing gum, potatoes, and sex, but none for the soft drink.[35] Occasionally a psychological test showing some effectiveness received trade press attention, including those conducted by Marvin Zuckerman of Indiana University.[36] The advertisement composer Glen Hurlburt developed a sub-audible recording technique, used in spots for Nucoa margarine on radio and television.[37] The ad agency responsible was one of the few that publicly acknowledged interest and experimentation in subliminal techniques.[38]

But others either chuckled at the idea or decried its ethics. Henry J. Engler, dean of the College of Business Administration at Loyola University, New Orleans, pooh-poohed the whole controversy, saying that people could not be "brainwashed" to do things that they wouldn't do anyway. But, he reasoned, this was because we had become accustomed to advertising overload, and have become skillful in discerning messages at a subconscious level.[39] In an era of outer-directedness, H. Radler of the Purdue Research Foundation worried that contemporary teenagers, conformist and fearful in character, were easy targets for hidden persuaders, "shoddy merchandise, shoddy morals or a patched-up police state philosophy."[40] One advertiser, R. M. Kidd, commented on the oddity of the bandwagon effect that surrounded the idea of subliminal suggestion, even without solid evidence, and then proceeded to outline some of the known psychological data.[41]

Steuart Britt, a marketing professor at Northwestern University, supported further tests and believed that there was some validity to the claims.[42] At a meeting of the Chicago chapter of the American Marketing Association, he gave an example of what control and comparison tests would look like, none of which Vicary had been careful enough to do.[43] Britt wryly summarized, "People today complain about the advertising they can see; if subliminal advertising becomes a reality, they'll complain about the advertising they can't see."[44] By 1960, though, Britt was convinced that there was no usefulness for advertisers: "Let's dismiss the subject by calling it the 'ghost of subliminal advertising.'"[45]

The Advertising Conference at the University of Michigan in 1958 took as its theme "Advertising and the Subconscious," with speakers from industry and academia primarily encouraging caution and skepticism, though with some interesting qualifications. Two advertising directors, W. B. Booth, vice-president and copy director of Campell-Ewald

Company, and A. B. Scott, senior art director of the same company, discussed "third communication," or the use of messages over and above copy and art. Their description of some extra impression, attitude, or opinion sounds very much like a Barthesian definition of connotation—Roland Barthes's *Mythologies* had just appeared in the original French in 1957—though the term was not used by these advertising executives.[46] Booth and Scott saw a glancing relation to subliminal influence: "You might also ask if we are dealing with some obtuse theory of subliminal perception. Not exactly, although we began some explorations into subliminal perception about two years ago. We did this, not with the Machiavellian hope of flashing unseen advertising messages all over the place, but to see if we could uncover the subconscious impact and meanings of various visual treatments and word arrangements. I understand that this subject of subliminal perception is to be treated here by far more learned hands than ours, but I should like to say that our explorations still continue and that they do tend to confirm the validity of the third communication."[47]

The featured speaker at the University of Michigan Advertising Conference was Vance Packard. He gave a talk titled "The Hidden Why's of Our Behavior," in which he argued against tapping into unconscious desires to promote irrational behaviors, citing the rising debate about the wastefulness of planned obsolescence as one example. Packard was somewhat gracious, perhaps because he was addressing an audience of advertisers, ultimately pleading for responsible uses of MR and making but an offhanded comment questioning the validity and ethics of subliminal advertising.[48] This theme was taken up in full by the next speaker, the psychology professor Richard I. Cutler, who decried the lack of solid scientific data for the claims being made for subliminal effects and spent time addressing the invalidity of Vicary's movie theater test.[49] This reasonable and rational response didn't stop Cutler's colleague Elton B. McNeil from painting a futuristic portrait of advertisers reminding housewives of their product by pushing a button to stimulate parts of their brains in his talk, "Subliminal Stimulation: Omen of Things to Come."[50] His view was that regardless of the uses to which subliminal influence might be put in the future, its prominence was a sign that "the unconscious is here to stay and you have to learn about it if you are going to do a complete job."[51] With some levity, McNeil ended the panel discussion by stating, "Until we find out whether Marilyn Monroe actually called Herb [Brean] . . . we will have to view subliminal communication with some skepticism, but not with complete indifference."[52]

Concurrently, attention to the issue mounted in the United Kingdom. Norman Dixon, a psychologist at the University of London who later wrote *Subliminal Perception: The Nature of a Controversy* (1971), appeared on the BBC's *Science Review* to say that in many ways advertising had always operated on a sub-threshold level, though without any evidence that the subliminal effect was greater than the supraliminal one.[53] This claim was cold comfort to those who were inclined to view advertisers as invasive and mendacious anyway. Sharps Toffee denied rumors of a six-week test of subliminal advertising in cinemas for its product, though a representative admitted that the company's ad agency might be experimenting.[54] The accepted view that subliminal techniques were ineffective and inconsequential did not lift the taint resulting from allegations of having used them. In a way, subliminal techniques were becoming synonymous with sneaky, underhanded, and unfair practice. The *Daily Herald*, a left-leaning paper, accused Television Wales and West of flashing a winking eye accompanied by the words "keep watching" for 1/25 of a second. Though an image shown for that long would have been consciously seen by many viewers, the broadcaster agreed to discontinue the practice.[55] The implied sneakiness of the technique led many to be cautious in how they dealt with the topic of subliminal suggestion, often making bold pronouncements about its unethical nature. The British Institute of Practitioners in Advertising formed a committee in December 1957 to examine subliminal techniques, with A. N. C. Varley of Colman Prentis as its chairman and an agenda of assuring that the industry was seen as honest and above board in its practices.[56] The committee submitted its report in May 1958, predictably with a ban on any use of subliminal content. It reasoned that the effectiveness of the technique was beside the point, and that full disclosure to consumers was a necessary requirement.[57]

A strange line of defense arose in the argument that subliminal messages were nothing new for consumers to worry about, as advertising at some level had always operated below consciousness and without awareness. To avoid tripping up on this approach, in the United States the Advertising Research Foundation (ARF) felt it necessary to prepare its own assessment, giving the task to its standing committee on MR. As a consequence of the negative impressions of the advertising industry that the subliminal scandal had sparked, the members were to produce a position statement on the subject. Called "one of the most controversial and pro-vocative developments in the history of advertising," subliminal advertising was the source of much confusion.[58] The ARF proposed to offer clear definitions and descriptions of the process, though it did not attempt to establish the related ethical boundaries for marketers. The most distin-guished member of the group was the chairwoman, Herta Herzog, an in-fluential early mass communication researcher with the Princeton Radio Research Project and the Bureau of Applied Social Research, a contribu-tor to Hadley Cantril's *The Invasion from Mars*, and now a vice-president and director of research at McCann-Erickson.[59] The ARF report, published in 1958, far from being a blanket condemnation of the invisible pitch, offered definitions and technical advice to those wishing to use it. The commissioners devoted the most space to descriptions of select psycho-logical experiments that had attempted to show discrimination below perceptual thresholds, including the "happy/angry" test conducted by George Klein and his team. Steering clear of the moral or ethical dimen-sion, they solidly backed the view that subliminal stimuli could be "felt," though the usefulness for advertising was undetermined.[60] So we see that exactly a year after Vicary's first bombshell of a press conference, Herta Herzog's commission announced that though psychologists could show some minor effects of subliminal messages under tightly controlled con-ditions, there was nothing that merited use for commercial purposes.[61]

An issue of the *American Psychologist* in May 1958 contained an elabo-rate critique of Vicary's claims and put his ideas, though without ex-plicitly mentioning him by name, into the context of a long history of psychological experimentation.[62] The authors opened by declaring the extraordinary nature of the public panic: "Seldom has anything in psy-chology caused such an immediate and widespread stir as the recent claim that the presentation of certain stimuli below the level of conscious awareness can influence people's behavior in a significant way."[63] Survey-ing advertising and psychology experiments, the authors reasoned that though some forms of unconscious influence by stimuli could be dem-onstrated, the methodological and ethical issues were complex enough to seriously limit the generalizability of those findings: "Anyone who wishes to utilize subliminal stimulation for commercial or other purposes can be likened to a stranger entering into a misty, confused countryside where there are but few landmarks."[64] Vicary responded in *Advertising Age*, reiterating points made in 1958 at the Advertising Conference in his defense.[65] Though he felt that he should have been named overtly in the issue — an anxiety of under-appreciation was a running theme in his life — he welcomed the sober discussion, maintaining yet again that he would not release details of the conditions under which the first surprising results were recorded.[66]

The presentations at the American Psychological Association in September 1958 only added to the growing consensus that advertising uses were minimal. Harry Walter Daniels, of Visual Impact Laboratory, Philadelphia, was careful to explain that his use of tachistoscopes to flash magazine copy for a test audience was not to be confused with subliminal advertising.[67] The debunking of what nearly everyone agreed was not anything substantive continued. On the first anniversary of Vicary's watershed press conference, *Advertising Age* reported that the idea "seemed to be getting nowhere fast," referring to bans by advertising organizations in Britain and Australia and by the National Association of Broadcasters, as well as to the widespread negative and dismissive response from the scientific community.[68]

Others weighed in, sometimes from unexpected corners. Herschel Gordon Lewis, soon to be an infamous director of cult horror films, argued in the pages of *Advertising Age* for separating subliminal perception and advertising. Citing several psychological studies, he wrote that rapid edits in film should not be lumped in with witchcraft and Ouija boards. From his experience in film he recounted that "punching a hole in a single frame of film, which is projected at 1/50 of a second, is glaringly obvious. An entire white frame looks like an explosion; yet a black frame may pass entirely unnoticed." Though I have no idea how he was doing his math here — single frames at the time moved at a standardized rate of 1/24 of a second — he rightly described the immense potential for emotional effect inherent in this simple technique. Yet when Lewis made this argument to clients for use in business films, they assumed, much to his consternation, that eliciting an emotional effect in this fashion was tantamount to brainwashing.[69] The budding artist Lewis, thwarted by ethically (or aesthetically) timid businessmen, would take his affective experiments elsewhere, turning his talents to make the splatter classics *Blood Feast* (1963) and *Two Thousand Maniacs!* (1964).

In Chicago Jack N. Peterman, director of psychological research for Buchen Co., and one of the members of the AFA Motivational Research committee, criticized Vicary's CBC television test, saying that the exposure rate was slow and relied upon a dim projection of the message for invisibility. Peterman, who had twenty years' experience working in audience research at CBS and the Mutual Broadcasting System and had been involved with U.S. Air Force audiovisual tests, said that the problem with a dim, slow message, rather than a bright, swift one, was that it would limit the ability of the subconscious to register it.[70] The marketing executive Bertrand Klass attributed the controversy to a semantic misapprehension of the distinction between the subconscious, which denotes what is just below the edge of awareness, and the unconscious, which denotes deeply held wishes and desires. The subconscious operates like any other form of liminal perception, Klass argued, and hence should be the topic of discussion about consumer behavior, regardless of whether messages have registered peripherally or not. Further, as with all advertising, merely noticing something does not translate automatically into doing something.[71] Taking aim at an elision resting at the heart of the debates about the impact of subliminal exposure, Klass pointed to the fast and unwarranted movement between a message that might register somewhere in the mind and a message that directly influenced behavior.

Supporters of subliminal techniques included Ross Wilhelm, marketing professor at the University of Michigan, who described at an AMA meeting that subliminal messages did not involve coercion or hypnotism, and could have enormous benefits, primarily the reduction of commercial interruptions.[72] In this reasoning, product placement in effect came to be seen as a reasonable and inevitable consequence of increased competition for new commercial space. Pushing even further to generalize the subliminal thesis, Wilhelm suggested that much media consumption was essentially without awareness: "Every time we drive our car and flash by a billboard we probably receive a subliminal suggestion. Each time we flip through a magazine or newspaper we probably receive subliminal messages from the ads and the pages we pass over. Whenever we switch our TV sets from channel to channel those channels we pass over which are delivering commercials probably deliver subliminal reminders to us—reminders of which we are not aware. And yet, have we to date seen any of the dire effects which the critics have feared?"[73] With this assessment Wilhelm saw the fleeting and the transient as part of the conditions of modern life. The image and informational clutter of contemporary media were transforming lived experience into something habitually gleaned from subliminal stimuli.

Others lent support to this view, like the advertiser Earle Ludgin, who argued to the Advertising Executives Club of Chicago that the high volume of commercial and promotional materials made them all somewhat subliminal. To demonstrate media clutter, he pasted onto a single roll of paper all 242 pages of an issue of the *Los Angeles Sunday Times*, pointing to how dwarfed a single ad would be. He also showed a seven-minute television sequence that included the end of one show, credits, sponsors, cross-promotion with other programs, local spots, the beginning of another show, a commercial, and opening credits. Using other examples from radio and magazines, he argued that this brand of flow and clutter was a defining attribute of the media, making any single spot essentially indistinguishable from the next.[74] In early 1959 Ludgin composed a feature article developing this argument for *Advertising Age*, which concluded that an ad would be effective if it could rise above the din created by the clutter of other ads. In the battle for attention, all ads were subliminal until they were able to do this, he reasoned. As an example of increased clutter Ludgin noted the growing practice of "triple spotting," in which several advertising appeals appeared one after another in radio and television.[75] In this way, he twisted the subliminal into an analogy for and commentary upon the whole of the contemporary advertising context.

Wilhelm's and Ludgin's assessments resonated. There was a sense that advertising was reaching a saturation point. Even before the term "information overload" gained popular currency, the noise of the glut of advertising was understood as a key contributing factor to media clutter. Advertising was held up by critics as an industry that participated in the most egregious misuse of media and as a cynical agent responsible for hijacking what might have otherwise been democratic tendencies in popular media. But the advertisers were not pleased about the climate either. Radio and television stations had begun to sell spots to multiple advertisers during commercial breaks, trimming the length of each commercial and increasing the number of products presented. This magazine format, with different commercials for different products placed side by side during a TV or radio broadcast, was not automatically welcomed by the advertising industry. Agencies complained vociferously about the practice, seeing their rates go up and the distinctiveness of their spots go down; some refused outright to accept double and triple spotting.[76]

The concept of "overload" in communication systems was just about to be recognized. In 1962 the economist Fritz Machlup published his highly influential book *The Production and Distribution of Knowledge in the United States*, which made a case for the rising economic might of a sector he called the "knowledge industry," a growing importance spurred on by its increased output.[77] The same year Richard Meier's groundbreaking study on urban growth appeared, arguing that because of the increased volume of communication, "cities face some unprecedented crisis in the not-too-distant future."[78] He proposed that the expanding city of the 1960s confronted a historically unique abundance of communication, largely technologically mediated, which pushed the upper limits of capacity for meaningful transactions between people and organizations. This argument drew upon cybernetic and information theory, most significantly the Shannon and Weaver model of communication, which featured channel capacity as a determination of efficient communication. Using as case studies a stock exchange and a university library, Meier concluded that there was the potential for a fatal overload of the communication system if steps were not taken to revise organizational procedures and decision making. With special attention to advertising, television, and telephony, he warned of a condition that became a core idea of the 1960s: information overload. The growth of the cultural sector, the concentration of people in large cities, and the increased volume of messages carried by communication systems pushed human sensory mechanisms and civilization to their structural limits. He predicted that "the problems of widespread saturation in communications flow may arise within the next half century."[79]

The historical origin of the feeling of being overwhelmed with cultural material certainly predated Meier. Some work, for instance, has documented a concern in the sixteenth century with an overabundance of books and sees the first European encyclopedia as symptomatic of a new age of information management.[80] And the special relationship between urban life and sensory bombardment has been developed at least since Georg Simmel's seminal essay "The Metropolis and Mental Life" (1903). In it he argued, "The deepest problems of modern life derive from the claim of the individual to preserve the autonomy and individuality of his existence in the face of overwhelming social forces, of historical heritage, of external culture, and of the technique of life." This challenge of modernity emerged from "the *intensification of nervous stimulation*" associated with city life, especially during periods of rapid change.[81]

But Meier's concept of overload linked specifically with a context of urban population growth, curiosity about electronic media, and new theories of how information systems operate. Moreover, scholarly and scientific discussion about the limits of the senses and consciousness, both of which were seen to be under threat from the flood of media signals, offered a physiological basis for his claims. Meier proposed the terms "attention overload" and "communication saturation" earlier in the 1950s, and the essayist Clifton Fadiman wrote of the decline of attention in 1951.[82] "Breakdown" due to information overload was so pervasive in so many different forms of performance tests, James G. Miller argued in 1960, that it could "explain some of the psychopathology of everyday life and clinical practice."[83] And Karl Deutsch elaborated these claims in 1961, with the metropolis as an engine of communication that produced, when its systems were taxed, "a pervasive condition of communication overload."[84] In these works there was an agreement upon the deleterious effect of urbanization and media upon sensory and information circuits.

The growing scholarly discussion about the impact of excessive sensory stimuli was a critique of what elsewhere was presented as the best product of the modern age. The language of overload challenged the desirability of technological progress and the necessity of a media-dominated everyday existence. As the subliminal thesis crossed into popular culture—on television shows, in comic strips, in the periodical press, etc.—it was part of a popular discussion about media clutter. Along with "information overload," the subliminal thesis expressed suspicion, and reservation, about the multitude of fleeting textual appeals that zip by us. As advanced by the subliminal thesis, though specific and isolated stimuli in an environment of overload may have been unnoticed, an effect was suggested nonetheless. Was it possible that we were reaching, or might soon reach, some ultimate structural limit to our sensory and cognitive apparatuses? Again, whether or not an absolute informational and sensory threshold exists is a matter of debate. But these terms captured an understanding that an accumulation and acceleration of the world of signs was a defining feature of contemporary society, that there was something particularly worrisome about the prominence of commercial appeals in this world of signs, and that these features warranted close monitoring, if not more extreme measures of resistance.

Supplementing the analyses of scholars, a popular critique of informational abundance, and its association with advertising, developed in the years leading up to the moment of the subliminal controversy beginning in 1957. Some works of fiction expressed terror about the prospects of an environment totally occupied by promotional pleas. Especially notable is Fritz Leiber Jr.'s "The Girl with the Hungry Eyes" (1949), in which a mysterious model becomes a national presence in magazine ads and on billboards, shaping the desires of millions. Depicted as a vampire consumer, the Girl is a serial killer who extracts the life from the men drawn to her varying images by sucking the spirit of those desiring her. In essence, she is pure, insatiable desire. Sounding like a psychotic child in the horrific conclusion, she reveals her murder method: "I want you. I want your high spots. I want everything that's made you happy and everything that's hurt you bad. I want your first girl. I want that shiny bicycle. I want that licking. I want that pinhole camera. I want Betty's legs. I want the blue sky filled with stars. I want your mother's death. I want your blood on the cobblestones. I want Mildred's mouth. I want the first picture you sold. I want the lights of Chicago. I want the gin. I want Gwen's hands. I want your wanting me. I want your life. Feed me, baby, feed me."[85] Key to this drama is the ubiquity of images and advertising, and the inescapability of the girl's face, always appearing and reappearing in magazines and on billboards. And most tellingly, in the story's conclusion this ubiquity connects with an insatiable consumer desire, which simply and ceaselessly wants everything.

Ann Warren Griffith's "Captive Audience," appearing in the *Magazine of Fantasy and Science Fiction* in 1953, depicts satirically the terrible surfeit of consumer desire and advertising appeals, prefiguring the subliminal controversy to follow.[86] The story describes domestic breakfast scenes in which spontaneous commercials emanating from food packages repeatedly interrupt conversation. The only way to stop the bread from singing its jingle is to put another slice in the toaster. The father, Fred, works for Master Ventriloquism Corporation of America, a company that produces "MVS," or pop-up commercials incorporated into product packaging. MVS are also broadcast messages to telephones, reminding people to look up phone numbers before dialing. The newspaper on the doorstep calls out, "Good morning, this is your *New York Times*! Wouldn't you like to have me delivered to your door *every* morning! Think of the added convenience."[87] A trip to the supermarket finds the mother, Mavis, in the noisy cereal aisle with ads, sound effects, and music blasting from each package, vying for her attention. When Mavis tells her daughter that one brand is simply too noisy to have at breakfast, the girl bursts into tears and threatens to tell her father. On this particular day Grandma is off to jail. Working with a radical protest group, she had refused to give up her earplugs, which were unconstitutional contraband because they contributed to "restraint of advertising."[88] On her ride to prison, "Grandmother was happy and at peace, thinking, as she listened to the gas tanks yelling to be filled up, the spark plugs crying to be cleaned, and all the other parts asking to be checked, or repaired, or replaced, that she was hearing MV for the last time."[89] It pleases her to be going to jail, where there are no such cacophonous advertisements. Fred then has a brainstorm. Why not place MVS in prison? They could be public service announcements, making sure that inmates don't lose their buying habits while incarcerated. Mavis is so proud that her husband thinks "not just of the moneymaking side, but of the welfare and betterment of all those poor prisoners!"[90] In its representation of generational difference in the experience and acceptance of the environment of clamorous publicity, the story presents an image of saturation that pushes us to the point of madness.

The sci-fi classic *The Space Merchants*, by Frederik Pohl and C.M. Kornbluth, also appeared in 1953.[91] Where Griffith's tale focused on the infernal experience and logic of advertising clutter, this novel depicted a fantasy of subconscious manipulation through techniques of motivational research. Revolving around an advertising campaign to sell the colonization of Venus, and efforts by the "Consies"—conservationists— to sabotage it, the novel depicts a world of complete commercial saturation, where the difference between ad agencies and governments has been eroded. Our narrator, the star advertiser Mitch Courtenay, describes being uneasy in a library, surrounded by books, because the absence of advertising seems so unproductive.[92] Beyond their socially beneficial contributions, ads now have a role as legitimate culture. While strolling through the Metropolitan Museum of Art, Mitch stops in front of "the big, late-period Maidenform—number thirty-five in the catalogue: 'I Dreamed I was Ice-Fishing in my Maidenform Bra.'"[93] The futuristic advertising forms described include "outlawed compulsive subsonics in our aural advertising," "semantic cue words that tie in with every basic trauma and neurosis in American life," "projecting our messages on aircar windows," and "a system that projects direct on the retina of the eye."[94]

The behaviorist and psychological influence on these imaginings is evident. The allusions to MR methods, at the time on the cusp of circulating as a popular concern, explore the implications of the impercep-tibility of the commercial environment in which we live. At one point Mitch points to all the name-brand products that a man wears. The man responds, "I never read the ads." Mitch grins at this, saying, "Our ulti-mate triumph is wrapped up in that statement."[95] The satire becomes a political morality tale, as Mitch grows to understand and support the Consies, abandoning his consumerism. So, like "The Captive Audience," *The Space Merchants* is also a story of rebellion against a dominant mode of capitalism. And behind this resolution is a popular sensibility about the powerful techniques of advertising that will later be represented in popular nonfiction by Vance Packard.

This popular and scholarly discussion of textual clutter, sensory over-stimulation, and commercial saturation both set the stage for and was advanced by the subliminal thesis, which arrived as the technological cut-ting edge of mass-mediated influence in late 1957. The sci-fi representa-tions of an eye-blearing, head-spinning, headache-inducing, and mur-derous future of advertising abundance captured familiar concerns. Did these tales not describe our present condition in some way too, or the direction in which the ever-ambitious aspirations of marketers wished to take us? Was it possible that the already noisy commercial realm would get even louder? And as manifest messages were overloaded, and as a re-sult, squeezed into imperceptible flashes, was it possible that the rumors of an unconscious, as yet untold, impact had some validity? What if the super-rapid appeal had an impact upon behavior and desire, despite its imperceptibility and its competition with a multitude of other appeals? Wouldn't agents of capital try to extend commercialization into the un-conscious if there was some gain to be made? Was it possible that perhaps competition for our sensory apparatus was not beneficial in the way that competition in the marketplace was assumed to be?

In the end, the subliminal thesis was a logical evolution of ideas and concerns about the total consumer environment. Echoing and extending the existing satirical and cynical tone of commentary about modern com-mercial culture, popular representations of subliminal communication techniques, even the most fanciful and outrageous of them, responded to an immediate experience of being overwhelmed and unduly influenced. And, most notably, this felt new. As the critics, satirists, and even adver-tisers themselves repeatedly claimed, the advertising and media environ-ment seemed different, more intense, than it had been in the recent past.

These concerns thus represented an anxiety about immediate and contemporary upheaval. And in this respect, information overload and the subliminal thesis were ways to talk about social change, over and above consumerism.

As should be evident from the preceding chapters, it is inaccurate to say that the late 1950s only and simply celebrated consumer society. Consumer society, its wastefulness, its perpetual transformation, its pandering, and its media abundance were equally seen as potentially fatal flaws in the capitalist system. By the time Daniel Boorstin published *The Image, or What Happened to the American Dream* in 1962, the problem of consumer capitalism was well established. His use of the term "pseudo-event" neatly summarized the sentiment that a media- and image-saturated world was not as materially real as other less mediated contexts.[96] For Boorstin, the image makers were tearing us from ourselves, alienating us, turning us into sleepwalkers, and leaving us disoriented in a hall of mirrors made up of product, cultural, and political appeals.

Though not always as eloquent as Boorstin, others leveled critiques of consumer capitalism in venues high and low. As the illustrations in this chapter show, there is a sizable record of satirical and pointed jabs at the manufacturers of images and desires, making ordinary the challenge to and suspicion about intensified commercial enterprises. The ad executive was an especially modern target for these critiques. He was about as with-it as a man in a gray flannel suit could be, rather like an artist, working in a creative capacity without strict nine-to-five expectations, but nonetheless associated with metropolitan excesses and addresses, martinis and Madison Avenue. Admen were at the heart of a new, intense, and cynical world of image makers, speaking a special lingo of statisticians and psychologists—a form of Freudian demography. Admen as media exploiters were emblematic of popular views about the encroachment of advertisements into our lives. Vicary was in many ways an exemplar of this popular idea about the Mad Ave set. The figure of the cynical adman, ambitiously exploiting unconscious desires, was already becoming a stock type in popular narratives. For example, *Ask Any Girl* (Charles Walters, 1959) narrates a tale of romantic success on the part of the newly urbanized young secretary, as she hunts for her perfect mate. The original novel by Winifred Wolfe, appearing in 1958, introduces motivational research tangentially, as a way for our protagonist to land a husband, but the later film makes it the central plot point.[97] The combination of matchmaking, advertising, and psychological influence appears again in the Kirk Douglas film *For Love or Money* (Michael Gordon, 1963), this time with Mitzi Gaynor playing a motivational researcher. In a sly reference to Vicary's work, Gaynor's character is introduced studying 16mm footage of supermarket shoppers, counting their eyeblinks.

But far from being heroic managers of the fast-paced urban contemporary, admen, and the occasional adwoman, were depicted in fiction as figures whose cynical ways took a toll on their character. As satirized in *Will Success Spoil Rock Hunter?* (Frank Tashlin, 1957), they were pill-popping nervous wrecks who crumbled under the weight of their ambitions, propped up by psychiatrists and girlfriend-secretaries while they enfeebled masses of people with their orchestration of consumer desires. Popular representations painted a sorry portrait of admen's masculinity, as seen with Rock Hunter, Don Knotts in the subliminal skit, and the nervous pitchman in the ad for Butter-Nut Coffee. Fear of his own smallness and inconsequentiality made the image maker's attempted manipulations more telling of individual weakness, rather than societal breakdown. Even in *The Incredible Shrinking Man* (Jack Arnold, 1957), the infinitely reducing titular character is none other than the prototypical suburban advertising man, losing accounts and his job, eventually everything, only to be reborn as some other being, but this time an elemental and universal one.

Writing in 1958, Arthur Schlesinger Jr. envisioned a crisis of masculinity prompted by the dominance of conformity and reliance upon herd instinct. He countered arguments that blamed this "unmanning" of the American male on the gains of women. Instead, a general unmooring of individual identity had taken the vigor and command from men and replaced it with timidity. He singled out "the spell cast on us" by mass cultural forms: "The popular addiction to prefabricated emotional clichés threatens to erode our capacity for fresh and direct aesthetic experience. Individual identity vanishes in the welter of machine-made reactions."[98] According to Schlesinger, the technologies of manufactured reactions included subconscious manipulation: "The subliminal invasion represents the climax of the assault on individual identity."[99] Distinction of individual identity and repossession of the self were the paths to reassert gender.

The outright fears about new forms of gender expression and experience were one facet of broader anxieties about the speed of social change and uncertainties about the positions available for mere mortals in a technologized, market-driven, information-saturated society. But so too was there a dream of smashing the image makers' world of pseudo-events, and of succeeding or triumphing over the demands of the artificiality and influence of media. Imagining what lay beyond was fuel for critics and artists as they worked through culturally and generically specific responses to the hidden messages and manipulations they had come to expect of mass culture. The advertising industry's reaction to subliminal communication and MR weighed effectiveness against ethics. But a popular discussion was already under way, assessing the texture and tone of the environment produced by commerce, media, and techniques of subconscious influence. What skills were necessary to survive and thrive in a world of image and information saturation?

From Mass Brainwashing
to Rapid Mass Learning

CHAPTER SEVEN

The condition of information abundance, and the concern about the cumulative effect of imperceptible media materials, were serious enough to warrant pointed and sustained attention by intellectuals and vernacular critics alike. Nonetheless, misunderstanding about subliminal influences was a running theme in editorials and commentaries. Often seeing popular response as irrational, these commentaries left the impression that a mass of citizens had shrieked in response to a nonexistent threat, as though these too were audiences running from the Martian invasion they had heard about on the radio.

And yet there really was no hysteria, unless a single instance of high school kids lobbying the state legislature for bans on hidden advertisements in movie theaters counts. The outrage about subliminal manipulation that found expression in periodical editorials was not matched by any groundswell of panicked and frightened citizens. A survey quantifying the understandings about subliminal advertising showed that in San Francisco, less than a year after the first articles on the technique appeared, 41 percent of the sample had heard of it, with the proportions higher among men and those current with the news. Among those who had heard of subliminal ads, only half thought there was anything unethical about them.[1] Although this was a limited study and a small sample, panic evidently was not the dominant sentiment.

Rather, the voluminous attention paid to subliminal manipulation showed that it was a sign of the age and a metaphor for a wrongheaded path of future development. When seen as the product of the darker side of consumer society, mass social control, and new media technology, it became a warning for an eventuality that needed to be guarded against. Its high visibility, the attention received, and the recorded debate suggest that the subliminal thesis was operating as a marker for the outer limits of social and technological progress rather than as a development to fear in and of itself. In this light, the subliminal thesis spoke to the context of change. Though the direct effectiveness of imperceptible stimuli was evidently not demonstrable—a fact amply reported in the popular press—the critical and comic responses suggested that the subliminal thesis stood for a historical moment when tinkering with human desire would be contemplated as a business enterprise. Were we truly only one technological discovery shy of total submission to media and corporate influence?

An ambivalence about the historical implications of the subliminal thesis was captured in the range of terms that described it. Its covert and suspicious nature is apparent in the descriptive phrases "silent sell,"[2] "secret sell,"[3] "secret pitch,"[4] and "sneak pitch,"[5] all of which appeared within the first six months of the breakthrough media event of September 1957. The habit of putting inverted commas around "invisible" was noticeable, a symptom of the uncertain material status of the ads. If they are "there" but not consciously perceived, do they really exist? If they exist, can we call them invisible, and if they "register" on our minds are they not visible, even if we can't see them? Some credited our growing understanding of the unconscious for the popular attention to subliminal communication. For instance, Harriett Moore wrote in *Art Direction*, "there is the satisfaction of seeing that the *possibility* of such a phenomenon seems to have done more to get acceptance of the unconscious than might have been assumed to exist."[6] Alongside, the subliminal thesis raised ethical issues about the unconscious, as distinguished from questions about codes of conduct for hidden intentions. The relatively new terrain of the psyche, now widely agreed upon in some fashion, must have boundaries that pertain to existing judicial, governmental, and commercial structures, so the reasoning went, but what on earth would these look like?

Essentially, the idea of unconscious manipulation was a stress upon democratic institutions. Even though it might not work, those concerned zeroed in on the idea of automatic control from a distance, short-circuiting human will. Subliminal advertising was a brand of persuasion, or preparation for persuasion, without rhetoric. Was subliminal communication therefore a form of speech, or merely an automatic response? If the former, then it should have its freedom protected, with the usual limits on paid speech applying. But attempts to place legal limits on concealed paid speech were a challenge. What would count as hidden expression? Utterly concealed advertisements were a clear-cut case. But what about more subtle manifestations like innuendo, suggestiveness, and allusion? Could one feasibly, or legally, restrict connotation?[7]

Intriguingly, the ethical dimension of subliminal messages impinged on issues of privacy.[8] As Norman Cousins put it in an October 1957 editorial in the *Saturday Review*, beginning with the prophetic "Welcome to 1984," "Nothing is more difficult in the modern world than to protect the privacy of the human soul. We live in an age where what we don't see and don't know can hurt us. It's serious enough to have to contend with the submicroscopic radioactive bullets flying crazily through the air without having to worry about contamination by sublimation."[9] After the demonstration for the FCC and Congress in January 1958, the editors of the *New York Times* echoed the Orwellian subtext, seeing subliminal communication as "an invasion of privacy."[10] In this view, the unconscious was a space that each person naturally owned, and was his or hers alone to sell. This view rested upon a proprietary right to one's own thoughts. The complications for intellectual property here would be enormous, and the possession of thought was clearly not the same as actually having or uttering thoughts that you alone owned. The best conceptual appraisal of the "invasion of privacy" argument was that people had the right not to be influenced, and that this right could not be exercised if the very moment of influence was disguised and unannounced. The mind was one's own to fill up or empty out, which meant that others could not traffic in that realm without notice. This was where Packard left the reader at the end of *The Hidden Persuaders*, advocating a right to privacy for our minds.[11] The aim was to reassert people's capacity to exercise when and in what manner they entered the market, either as consumers, with bodies and psyches, or as commodities. In a solidly liberal notion of property rights and individual rationality, advertisers should not sneak into our heads—trespass, as it were—and erect billboards without forewarning or compensation. In this view, each person was much like a network executive or magazine editor, selling spots in his or her own unconscious to advertisers.

Even as the first wave of outcry faded, subliminal influences continued to figure in the imagining of tyranny. As Soviet satellites were being launched in the fall of 1957, who knew what manner of mind-controlling broadcasts were emanating from above, perfectly positioned as the satellites were to launch invading ideas? Inspired by presentations at an electronics conference, John Benedict wrote distressingly of "bio-control" in the April 1960 issue of *American Mercury*. The piece closely resembled dystopic science fiction: "a conquering nation . . . could equip each child soon after birth with a socket mounted under the scalp and electrodes reaching selected brain areas. A year or two later, a miniature radio receiver and antenna would be plugged into the socket. This would mean complete human control of thought and action and would make obsolete the newspaper, radio and television because information would be transmitted directly to the individual brain."[12] Benedict complained that the FCC had been just as lax with subliminal advertising as it had been with quiz shows.[13] He placed communist brainwashing, fluoridation, lobotomies, LSD, and motivational research side by side as threats, with praise going to those sounding the alarm, including Edward Hunter, William Whyte Jr., and Vance Packard. Benedict's tone was in keeping with the conservative politics of *American Mercury*. Nonetheless, in this particular example of Cold War paranoia, we can evince quite concretely sites of anxious speculation, all of which continue to agitate those on both the right and the left fifty years later: the globalization of media, the fearsome prospects of biotechnology, the centralization of governmental powers, the limited democratic potential of mass society, and the functional control of a nation's thinking through scientific means.

The most alarmist voices on subliminal communication linked it with brainwashing. Beginning as an explanation for what was seen as an unimaginable betrayal—how could good American boys decide that they did not want to return to the United States after time in a North Korean prison?—brainwashing first appeared in the English language in the early 1950s. The idea, though, already had some degree of currency. Orwell's *1984* (1949) depicted not only a dystopian world of enslavement and thought control but a lengthy and precise scene of brainwashing, though that term was never used in the novel. In his history of mind manipulation, Dominic Streatfeild put special emphasis on Stalin's show trials of the 1930s in Moscow, at which defendants appeared to willingly incriminate themselves without evidence that they had committed the crimes of which they stood accused. The apparent ability to control people's behavior to such extreme lengths intrigued western intelligence agencies, especially the CIA (formed after the Second World War), which began to experiment with a variety of pharmaceuticals and torture techniques to influence thoughts, beliefs, and behaviors.[14] The Americans, though, had in place an even more expansive program of mass influence with the psychological warfare research of the 1940s, as detailed in a groundbreaking book by Daniel Lerner, *Sykewar: Psychological Warfare against Germany, D-Day to VE-Day* (1949).[15] In many ways, despite their fundamentally antidemocratic impulse the programs studied and recommended by Lerner and others were seen as more legitimate scholarship, even more ethical, than the more clandestine and injurious brainwashing experiments. But these Cold War psychology and communication researchers shared a paranoia about communism at home and abroad, and both groups saw the new findings related to influence, propaganda, and behavior as necessary tools in the project of running and protecting contemporary mass society. Books, studies, and news coverage presented brainwashing in particular, feared as a communist ploy, as a test case for the nefarious possibilities of the findings of psychology and behaviorism.

The authors William Sargant, Edward Hunter, and Robert Jay Lifton all contributed to the popular understanding of brainwashing.[16] Films like *Time Limit* (Karl Malden, 1957) and *The Rack* (Arnold Laven, 1956), and television episodes like "The Brainwashing of John Hayes" (Harry Horner, 1955) on *TV Reader's Digest*, also kept brainwashing visible. And as a result, American audiences were presented with a way to understand and talk about the psyche of prisoners of war, the camps in which they were held, and military justice. Importantly, brainwashing was a weapon primarily associated with Soviet expansionism. An editor of *America* asked in 1960, "Is Nikita Khrushchev trying to practice brainwashing on a global scale?," and speculated that the world was subject to "some low-level form of brainwashing that can be employed to soften us up and achieve limited objectives in the strategy of conquest."[17]

Brainwashing—a translation of the Chinese word *xǐnǎo*, which referred to an assortment of procedures of intensive reeducation under conditions of stress—was seen as a form of scientifically fortified behaviorism. The term was occasionally applied to describe propaganda.

But though partisan and one-sided, and however much it limited debate, propaganda still referred to making a case and presenting an argument. Even in its most extreme manifestations, propaganda involved rhetorical persuasion. Contrarily, brainwashing was seen as sidestepping persuasion in favor of fearsome physiological intervention, conditions of physical exhaustion and torture, and exploitation of root psychological states. Selma Fraiberg captured this distinction: "The methods of enslaving the ego and even the methods of 'thought reform' are not entirely new. But we are the first generation in history to acquire a scientific psychology of tyranny and mental enslavement."[18]

These tyrannical possibilities pointed to a relationship between modern life and brainwashing. The history of the modern crowd was in part understood to be a history of the loss of self and the hypnotic trance that one enters into with the mechanization and atomization of society. For Gustave Le Bon, this era had primed popular audiences for these conditions, putting them in a dream state, half-conscious. It is worth remembering that the years after the Second World War were fraught with efforts to comprehend Nazi atrocities. The grisly mechanics of concentration camps and of human conduct in extraordinarily inhuman circumstances pushed the limits of the imagination. Many authors, among them Bruno Bettelheim and Hannah Arendt, worked to understand the cultural and psychological conditions of this horrific conduct. After the full exposure of the Holocaust, the capacity for a banal, yet extreme, evil on the part of ordinary people seemed boundless. But it was not fascism alone that embodied this submissive nature of the "massified" individual. Even experiments in mass democracy could be shown to harbor the grains of totalitarianism, whether in the form of unshakable hierarchical powers or in the apparent willingness of populations to surrender hard-won rights and freedoms. According to this dark view, modern life itself was a condition of sleep from which one had to be awakened.

Brainwashing began as a specialized technique of reeducation premised upon physical and mental exhaustion, with intense individualized isolation and attention. With unusual speed, the term became transformed to describe a widespread state of contemporary existence. At public hearings about the brainwashing of American POWs during the Korean War, Colonel Frank H. Schwable compared his own brainwashing, after which he signed a false statement confessing to the use of germ warfare by the United States in Korea, with the sensory bombardment and repetition of advertising.[19] This was an astonishing and telling association, utterly absent in the scientific literature on brainwashing. Nonetheless, some observers did find similarities between brainwashing and the broad condition of mass and consumer society, just as others insisted on emphasizing its communist pedigree. For example, the head of the National Conference of Christians and Jews alarmingly claimed in 1958 that the methods of psychological control employed by advertisers and government were forms of brainwashing that were leading toward the society depicted in *1984*.[20]

Consider the following two dictionary definitions. The Random House dictionary described brainwashing as "a method for systematically changing attitudes or altering beliefs, originated in totalitarian countries, esp. through the use of torture, drugs, or psychological stress techniques" and "any method of controlled systematic indoctrination, esp. one based on repetition or confusion: *brainwashing by TV commercials*."[21] Merriam-Webster similarly defined brainwashing as "a forcible indoctrination to induce someone to give up basic political, social, or religious beliefs and attitudes and to accept contrasting regimented ideas" and "persuasion by propaganda or salesmanship."[22] In its joining of all methods of indoctrination, of totalitarian countries *and* television commercials, "forcible" *and* persuasive salesmanship, "brainwashing" was a perfect term for the era, one that saw its specificity disappear upon popular deployment. It offered a homologous relationship between indoctrination and salesmanship—torture and television commercials—essentially compelling the interpretation that the experience of being subjected to advertising clutter had connections to the experience of those unfortunate POWs.

Some claimed that the contemporary experience of speed, repetition, and media abundance left us in a weakened rational state. In a book that notably links brainwashing to hypnosis, the psychologists Merton M. Gill and Margaret Brenman wrote in 1959 of the forces that whittle away an individual's autonomy: "A strong social press may range all the way from 'keeping up with the Joneses' to brain-washing. A strong non-social press may be pressure to attend carefully and for a prolonged period to a space-time stimulus, for instance, driving along a super-highway, flying a plane in close formation, or attending vigilantly to a radar screen."[23] For Gill and Brenman, the social demands of consumerist conformity and the psychological demands of highway driving and radar watching exemplify the ordinariness of states of suggestibility. Brainwashing was a product of new developments in understanding the mind and the conditions under which it could be influenced. More dramatically, according to the authors, we appeared to be living under near-approximations of those conditions all the time. The fantasy of the brainwashed war veteran controlled to respond robotically to murderous commands—in *The Manchurian Candidate*, film and novel, the appearance of the Queen of Diamonds during a game of solitaire is the trigger sparking the sleeper assassin—bled into an image of entire populations in sleeplike states, awaiting their triggers.

In an article in *American Mercury* in 1959, Alfred Pritchard, after writing about the mass hypnotism used by Hitler, alerted readers to the phenomenon of "waking hypnosis" and to the "large number [of psychologists and hypnotists] employed by corporations designing new, more subtle, more powerful ways to use this power to move the people in the direction of their desires, *through the printed word and picture, through the spoken word in person or on the radio and television, and by means of the television picture*."[24] This psychological war for the minds of United States citizens meant that the media had to be held accountable for the ideas they circulated. "The radio and television directors should be challenged whenever their programs support any part of the current Communist Party 'line.'"[25] Senator John L. McClellan (Democrat of Arkansas), chairman of the Senate Permanent Investigating Subcommittee on Brainwashing in Korea, said, "It is the aim of the Communist system to not only control the land areas of the world but the minds and souls of the human race."[26] As Edward Hunter put it in closing his popular book on brainwashing, "There is no 'behind the lines' any longer."[27]

Ideological control was more than a technique of a foreign power; it equally applied to local sympathizers. Several public scandals arose in the mid-1950s in which teachers were suspected of trafficking in leftist thinking. A psychology professor at the University of Alabama was attacked in print for "brainwashing" students into supporting racial integration with such apparently incendiary statements as "I haven't seen anything harmful about mixing the races. I have seen many Negro women I would rather marry than white women. Segregation is illegal and unreligious."[28] Bishop Mark K. Carroll of Kansas recommended that Catholic college students avoid some psychology and philosophy courses that were "brainwashing" them.[29] AWARE, Inc., "a private organization devoted to fighting communism in entertainment, communications, and the fine arts," charged that left-wing professors were brainwashing students at universities and colleges.[30] E. Merrill Root examined eleven high school textbooks to show that American students were being "brainwashed" to think favorably about collectivism and unfavorably about individualism.[31]

The most historically significant of these accusations involved Governor Orval E. Faubus of Arkansas, a Democrat who closed four high schools in Little Rock to prevent desegregation in September 1958, pending a referendum on the issue. This was on the heels of his having called out the National Guard to halt the integration process. Faubus said that if voters gave him a mandate to integrate the schools, he would privatize them to circumvent the Supreme Court's ruling on desegregation.[32] When members of the Presbyterian clergy spoke out against these attempts, Faubus declared that they were either left-wingers or had been brainwashed by communists.[33] The battle of hidden ideological agendas could be thrown occasionally in the opposite direction, as was seen when one southern newspaper wrote that Negroes had been "brain-washed by generations of white supremacy" while another wrote that desegregation was "a result of outside propaganda."[34] However, so strong was the association between brainwashing and civil rights that even in 1964, Senator Richard Russell Jr. of Georgia could claim that the rise of pro-integration sentiment was the result of mind-control techniques.[35] These associations presented a sense that American values—at least as understood by right-wing ideologues—were vulnerable and frail, reflecting what the historian Martin Walker has called the national inferiority and insecurity complex of the late 1950s.[36]

There were no limits to the suspicions that governmental agencies used brainwashing techniques: one defendant in an acid-throwing case claimed to have been brainwashed by the FBI.[37] Governor George Romney of Michigan, father of Governor Mitt Romney of Massachusetts, did serious damage to his prospects for reelection, and effectively ended his presidential campaign in 1968, when he claimed to have been "brainwashed" during a visit to Vietnam by army and government officials, including Ambassador Henry Cabot Lodge and General William Westmoreland.[38] He made matters worse in a press conference when he attempted to clarify his remark by saying that he had not meant "Russian-type brainwashing, but LBJ-type brainwashing."[39]

Politicians and spokespeople who referred to brainwashing may have been skilled rhetoricians tapping into a stream of popular thought. Or they may have been clumsy speakers, seeking to shock and haphazardly striking an alarmist chord. But whatever the reason, the preoccupation with brainwashing shows that it captured a manifest worry over a potential loss of individual and democratic freedoms. Even as a still novel expression, the term muddied the distinction between learning and mind control, between willful action and manipulation. The concept of brainwashing, like the subliminal thesis, was a convenient category in which the circulation of unfamiliar or unsavory ideas could be associated with an inhuman injection of thoughts designed to drain people of their willfulness. Here, during the triumphal era of the end of ideology, was a powerful and popular understanding of, and debate about, false consciousness.

Modern life and mind manipulation are linked in Aldous Huxley's *Brave New World Revisited* (1958), an expanded version of a series of newspaper articles published late in 1957 that reconsidered his famous novel twenty-five years after its appearance.[40] Having generated great interest in drug experimentation with *The Doors of Perception*, in many ways initiating the psychotropic era to come, Huxley remained a critic of modern technological society's damaging impact upon the individual. The original title of the newspaper series was *Tyranny over the Mind*, echoing William Sargant's book on brainwashing of the same year, *Battle for the Mind*. A frighteningly conservative treatise, *Brave New World Revisited* worried about how fast the world of Huxley's novel had arrived. Referring to brainwashing, subliminal projections, chemical induced consciousness, and sleep-learning, Huxley argued that our overpopulated and over-organized world had erased true individual will, leaving us the pawns of "Big Government" and "Big Business." The techniques of mass mind manipulation, as he saw it, drew from insights of psychology, especially what he called "post-Freudian" methods. Huxley ended with a call for education, the "proper" use of language, and modified, nonhierarchical social organization. He defended proposals for a return to a smaller, more communal way of life, including B. F. Skinner's *Walden Two*—and oddly so, because in an earlier chapter Huxley had challenged Skinner's emphasis on environment over genetics. Assuming the role of public intellectual, Huxley brought these ideas to other popular venues. Speaking on ABC's *The Mike Wallace Interview*, Huxley described the antidemocratic tendency of mass media and technological development, singling out subliminal techniques.[41]

Huxley's call for educational investment was timely, as the entire field of education was about to undergo unprecedented revision. Just as assessments of mind manipulation were evident as organizing factors of public debate, and just weeks after the jolt of Vicary's press conference in September 1957 prompted popular investigations into hidden messages, the Soviet Union's launch of Sputnik I on 4 October and Sputnik II on 3 November created a sense of urgency among Americans, who received the news of these satellite launches as a national defeat. Comparisons with the surprise attack on Pearl Harbor abounded.[42] As Stephen J. Whitfield commented, the Sputnik launches "had shaken American confidence in its technological superiority and educational advantages."[43] One prominent view was that the American failure to lead in the conquest of space was due to a preoccupation with the inconsequential pleasures of the marketplace. Though Whitfield went on to indicate that consumer capitalism presumably offered a "war" that Americans could win, the "trivial" preoccupations of the American public were also the target of scorn, and were blamed for weakening national fortitude. William O'Neill emphasized the introspection and criticism ignited by the revelation of Soviet technological superiority, writing, "Sputnik proved that the United States was smug, lazy, and second rate, also that Russia was ambitious, disciplined, and ahead in crucial areas."[44] The breadth of challenge to national priorities was such that even Roger Corman described his film *War of the Satellites* (1958) as a critique of the government's failure to keep pace with the USSR.[45]

Packard's first feature article after both the breaking of the subliminal controversy and the Sputnik launches, "The Mass Manipulation of Human Behavior" (1957), explored "some shocking implications of what we often think of as the American way of life," as the editors of *America* put it.[46] After reasserting the core arguments of *The Hidden Persuaders*, and staking a claim for a public awakening with respect to subliminal methods, Packard went further than he had gone in his book to attack the wastefulness of affluence. In a way we can see the beginning of a book that would appear three years later, *The Waste Makers*, which demonstrated the illogic of rampant, endlessly increasing rates of consumption and popularized a new term, "consumerism."[47] In the magazine article Packard compared Americans to force-fed geese: "I do suggest we are starting to become a bit overstuffed with material goods and that our livers are starting to enlarge."[48] He saw this as a consequence of a "new softness," using the "give-up-itis" of U.S. soldiers in the Korean War as an illustration.[49] He told of GIs leaving behind the wounded and stealing food from weaker soldiers. Acknowledging the cruelty of brainwashing, he also claimed, "In some cases the 'cruel' Chinese simply smiled at the Americans, slapped them on the back and offered them cigarettes."[50] He compared the Soviet interest in satellites with Americans' love for tail fins on cars, and found the latter a symptom of a self-indulgent nation.[51] Here again, as Penny Sparke and others have detailed, the liberal critique of consumer society slips into a masculinist posturing against a feminized mass culture, a stance that remains a most resilient aspect of theories of the modern crowd.[52]

Reevaluations of American consumerism were soon joined by works like John Kenneth Galbraith's *The Affluent Society* (1958), which, as William O'Neill pointed out, "laid the intellectual basis for the Kennedy-Johnson crusade against poverty."[53] But by all accounts and assessments, a crisis of character was afoot, with the American citizen ostensibly adrift in wasteful and spirit-draining pastimes. The institution charged with the making of citizens, and hence expected to be ballast countering this unsteadiness—namely, education—was itself in crisis. Despite the affluence of the United States, an increasing number of students confronted fewer teachers and fewer resources per student. In the summer of 1957 the National Educational Association estimated that during the following year 328 classrooms had to be built and 493 teachers hired every day just to maintain existing standards, which was an impossible rate of renewal.[54] What followed was a collective rush to reorient the direction of the next generation, and educational programs and standards were high on the agenda, made even more so by the assessments following the Sputnik launches. As Barbara Barksdale Clowse put it, "A consensus grew that the nation's educational institutions were largely to blame for this Cold War defeat," essentially transforming the Sputnik crisis into an educational crisis.[55] David Halberstam characterized subsequent events by pointing out that an undistinguished two-year-old book, *Why Johnny Can't Read—And What You Can Do about It*, "suddenly became a smash best-seller."[56]

What had been called visual education at the beginning of the twentieth century, then audiovisual education in the 1940s, had long been explored as a magical solution to increase the efficiency of schools. There had already been decades of educational experiments with film, stereoscopes, filmstrips, projection devices, records, and radio, typically premised on the need to modernize the classroom, keep up with the times, and maintain students' interest. By the mid-1950s instructional technology had become something more basic, namely a way for schools to meet even the most rudimentary educational needs. The failure of public education seemed imminent; resources and teachers were simply too scarce, and classrooms too small, to confront an expanding student population and the skills supposedly required in a changing world. The future of education was "rapid mass learning," as Charles Hoban and Edward B. van Ormer called it, requiring techniques that could accelerate and direct the learning process, techniques that could be transported from metropolitan centers to the most remote regions.[57] The Second World War saw massive amounts of support going to the testing of new technologically driven forms of instruction, of which Samuel Renshaw's tachistoscopic training of naval pilots was one celebrated example. These rapid mass learning techniques required the full incorporation and integration of instructional media into classrooms. So, after decades of lobbying and experimentation, AV instruction was now about to move to center stage as a way to reorient the American public toward the skills of the future.

As a guiding rule for bringing technology into the classroom, in 1962 James D. Finn of the University of Southern California named seven aids as essential components in contemporary teaching: the 16-millimeter sound film projector, the filmstrip projector, the overhead projector, the radio, the record player, the tape recorder, and the television. He recommended that at least five of these be made available to every classroom.[58] But there were other, more novel technologies available for consideration. Teaching machines, the pushbutton individualized learning units that guided a student through a lesson mechanically, and specialized audiovisual facilities, like language learning labs, became pedagogical and funding priorities at the time as well. The mythic little red schoolhouse was now seen as an inappropriately pastoral and nostalgic ideal of close relations between teacher and student, its environment irrelevant and rustic when compared to the flashy, technologically sophisticated world outside its walls. By the late 1950s the place of audiovisual equipment in schools was virtually beyond discussion. Instead, the focus was upon the standards for what was to be integrated, and how. The advocates of AV instruction had succeeded in fully co-articulating its family of technologies with educational efficiency *and* modernization.

LOOK MAGAZINE PHOTO

It's a world of pictures . . . and of sounds.

Much of our
knowledge
comes through
what we see
and hear,
either
directly . . .

Audiovisual pamphlet, promising special access to the world and speed of instruction through technological means, ca. 1960, from "Gateway to Learning," Audio-Visual Commission on Public Information. Courtesy of National Public Broadcasting Archives, University of Maryland.

. . . or through the modern tools of learning we call

AUDIO-VISUALS

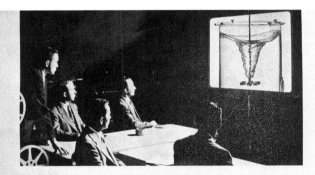

Today, audio-visuals are helping people everywhere to *learn more in less time.*

These powerful learning tools have many advantages . . .

With a budding expansion of the dispersed educational market already in formation, the National Defense Education Act of 1958 institutionalized, and accelerated, much of the activity of earlier decades. This act was President Eisenhower's response to the Sputnik crisis, elements of which—for instance the student loan programs—continue to this day, though in a hobbled form. Many of the targeted areas were explicitly defense-related, like funds to establish technologically advanced language learning centers and support for math, sciences, and area studies. Title VII of the act established a New Educational Media Program at the Office of Education for "research and experimentation in more effective utilization of television, radio, motion pictures, and related media for educational purposes." Marshall McLuhan received $35,000 under that program in 1959 to write his *Report on Project in Understanding New Media* for the National Association of Educational Broadcasters.[59] The body that made decisions about Title VII research funding was the Advisory Committee on New Educational Media, which included leading figures in the AV movement of the postwar period, with Scott Fletcher of Encyclopaedia Britannica Films and the Ford Foundation for Adult Education as the first charter director. The phrase "new educational media" was used for several years by Title VII authors, administrators, and instructional media specialists as a catch-all category for a range of AV technologies, though by 1960 some Title VII authors joined McLuhan in referring simply to "new media," thus launching our contemporary usage.

For the education technology historian Paul Saettler, the National Defense Education Act was a turning point in the history of media education in the United States: "There can be little question that it supplied a historic stimulus to an unprecedented, massive instructional media research program throughout the country."[60] With $9 million dollars in appropriations, the act supported 150 research projects and 93 programs to collect and circulate information within the first three years.[61] By June 1963 the act had funded 277 research projects and 160 information dissemination projects,[62] and by 1968 six hundred research projects totaling $40.3 million had been funded through Title VII.[63] Compare this, though, to the new money made available to purchase equipment and remodel schools under Title III—$280 million in the first four years and nearly half a million teaching modernization projects funded in the first ten years, which required matching funds from states and school boards.[64] The boom in AV was astonishing.

In the United States a number of organizations sponsored this new world of instructional technology, and benefited greatly from the National Defense Education Act. For example, the National Education Association (NEA), a leading agenda-setting organization for educational policy established in 1848, launched its Department of Visual Instruction in 1923, changing its name to the Department of Audio-Visual Instruction (DAVI) in 1947; this became a separate organization, the Association for Educational Communications and Technology, in 1971. DAVI and others produced and circulated AV catalogues, policy documents, and scholarly research, all with the intention of advancing the beneficial instructional use of AV materials. A prime beneficiary of the AV boom, DAVI saw its membership grow from three thousand in 1958 to eleven thousand in 1970.[65]

The NEA's recommendation in 1963 for "new media" for schools of the 1960s asserted that "new concepts of space, time, and instructional resources emphasize new functional definitions of the roles of teachers and students."[66] New concepts of space and time referred to lesson schedules and physical plant commitments, but comparable assessments by the NEA and others also described a certain experiential shift: contemporary life created new conditions of sensory and mental awareness that had to be accommodated by teachers. This is to say that McLuhan's contemporaneous views on the changing sensorium of modern media, and the related challenges to traditional ideas about literacy and education, were evident in educational policy conclusions even before he published his widely read work *Understanding Media* (1964), a book whose origins are found in his Title VII report.[67] For the NEA and McLuhan alike, schools needed technologically equipped classrooms and audiovisual centers with a special eye on self-instruction and individual student learning, as well as promotion of "informal" learning as a pedagogical approach and as a way to understand education beyond the walls of the classroom.

McLuhan described his *Report on Project in Understanding New Media* as a study of the subliminal patterning of consciousness by the media and of how syllabi might be altered to best take advantage of this. His research for this project included visits with sociologists, psychologists, and audiovisual experts, including Gilbert Seldes, David Riesman, and the tachistoscope educator Samuel Renshaw. Some of McLuhan's core ideas are found in this report, in particular his assertion that electronic media are moving western culture from linear, print-based Euclidean space to mosaic, field, or auditory space.[68] Among his axioms was the soon-to-be-indispensable McLuhanism *the 'content' of any medium is another medium.*[69] In this report cool, participatory, and teacher-friendly media (e.g. television) were categorized as low-definition, while hot, non-participatory, propaganda-friendly media (e.g. film) were categorized as high-definition. McLuhan further characterized the low-definition media as subliminal, meaning that they tended to fade into the background and become part of the environment.[70] He concluded that the consequences for educators were profound, and he was "not optimistic about saving any of the traditional qualities in education from the electronic bombardment."[71] Articulating his thesis of "information overload," McLuhan felt that new media telescope "centuries of development and evolution into weeks or months. In speeding up actual change, it makes the understanding of change much more feasible just as a movie of an organic process may reveal years of growth in seconds. But such acceleration of growth in no way prepares the human community to adapt to it. Suddenly there is a nine foot redwood where in the morning you had experienced a bedroom."[72] This psychedelic image suited the sort of phantasmagoria for which McLuhan was to become known, and it looked ahead to a coming age of everyday surrealism.

In reworking the report into *Understanding Media: The Extensions of Man* (1964), McLuhan elaborated the idea that the major impact of media went unnoticed, involved technological form over media content, and reoriented sense and perception: "Program and 'content' analysis offer no clues to the magic of these media or to their subliminal charge."[73] Throughout the book he returned to this claim, demonstrating the powerful influence the then recent subliminal controversy had on his ideas and rhetoric. Film viewers "accept [the reality of the film world] subliminally and without critical awareness," the TV mosaic was its "subliminal message," and, with classic McLuhanesque bombast, "the subliminal depths of radio are charged with the resonating echoes of tribal horns and antique drums."[74] Given the omnipresence of the revolutionary, though imperceptible, effects of media technology, McLuhan found it amusing that a fuss should be made about a specific instance of hidden influence, such as subliminal advertising. He commented, with a noticeable lack of historical precision, "When early in TV broadcasting hidden ads were tried out, the literate were in a great panic until they were dropped. The fact that typography is itself mainly subliminal in effect and that pictures are, as well, is a secret that is safe from the book-oriented community."[75] In 1968 he succinctly summarized all of his recommendations as follows: "Study the modes of media, in order to hoick all assumptions out of the subliminal, nonverbal realm for scrutiny and for prediction and control of human purposes."[76]

Though McLuhan's position had been stated more forcefully in his earlier report, *Understanding Media* also included recommendations for technologically supported rapid mass learning, with similar claims about the special pedagogical effectiveness of television. Remaining perfectly in step with the reigning instrumental views of education, McLuhan found teaching machines superior to books because of their interactivity: "These devices are adaptations of the book in the direction of dialogue."[77] The totalizing new media environment, which effected an unconscious recalibration of thought and perception, necessitated an expanded view of education, an acknowledgment that students in their daily lives inhabited an immense "classroom without walls."[78] As McLuhan saw it, "the ordinary child lives in an electronic environment; he lives in a world of information overload . . . The children so accustomed to a Niagara of data in their ordinary environments, are introduced to nineteenth-century classrooms and curricula, where data flow is not only small in quantity but fragmented in pattern. The subjects are unrelated. The environmental class can mollify motivation in learning."[79] For all of his wily oscillation between skepticism and celebration, McLuhan's ideas during this period ran essentially synchronously with those of the AV educationalist, advancing the necessity of a technologically enhanced curriculum.

As part of the National Defense Act funding programs, the NEA received $102,980 in 1960 for a study of the effects and teaching opportunities of teaching machines, television, and various other audiovisual instruments.[80] First word of their findings in the following year was "that the teaching machine industry was growing so fast that not even the experts could keep up with it."[81] It released "A Survey of the Industry" in November 1962.[82] Two years hence, in 1964, the Act led to the availability of $76.6 million for schools to acquire instructional technology and material, to retrain teachers, and to redesign classrooms to accommodate new media.[83] Such legislation created what the U.S. commissioner of education, Harold Howe II, referred to as a "'revolution' in the capacity of schools to purchase apparatus and equipment to serve learning and teaching."[84] Howe's predecessor, Francis Keppel, departed from his position to become the chairman of the newly established General Learning Corporation, a joint venture between Time-Life and General Electric in instructional technology supplies that illustrated the close ties between industry and government on the issue of educational technology.[85]

The more widely accepted and tested media itemized by Finn were only part of the burgeoning industry of educational technology. Experiments in machine teaching and programmed instruction abounded. The renowned behaviorist B. F. Skinner's teaching machine—an individualized, pushbutton lesson box—received much attention. Promising that with the machine students would "learn in one hour what it takes a human teacher a whole day to teach them in laborious classroom instruction," Skinner maintained that only the absence of actual lessons would slow the technology's introduction, as the machines themselves were ready to be built by Rheem Manufacturing.[86] Early competitors included Grolier, Inc., which formed Teaching Machines, Inc., and U.S. Industries, Inc., manufacturer of the Mark II Auto-tutor, which was thousands of dollars cheaper than its Mark I.[87] Grolier, an encyclopedia publisher with a door-to-door sales force, introduced its Min-Max teaching machine with the same door-to-door strategy.[88] In less than a year Grolier had sold more than twenty thousand of its machines, mostly to homes, and was shifting its focus to schools.[89] Elizabeth Fowler of the *New York Times* described the situation as follows: "Uranium, Canadian oils, computers, space-age electronics, bowling, boats and book publishing are some of the industries that have captured profits and investor interest since World War II. Now, a new one may be added to the list—teaching machines. . . . The machines are an outgrowth of the surge in educational interest partly inspired by the space age race, partly by world problems, and partly by previous neglect of this field. The shortage of teachers and the need to modernize methods have also spurred many school boards to investigate its use."[90] Perhaps few signs are as telling of the relevance of the teaching machine as the Smithsonian's acquisition in 1963 of Sidney L. Pressey's prototype, built in 1925.[91] The teaching machines were thought to be no longer experimental, but as steps toward a Skinnerian utopia.

Mass-marketed teaching machines grew out of the machines developed for testing of personnel at the Air Force's Air Research and Development Command.[92] As reported in *Fortune*, programmed instruction was to be comparable to the revolutionary change that followed the pedagogical philosophy of John Dewey,[93] though in fact it represented a culmination of critiques of progressive education that gained widespread legitimacy after the Sputnik launches.[94] Reports on the rush to introduce teaching machines were careful to indicate that the intent was to integrate them with more conventional educational strategies, not to replace teachers.[95] Nevertheless, the teaching machines' contributions to modern education were never said to be to elevate critical faculties, to improve sociability among students, and to gain a richer understanding of the physical world. Consistently, they were to increase learning speed, to put the rate of learning into the hands of individual pupils, and to decrease the involvement of that arcane, unpredictable, and expensive human component in education, the teacher.[96] Thus, an individualized technological interface promised to close the missile gap.

As influential as the new research being done on technologized classrooms were the efforts to consolidate and disseminate findings and policy recommendations. These schemes established clearinghouse operations to help educators navigate the tangles of new technology and its implications for curriculum design. In 1959 the Council of Chief State School Officers released a "Purchasing Guide" describing 954 technological apparatuses for schools.[97] In 1961 the first issue of *Programmed Instruction* appeared, a periodical intended as a single source for news and information on machine learning for teachers, and to which the prominent communication scholar Wilbur Schramm contributed.[98] And publishers in the educational market helped to organize school purchases with up-to-date catalogues. According to one commentator, "there seems little doubt that it is only a matter of time before automation comes to American schools."[99]

Assisting in the task of confronting the audiovisual revolution, government agencies were acting as marketers for a growing educational industry. For example, McGraw-Hill released the fourteen-volume *Educational Media Index* in 1964, a comprehensive and annotated compilation of audiovisual materials covering films, maps, kinescopes, models, programmed instruction, and transparencies, among other items; in other words, it compiled virtually all educational media except books.[100] A product of the National Defense Education Act, hence a joint initiative between industry and government, the index was, according to Paul Saettler, one of the most notable accomplishments of the New Educational Media Program of the Defense Act.[101] Not only did government support the technologizing of classrooms by providing funds; they also helped teachers to technologize their teaching by providing lists of what to buy, how it would be used, and from whom to buy it. Howe similarly made money available for informational agencies, the main purpose of which was "to evaluate educational television, films, books and other teaching aids and advise public and private elementary and secondary schools throughout the country on what to buy and how to use it."[102]

I see the consequences of these initiatives as monumental. Remember that they took place just before the full-scale introduction of computers into classrooms, and in fact the first reports of this prospect appeared in news on programmed instruction and teaching machines.[103] In this environment of technological solutions, an industry took off. Since the early decades of the twentieth century, commercial interests had seen classrooms as an untapped or at least underexploited market for motion pictures and other media forms. From the late 1950s on, a new technology industry expanded its reliance upon educational clients with financial, institutional, and governmental support across media. This would not have happened without the widespread belief that school curricula and physical resources required radical revision and updating in the wake of the Sputnik launches. Though some rumblings about curriculum reform were evident in the early 1950s, it was in late 1957 that reform as a technological matter took shape as a full-fledged movement.[104] For example, though instructional films were evident in the first decade of cinema, and their availability grew with the introduction of 16mm gauge "safety" film in the 1920s, Robert Filep and Wilbur Schramm observed that the use of such films "was negligible until the launching of Sputnik sparked an unprecedented concern and dissatisfaction with the learning devices and practices of the time."[105] "Negligible" is not an entirely accurate assessment, but since the 1930s there most certainly had been a sense that institutional media, in particular film, were underutilized because of confusion among teachers and community leaders, lack of training, and lack of coordination between users and producers. After the National Defense Education Act, the growth of this market was phenomenal.

Not surprisingly, soon after the federal incentives were in place, corporate consolidation followed between those who manufactured the apparatuses and those who provided the content. The first popular uses of the terms "hardware" and "software" appeared in the mid-1960s to describe the different components of device and content that now required joint coordination to produce, whether for technological reasons or for economic advantage. Prentice Hall and Litton Industries agreed to jointly produce teaching machines and lessons.[106] Harcourt, Brace and World aligned itself with Rheem in producing teaching machines and content. U.S. Industries enlisted Doubleday to provide content for its AutoTutor.[107] Corporations understood that making the curriculum rely upon their devices lent longevity to the market. Minnesota Manufacturing and Mining (3M) gave overhead projectors, transparency supplies, and teacher training to five hundred schools, donations worth $3,000 each and $1.5 million all told.[108] Over the years of a projector's use, 3M could reap ongoing financial benefits from the sale of parts and additional transparencies, as well as pre-packaged lessons. To serve this newly vibrant sector, in 1965 the American Management Association launched regular conferences and trade exhibits specifically for businesses courting the educational market and for producers of educational technology.[109]

Throughout the 1960s electronics manufacturers acquired or struck deals with educational publishers, foreshadowing a trend toward "convergence" and "synergy" that some myopically assume is unique to our era of digital media. Xerox bought Basic Systems and American Education Publication (1965); RCA bought Random House (1966); IBM acquired Science Research Associates (1964); General Electric formed a joint venture with *Time* (the General Learning Corp, 1965), as did 3M with *Newsweek* (1966) and Sylvania with *Reader's Digest* (1966).[110] In an arrangement that prefigured Channel One two decades later, 3M marketed and distributed a weekly publication prepared by *Newsweek*. News Focus, as the venture was called, was made up of texts and transparencies of current events, thus providing content for overhead projectors.[111] As one industry reporter put it on the occasion of the deal between *Time* and General Electric, "The companies' arrangement is the latest in a series of moves by leading industrial concerns into the fast growing multi-billion dollar 'knowledge industry.'"[112] Hillel Black tallied the mergers and ventures intending to take advantage of the educational market between 1966 and 1968 at over 120.[113]

Saettler's history of educational technology revealed the rich and complex interaction between media and teaching. But as he pointed out, nothing compares with the upsurge in activity from the late 1950s onward. As the veteran educational technology researcher and advocate Dean McClusky wrote in the introduction to Saettler's seminal text, "Despite the slow pace with which the use of instructional media progressed at first, the growth in acceptance and use of the products of technology has been substantial and has accelerated during the past twenty-five years. This has been particularly true since World War II, during which instructional technology made an immeasurable contribution to the rapid training of millions of people who served in the Armed Forces and in industry."[114] Estimates of the knowledge industry sector's total production and distribution costs for 1958 were $136 billion. This jumped to $195 billion by 1963.[115] Educational spending was $39 billion, second only to spending on national defense, at $49 billion, in 1965.[116] A survey for the Society of Motion Picture and Television Engineers put spending on audiovisual equipment and supplies at $667 million in 1964, a 4.5 percent increase over the previous year.[117] Total educational spending rose from $9.3 billion in 1950 (3.5 percent of gross national product) to $33.7 billion (5.4 percent of GNP) in 1964.[118]

The technologizing of the classroom did not progress unfettered. Concerns about automation and teacherless environments were heard from all quarters. Howe, making a point of using the new lingo of the day, expressed caution and encouraged reflection as the "hardware" of overhead projectors, teaching machines, and various audiovisual technologies seemed to take precedence over the "software" of actual lessons.[119] He challenged industry to provide content as innovative as the instruments: "I would caution the businessman not to venture into hardware unless he is prepared to go all the way into printed materials and programming. Otherwise he will have created an empty vessel or simply a glorified page-turner."[120] Even business leaders thought it prudent to assess the path they were pushing schools to pursue. J. Sterling Livingston, of the Harvard Graduate School of Business, commented that despite the continuing vogue for speed-reading courses, "the most critical problem remains to teach people to write things that are worth reading slowly."[121] The *New York Times* depicted an unimpressive demonstration at a major conference on educational technology, where speakers "almost without exception . . . used projectors ineptly and redundantly. They seem to believe that a dull lecture can be saved by dull, repetitious pictures shown by an overhead projector."[122]

In its recommendations of priorities for schools in the 1960s, the NEA supported broader use of educational television, radio, and programmed instruction, though "accompanied by a vigorous program of research and experimentation."[123] Among technological enhancements of schools, it recommended, "School authorities should examine the potentialities of automation for storage and retrieval of pupil personal data and instructional materials."[124] With these and other priorities the ideological and procedural course for the next few decades was falling into place. The changing conditions of modern society, notably a totalizing sense of media presence, required educational institutions to similarly integrate media into their lessons. The assessment that contemporary experience was approaching some ultimate sensory and informational saturation point could be addressed, counterintuitively, with an increase in sensory and informational materials in schools. The terrified view of technologically facilitated mind control could be allayed by an augmented incorporation of technologically assisted instruction. The recommendation, taken up in policy and by the most prominent of media scholars, from the esoteric McLuhan to the instrumentalist Schramm, was that a technological problem required a technological fix, and that an adequate response to the felt crisis of the speed, clutter, and overload of modern life was more speed, clutter, and overload.

As the scandalous possibility of manipulation of our unconscious was being decried, an underlying belief arose that mass social engineering was feasible, even necessary. Programmed learning and the panoply of other forms of instructional media entered as the reasonable pedagogical option. Thus the challenge of contemporary education did not stem from the impact of media or from concerns about the effectiveness of particular technological forms. The extreme vision of mass brain manipulation could be quelled by a promise of the supreme individualization of learning needs, even though part of the appeal of programmed instruction was its centralized formulation of materials and curricula. The discursive arrangement was such that by 1973, Wilson Bryan Key could write that successful experiments in educational television were actually capitalizing upon the special powers of the medium to manipulate minds. "As an educational tool . . . television is a disaster area," but "these experiments have established most emphatically that as a *training* device, or if you will, *brainwashing* or *conditioning* device, television has an enormous potential."[125] In other words, efforts to improve education through audiovisual systems post-Sputnik both responded to and fueled fearful notions about the media manipulations of populations.

Teaching machines were relatively quick to join the junk pile. When Robert Filep and Wilbur Schramm wrote their summary report on the impact of Title VII in 1970, they did not have kind words for the introduction of programmed instruction: "Expectations for programmed instruction outran the materials. The new method passed quickly into commercial hands. A false start was made with 'teaching machines,' thousands of which were sold to schools before there were adequate programs for them. Publishers offered programs that had not been adequately tested. There were no concentrations of scholarly talent such as had been gathered around the curriculum revisions, and no general evaluations of materials. Schools adopted many such materials, and promptly began to have doubts about their quality and value. Simultaneously, teachers found that some programs did not work well at all or else did not fit into their curricula."[126] This damning conclusion, though, did not convince the authors to steer away from their support for the idea of programmed instruction. And we know how this story ends. Teaching machines found their way to the scrap heap; computers stepped in as the future of programmable lessons.

From the press conference in September 1957 announcing the formation of a company, Subliminal Projection, the cultural work of the subliminal thesis impinged on the limits of advertising's influence. Almost immediately the technique was denounced as inappropriate, with some exceptions, regardless of whether it worked. Various defenses of ethical advertising arose against Vicary's brand of "psychic hucksterism."[127] But Subliminal Projection was more than an advertising research firm; it promised a form of mass instruction, and the company's goals were consistent with the sharp growth of corporate involvement in education. The tachistoscope—the technology at the heart of concerns about subliminal influences—had already been used in educational contexts, and was an indispensable tool in the then current craze for speed-reading. Vicary's patent for his tachistoscope was never granted. Precon's was, in 1962, its uses described in the patent application as education and psychotherapy, in addition to marketing and promotion. To be sure, education and psychotherapy may have been mentioned to assure the patent office that the device would not be used to sell the unconscious for advertising space. Still, Precon's device joined the variety of other educational technologies developed and marketed during the 1960s with similar goals of rapid mass learning. In short, the first popular subliminal event was the outermost layer of a discussion about the relationship between mind manipulation, media consumption, affluence, and educational technologies.

Even as new technology was being advocated as a necessary mechanism of social progress and disseminated with increasing vigor through the 1960s, the subliminal thesis was a site at which the place of technology in our lives was being assessed and sorted through.

Vicary's press conference marked one entry point for a popular discussion about injecting ideas into minds without awareness. As Alvin Rose wrote at the time, "underneath the popular interest in motivation research and subliminal advertising there may be developing a considerable, silent, as yet unarticulated public anxiety regarding the emergence of a new segment of power in contemporary society—that of mass-communications media."[128] He saw in this anxiety a "creative skepticism" that might "be brought to consider the larger issues of the ethical relationship of psychological science and scientists to industry, the obligation of industry to the consumer public, and the responsibility and morality of a free press, of popular journalism, in a democratic society."[129] Challenges to the subliminal idea were about the fearsome ease with which our age of progress, especially its new understandings of the human mind, could take a turn for the loathsome. Commentators like Aldous Huxley and Marshall McLuhan participated in public and policy debates that exposed and managed the related failings of American society, for which the idea of subliminal influence was either a harbinger or a symptom. Indeed, the most lasting contribution of the term "subliminal" may be its stabilization as a Cold War trope of totalitarianism, and a schematizing of the path of power from an abstract centralized agency (government, business, media élites) to the concrete site of the individual body and mind. The concept of subliminal manipulation became a way to make imaginable and imminent the extreme undermining of individual will, and with it the undermining of democratic ideals for contemporary mass society. Curiously, a core response to the subliminal threat was that in the end the individual would prevail if properly armed with a modern education. This modern education could only be achieved, it was thought, through the deployment of a catalogue of new audiovisual instruments, *some of which were the same type of instruments that sparked the first scandalized reactions*. Machine-oriented learning was seen as reasonable and desirable, and the practice, along with its commercial backbone, flourished.

Textual Strategies for Media Saturation

CHAPTER EIGHT

Wake Up!

The imaginative extensions of scientific and technological discovery have produced some amazing curiosities of popular culture. *Invisible Invaders* (Edward L. Cahn, 1959) begins with narration warning that the global race for "atom supremacy" is going too far, accompanied by documentary footage of an atomic blast. As the story develops, we find that invisible alien residents of the Moon agree. Having watched humans for thousands of years, they are now worried that our ambitions in space will encroach on their empire. They decide to take over Earth before our technological capabilities pose a real challenge to them. Their manner of invasion is to inhabit the bodies of the dead, effectively bringing them back to life. But the aliens have underestimated the speed of research, especially when defense is an issue. The front line of human defenders inadvertently realizes that sound vibrations not only make the invaders visible but destroy them. In *Invisible Invaders* scientific progress both sparks the conflict and resolves it.

While giant insects and alien monsters populate the science fiction of the postwar period, there are also ample illustrations of nonhuman humans in various forms of zombies and pod-people. Loved ones could be transformed into vegetative aliens, children could be stoic agents of an evil plot, corpses could be inhabited and reanimated, and the dead could run. In the most celebrated versions, including Robert A. Heinlein's *The Puppet Masters* (1951), Jack Finney's *The Body Snatchers* (1955), Richard Matheson's *I Am Legend* (1954), and Murray Leinster's *The Brain-Stealers* (1954), the story involves a national or global attack on thought, rationality, and free will. As shown by Mark Jancovich's detailed study of American horror and science fiction films and literature of the 1950s, anxieties about conformity and depersonalization, as well as masculinity, pervade these genres.[1] The dramas conventionally focus on the struggles of a male protagonist, accompanying him as he witnesses the destruction of his immediate world and furiously tries to defend himself against a threatening force. And that threatening force is invariably a broad attack on the entirety of a population and way of life. Threats are directed against the multitudes, and catastrophe confronts the totality of society, with plentiful pseudoscientific explanations of the control of body, brains, and will. As the populace transforms into a subservient mass, an alternative social order emerges, a horrifying inverted image of democracy. In this respect the stories are at root depictions of revolutionary change. They reflect fears of individuality subsumed into a crowded world, leaving behind a glassy-eyed populace or human husks driven by violent impulses to attack even more people. As allegories of change, they express alarm about an alternative social order, in which individuality is erased and aliens control a totalitarian society. They show that "one-dimensional man" was a prominent theme well before Herbert Marcuse published his book with that title phrase in 1964.

In the most terrifying iterations the battleground is the mind, where external powers plant and direct thoughts and desires and one cannot always identify allegiance from outward appearance. Everyone you thought you knew becomes suspect, and the moment of transformation from friend to mortal enemy might itself be ambiguous. When exactly has a husband, wife, boss, and politician been taken over? In Jack Finney's *The Body Snatchers* the drama begins with concern expressed to a doctor that a man's wife is not his wife anymore. In the first film version, *Invasion of the Body Snatchers* (Don Siegel, 1956), a niece knows that her uncle is not really her uncle and a boy knows that his mother is no longer his mother. As the protagonist Miles narrates, "At first glance everything looked the same. It wasn't. Something evil had taken possession of the town." Importantly, the difference cannot be seen, but it can

Individuality under attack: *Invasion of the Body Snatchers,*1956. Source: BFI Stills.

be felt. Toward the end of the film, after a kiss between Miles and his wife, Becky, a close-up of her blank face tells Miles that she has been taken over. This intimate scene establishes body snatching as both seductive and horrific. The revelation that his love is already a pod-person is a betrayal, as she calls to the others to catch and convert Miles.

As they approach the dreadful border that separates human essence from "thingness," fiction and films about "body snatching" capture worries about the troubled future of mass society. They are in equal measure allegories of fascism, communism, and consumerism. But propping up the political allegories is a thesis about mind and the nature of manipulation. In Robert A. Heinlein's *The Puppet Masters,* the United States is being taken over by invaders who can colonize and control minds. As the protagonist Sam Kavanaugh understands it, such occupation of brains transforms people into communication devices, no different from telephones or radio receivers, and one's body becomes a subservient tool for new masters. But he fights these invaders, as well as his own mental and corporeal colonization, to dramatic success. Sam appears not just as a survivalist but as a traditionalist. He likes things the way they used to be.

The narrative function of change in these works is to depict total upheaval. We may begin with the calm of a small community, but soon we are witnessing national or global cataclysms. The stories play with this scale, connecting a quotidian disruption to earth-shattering devastation. The whole of human society is being reworked; everyone is implicated and everyone will be affected. The sweeping nature of the threats means that these accounts are often described as conspiratorial and paranoid. And many cultural critics and historians take the investigation of paranoia in popular texts as a mirror for the tone of the postwar era. It would be a mistake, though, to limit the paranoid reading to a study of individual states of mind, as though this vision were traced to a central hero alone. In fact, the convention of focusing on a protagonist is more accurately understood as a vehicle through which a more elaborate social portrait is painted. The outer edges of commonsense and popular science found in this strain of science fiction, a subgenre that in hindsight can appear now as simply campy or ridiculous, nonetheless elaborated and speculated upon contemporary issues in the language of the day. Narratives of what Ray Pratt calls "visionary paranoia" may be a sign of heightened political awareness, despite their fallacies and exaggerations.[2]

A case in point is *The Brain-Stealers* by Murray Leinster (pseudonym for Will F. Jenkins), a novel expanded from his short story of 1947. It depicts a future totalitarian society in which it is illegal to experiment with thought-control transmission. Jim Hunt refuses to comply with this restriction on scientific research and violates the law by continuing his experiments. State security pursues him, but another threat is more pressing. Aliens are enslaving people and feeding on them parasitically. Hunt wages a battle on two fronts, one against alien invaders using mind control and the other against a strong-arm security state that disallows exploration of the powers of the mind. As our protagonist sees it, the State and the so-called Things complement one another, as they both produce a servile and complacent populace. Hunt covertly continues his rebellion, and frees people by building an especially powerful thought transmitter. Consequently the vampiric Things are themselves enslaved, tortured, and gruesomely brutalized in the name of revenge, science, and security. In the novel's finale, expecting to be imprisoned for his contraband mind-control device, Hunt is confronted by the director general of security, described as the most powerful man in the world, who instead offers him a job with the state agency that Hunt has been fighting. The director general, taking a new preventative defense tactic, promises to end the State's policy of isolationism and to begin colonizing other creatures and planets. Hunt enthusiastically accepts the offer.

The Brain-Stealers has many of the attributes of a Cold War story, including an alien Other that dehumanizes people and an imagined threat of future invaders. The reference to the end of isolationism matches a brand of aggressive liberalism, characterized by a global, or in this instance interplanetary, attentiveness to the exportation of a domestic way of life, backed by a military campaign with undisguised imperialist ambitions. And it also presents a battle for minds, or what can be read as an ideological struggle between two opposing modes of citizenship. One may champion free will and the other life-draining enslavement, but both conduct their matters with the same method of long-distance mass mind control. All forces are in the end brain stealers, and the conflict is between different versions of what people will be controlled to think and do. In a way this is a war between broadcasters acting in the service of two state powers. And their propagandistic endeavors are not only massively effective but necessary: brain stealing here is realpolitik.[3]

Paranoid tales, as represented by these Earth-bound sci-fi classics in which enemies are everywhere and their menace is universal, display a brand of global consciousness. Nuclear, bacterial, televisual, or alien dangers unite the world because the world in its entirety is at risk. In addition to the global outlook sparked by Sputnik, the dominant internationalism of political bodies like the United Nations and the World Health Organization made the possibility of world-governing powers imaginable and immediate. With visionary paranoia, it is a small step from supranational organizations to secret plans for the control of mass populations. James Bond, Matt Helm, and the men and women from UNCLE all battled organized world criminal agencies guided by megalomaniacs—respectively Specter, Smerch, and Thrush—with each at times having to battle modes of mass mind control.

Another exceedingly popular mid-century cultural form, the superhero comic, took up these themes of mind manipulation, depicting a world similarly replete with despotic aspirants and their totalitarian ambitions, plans that often involved constructing the conditions for mass acquiescence. A sampling of the appearance of mind manipulators that have appeared in comic books provides an illustration of the types and narrative functions of the idea of extreme media effects.[4] In addition to the sheer number of examples, the variety of hypnotizing and illusion-making devices displays the wildly imaginative flourishes that one expects of American comics. Still, certain patterns emerge to reveal dominant sensibilities concerning the largely nefarious uses of mediating technologies. Heroic demonstrations of mind reading and telekinesis figure. But villains notably use their mind-reading or telekinetic powers as illusion-making weapons, deceiving or brainwashing either individuals or entire cities and countries. Not only are these treatments numerous, but they are expansive in scope and present simple, if baroque, accounts of occupying the mass mind.

There are those with natural manipulating capabilities, sometimes mutants, aliens, or the gifted. For example, the Brain Wave is a mutant hypnotizer and conjurer of 3-D illusions from the early 1940s (*All Star Comics* #23, 1940). The Wizard uses illusions and hypnosis to execute his crimes (*All Star Comics* #34, 1947). Mind-controlling powers are often the product of research, technological innovation, or industrial accident. Not surprisingly, many criminals with visions of global domination are highly educated figures of scientific authority, including doctors and professors. Though the indefatigable superheroes have their own extraordinary traits, many villains make unethical uses of the benefits of progress for their own gain and physical enhancement. This is in part an acknowledgement of the power that resides among such authoritative institutions as the military, government, medical, scientific, university, and industrial establishments. Many superheroes make appropriate, ethical, and cautious uses of the products of these institutions. For this reason superhero narratives tend to betray a conservative impulse, legitimating and restoring the power located in those familiar institutions. But these narratives also explore, and indeed revel in, the willful misuse of this power. Even as our valiant gods and goddesses toil to reinstall peace and order, the most exciting and dramatically rendered moments are those of the spectacular destruction of familiar sites and agencies.

Quite a bit of attention is conventionally given to the methods of creating deception. Among the multiple moonlighting professors in the comic book world is the psychologist Jonathan Crane, also known as the Scarecrow (*World's Finest Comics* #3, 1941). This criminal mastermind develops gases and electrical gadgets to create fear. The *Batman* character the Mad Hatter, a computer genius first appearing in 1948 with a mind-reading device (*Batman* #41, though #49 according to Mark Waid's *Who's*

Who), subsequently develops hypnotizing and amnesia-inducing talents in 1956 (*Detective Comics* #230).

Among the brainwashing machines and chemicals, prosthetic brain-enhancing devices are plentiful and appear as elaborate headgear. The villainous artist Crazy Quilt bewilders people with a dazzling helmet that projects colored lights (*Boy Commandos* #15, 1946). Flash's nemesis the Thinker increases his intellect, hypnotic control, and telekinetic abilities when he wears his "thinking cap" (*All-Flash* #12, 1943). An early Wonder Woman foe is Dr. Psycho (*Wonder Woman* #5, 1943), whose experiments in hypnosis lead to the discovery that he can change matter with the assistance of an entranced subject, Marva. Optical instruments are also a popular part of the hypnotic arsenal, effectively transforming one recognizable symbol of the egghead—eyewear—into a dangerous weapon. For instance, the hypnotic monocle is the weapon of choice for the Mad Thinker, who faced the Fantastic Four in 1963 (#15).

Several stories and characters exploit and exaggerate the entrancing qualities of music and sound waves to the point at which they become weapons. Music figures as a method of mind control especially in the D.C. universe. The Fiddler (*All Flash* #32, 1947–48) can destroy things, create shields, and hypnotize with his music, talents acquired from a Hindu fakir in prison. Building upon the familiar folktale, *Flash* (#106, 1959) introduces the Pied Piper, whose arsenal contains hypnotizing pipes and Sonic Boomatron bagpipes. A parallel criminal, also a D.C. Comics creation, is the Pied Piper of Pluto (*Mystery in Space* #110, 1966), whose favored instrument is a hypnotizing flute. Sonar fights the Green Lantern with his powerful, brainwave-distorting tuning fork (*Green Lantern* #14, 1962). The weapon of musical entrancement is a favorite of several story lines of the Justice League of America. Kanjar Ro (*Justice League of America* #3, 1961) threatens his adversaries with a paralyzing sonic gong. The chemically enhanced villain The Key uses a keyboard to achieve his psychic control of people (*Justice League of America* #41, 1965). The Justice League also faces the Maestro (#16, 1962), who manipulates minds with a radio beam hidden in music, debilitating people by making them dance to exhaustion, the ultimate fear of a youth culture entranced by popular music.

Asian stereotypes figure prominently, of which Flash Gordon's nemesis Ming the Merciless, introduced in the 1930s, is a longstanding example. In addition to an all-seeing television, Ming develops a machine that transforms people into slaves. Decades later the ancient wizard Dormammu (*Strange Tales* #126, 1964) has mind-control abilities, and *Tales of Suspense* (#50, 1964) introduces the Mandarin, an English-Chinese lunatic with magical rings, one of which allows him to control minds.

The above characters, plots, and criminal methods far from exhaust the range of depictions, but this overview helps to present some of the manifold appearances of the mind-control theme. Some patterns are evident. Scientific intervention, motivated by unethical desires, is a recurring origin of these powers. Devices include monocles and gemstones, and they may affect single people or mass populations, but the overall impression is that a mad logic generates the battles that ensue. Brains are programmable in these worlds, and efforts to develop technological modes of programming are rampant. This universe (and technically "universe" should be plural in the world of comic books) is one where the hidden depths of the mind can be accessed with the right substance, procedure, or machine. The more archaic-appearing magicians favor inexplicable magical artifacts or talismans. Aliens and characters from across time and space may have inborn mental abilities. But the essentially contemporary dramas tend to focus upon the harnessing of mental energy, with scientific discovery a main source of newfound manipulative powers.

A Cold War fascination with controlling emotions is noteworthy. The struggle over the use of fear, hate, and doubt as harnessed by Psycho-man (*The Fantastic Four Annual* #5, 1967) aligns well with a psychological battle for hearts and minds. The continuing appearance of Nazi villains keeps the horror of fascism prominent, and reinforces the claim that at the root of evil lies the manipulation of people and the stifling of individual emotion, expression, and will. A related thread concerns the potentially debilitating effect of sight and sound. The senses and perception are playgrounds of malleable possibilities. Sometimes the lines are blurred between illusion and materiality, between the imagined and the physical. Other dramas concern the disorientation of music, noise, color, and light. Related to this, the conventions of superhero representational style developed ways to depict the extreme impact of invisible forces. The dazzling presentation of climactic scenes, with obsessive attention to muscles in motion and contorted faces of anguish and concentration, connotes graphically the exertion of force. Heroes are thrown backward by invisible barriers, with jagged lightning bolts of color depicting waves of mental, light, or sound energy. Squiggly rays emitted from foreheads, fingertips, pendants, monocles, jewels, helmets, and radar all capture on the illustrated page an idea of control from a distance.

It is especially significant that there was a surge of new characters in the 1960s. There had been a similar abundance of new characters in the 1940s, the so-called golden age of comics, followed by a period of retrenchment in the mid-1950s. The appearance of so many brainwashers and mind controllers in the 1960s led to an intensified investment in media effects and references to illusion-as-weapon in comics. There is a self-reflexivity evident here. This wave of mind controllers occurs in the wake of the moral panic of the 1950s about the effect of comics on youth, in which cultural authorities claimed that their composition, color, layout, and story were detrimental to the development of young minds.[5]

Beyond the world of comics, stories of mind control, evil scientists, revolutionary change, and heroic battles against nefarious plots were the province of science fiction literature. And by 1958 the subliminal version of mind control continued these themes. The most direct precursors were *The Space Merchants* (1953) and "Captive Audience" (1953), discussed in chapter 6. On the heels of Vicary's press release on subliminal communication were several works of fiction that explored the extreme consequences of subliminal techniques. In June 1958 perhaps the first such work came from the prolific mass-market spy author Edward S. Aarons, "The Communicators" in the *Magazine of Fantasy and Science Fiction*.[6] As the title signals, concern about mass media is the central theme. The sci-fi short story recounts a futuristic civil war in the United States, with an army of rebels set to establish a sovereign republic in Texas on the very day the story takes place. The dramatic opening lines introduce the mind-control theme: "The animals screamed. They moved through his mind like stealthy beasts in a green, humid jungle, making shadow patterns across the web of his thoughts."[7] In this scenario of a centralized, totalitarian society, government leaders are Protectors and their functionaries are Communicators. A lead revolutionary, Hennery Davis, describes the state-controlled television as an opiate. With video screens covering entire walls, it is not hidden messages but the genre of soap opera that is being described in this way. But Davis is able to slow the broadcast images to reveal that there are also embedded subliminal messages used to maintain social order. In statements strongly reminiscent of the slogans of Big Brother in *1984*, they command, "Citizens of Texas! The Communicators are your friends! Obey the Austerity Program! Be strong! Be disciplined! Work and Obey!"[8] Aarons takes time to explain subliminal methods, with oblique reference to the controversy of 1957: "Long ago, before the Ten Day War, when free enterprise was the rule, various commercial organizations had experimented with subliminal broadcasting for merchandising impact. It hadn't worked very well then, because the TV tubes of those days scanned an image in more time than a subliminal message should take. But with the development of tubes capable of almost instantaneous scanning, subliminals became practicable after the initial failures."[9] Vicary's experiment thus became the real-world, contemporary evidence of hidden influences, lending topicality to the fiction, regardless of the experiment's questionable results. After all, the story makes a distinction between Vicary's initial failure and future manipulative success.

"The Communicators" continues with details of the civil war. There is a plot to attack and destroy the Dallas Communicator Tower, the source of broadcasts and subliminal controlling messages and the basis of the dominant regime. Dr. Soong, a Fu Manchu–like psychiatrist, helps Davis in this plot, but Mugrath, a telepath who supports the coup and does so under orders from the North, "sees" him. Mugrath uncovers Dr. Soong's true intentions to control a post-revolutionary Texas. This leads him to kill Dr. Soong in gruesome fashion, but not before the evil doctor accuses Mugrath of being an automaton carrying out the orders of others. Mugrath then discovers how Dr. Soong has been manipulating Davis with his own subliminals. The rebellion is a success, Davis is now the new Protector, and Mugrath types out a new subliminal message for invisible broadcast, one that champions the importance of the Union. Though the hero of the piece, Mugrath dons the doctor's old clothes, which fit him well, suggesting that his counterrevolutionary position is not so easily distinguishable from the despotic, rebellious zeal of Dr. Soong. In a despairing conclusion, Mugrath expresses his dilemma:

> Again he became aware of the inflexible net of forged obedience skillfully built into him by surgeons' scalpels. What difference did it make? But it made a difference. These strange storms, these stresses of pulling and pushing within him, as the man he once was still struggled feebly against the man he had become, were intolerable. He felt the burden of a great, overwhelming sorrow rise within him.
>
> And Mugrath sat down and wept for himself and the world.[10]

The convention of the mysterious Chinese villain and his special mental powers figures yet again, and there are references to "Eastern decadence,"[11] though it is not clear whether this phrase refers to the Far East or the eastern United States; the story is, of course, set in revolutionary Texas. Other instances of southern antipathy toward the North appear, and Mugrath is described disparagingly as a "damnyankee" and "a North Unionist, a Federalist, a Communicator."[12] But this tritely xenophobic kernel of Aarons's fantasy is less provocative than the maze of media influence that he foresees. Political actions in support of a stable federation, an independence movement, or a foreign imperial regime all rely upon media manipulation. This control acts upon a general population as much as it does upon any specific individual key to internal power struggles. The revolution both succeeds and fails, as does preservation of the Union. Mugrath's closing despair is a cry of frustration, as our classical hero acknowledges that his actions and decisions are being guided by someone else. This conventional science fiction narrative has at its heart the paradox of a protagonist, a "man of action," whose will and actions are not his own. And they are not his own because of media influence and technological intervention.

In a most trim and efficient story of totalitarian media control and revolution, one that reiterates that paradox of the will-less man of action, Ray Faraday Nelson's "Eight o' Clock in the Morning" (1963) portrays a battle of control over the airwaves and minds.[13] The society depicted is stifled by its willful ignorance of the controllers in its midst. In a clever allusion to the place of mesmerism in the history of popular entertainment, the story opens with the performance of a stage hypnotist who during the course of his act awakens his audience and inadvertently causes our hero, George Nada, to truly awaken. In his newly aware state he can see that the crowd is made up of humans and nonhuman, reptilian Fascinators. These creatures rule and manipulate the world, keeping the population subdued by mind control. As he returns home, being careful not to show his newly perceptive state, Nada sees the Fascinators' commands hidden in posters and television broadcasts: "Work eight hours, play eight hours, sleep eight hours," "Marry and Reproduce," "Stay tuned to this station," "Obey the government," "We are the government," and "We are your friends, you'd do anything for a friend, wouldn't you." Interestingly, these commands are rather banal and peaceful, and mostly mirror ordinary expectations for middle-class American lives. Nada's rebellion and his awakening are in response to the conformist pressures of this version of normalcy. At home, in a classic gesture of media refusal, he immediately disconnects his television set. But he is not safe, and he receives a phone call from a Fascinator who commands his heart to stop the next day at 8:00 a.m.

A race against time ensues, with Nada trying to awaken as many people as he can to the existence and designs of the Fascinators before the ominous hour of the next morning arrives. He finds that for the Fascinators' power to work these rulers must believe that they have the power. Showing resistance is therefore effective in loosening the dominant faction's grip on social control, which is of course the dream of rebel protesters everywhere. Nada fights his way into a television studio, and in his own act of media manipulation broadcasts a plea for people to wake up by being the off-camera voice to an on-camera dead Fascinator. This tactic is a striking echo of the Superman comic discussed in the Prologue of this book, in which Orson Welles convincingly broadcasts a ventriloquized message of peace from an otherwise unconscious leader. And in Nelson's version the tactic is just as effective. This city wakes up to the domination of the Fascinators, and the war for liberation begins. Still, as commanded, Nada dies at the appointed hour.

The conclusion seems oddly contradictory. Though Nada has awakened, the ending suggests that he remains under control; he obeys the Fascinators' command and dies. But his border state between sleep and wakefulness is such that several times throughout the story Nada experiences a slippage, and people flicker between their human and nonhuman forms before his eyes. In this account, an awakened state is not a pure state. And yet, importantly, Nada believes that he can see clear demarcations between the manipulators and the manipulated, between the aliens and the humans. Nada's acts of violence are heroic precisely because he has the power to recognize with absolute confidence who the aliens are, or at least he believes he has this power. This dream of a stable and identifiable Other, as well as its equally stable menace, authorizes his casual dispatching of these creatures. In one episode, while Nada is visiting his girlfriend, Lil, a Fascinator comes to her door. Nada promptly stabs him in the throat, though Lil can only see her familiar middle-aged neighbor dead on the floor. Lil, as a horrified sympathetic citizen, is exposed as somnambulistic. "Eight o' Clock in the Morning" leaves the reader unclear about the outcome of the rebellion, with Nada's residual control leading to his demise. But unambiguous is the will to fight. This is not just a story of totalitarianism, conventionality, or paranoid accusations of conspiracy. It is a story of valiant efforts to resist and struggle against oppressive forces and manipulative tactics. As in *The Puppet Masters*, *The Brain-Stealers*, *The Body Snatchers*, and *I Am Legend*, the protagonist is not just a conspiracy believer, but a conspiracy fighter.

"Eight o' Clock in the Morning" was later reimagined as a vehicle for the wrestler Rowdy Roddy Piper, with more attention to action sequences, in the film *They Live* (John Carpenter, 1988). The movie version focuses on a depiction of economic hardship, representing squatter camps of the homeless and working poor. The aliens are the élite of society, benefiting economically from their control of an underclass. Carpenter's film is an obvious critique of capitalism: Adorno for teenagers. The most visually distinctive element in the film is the introduction of special sunglasses that let the hero, and the cinema spectator, see through the surface skin of people to the alien musculature beneath, and through the colorful veil of media to the black-and-white hidden commands below. This accessory is rather like the x-ray specs sold in the classified ads of comic books. Unfortunately, the decision to introduce this device erases the ambiguity between the states of ignorance and awareness found in the short story. Without a technological apparatus through which to see the world as it truly is, the original version makes the battle against governmental and commercial oppression a matter of continual media consciousness. "Eight o' Clock," even with its substantial action components, advocates media literacy rather than a technological fix.

J. G. Ballard's short story "The Subliminal Man" (1963) is another contribution to the media conspiracy–fighter cycle, this time as Vance Packard's worst nightmare.[14] Hathaway, who with his long hair, sandals, and dirty jeans is a hippie radical *avant la lettre*, cries a warning to his friend Dr. Franklin about the large public signs that are being erected everywhere—signs, he claims, that inhibit thought. Simultaneously dismissing and validating Hathaway's concern, Dr. Franklin admonishes him for thinking too much, and asks for confirmation of these claims. Secretly envying the bohemian life of Hathaway, Franklin drives by the signs in question, spontaneously exiting the highway to purchase cigarettes, only to find three other cartons already in his glove compartment.

At home, domestic consumption appears to be the only topic of discussion or activity. With product obsolescence contractually enforced,

Franklin and his wife Judith feel compelled to replace consumer items even faster than necessary. In this consumption-driven economy, other contracts oblige households to purchase in bulk, to the point of physical exhaustion, and to buy enough to meet a neighborhood standard. Advertising is pervasive, including five-second commercials that interrupt telephone calls. Hathaway witnesses firsthand the hidden workings of the giant electronic billboards—the hundreds of gun-like stroboscopes that flash imperceptible messages at passersby. He tries to convince Franklin that these subliminal messages compel excessive shopping. Franklin, the white-collar professional, keeps track of his expenditures and realizes that something is afoot with his illogically inflated consumer desire, but he is not compelled to resist. Hathaway, for his part, wages a solitary battle against advertising, blowing up the offending signs and, in a fatal disruptive effort, arresting a billboard's flickering so that people can read the crass demands to "buynowbuynow." Moments after this protest the police gun him down. Disturbed by the violence, and now believing Hathaway's accusations, Franklin and his wife go shopping. Like "Eight o' Clock in the Morning," the story passes the need to wake up from the protagonist to other characters, and in so doing it slyly includes the reader among the sleepers. But where Nelson's story ends with the start of a war against the manufacture of mass mental acquiescence, the dead radical of "The Subliminal Man" has disturbed the bourgeois family, but not enough for its members to imagine an alternative life.

Science fiction novels, short stories, and superhero comics offered sustained narrative and formal investigation of oppressive manipulation and individualist battles for freedom. And one of the dominant themes in narratives about mass hypnosis, brainwashing, and subliminal control, running from the novel *1984* through the film *The Matrix* (Andy and Lana Wachowski, 1999), is the adventure of waking up and becoming aware of the limits of freedom. In this way the stories are about survival, recovery, and preparedness, with generally reverential treatments of the political rebel, renegade scientist, and social malcontent bent on breaking free from restrictions on individuality. Even though events may end terribly for the protagonist, we are left with not just a study of conformity and totalitarianism but a study of resistance to conformity and totalitarianism. That mass suggestibility is envisioned as a general state, one to be explored through varieties of performance or to be challenged as an endpoint for rationality, makes these tales more than documents of the outrageous and fanciful. They become full and anxious expressions of the qualities of the age, but with a singular, masculine hero who can see through the mass illusions to fight them. The results may vary, as with Mugrath (alive and revolution finished, though perhaps a false one), Nada (dead and revolution commencing), and Hathaway (dead and no revolution), but their actions affirm a struggle to recover individual self from the gravitational pull of a stifling social order. These stories configure the subliminal as something that you fight.

Represented here too is a form of awareness about the media in our midst. Their media consciousness depicts a disorienting world of abundant images. This abundance challenges basic abilities to discern the difference between the manufactured and the natural, thus making unreliable the perceptual functions of characters. The mediated sci-fi world is a particular kind of lonely crowd, isolating people and alienating them even from themselves. Outer-directedness still characterizes most in these stories of mass deception. The self-reliant orientation of inner-directedness distinguishes our protagonists, or at least they come to recognize that this is what they and others lack. With this self-consciousness, they are able to stand out from the deceived.

One textual strategy in the depictions of this culture of abundance is a radical break with reason through total sensory and mental saturation, and an embrace of disorientation. No author has produced as sustained an investigation of the themes of the perceptual limits of consciousness as Philip K. Dick. In one of Dick's masterpiece novels, *Time Out of Joint* (1959), Ragle Gumm, a champion newspaper puzzle contestant living in a suburb in the late 1950s, grows to realize that he is really living in 1998 and has been kept in an illusory world in order to predict missile targets for one side of a ferocious civil war.[15] Though his managers closely oversee the closed environment of the past, slips occur. Objects melt into pieces of paper on which the names of the objects appear. While he first believes he is having some sort of mental breakdown, Gumm is finally able to tear through the fabricated peacefulness he enjoys to see the violent conflict that it masked. The artificiality of his surroundings connects to the manufacture of consciousness, but in Dick's novel these surroundings are far from seamless, and instead are full of gaps and errors. The novel is concerned with the welling up of that ugly truth, and about the incomplete illusions that try to keep it hidden.

A recurring element in Dick's work is the role of corporations in manipulating and exploiting consciousness. *The Three Stigmata of Palmer Eldritch* (1965) is about the marketing of illusions. Through the use of drugs, people are able to "translate" themselves into the universe of a popular toy, the Barbie-like Perky Pat doll, and its accessories. But for some characters the nature of entering this miniature universe is not clear. Even when using the drug Can-D, only true believers can experience this "miracle of translation—the near-sacred moment in which the miniature artifacts of the layout no longer merely represented Earth but *became* Earth."[16] Similarly, by using a competing drug, Chew-Z, one does more than inhabit this simulacrum: one becomes other life forms. But one character wonders if the experience is "a form of what they used to call brainwashing."[17] It becomes apparent that what one experiences is entirely artificial, hypnotically induced. Building up these uncertain boundaries between the real and the manufactured is advertising and marketing. As depicted here, competition between corporations involves creating and maintaining a world of illusion.

Another exemplar of the investigation into perceptual limits is the work of William S. Burroughs, who built a pansexual universe of blood, semen, and drugs in which government control and mind expansion intersect. His celebrated *Naked Lunch* (1959), with humorous and vivid episodes of sex, hypnosis, and bureaucracy, drew from that era of brainwashing and global conspiracy, and in the process became a document of the creative and social struggles to push beyond reigning norms. Dr. Benway uses hypnosis to operate the Reconditioning Center in Freeland, where even his own face "flickers like a picture moving in and out of focus."[18] The National Electronic Conference describes radio implants and telepathic transmission used for control by the State.[19] For Burroughs the "algebra of need" makes the junkie's addiction comparable to other controlling obsessions, from the sexual to the materialistic. This world of doctors, government agents, and alien beings is stifled by forces of domination, but it still includes efforts to experience freedom. Burroughs captures this paradox in what should be read as a hopeful statement, a glimmer of light breaking through an iron door: "A *functioning* police state needs no police."[20]

Burroughs and his fellow Beat artist Brion Gysin spent considerable time performing their own consciousness-expansion experiments. Through Gysin's influence, the hypnotic and hallucinogenic properties of flickering light became habitually applied and sought out by Burroughs.

Gysin introduced Burroughs to the grandiosely named Dream Machine, which was actually a simple homemade mechanical device consisting of a rotating cylinder, cutouts of Moroccan-inspired motifs, and a light source at the center. The user would lean into the resulting flicker, eyes closed, making one's own face the screen across which the light passed. Doing so would eventually produce visions and images in the mind of the user. Burroughs claimed to use the device regularly throughout his life, and several novels make reference to it, most elaborately evident in his collage-like "cut-up" works.[21] For instance, *The Ticket That Exploded* (1962/1968) is a delirious journey through a sci-fi, sexual underground. The disjointed prose-poetry style makes digging for a narrative thread beside the point. The cut-up method is in full form, and one reads groups of phrases repeatedly in various sequences. Despite the lack of a general narrative thrust, the characters, a mix of fictional, semifictional, and real people (Gysin, for instance, makes an appearance), spend a good deal of their time narrating. Many describe activities undertaken to enrich their participation in that utopian fantasy of an underground. The result is an intensely self-reflexive book. Just as Burroughs experiments with cut-ups to expand his expressive capability, so too do his characters employ these techniques as part of the novel's content.

The Ticket That Exploded opens with a traveling companion, who describes a science fiction book he is reading called *The Ticket That Exploded*. The narrator romantically feels that the companion's voice "has been spliced in 24 times per second with the sound of my breathing and the beating of my heart."[22] One later episode, "writing machine," involves a multimedia exhibition with pools, canals, flickering light, showers of sparks, calligraphs of iron filings, movies projected on top of one another, and a writing machine "that shifts one half one text and half the other through a page frame on conveyor belts."[23] Short Time Hyp is another such experiment, described as "subliminal slow motion" of a 35-frames-per-second film run at 24 frames per second.[24] Later the Subliminal Kid proposes an elaborate sound-splicing experiment using three tape recorders, which expands into a total sound and image cut-up of everybody and everything.[25] With revolutionary zeal that would be familiar to Nada or Hathaway, the narrator cries, "Carry your Carry Corders down Fleet St. and Madison Avenue . . . Sublimate the subliminators . . . Carry Corders of the world unite. You have nothing to lose but your pre-recordings."[26]

The number of pranks and perceptual experiments depicted in *The Ticket That Exploded* make this a cut-up about cut-ups, a collage about collage. As much as it is a Reichian treatise on bodily liberation, it is also about how one pursues this liberation by manipulating media. At times the novel reads like the technical instructions for an artist's installation. There is freedom to be found in the infinitesimal hidden bits of sound and vision, isolated and remixed with others (and it's no wonder that at least one contemporary hip-hop artist has seen the connection to his art: DJ Spooky, also known as That Subliminal Kid).[27] In Burroughs's battle for liberation, one wakes up from totalitarian control through art. And the art described, and represented by the novel itself in literary form, mirrors McLuhanesque reveling in the chaos of modern media. Significantly, these ideas about sensory overload, as represented in comic books and genre fiction as well as underground literature, coalesced in an emerging psychedelia in which thunderous multimedia bombardment opened a portal to a freer dimension. The champions of psychedelia were the next generation of sailors who stopped swimming and embraced the whirlpool to save themselves from drowning.

Flicker

William Burroughs's prose media installations were in essence a record of what was happening in both avant-garde and popular art as visual media pushed the exploration of representational and material clutter to the extremes of perceptual limits. A world of excitement and possibility was found hidden in flickering light. "The happening," with rotating colored lights, loud, chaotic music, and audience participation, was one brand of multimedia sensual art event that pursued these limits. The act of seeing swiftly was a document of a time, an aesthetic strategy to reveal hidden mental states as well as a form of emotional and perceptual manipulation.

Perfectly in tune with McLuhan's core hypothesis—the medium is the message—multimedia art events constructed environments to be experienced rather than static objects to be looked upon. Jordan Belson and Henry Jacobs produced the sound-and-light experience of Vortex for the world exposition of 1958 in Brussels and for Morrison Planetarium in San

Francisco in 1959, with flickering strobes, slide projectors, and dream-machine-like devices. Concurrently, Ray and Charles Eames were beginning to construct their multimedia pavilions. By the mid-1960s there were manifold expanded screen experiments, perhaps best exemplified by numerous installations at Expo '67 in Montreal.

Visual artists pursued strategies that capitalized on new media forms of expression and installation, which themselves often made direct reference to the historically specific condition of living among new media forms. Where Pop Art reworked the status of the art object, with attention to low forms and media saturation, Op Art explored the physiological conditions of perception with an extreme formalism. Bridget Riley painted simple lines, curves, and colors to create complex, nonrepresentational optical illusions. The groundbreaking show "The Responsive Eye" at the Museum of Modern Art (1965), curated by William C. Seitz, was initially to be a survey from Impressionism to contemporary optical art, but the interest in the latter led to a decision to focus on it alone. Highlighting its physiological basis, this wave of practice was first referred to as "retinal art," but by the mid-1960s Op Art was the accepted term. Even with its universal nonrepresentational heart, Op Art was a response to contemporary conditions of media flow. As the art historian John Lancaster put it, "In a peculiar way its optical patterns also reflect dynamic sensations evoked by the flickering imagery of cinema and television screens, whose moving forms can often be bemusing or even hypnotic to the viewer."[28]

We see a taste of similar perceptual and libidinal trickery in less esoteric cultural venues. Pacific International and William S. Edwards produced the second Psychorama film, *Date with Death* (1959). The exhibition gimmick Psychorama, first used in the feature *My World Dies Screaming* (1958), again consisted of words and images flashed subliminally at moments of dramatic or romantic tension. As the *Motion Picture Herald* favorably noted about its use, "exploitationwise, the undertaking has distinct showmanship possibilities."[29] *Date with Death* is a film noir about a drifter, played by Gerald Mohr, arriving in a gangster-ridden town, which he proceeds to clean up. The low-rent execution of this tale made certain that the Psychorama process, developed by the subliminal marketing company Precon, was the film's main, perhaps only, attraction. Indeed, the opening credits include the unique acknowledgement "Subliminal Communication by Precon," listing the company's founders

Title credit, *Date with Death*, 1959. Author's collection.

Precon credit, opening of *Date with Death*, 1959. Author's collection.

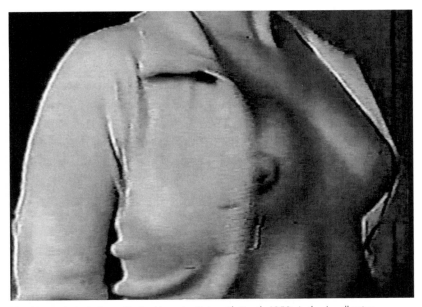

Unadvertised single frame flash of breasts, *Date with Death*, 1959. Author's collection.

Hal Becker as engineer and R. C. Corrigan as psychologist. The actual success of Psychorama in heightening emotional involvement, in this film and the earlier one, can safely be assumed to be nil. Yet the film-makers were bold enough to push the limits of censorship by including (at least) a single frame of the naked breasts of the comely shopkeeper's daughter when she is roughed up early in the film. This insert had nothing to do with the advertised attraction of Psychorama, a process that found itself in the dustbin of forgotten cinema technologies after the film's run. But it did signal a direction actively pursued for the rest of the next decade: the flash-edit as a way to tease audiences and censors alike.

The October 1962 issue of the men's magazine *Gent* includes a pictorial feature on a "new wave in titillation."[30] Using frame stills from several French films and a single Italian one, the photo essay highlights beautiful European stars and the occasional moment of flesh they bare on screen. The appealing sexual frankness of this new wave of cinema is an unsatisfying tease, however, because those explicit views pass by all too quickly in the theater. As the article explains, "the frames pass your eye so fast that you've usually had, at best, a subliminal titillation."[31] Freezing erotic images from *Violent Summer* (Valorio Zurlini, 1959), *Come Dance with Me* (Michel Boisrond, 1959), and *La Fille aux yeux d'or* (Jean-Gabriel Albicocco, 1961) on the pages of a magazine allows for an extended, concentrated gaze. Interestingly, the pictorial connects these adult art films with the advertising industry, claiming that "taking their cue from Mad Alley, foreign film producers are now packaging subliminal kicks!"[32] This is less a claim of cynicism on the part of European filmmakers, or even domestic distributors, than it is a confirmation that the rumors are true, so to speak, and yes, there is indeed a new world of eroticism opening up at the movie house.

In the late 1950s and early 1960s the flash-edit of some taboo material was a challenge to the censor, just as the industry self-regulation of the Hollywood Production Code was appreciably loosening and just before its wholesale revamping as an age-graded ratings system in 1966. The flash was also an invitation to the prurient viewer to pay attention, for there was the possible reward of a glimpse of something naughty or gruesome. The brilliant and resonant influence on popular cinema of the shower sequence in *Psycho* (Alfred Hitchcock, 1960) comes to mind. Its collision of shots and angles harkened back to Eisensteinian montage. It was also perfectly contemporary to the formal breaks with conventions of editing seen in the films of the Nouvelle Vague. To this we must add that in the American context the sequence capitalized on a popular awareness of and concern about the effects of swiftly moving images on cognition and emotion. Let us remember that the shower sequence included unusually graphic images of nudity and violence for mainstream cinema. With the momentary appearance of the curve of a breast and a naked torso, with the flash of a knife cutting skin and the splattering of blood, audiences were getting a glimpse of an adult cinema to come. This was the thrill of the potential of what one might see, and the anticipation about the next sight, which in many ways is a lasting feature of popular pleasure.

As the curiosity of Psychorama vanished, film efforts to push audiences to watch closely and think fast abounded. Mainstream cinema took the flashing image as a way to connote confusion, memories, and fragmented thinking, and to offer a sort of experiential sense of those states. *The Pawnbroker* (Sidney Lumet, 1964) uses extremely rapid inserts to signify the welling-up of terrible memories of a concentration camp for a Nazi holocaust survivor living in New York City. These flash-edited

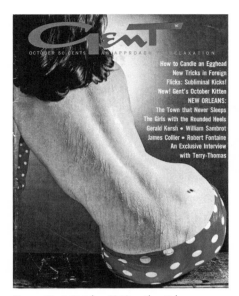

Cover, *Gent*, October 1962, with article on "Subliminal Kicks," Gent Publications, Inc.

"New Wave in Titillation," *Gent*, October 1962, Gent Publications, Inc.

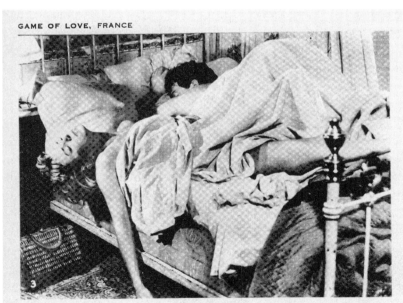

Mad Alley's subliminal kicks in art films, *Gent*, October 1962, Gent Publications, Inc.

flashbacks convey the uncontrollability of traumatic memory. The Puerto Rican prostitute who disrobes for the pawnbroker and the interrupting flashes of the concentration camp, among which are shots of a topless woman, were the first such images of nudity to be deemed acceptable by the Hollywood Production Code.

European cinema was opening a language of explicitness, but also one of filmic disjunction for American audiences. The jitteriness of *À Bout de souffle* (Jean-Luc Godard, 1960) makes visible the seams of film construction, using jump-cuts to highlight rather than conceal the connections between shots within scenes. The technique creates a feeling of acceleration, as though dramatic action were being bumped forward, like a needle skipping ahead on an LP. And it makes spectators attentive to the film material as well as to the proceedings. One must concentrate, and not blink, lest something be missed. By the time *Persona* (Ingmar Bergman, 1966) hit screens in the United States, non-narrative collage and disjointed editing were becoming familiar enough, if not exactly common. The images that open *Persona*, however brief, of animal evisceration, self-immolation, and crucifixion were most definitely unsettling. In a film about the limits of language and the impossibility of communicative connection between people, Bergman draws attention to the form of expression, presenting the film as a self-generative mechanism, guiding us through a veritable history of cinema in miniature at the film's opening, and then having the celluloid appear to break at a key dramatic moment later, halfway through the film. Even the title sequence suggests a negative photographic image, with dark lettering against a white background, percussive music, and rapid-fire cuts making a jarring assault on the viewer. The world of indescribable violence still enters the dreamlike calm of our characters' minimal sensory existence, both at a hospital and at a beach house, through radio and television broadcasts. Even the core betrayal in the film arrives by a personal correspondence read by a character who was to have simply mailed it. Bergman quite plainly proposes an experiential relation between the environment of media and the cruelty and distance between people.

The subliminal flash first alarmed the public as an advertising technique; soon the split-second insert was a way to depict the subliminal and the depths of consciousness. The flash-edit became a representational convention for the nearly imperceptible and for the general experience of media saturation. Television advertising too made use of rapid editing in a serious way, in contradistinction to the ironic use in the spot for Chevy in 1959 mentioned in chapter 6. A commercial, shown in 1966, alternates between color footage of a housewife getting into her Toyota and bursts of black-and-white footage of her in a racing car. The woman is Lee Breedlove, the women's speed record holder. This quasi-feminist confounding of conventional gender roles is arguably the first deliberate aesthetic use of integrated visual jolts in a television commercial, reportedly inspired by the flash-edits used in *The Pawnbroker*.[33]

Such instances were not below any threshold of perception, sensation, or awareness, but they worked to approach or suggest those thresholds. Some referred directly to the hidden, sneaky pleas of promotional agencies. The première episode of the television news magazine *Ad World* in 1958 used what it called subliminal messages for the Red Cross, lasting a fraction of a second, throughout the show. A review dismissed the program as "a thirty-minute promotional handout for the advertising business," and said that the "flashes were merely annoying and intrusive."[34] As the reviewer wrote, "The familiar Red Cross symbol was recognizable part of the time but the accompanying message was never clear."[35] In other words, at least part of the public service announcement was not subliminal at all but perfectly perceptible, if blinking fleetingly. Similarly, Norman McLaren scratched directly onto black film stock to create a public service announcement for Canada Post. *Mail Early for Christmas* (1959) is a forty-second short consisting of dancing, multicolored geometric shapes, accompanied by a musical fanfare reminiscent of vaudeville. Nearly unnoticed are the words of the title, scratched onto four frames and bursting momentarily on the screen to interrupt the dance.

This aesthetic dimension is worth emphasizing in that extraordinarily fast images were taken as subliminal nonetheless. The impossibility of signifying something that was imperceptible meant that in film, at least, the flash-edit was the representational stand-in for the subliminal. And this representational transference was part of a developing iconography of rapidity. This iconography did not necessarily attempt to produce the psychological effects of sub-threshold sensations, but was marshaled as a graphic and design choice to represent and allude to supposed psychological effects. A representational convention was in formation. Just as the double lines and puffs of smoke near the heels of a cartoon character signify movement, fleeting images evoke hidden desires, resurfacing memories, the unconscious, and confusion. And these qualities together offered another connotation: the contemporary. Blinking lights, flashing images, and graphic clutter were *now*.

Experimental filmmakers were especially active in deploying this vocabulary. The poetics of the flicker was one strategy to bring the mechanics of the cinema to the fore, explored by several, including Norman McLaren in his unreleased *The Flicker Film* (1960). A nearly perfect example of these poetics is Tony Conrad's notorious *The Flicker* (1965), whose elemental nonrepresentational construct was a hallucinogenic binary alteration between black-and-white frames of celluloid. It is possible to make people dizzy or induce fits with Conrad's spliced flickers of light, but most experimental uses of extremely rapid editing did not try to provoke such responses and instead explored the iconography and pace of consumer society. For instance, Arthur Lipsett's groundbreaking and celebrated *Very Nice, Very Nice* (1961) is a document of contemporary abundance and clutter employing extremely quick editing of images of city life, faces, posters, parades, and machinery, always rhythmically and often humorously. Robert Breer's *Fist Fight* (1964) consists of thirteen thousand single-frame images over its nine-minute length, and presents no illusion of movement, just assault. Peter Kubelka's *Schwechater* (1958), commissioned as a beer advertisement though never used as such, is an abstract film of abrupt edits and a loop of barely perceptible forms, most identifiably a woman drinking something, perhaps a pint of beer.

So routine was the barrage montage that versions could be found in such cheap-o films as *The Monitors* (Jack Shea, 1969), a sci-fi satire of a police state and a rebellious underground produced by Bell & Howell and Second City. Even the tag line on the poster creates a collage of contemporary issues: "If you don't like air pollution, war, body odor, hard pizza rolls, exercise, hairy musicians, sexy blonds, tooth decay, smiling heroes, population explosion . . . you'll love *The Monitors*." Certain sequences are punctuated with flashes of nudity and sexuality, and at one point a Lipsett-like commentary overtakes the narrative, complete with juxtaposed images of tanks, traffic signs, and urban decay.

These examples of editing bombardment had affiliations with psychedelia and displayed links between the Dream Machine, happenings, and the representation or attempted replication of psychedelic experiences in narrative cinema. Roger Corman's infamous art-cum-exploitation movie *The Trip* (1967) makes full use of the flash-edit to suggest destabilized perception. From the opening moment there are barely perceptible in-

Bursts of seemingly random images as social commentary, montage sequence in *The Monitors*, 1969.

serts of geometric and kaleidoscopic images. A full range of stroboscopes and light projections appears throughout, and the slim narrative frame of one person's experiences with LSD forms a backdrop to a dream-like pursuit by medieval midgets, random home intrusions, and body painting. Stylistic and narrative disruption is intended to capture the experience of an LSD trip, at least as the promotional material hyped it, opening minds to visions and memories. But in actuality the disruption is of realist film conventions. In *The Trip* the standards of continuity editing are the representational real not only of the spatial and temporal unity of the film world but of the spectator's consciousness; thus, flash-editing opens an alternative realm. *The Trip* is not alone in this reconfiguration. Any number of experimental films from the late 1950s onward promise, or at least dream of, taking their audiences on some sort of experiential trip. And so, true to an avant-gardist manifesto, the break with conventional narrative cinema and the exploration of alternative film languages is meant to be an expansion of the audience's minds as well.

Corman's film directly connects the manufacture of consciousness to advertising. Paul (Peter Fonda) is a director of television commercials, and the film opens with a sequence that is revealed shortly afterward to be a film shoot for a perfume ad. The trip in question is partly a drug adventure and partly an exploration of a personal crisis involving Paul's ex-wife and his own uncertainty about the world of advertising. In one extended segment Paul runs through the city, with streetlights and the flashes of advertising appeals mirroring or perhaps augmenting his confusion. Later there is a ten-minute sequence of flashing images, symbols, and flashbacks. At this point we are fully immersed in the internal voyage, away from the real and far from conventional representational sense.

A telling sequence involves Max (Dennis Hopper) interrogating Paul in such a way as to suggest that Paul is on trial. Paul sits in a chair wearing a metal cap and watching a series of screen images. He "can't see the message" that Max insists is right there in front of him. The images, flashing in a combination of slideshow and film or television montage, are scenes from Paul's life as well as commercials (presumably some of which he made). A question is posed: What word comes to mind when you think of television commercials? To this a disembodied female voice (possibly Paul's ex-wife) responds, "lies." Again, truth about the lies of the manufacture of commercial images peeks through, facilitated by pharmaceuticals and the right montage sequence. In this diegetic context the collage is not a convention in and of itself. It is the experimental bearer of a real that is masked by representational convention. When Paul returns from his "trip," the film closes with a long take as he moves from his bed to the beach outside his bedroom. A final freeze-frame, after a sharp zoom-in on the image of his face, cracks like a mirror, as Paul says he'll worry about tomorrow . . . tomorrow. Despite his cynical or fatalist tone, the conclusion foregrounds the artificiality of the screen image, literally breaking the window to the diegetic world into which the spectator is gazing. The full manipulative force here is not the constructed fiction but the artist's—in this instance Roger Corman's—claims to be able to reveal the simulated world and the lies of advertisers.

The poetics of the flashing, flickering image settled into the barrage montage sequence *and* remained a touchstone for pushing experiential limits by media artists. "Expanded cinema," as deftly elaborated by Gene Youngblood in his book from 1970, investigates the material conditions of the illusion of movement and the perceptual demands on viewers, moving cinema beyond a standardized apparatus to a multimedia form. While this aesthetic tack is especially associated with the 1960s, at the time it connoted artfulness, or simply youthful artiness. The Monkees' feature film *Head* (Bob Rafelson, 1968) shows how this artiness could dominate even a vehicle for a teen pop act. Far beyond the frantic pace of the Beatles' *A Hard Day's Night* (Richard Lester, 1964), *Head* is on the one hand a cut-up film and a mess of a movie, and on the other hand a perfectly appropriate rendition of a psychedelic backstage musical (or, more accurately, backlot musical). It is a mix of star cameos, Vietnam war footage, and old film clips, with episodic skits that plunder a variety of Hollywood genres, presenting a roughly anti-commercial, antiwar theme. The jokes frequently turn inward, scathingly commenting on the band's own manufactured status: "Well, if it isn't God's gift to the eight-year-old," says a sarcastic waitress (played by a cross-dressing T. C. Jones). The theme of artificiality extends to *Head*'s materialist film aesthetic, which includes distorted sound, approximate framing, and blurred focus, as well as continual talk about the film, its construction, and the potential audience. And with the speed of the editing, inserts, and montage, *Head* announces its pretensions to serious social critique.

In a way cinema, as a mechanism trafficking in the arrival and departure of images, has long explored sensory bounty. In a manner consistent

Paul (Peter Fonda) tripping on the absurdities of billboard advertising during a rapidly cut montage sequence in *The Trip*, 1967.

with Tom Gunning's classic argument about early cinema's "attractions," the cinematic flow of images has exerted an appeal partly by facilitating an encounter with the shock of modern visual trauma.[36] The formal techniques of producing visual trauma in the 1960s consisted of changing angles, jumping from close-up to medium shot to extreme close-up, and interposing jarring inserts. Barrage montages were found in the work of lesser experimental filmmakers and of film school novices. The sequences, whether in *Very Nice, Very Nice* or *The Monitors*, are noticeably invested in images of images—marquees, film clips, advertisements, posters, magazine covers, billboards, and television ads. The subject matter included tanks, bombs, corpses, stars, ghettos, ruins, young women, and parades. The flood of images, especially grave and violent ones, must add up to profundity, right? Perhaps not. Most assuredly, though, what we had was the iconography of rapidity, that is, imagistic multitudes and their fleeting appearance. Contemplation, if there was any, focused on the tempo of the sequence rather than individual images. The semiotic weight of each image was leveled out, perhaps trivialized as disposable, undifferentiated, and ordinary. The continuous pace suggested a lulling surrender to the flow of images, or a speeding-up to the trance-inducing nonrepresentational pace realized most completely by Conrad's *The Flicker*.

The simultaneous arrival of information—the speedy overlay of signs—was precisely what McLuhan identified as emblematic of our shift to acoustic culture. In this state, he thought, images and data arrived like music, from everywhere, with multiple registers, countermelodies, and ornamentation. He wrote of the characteristics of a waning linear, literate society and the rise of a post-literate, nonlinear world—his global village—taking television as especially characteristic of the time. McLuhan is a controversial figure, politically conservative and technologically deterministic. Yet his proposal is an inventive and prescient reorientation of the meaning of total media environments, one symptomatic of a context that is trying to represent the speed and disorientation it is experiencing. To that end, in the late 1960s McLuhan expanded on the typographical play of *The Mechanical Bride* (1951) in collaborative works with designers. With Quentin Fiore, *The Medium Is the Massage: An Inventory of Effects* (1967) emphasized images breaking up text or taking over entire pages, with short accompanying statements from McLuhan, selected by Jerome Agel.[37] The images dominated and worked as counterpoints to commentary, which consisted of a few paragraphs, slogans, and photo

BLSS
SS BL
SS

MADISON AVE

FOR RESTORING THE
maGical ART
OF THE
(AVEMEN
TO
SUBURBIA

Graphic play and clutter: Marshall McLuhan, *Counterblast*, designed by Harley Parker, 1969. Courtesy of Estates of Marshall McLuhan and Harley Parker.

captions. The next photographic essay collaboration was *War and Peace in the Global Village* (1968), for which McLuhan offered a more substantial essay, and in which the photos performed more of an illustrative function than in the previous book.[38] *Counterblast* (1969) was a collaboration with the designer Harley Parker, exploring typographical visual space.[39] A mélange of fonts and font sizes with flashes of color, the book, like the two previous ones, presented a formal breakdown of linear argument and a collage of aphoristic impressions of media change, drawing inspiration from Wyndham Lewis's short-lived experimental journal *Blast* (1914). *Through the Vanishing Point (1968)* and *Culture Is Our Business* (1970) push McLuhan's role as author from composer of original ideas to curator of quotations.[40] The busy presentational style of these works encourages browsing, glancing, and nonsequential reading. It also tries to reproduce the sensation of full environmental message sources, with all print elements varying—from placement on the page and placement in relation to image, to font type and size, to use of collage effects—and hence made presumably significant, in some way communicating something more than the meaning of the words alone. These books explored the mechanics of media speed and perceptual disorientation. In them we witness the emergence of an aesthetic of covert meanings, a way to connote a technologically driven state of multiple layers of signification. As McLuhan commented, "Faced with information overload, we have no alternative but pattern-recognition."[41]

With these illustrations and textual examples we are well beyond the specific psychological effects of sub-threshold exposures. These artworks—*Very Nice, Very Nice, Head, Counterblast*, and so on—were about the speedy and disorienting overlay of images and texts as a legible product of the decade following the subliminal controversy. Graphic play in print, and dazzling montage in film, signaled semiotic complexity, ideological intent, and information overload. They were also an attempt to address the velocity of these things. Remember, this was one of the ways the subliminal was codified in periodical press reports of 1957–58—as textual play with embedded inserts of notably different fonts. And in this there was a triple conceptual intersection: the signification of image and textual abundance, the exploration of the experience of perceptual limits, and the circulation of a popular idea about media effects, especially as implicated in commercial pursuits. The plenitude of light and sound, circulated by a newly intensified multimedia environment, was both a symptom of contemporary alienation and a way to navigate that same inhumanity.

Critical Reasoning
in a Cluttered Age

CHAPTER NINE

After years of shying away from the topic, James M. Vicary agreed to be interviewed for *Advertising Age* in June 1962 about the subliminal controversy. However, once the interview had been conducted he had second thoughts about how it might affect his employability, with the firm Dun and Bradstreet interested in engaging him at the time. He remained eager to prove himself an innovative market researcher, and fought against his popular and professional reputation as a psychic huckster. Still, he felt that vitriol from all sides had tainted him. Vicary fretted enough about this to persuade the interviewer, Fred Danzig, to withhold the article's publication until September, when it eventually appeared on the fifth anniversary of Subliminal Projection's original press conference on subliminal advertising and on the occasion of Vicary's appointment as director of survey research for Dun and Bradstreet.[1] In the interview Vicary expressed delight about leaving the controversy behind, and about no longer being "Mr. Subliminal." This was fruitlessly optimistic on his part. He would always be Mr. Subliminal.

Speaking to Danzig, Vicary intimated that though tests had been done in Fort Lee, Subliminal Projections "hadn't done any research, except what was needed for filing a patent,"[2] leading one to wonder whether the 45,699 research subjects whom Vicary once claimed to have studied ever existed, or whether the figure was but a wild estimate of attendance at the Fort Lee Theater. Vicary's tone is difficult to interpret. He expressed regret about his role in the subliminal uproar, but some statements made him sound insincere. He seemed surprised that critics related his ideas about advertising to Vance Packard's *The Hidden Persuaders*, when in fact he had known about the book and its direct references to his various research projects before he planned the original press conference. It was already an impressive bestseller and Vicary even discussed subliminal advertising in relation to Packard's arguments at that first media event. Vicary downplayed his actions as "high jinks" that he "didn't want to have anything to do with" and as "a big joke," even though at the time he was serious enough to attract investors, incorporate a firm, and seek patent protection.[3] Further, far from being an anomaly in his career, Vicary's interest in tachistoscopic influence was consistent with his earlier empirical physiological marketing research on word associations. Even in this relatively brief printed interview he shifted opinions about his intentions. In revisiting five-year-old events, he defended subliminal advertising as "innocent." Vicary said, "I really thought it would help increase the commercial time for broadcast media,"[4] which suggested in the very least that he did take the idea seriously on some level and that it was not "a big joke." Despite this confused attempt to reexamine the issue, *Advertising Age* was "upset" by Vicary's cavalier attitude about the controversy he sparked, and published an editorial to that effect.[5] And two decades later the magazine returned to the topic to remind readers of what they called Vicary's con in fabricating evidence.[6]

In an effort to move beyond the anger, Vicary had incorporated another business concern in the fall of 1959. Continuing his interest in word associations and the naming of products and companies, he established Trademark Management Institute (TMI), owned and operated by him alone. Aside from the testing and development of trademarks, TMI offered more inventive services. To assist in brainstorming for brand and company names, Vicary developed a Trademark Sliderule that could easily combine a range of single- and double-syllable words, with pronunciations indicated. He also proposed to focus on slang, compiling a list of taboo words and connotations to alert trademark developers of inadvertently offensive selections.[7] Noting the growing interest in global markets, Vicary ambitiously proposed to compile lists for languages other than English as well, to be presented in the form of a newsletter to subscribers that would inform business executives of, for instance, the Danish words for "nipples," "fart," and "unpleasant old woman."[8] Some complications ensued in relation to this work, with customs agents seizing what they saw as obscene material that Vicary had tried to bring into the country, supposedly for this new research venture.[9]

By 1962 Vicary had, in his words, a "deliberate policy" of disassociating himself from subliminal advertising.[10] While expecting TMI to soar, Vicary began to do something he had avoided doing as a self-employed businessman: he took a series of jobs with big companies. He hoped that Dun and Bradstreet would buy TMI, but it did not.[11] Hired at McGraw-Hill in September 1964 to be part of its research department, he lasted only eight months, the official reason for termination being "lack of qualifications for the job."[12] After moving to California in the late summer of 1966, then back east to Massachusetts a year later, he died in 1977.[13]

Though Vicary may have wished to leave behind the whole Fort Lee episode, others did not. Soon after Vicary's interview appeared, one of his chief competitors in the subliminal market, Precon, received a patent for its subliminal projector, intended for entertainment, psychotherapy, and educational uses.[14] The company continued product development over the decades and developed a line of audio tapes with subliminal messages in the 1970s. It gained special attention for a "black box" device, which promised to emit inaudible but emotionally effective sounds intended for use by retailers.

In the end, subliminal influence is fixed as part of our era and as a command metaphor for powerful media effects. Stuart Ewen commented that the mythology "verbalizes the dissatisfaction that flows in a world where image-management and spin-doctoring have become social norms. To some extent, the folklore of subliminal advertising that runs—mostly by word of mouth—through the byways of American culture is an example of the 'consumer resistance' that advertisers, in their marketing plans, are perpetually attempting to 'break through.'"[15] In other words, the folkloric status of the "subliminal" holds a set of ideas that feeds suspicions that there is more going on than meets the eye. Most significantly, with the subliminal thesis and the attendant speculations about mass brainwashing, a resonant way to understand ideological control is available to a wide population. It was, and is, *practical consciousness about false consciousness*. The notion of subliminal communication thins out a thick knot of media information. It effectively squeezes the social world into root messages of consumption (eat, drink, buy) and civic duty (fight polio, donate blood). After all, the presumptions about unconscious mechanisms reading and responding to statements such as these are grounded in an extraordinary faith in the power of the written word and the rush of images. That faith puts forward a seemingly hyper-rhetorical belief that textual assertions could effectuate some level of individual and perhaps social change. Friedrich Kittler noted this, positing that the tachistoscope marked "probably the first time that people in a writing culture were reduced to the naked recognition of signs."[16]

A chorus of voices warned about the dangers implicit in the mechanization of minds. To some, the coming automatization of human thought was yet another ethical failing of the modern world. Arthur Koestler's *The Ghost in the Machine* attacked the ideas of behaviorists and the "poverty of psychology" for contributing to the dehumanization of contemporary society.[17] C. Wright Mills worried about the rise of the Cheerful Robot, that compliant and alienated citizen of postmodernity produced by the ultimate failure of modern society—rationality without reason.[18] These critics cited a devotion to the logic of scientific progress, and the pursuit of efficiency through technological means, as catalysts for the apparent loss of human willfulness and independence of thought.

Theodor Adorno had already been warning that conditions were ripe for the nurture of authoritarian irrationality. In his study of newspaper astrology columns he concluded that their audiences displayed a weak and regressive ego, and that their sense of agency was reduced to the appearance of action. These readers were symptomatic of an entire population given over to a closed system of fatalism and conformity. They operated with pseudo-rationality, that "twilight zone between reason and unconscious urges."[19] Adorno's warning about authoritarian irrationality included details about the psychological reassurances offered by totalizing and closed systems of understanding the world: "Within the pattern of modern mass delusions, the idea of conspiracies is always present—an idea doubtlessly of a protective nature." He continued, missing an opportunity for self-reflection, "Those who persistently blame others for indulging in conspiracies have a strong tendency to engage in plots themselves."[20] Moreover, Adorno worried about the pseudo-individuals he observed who saw the world "more as a 'system' than ever before, covered by an all-comprising net of organization with no loopholes where the individual could 'hide' in face of the ever-present demands and tests of a society ruled by a hierarchical business set-up and coming pretty close to what we called '*verwaltete Welt*', a world caught by administration."[21] The resulting paranoid and doomed perspective can also be seen in the popularity of the subliminal thesis, which similarly offered no loopholes and no hiding places in its strongest manifestations. Following Adorno, the very idea of a total persuasive unconscious effect—regardless of whether there was an *actual* effect—readied people for manipulation and pointed to the ever-present prospect for fascism that existed in advanced capitalism. In one respect the subliminal thesis worked as a universal automatic critique, a one-dimensional criticality for a complex system of media influences.

Media industries had created what appeared to be a total environment of cultural materials. The "graphic revolution," which Daniel Boorstin said characterized the image and media saturation of everyday life from the mid-nineteenth century onward, helped lead us into a world of artificiality and pseudo-events. In *The Image*, Boorstin blamed advertising and consumerism for the creation of a semi-hypnotized population that was nonetheless culpable, because "each of us individually provides the market and the demand for the illusions which flood our experience."[22] He saw people guided by "extravagant expectations" for the world and their power to affect it, and believed that the production of illusions to feed those expectations had "become the business of America."[23] With direct reference to the hidden persuader critic Vance Packard, Boorstin claimed that advertising was coming to rely on the hypnotic power of images rather than rhetorical persuasiveness. Significantly, he pushed his argument beyond the cynicism of a single industry to point to the density and pace of media texts. He referred to the technological ability to produce an unprecedented multiplication of images, creating the experience of living amid a veritable flood, as he described it.

The very qualities of a set of conditions that came to be called the information or knowledge society were beginning to settle. Boorstin in particular was responding to a new way to conceptualize a prominent business and educational challenge: the information explosion. One of the earliest uses of this phrase was as the title of an advertising supplement by IBM in the *New York Times* in April 1961. Including short essays on computers, mathematics, and a humanistic plea from Arnold Toynbee, the insert began with a declaration, from IBM's president Thomas J. Watson Jr., that communication problems were the central concern of the era: "There never has been a time when more information was available to more people than at the beginning of this promising decade. Not only are more people doing more things that are worth knowing about, but the means for communicating information have never been so effective and far reaching as they are today. With radio and television, jet travel, countless libraries, and a highly articulate press, it is a remote and highly insulated individual who is not exposed to immense quantities of information."[24] Conditions, it seemed, were such that the flood of materials, and the demand to process them swiftly, could be managed with the assistance of IBM's new products.

Here, on the threshold of the computer revolution, the advertisement characterized the dawning age as a global one, with an image of a woman sorting computer cards in Thailand and a map of IBM's international operations. The description of this global computer experience would not be out of place in more recent advertisements by the likes of Apple and Cisco Systems: "In Bolzano, Italy, a restaurateur uses punched cards to keep track of the spaghetti for several restaurants. A fruit exporter in the same town uses punched cards to prevent overstocking of apples. In Brazil they use IBM equipment to compute statistics on coffee crops and exports. In England, IBM equipment helps in educating new drivers. The University of Vienna has used an IBM computer to create a whole new traffic pattern for the city. For Canada, IBM has developed special census equipment."[25] The parallels set up between local character (spaghetti and coffee), modern bureaucratic demands (traffic patterns and census taking), and global business enterprise (IBM) took the condition of "information explosion" from a threat to human values to a recipe for international connections and corporate success.

Information explosion and overload were concepts that circulated a sense of social and technological upheaval. In a magazine advertisement from 1964, *Fortune* promises to help orient the regular subscriber immersed in this upheaval, and indeed appeals to an already engaged reader who knows "what more than half of these words mean." First, though, the ad establishes the confusion brought on by the "information explosion." The ad challenges the reader to be conversant with many new economic, scientific, and technological terms: data bank, software, silicon, solid state, etc. But there is an additional urgency conveyed. The words are off-kilter and "explode" outward. More than an expansion of word power, the ad confronts the reader with the "radical change" that has produced this vortex of concepts. Non-regimented, non-linear, non-justified type—examples

THE INFORMATION EXPLOSION

If you know what more than half of these
words mean, you should be a FORTUNE reader now,
in this era of radical change

Information explosion as typographical clutter: newspaper ad for *Fortune*, 1964.
Author's collection.

of which include the illustration that introduces Vicary's article on brand names (page 97) as well as many of McLuhan's design collaborations (page 225)—visualized what we call the information age, highlighting an anxiety about the confusion it would produce even as it signaled excitement and opportunity. This style is still with us, having been conventionalized as the "word cloud," especially as incorporated into website interfaces. The difference between the word cloud and these earlier graphic examples is that the explosion of non-linear type now offers a hyperlink and the presumption of order and control in the information society.

Media clutter was a major part of the texture—or what Raymond Williams would call the "structure of feeling"—of the late 1950s and 1960s.

The speed, intricacy, and density of the media environment made interpretive capacities, assisted by new technologies, a matter of survival as much as a concern about totalitarian rule. In this respect, the rise of the vernacular critique of the subliminal is a symptom of this experience of total media immersion. The subliminal is a lasting idea about the information society, itself an interpretive apparatus for accumulating ideas about "future shock," to use Alvin Toffler's soon-to-be popular phrase describing the disorienting experience of living with the onslaught of new technology.[26]

The legacy of that period's influence on the knowledge society is evident decades later, with attendant worries about the diminishing returns of informational abundance. In the mid-1980s Orrin Klapp linked irrationality to information overload. The habitual condition of non-contemplation, effectively a gap between the signs in one's sensory field and an ability to interpret them adequately, led to "a flood of cultic movements, within and outside conventional churches, groping for meaning, as seekers shop from guru to guru for something to believe in or a glimpse of reality beyond ordinary consciousness. Nor can one ignore millions of people turning to magic, horoscopes, divination, I Ching, and so on for interpretation of what is happening or about to happen. In this crisis of meaning, the contemporary rush to personal computers seems a last desperate attempt to master the tidal wave of incoming information."[27] Astrology, magic, personal computers, and subliminal communication: an odd assortment of coping mechanisms, but all were seen as sharing a root condition, namely the perceptual and rational limitations engendered by a saturation of texts and materials.

Questions about information abundance are as prominent a language of our world as ever. On the cusp of the Internet age, Richard Saul Wurman offered help to a new condition that was debilitating businessmen—"information anxiety." In Information Anxiety (1990), divided into easy-to-read sections decorated with pithy quotes, notable trivia, illustrations, and font-play that mimicked McLuhan's typographical design experiments, the author clearly did not want to contribute further to that anxiety. He included a list of symptoms for a reader's self-diagnosis, with a check box beside each to facilitate a tally. Symptoms included "chronically talking about not keeping up with what's going on around you," "feeling guilty about that ever-higher stack of periodicals waiting to be read," "nodding your head knowingly when someone mentions a book, an artist, or a news story that you have actually never heard of before," and "feeling depressed because you don't know what all the buttons are for on your vcr."[28] Being lost in a sea of data might mean lost professional status, but it was also presented as a source of embarrassment about not being current with media and technology.

The experience addressed by Wurman mirrors current dominant sensibilities. Our context of the "googlization" of everything written, photographed, recorded, and mapped is best seen as a logical extension of the last few decades of abundance and clutter. And the lack of confidence in our human ability to handle and navigate the resulting heap of textual materials is a relatively stable condition of contemporary life. Malcolm Gladwell's *The Tipping Point: How Little Things Can Make a Big Difference* (2000) describes the "Stickiness Factor" to explain how certain ideas catch on and others do not. In many ways it is the "stickiness" of the subliminal thesis that has been the subject of this book. But for Gladwell, "stickiness" becomes an ever more potent challenge in light of what the advertising business sees as "this surfeit of information that is called the 'clutter' problem."[29] Instead, I maintain that the subliminal thesis is precisely, and simultaneously, a product of, and a balm for, the surfeit of information. Gladwell's follow-up book, *Blink: The Power of Thinking without Thinking* (2007), links the necessity of speedy, gut-level, nearly unconscious decision making as not only a path to making accurate assessments and choices but a survival strategy for the demands of our era. Explaining the success of this book in an afterword to the paperback edition, Gladwell writes, "We live in a world saturated with information. We have virtually unlimited amounts of data at our fingertips at all times, and we're well versed in the arguments about the dangers of not knowing enough and not doing our homework. But what I have sensed is an enormous frustration with the unexpected costs of knowing too much, of being inundated with information. We have come to confuse information with understanding."[30] Given how long commentators have been making similar claims, I am not convinced about the uniqueness of our situation. Wider access to textual materials in a range of forms might confront more people with the complications and difficulties of judgment. And increasing uncertainties in job markets, and the carving away of basic labor rights, have put more pressure on people to maintain their competitiveness individually. But posing "knowing too much" as a cost or hazard seems antidemocratic in the extreme. However, Gladwell's two enormously successful bestsellers suggest an enduring popular faith in the truth-value of a strain of social psychology, and they quite expertly tap into anxiousness about sensory and informational clutter, as well as a desire to navigate it, or at least handle it better than one's competition.

This book has tried to show that the movement of the subliminal thesis into a lasting position as a popular media critique cannot be dismissed as the product of Cold War paranoia or the province of the simpleton. Its popular life began at the dawn of the information age, an age when concerns about new media and the associated clutter were to become a central topic. The discernment of information from noise, the boundary between the real and the fabricated, and the prospects for authentic individual willfulness, contra a totalitarian drift, became focal points for assessing the quality of life offered up by the world of media. The subliminal thesis continues to help specify contemporary media experience as overwhelming and chaotic. It has made available a framework that proposes the influence of fleeting images on the unconscious. With it, an everyday understanding of the workings of the unconscious was fed through worries about the cost of affluence and conformity, about the boundaries of commercial culture, about media representation, and about social control. It was equally a site at which the place of technology in our lives was being assessed and sorted through, or more appropriately, the imperative of new technology as a mechanism of social progress was being advocated, disseminated, and critiqued. Thus the irrational dimension preyed upon by supposed subliminal influences was to be fortified by an amplification of a multimedia educational environment.

In closing, I want to clarify that the late 1950s and early 1960s were not the only years when art and culture confronted conditions of speed and fragmentation. Nor do I say that the critics of new media and the aesthetics of the 1960s owe their innovations to an advertising controversy. I do contend that the subliminal debate sparked by Vicary and his entrepreneurial ambitions was a major event in the conjoining of a set of presumptions and anxieties about media, the unconscious, social and technological change, and the condition of textual clutter. It was one significant contribution to the conditions that would come to characterize the information society of the 1960s, and it was a vehicle through which a popular understanding about those conditions circulated. As Adorno commented, "Astrology, just as other irrational creeds such as racism, provides a short cut by bringing the complex to a handy formula and offering at the same time the pleasant gratification that he who feels to be excluded from educational privileges nevertheless belongs to the minority of those who are 'in the know.'"[31] Like Adorno's astrology, the subliminal thesis is a system of knowledge that works in everyday life, a form of expression of intellect that is deeply suspicious, conceptually abstract, though totalizing and understandable. In a comparable fashion, the subliminal thesis can be a form of semi-erudition. Like astrology, it is a "middle way between realism and paranoid fantasies."[32]

Though I have focused on the early years of this vernacular media critique, commentators continue to describe barely visible flashes as subliminal. And controversy is rekindled with regularity. In the fall of 1973 the FCC received complaints about commercials for a toy called Hüsker Dü, which had used quick flashes of "get it."[33] In 1974 the FCC summarized its stance, saying that though subliminal advertising did not violate any official sanction, it was not in the public interest: "Whether effective or not, such broadcasts clearly are intended to be deceptive."[34] In 1975 the Canadian Radio and Television-Telecommunication Council held hearings on subliminal advertising on television after a ban was proposed. The Canadian Advertising Advisory Board worried that the definition of subliminal was too broad, potentially encompassing any sound or image of "very brief duration," including background music.[35] Kansas police in Wichita tried to catch the so-called BTK serial killer with near subliminal flashes of "call the chief" in television news reports, presuming that the perpetrator would be watching and would find the messages too personal and mysterious to ignore. He wasn't and didn't. And in 1984 a Congressional subcommittee revisited the issue, with Precon's founder Hal Becker appearing to demonstrate his products.[36] The future head of the Motion Picture Association of America, Dan Glickman, chaired the subcommittee. The recorded proceedings comment heavily on the sci-fi aspect of subliminal suggestion, though participants agreed it was still necessary to consider, especially because it might have implications for computer security. The FCC's stance remained the same, reaffirming its jurisdiction to regulate such broadcasting transmissions and the view that they were tantamount to deception, regardless of effectiveness. Perhaps priming him for the accusations that he would levy against Bush during his presidential run sixteen years later (see chapter 1), the subcommittee included a young congressman from Tennessee, Al Gore.

Does the subliminal thesis serve to trivialize critiques of image culture, placing valid concerns in the same category as alien abductors and Elvis spotters? At times, yes. Yet in other moments, it has served to inspire. Playing with an interest in subliminal messages, the amateur website www.starterupsteve.com promises to demonstrate the existence of hidden appeals. The site prompts the visitor to look closely at the images on the screen, and after a few seconds an embedded or concealed icon appears. Several images are from Key's *Subliminal Seduction*, including the magazine ads with orgies in the ice cubes. The visitor also sees more conventional trompe-l'oeil images commonly found in psychology textbooks, such as a drawing of a young beauty who becomes an old woman when inverted. Suddenly, jarringly, the screen presents a blast of horrific images — corpses, devils, monsters — all assaulting the visitor, accompanied by a piercing screech, followed by an insulting notice questioning how the visitor could be so stupid as to believe in such a ridiculous idea as subliminal messages. It is impossible not to leap back from the computer when first surprised by this with one's heart racing and pride deflated, after being taken by such an obvious prank. I know this from experience.

But there is something quite wonderful about the impulse on which this site bases its joke: the desire to look closely. The aesthetic of flicker is a warning about the fearsome abundance of images, choosing to head into the maelstrom like Poe's drowning sailor. But there is also a call to hermeneutic action being sounded, a plea for vigilance in meaning. The pledge is that close attention to the world of signs will lead to a revelation of some sort. By being scavengers of interpretive surfaces, we will see something significant and meaningful from below come into view. Such an augmentation of the singular and immediately legible meanings of signs is not, in and of itself, a foreclosure of analysis. It is a symptom of the rich, polyvocal dialogue with the image-world that we initiate daily. The desire to look closely, to examine, and to unearth reveals a faith in interpretation, even if it is a socio-psychological reverie of perfect correspondence between meaning and effect. Here is language in action, here are minds engaged with texts, and here are individuals sharing their skepticism about their environment. Even though there is an overvaluation of the presumption of effect, and an over-localization of power into single images, the subliminal thesis has become a fundamental preparatory vehicle for the necessary condition of perpetual vigilance of our media culture. This is the case, even if the last word is, simply, "boo."

Notes

Black Magic on Mars

1. Cantril with Gaudet and Herzog, *The Invasion from Mars*, 3.
2. Cf. Gary, *The Nervous Liberals*, and Glander, *Origins of Mass Communications Research*. Lazarsfeld settled at Columbia University with the PRRP in 1939, renaming it the Bureau of Applied Social Research. The Rockefeller Foundation's communication and culture work in the 1930s was capped by the policy document "Research in Mass Communication," which outlined the range of research domains that needed to be developed to provide information vital to the new communication-rich context. Addressing a brain trust of leading academics, including Harold Lasswell, Charles Seipman, Robert Lynd, Donald Slesinger, and Paul Lazarsfeld, the policy document recorded the essential questions of mass communication research: who says what to whom, with what goals, and to what effect.
3. Buxton and Acland, "Interview with Dr. Frank N. Stanton."
4. Cantril with Gaudet and Herzog, *The Invasion from Mars*, 60.
5. Ibid., 147.
6. Ibid., 189.
7. Ibid., 158.
8. Ibid., 158.
9. Ibid., 204.
10. Ibid., 204.
11. Flournoy, *From India to the Planet Mars*.
12. Cantril with Gaudet and Herzog, *The Invasion from Mars*, 161.
13. Ibid., 57–58.
14. Ibid., 214.
15. During, *Modern Enchantments*, 50.
16. Cantril with Gaudet and Herzog, *The Invasion from Mars*, 214.

17. Ibid., 98–100.

18. Le Bon, *The Crowd*.

19. Sconce, *Haunted Media*, 110–11. Sconce points out that most of the contemporary media responses immediately following the broadcast addressed media power, with few covering the panic itself. He adds that what Cantril included were people retrospectively claiming to have been frightened. Moreover, Sconce argues that the event coincided with the rise of broadcast networks and the conventionalizing of broadcast codes, seeing it as a parable about "invading" broadcasters and national networks. Ibid., 115–16.

20. Fearing, *Clark Gifford's Body*, 64.

21. "That Old Black Magic."

22. "$250,000 Ad Budget for 'Black Magic,'" *Motion Picture Daily*, 7 June 1949, *Black Magic* clippings file, Margaret Herrick Library, Academy of Motion Picture Arts and Sciences.

23. "Orson Welles Pulls Mass Hypnosis Act on Us All," *Los Angeles Times*, 19 August 1949, *Black Magic* clippings file, Margaret Herrick Library, Academy of Motion Picture Arts and Sciences.

Chapter 1: Subliminal Communication

1. Jamieson, *Dirty Politics*, 97–100.

2. *Inside Politics*, CNN, 11 September 2000.

3. *NBC Nightly News*, 11 September 2000.

4. "Campaign Laugh Track."

5. "Agency Investigates 'Rats' Ad"; "No Penalty for Stations that Showed 'Rats' Ad."

6. "Aclara Sabritas spot sobre elecciones," *¡Ehui!*, 1 November 2006, www.ehui.com.

7. Zanot, Pincus, and Lamp, "Public Perceptions of Subliminal Advertising."

8. Rogers and Seiler, "The Answer Is No," 36.

9. Fernald and Fernald, *Introduction to Psychology*, 601.

10. Reichert, *The Erotic History of Advertising*, 40.

11. Ewen, *All Consuming Images*, 48, 51.

12. Reeves and Nass, *The Media Equation*.

13. Twitchell, *Adcult USA*, 116.

14. Messaris, *Visual Persuasion*, 65–89.

15. Sutherland, *Advertising and the Mind of the Consumer*, 4.

16. Ibid., 27.

17. Ibid., 30.

18. Cook, "Lurking behind the Ice Cubes," 7.

19. Ibid., 8.

20. Moore, "Subliminal Advertising."

21. Hawkins, "The Effects of Subliminal Stimulation on Drive Level and Brand Preference."

22. Beatty and Hawkins, "Subliminal Stimulation."

23. Rose, "Motivation Research and Subliminal Advertising," 281.

24. Edwards, "Subliminal Tachistoscopic Perception as a Function of Threshold Method."

25. Bevan, "Subliminal Stimulation," 84.

26. Rees, "On the Terms 'Subliminal Perception' and 'Subception.'"

27. Dixon, *Subliminal Perception*; see also his revised version of that book, *Preconscious Processing*.

28. "The New Charm of Black."

29. Rogers and Seiler, "The Answer Is No"; Haberstroh, *Ice Cube Sex*, 39–52.

30. Rogers and Seiler, "The Answer Is No," 44.

31. Krajick, "Sound Too Good to Be True?"

32. Suzuki, *Ring*.

33. Koontz, *Night Chills*.

34. Ibid., 69.

35. Roszak, *Flicker*.

36. Robbins, *Still Life with Woodpecker*.

37. Stam, Burgoyne, and Flitterman-Lewis, *New Vocabularies in Film Semiotics*, 26.

38. Kellner, *Media Culture*, 97.

39. Bordwell, *The Way Hollywood Tells It*, 44.

40. Miller, "Hollywood the Ad."

41. James, *The Essential Writings*, 257.

42. Lazarsfeld and Merton, "Mass Communication, Popular Taste and Organized Social Action"; Lerner, *Sykewar*.

43. I am appropriating the phrase "command metaphor" from Cunningham, *Framing Culture*. In his usage, Cunningham critiqued the prominence of resistance as a "command metaphor" for cultural studies (9).

44. McRobbie, "The Moral Panic in the Age of the Postmodern Mass Media," *Postmodernism and Popular Culture*, 198–219.

45. Gladwell, *The Tipping Point*.

46. Gramsci, "The Intellectuals," *Selections from the Prison Notebooks*, 9.

47. Williams, *Marxism and Literature*, 132.

48. Klapp, *Overload and Boredom*, 97.

49. A case in point is Bullock, *The Secret Sales Pitch*.

50. Haberstroh, *Ice Cube Sex*, 11.

51. Key, *Subliminal Ad-ventures in Erotic Art*.

52. Key, *Subliminal Seduction*, 187.

53. Ibid., 199; and McLuhan, *Letters of Marshall McLuhan*, editors' footnote on 501.

54. Key, *Subliminal Seduction*, 24.

55. Key, "Watch the Background, Not the Figure," 189–90.

56. Ibid., 189–94.

57. McLuhan, *Letters of Marshall McLuhan*, 507.

58. McLuhan, *The Mechanical Bride*, v.

59. Ibid., 93.

60. Ibid., 97.

61. Fond as he was of jokes, McLuhan later recounted the story of the Scotsman who,

upon arriving at the scene of a terrible car accident, asks a victim whether the insurance agents had been by yet. When the unfortunate wounded soul answers in the negative, the Scot says, "Do you mind if I lay down next to you?" This bears some resemblance to the Poe tale, in which one seeks advantage not by struggling, resisting, or helping others but by cynically cooperating with the conditions one discovers. McLuhan, *Letters of Marshall McLuhan*, 423.

62. Marshall McLuhan, "Media Ad-vice: An Introduction," *Subliminal Seduction*, by Key, vii.

63. McLuhan, *Letters of Marshall McLuhan*, 501. D. Carleton Williams had been an associate editor of *Explorations* when he was at the University of Toronto with McLuhan. In 1974, when the letter was sent, Williams was president of the University of Western Ontario, which would soon be dismissing the tenured Wilson Bryan Key.

64. McLuhan, "Media Ad-vice," vii.

65. Ibid., viii.

66. Ibid., ix.

67. Ibid.

68. Ibid., x, xii.

69. Ibid., xii.

70. Ibid., xvi–xvii.

71. Ibid., xviii.

72. Ibid.

73. Key, "'Cloze Procedure.'"

74. Key, *Media Sexploitation*.

75. Key, *The Clam-Plate Orgy*; Key, *The Age of Manipulation*.

76. Tankard, "Whose Seduction?," 221.

77. Ibid., 222.

78. Baldwin, "Review: N. F. Dixon's *Subliminal Perception* and Wilson Bryan Key's *Subliminal Seduction*."

79. Baldwin had created an installation piece that included supraliminal images of hangings and subliminal images of victims of bombing raids during the Second World War. Baldwin, "Kinetic Art."

Chapter 2: Mind, Media, and Remote Control

1. Schneck, "A Reevaluation of Freud's Abandonment of Hypnosis."

2. Ellenberger, *The Discovery of the Unconscious*, 208–9.

3. Ibid., 321.

4. Caplan, *Mind Games*, 8.

5. Hackett and Burke, *80 Years of Best Sellers*, 78.

6. Ellenberger, *The Discovery of the Unconscious*, 174.

7. Ibid., 311.

8. For a comparative assessment of the contributions of Myers and Janet to the psy-

chology of the unconscious, see Crabtree, "'Automatism' and the Emergence of Dynamic Psychiatry."

9. Quoted in "What Hypnotism Is and Is Not."

10. Pearson, "Sub-human Consciousness," 583.

11. Bent, "Dethroning the Will."

12. Fishman, "James and Lewes on Unconscious Judgment."

13. James, *The Essential Writings*, 162–74.

14. James, from *Varieties of Religious Experience* (1902), in *The Essential Writings*, 257.

15. Tweedy, "The Subliminal Brute."

16. Valsiner and van der Veer, *The Social Mind*, and Ellenberger, *The Discovery of the Unconscious*, both devote chapters to the substantial and underacknowledged influence of Pierre Janet on psychology and psychiatry.

17. Valsiner and van der Veer, *The Social Mind*, 66.

18. Janet, "Report on Some Phenomena of Somnambulism." Janet provided a detailed description of Léonie B. in "Note sur quelques phénomènes de somnambulisme" and "Deuxième note sur le sommeil provoqué à distance et la suggestion mentale pendant l'état somnambulistique," translated into English in 1968.

19. Valsiner and van der Veer, *The Social Mind*, 63–64; Ellenberger, *The Discovery of the Unconscious*, 338; Janet, "Second Observation of Sleep Provoked from a Distance and the Mental Suggestions during Somnambulistic Sleep," 265.

20. Janet, "Second Observation of Sleep Provoked from a Distance and the Mental Suggestions during Somnambulistic Sleep," 263.

21. Quoted in Forrest, *Hypnotism*, 25.

22. Peters, *Speaking into the Air*, 89. For a full account of the political and cultural forces involved in the official discrediting of mesmerism see Darnton, *Mesmerism and the End of the Enlightenment in France*. Winter, *Mesmerized*, is a detailed cultural history of the practice in Victorian Britain. And Nadis, *Wonder Shows*, documents the relationship between science and entertainment in nineteenth-century America, with special attention to stage hypnotism.

23. Kopell, "Pierre Janet's Description of Hypnotic Sleep Provoked from a Distance," 122.

24. Quoted in ibid.

25. Freud, "Group Psychology and the Analysis of the Ego."

26. Ellenberger, *The Discovery of the Unconscious*, 338.

27. See Forrest, *Hypnotism*, 229–53.

28. In Forrest, *Hypnotism*, 244. Versions of this scene have been restaged in films including *The Manchurian Candidate* (John Frankenheimer, 1962) and *Devil Doll* (Lindsay Shonteff, 1964).

29. Barrows, *Distorting Mirrors*, 121.

30. Le Bon, *The Crowd*, xviii.

31. Ibid., 8.

32. Ibid., 12.

33. Ibid., 21.

34. Ibid., 47.

35. Ibid., 54.

36. Ibid.

37. McClelland, *The Crowd and the Mob*, 235 n. 1.

38. Barrows, *Distorting Mirrors*, 20–22.

39. Ibid., 124.

40. Münsterberg, "Psychology and the Market."

41. Ibid., 89.

42. Münsterberg, *Psychotherapy*; "A Psychologist's Denial of the Existence of the Subconscious Mind."

43. "Misuse of Hypnotism in Securing Confessions of Crime."

44. Münsterberg, "Hypnotism and Crime," 317.

45. Ibid.

46. Ibid., 318.

47. Ibid., 319.

48. Ibid., 320.

49. Ibid., 321.

50. Münsterberg, *Psychotherapy*, 112.

51. Münsterberg, "The Prevention of Crime," 755.

52. Ibid., 753.

53. Münsterberg, "Prohibition and Social Psychology," 443. "Dr. Münsterberg on the Emotional Desiccation of the American People" reproduced this argument.

54. Münsterberg, *Hugo Münsterberg on Film*, 97. For more on Münsterberg's impact on ideas about the effects of motion pictures see Grieveson, "Cinema Studies and the Conduct of Conduct."

55. "Good and Bad Effects of Mental Suggestion in the Theater."

56. "Max Reinhardt Hypnotizing the World."

57. "Newspapers' Sensations and Suggestion."

58. Dench, "Strange Effect of Photoplays on Spectators."

59. Peters, *Speaking into the Air*, 106.

60. Ibid., 99.

61. Sconce, *Haunted Media*.

62. Gregory, "Telepathy, Radiation and the Unconscious."

63. For thorough documentation of the machines and ideas about the reformation of human bodies through electrical means from 1850 to 1950 see de la Peña, *The Body Electric*.

64. Peters, *Speaking into the Air*, 249.

65. "Images Reproduced in Brain as in Television Receiver."

66. Free, "Radio's Aid Is Invoked to Explore Telepathy."

67. Quoted in Caplan, *Mind Games*, 74.

68. Cited in Hilliard and Keith, *The Broadcast Century and Beyond*, 4, and in Hamilton, "Unearthing Broadcasting in the Anglophone World," 292.

69. Knowles, "Wireless Telegraphy and 'Brain-Waves,'" 857.

70. Peters, *Speaking into the Air*, 104.
71. "Navy Novices Learn Radio while Asleep through Telephones Strapped to Ears."
72. "Topics of the Times."
73. "Learn While You Sleep."
74. "Deeper . . . Deeper . . . Dee . . ."
75. "Performances to Be Discouraged."
76. "Hypnotized Policeman Kills Three at a Séance."
77. "Hypnotized Girls Sleep Months."
78. "Thought Waves by Radio Tested in Chicago"; "Dr. Murphy Tells of Telepathy Data."
79. "Thought and Electricity."
80. "Propose to Send Thought across the Atlantic Ocean"; "Telepathy Put to Real Tests."
81. "Thought Is Not Like Radio."
82. "Hypnotism by Radio Is Latest Claim."
83. "Radio to Be Tried as Anaesthetizer."
84. Ibid.
85. Discussed in Sconce, *Haunted Media*, 76–77.
86. "'Radio Telepathy.'"
87. Lloyd, "Mental Contagion and Popular Crazes."
88. Ibid., 202.
89. Ibid., 203.
90. "165 Girls Faint at Football Game."
91. Illingworth, "The Future of Hypnotism," 230.
92. "Brr."
93. "Youth Confesses Strangling Boy, 4."
94. Wertham, *Seduction of the Innocent*, 10.
95. Hansen, "The Mass Production of the Senses."
96. Williams, *The Long Revolution*.

Chapter 3: The Swift View

1. Heinlein, *Stranger in a Strange Land*, 72.
2. Keyes, *Flowers for Algernon*.
3. Condon, *The Manchurian Candidate*, 30.
4. Benschop, "What Is a Tachistoscope?," 30.
5. Woodworth, *Experimental Psychology*, 688; Cattell, "The Inertia of the Eye and Brain."
6. Benschop, "What Is a Tachistoscope?," 27.
7. Benschop, *Unassuming Instruments*.
8. Seltzer, *Bodies and Machines*.
9. Benjamin, "The Work of Art in the Age of Its Technological Reproducibility," *Selected Writings*, vol. 3, 1935–38, 101–33.

10. Tracy, "Must Be Unseen to Be Believed," 812.

11. Dodge, "An Improved Exposure Apparatus"; Dodge, "An Experimental Study of Visual Fixation."

12. Netschajeff, "Zur Frage über die qualitative Wahrnehmungsform."

13. Wolfle, "The Improved Form of the Gulliksen Tachistoscope"; Renshaw and Hampton, "A Combined Chronoscope and Interval Timer."

14. Grindley, "A New Form of Tachistoscope."

15. Tinker, "A Flexible Apparatus for Recording Reading Reactions."

16. Jenkins, "A Simple Tachistoscope of Many Uses"; Evans, "A Tachistoscope for Exposing Large Areas."

17. Harvey, "Space Illusions."

18. Newhall, "Projection Tachistoscopy"; Schlosberg, "A Projection Tachistoscope."

19. Kittler, *Discourse Networks*, 222.

20. I have not found examples of bodies being secured in any violent fashion. After all, the tests were generally performed on colleagues, students, relatives and acquaintances, whom (for the most part) one would not want to subject to petty tortures, even in the name of scientific investigation. Much of this early research was not the more ethically suspect work in asylums or work that exploited subjugated persons. For a good image of the relatively comfortable, if immobile, bodily situation see Whipple, "The Effect of Practice upon the Range of Visual Attention and of Visual Apprehension," 252.

21. Crary, *Suspensions of Perception*, 306.

22. Ibid., 311. Building on Crary's claims, Martin Thomasson offers a perceptive commentary linking Hugo Münsterberg and Wundt to argue that tachistoscopes and motion pictures together helped produce an idea of machine management of minds; see his essay "Machines at the Scene."

23. Cf. Ellenberger, *The Discovery of the Unconscious*.

24. Watson, *The Great Psychologists*.

25. Harvey, "Space Illusions."

26. Kittler, *Discourse Networks*, 223.

27. Crary, *Suspensions of Perception*, 307.

28. Ibid., 344–45.

29. Kittler, *Gramophone, Film, Typewriter*, 122.

30. Kittler, *Discourse Networks*, 251.

31. Ibid., 252. Actually, unless it is not operating as it should, a projector does not "chop up" the flow of images. Kittler is likely referring to the technologies of film editing, not projection.

32. Crary, *Suspensions of Perception*, 306.

33. Esper, "The Bradyscope."

34. A discussion of film and flicker, presented as a critique of the myth of "persistence of vision" among film scholars, appears in Lederman and Nichols, "Flicker and Motion in Film."

35. Benschop, "What Is a Tachistoscope?," 31.

36. Crary, *Suspensions of Perception*, 307.

37. Benschop, *Unassuming Instruments*, 90, cites experimental classroom use of a ta-chistoscope in 1923.

38. Woodworth, *Experimental Psychology*, 696.

39. Aiken, *Method of Mind-Training*; Aiken, *Exercises in Mind-Training*.

40. Whipple, "The Effect of Practice upon the Range of Visual Attention and of Visual Apprehension."

41. Machaver and Borrie, "A Reading Improvement Program for Industry"; Hurt, "Perception Training for Telephone Information Operators."

42. Hische, "Identifikation und Psychotechnik."

43. Sarris and Wertheimer, "Max Wertheimer's Research on Aphasia and Brain Dis-orders."

44. Kittler, *Discourse Networks*, 223.

45. Thurstone, *Primary Mental Abilities*.

46. For more on machine-assisted reading see Currell, "Streamlining the Eye."

47. Grund, "Das Lessen des Wortanfanges bei Volkschulkindern verschiedener Al-tersstufen."

48. Stein, "Tachistoskopische Untersuchungen über das Lesen mit sukzessiver Dar-bietung."

49. Weber, "The Use of Tachistoscopic Exercises in the Improvement of Reading Speed."

50. Swanson, "Common Elements in Silent and Oral Reading."

51. Dearborn, "The Tachistoscope in Diagnostic Reading."

52. Taylor, *Controlled Reading*.

53. Renshaw, Miller, and Marquis, *Children's Sleep*.

54. Larsen, "Obituary: Samuel Renshaw."

55. Renshaw, "The Visual Perception and Reproduction of Forms by Tachistoscopic Methods."

56. "Recognizing Planes."

57. Larsen, "Obituary: Samuel Renshaw," 226.

58. Price, "New Ways to Learn Faster."

59. "Fast Looks."

60. Renshaw, *How to Use the Renshaw Tachistoscopic Trainer*. In a curious parallel de-velopment, Michael Lobel examines how Roy Lichtenstein's paintings explore "the interrelation between machines and visual perception." Lobel argues that this interest grew from one of his early teachers, Hoyt Sherman, who at Ohio State University used tachistoscopes to flash images in a darkened room and had students draw what they had barely seen. Lichtenstein apparently taught in this flash lab between 1946 and 1949 and tried to establish similar labs elsewhere. The artist himself implied that Renshaw had snatched the idea for tachistoscopic training from Sherman, which is unlikely given how long Renshaw had been doing his studies. Lobel, "Technology Envisioned"; and Lobel, *Image Duplica-tor*. Where Lobel associates tachistoscopic training with the flatness of pop art, I would point to what we could reasonably call an emergent aesthetic of flicker in the early 1960s. Here artists, and especially avant-garde filmmakers, take the raw

physiological disorientation of flashing light as formal experiment and as reference to the psychological shock of modern life, a topic to be discussed in chapter 8.

61. Snyder, "The Flashreader in the Reading Laboratory."
62. Melcer and Brown, "Tachistoscopic Training in the First Grade."
63. Arnoult, "Accuracy of Shape Discrimination as a Function of the Range of Exposure Intervals," 12.
64. Wilson, *The Manual-Verbal Response Tachistoscope*, ii, 17.
65. Smith and Tate, "Improvements in Reading Rate and Comprehension of Subjects Training with the Tachistoscope."
66. Schaffer and Gould, "Eye Movement Patterns as a Function of Previous Tachistoscopic Practice."
67. Winick, "An Investigation of the Group Tachistoscopic Method of Evaluating Magazine Advertisements"; Taylor, "A Study of the Tachistoscope."
68. Lucas, "The Optimum Length of Advertising Headline"; Nixon, "A Study of Perception of Advertisements."
69. Lucas and Britt, *Advertising Psychology and Research*, 16.
70. Ibid., 471–72.
71. Caffyn, "Psychological Laboratory Techniques in Copy Research."
72. Smith, "Total Measurements, Evaluating All Promotional Factors in a Campaign."
73. "Tachistoscope," *Dictionary of Business* (Oxford: Oxford University Press, 1996).
74. Caffyn, "Psychological Laboratory Techniques in Copy Research," 48.
75. Newson, "A Projection Tachistoscope."
76. Deutsch, "The Reflecting Shutter Principle and Mechanical Tachistoscopes."
77. Boyd, "Portable Tachistoscope Based on a Commercial Slide-Viewer."
78. Dumler, "A Study of Factors Related to Gains in the Reading Rate of College Students Trained with the Tachistoscope and Accelerator"; Mackinney, "A Validation of Tachistoscopic Training for Clerical Workers."
79. Luce, "Flashfilm."
80. Brown, "Vocabulary via Tachistoscope"; Benson, "We Improved Spelling with the Tachistoscope"; Alterman, "Tachistoscopic Teaching."
81. Burmeister, *Foundations and Strategies for Teaching Children to Read*, 466.
82. *General Manual of Instructions*.
83. Barnette, *Learning through Seeing*.
84. Brown and Wright, *Manual of Instructions for Use with the Minnesota Efficient Reading Series*.
85. Ibid.
86. Masson, "Read with Speed."
87. Snyder, "The Flashreader in the Reading Laboratory"; Pringle and Pringle, "Time Yourself Reading This."
88. "Fast Reading vs. Fast Thinking."
89. Marvel, "Acquisition and Retention of Reading Performance on Two Response Dimensions as Related to 'Set' and Tachistoscopic Training."

90. Mathis and Senter, "Quantification of Contributions Made by Various Reading Instrument Combinations to the Reading Process," iii–v.

91. Ibid., v–vi.

92. Ibid., 13.

93. Galton, "2,000 WPM — but Is It Reading?," 60.

94. Keystone View Company, *Users of the Keystone Tachistoscopic Services* (Meadville, Penn.: Keystone View Company, 1962), Crawford County Historical Society, Keystone View Company Collection.

95. Stanford Taylor, personal interview, 13 November 2002.

96. Lloyd Silverman, quoted in Adams, "'Mommy and I Are One,'" 27.

97. "History and Evolution," Subliminal Dynamics (Centennial, Colo.) website, http://www.subdyn.com/subwel.html [accessed 8 February 2010].

98. Ibid.

99. Benjamin, "Little History of Photography," *Selected Writings, vol. 2, 1927–1934,* 510.

100. Simley, "The Relation of Subliminal to Supraliminal Learning."

101. Kittler, *Discourse Networks,* 223.

102. Ibid., 223–24.

103. Crary, *Suspensions of Perception,* 305.

Chapter 4: Mind-Probing Admen

1. "'Invisible' Ads Tested."

2. Danzig, "Subliminal Advertising."

3. Fort Lee is also considered by film historians to be the birthplace of the U.S. film industry, where the Edison branch of the industry first set up shop.

4. Rogers, "How a Publicity Blitz Created the Myth of Subliminal Advertising."

5. Ibid., 16.

6. Rogers, "People Love to Be Fooled."

7. Twitchell, *Adcult USA,* 116.

8. James M. Vicary, notes for an article to be titled "Creative Marketing Research," in James M. Vicary Papers, Archives and Special Collections, Thomas J. Dodd Research Center, University of Connecticut (hereafter JMV), box 1, folder 19, n.d. [post–February 1962].

9. Pooler, "Ex–Office Boy Borrows from Psychiatry to Add New Touch to Poll-Taking."

10. "Stereotypes: Student Poll Indicates Propaganda Value of Catch-words," *Michigan Daily,* JMV Papers, box 4, James Vicary Company Papers, vol. 15, 13381.

11. Application for Employment, Dun and Bradstreet, Inc., 16 July 1962, JMV Papers, box 1, folder 11.

12. Company listing in *Advertising Agency Magazine,* 1 March 1957, JMV Papers, box 1, folder 1.

13. "'Invisible' Ads Tested."

14. Offprint, James M. Vicary, "How to Think about a Brand Name for a New Prod-

uct," *Sales Management*, 3 August 1956, JMV Papers, box 1, folder 1; Vicary, "What's in a Name Change"; offprint, James M. Vicary, "What's in a Company Name?," *Dun's Review and Modern Industry*, June 1957, JMV Papers, box 1, folder 9; offprint, James M. Vicary, "When You Outgrow Your Company Name," *Dun's Review and Modern Industry*, May 1960, JMV Papers, box 1, folder 9.

15. The James M. Vicary Company Papers, JMV Papers, boxes 2, 3, and 4, consist of thirteen bound volumes and one unbound volume of the firm's research from 1946 to 1959, totaling twelve thousand pages. Complete tables of contents exist for another six volumes, though they are not in the collection. In one of these missing volumes are three hundred pages of material on Vicary's subliminal advertising enterprise. It is unclear how much of this material is duplicated by what is available elsewhere in the papers.

16. James M. Vicary Company, press releases for 4 May 1954, 4 June 1954, and 16 September 1955, JMV Papers, box 1, folder 1; Graham, "Adman's Nightmare"; Longgood, "Shop Spy Tells Why of Baking."

17. Britt, *The Spenders*, 214–15, 219.

18. "Mass Observation."

19. Vicary, "Labor, Management and Food."

20. Bartos, "Ernest Dichter."

21. Rogers, "How a Publicity Blitz Created the Myth of Subliminal Advertising," 13. For a full account of Ernest Dichter, his relationship to Vicary, and the rise of motivational research, see Samuel, *Freud on Madison Avenue*.

22. James M. Vicary, "Applying Projective Techniques to Marketing Problems," talk presented to the American Marketing Association, Chicago, 1952, JMV Papers, box 1, folder 19, 1.

23. Vicary, "Word Association and Opinion Research," 81.

24. Vicary, "*Gestalt* Theory and Paired Comparisons."

25. Vicary, *Annotated Bibliography of Word Association References Important to Marketing Researchers*.

26. Vicary, "Seasonal Psychology," 397.

27. "Marketing Men Hear about 'Mind Probing.'"

28. Cooper, "Man, Dig These Crazy Tests!"

29. Script from *Dorothy and Dick*, 6 January 1953, JMV Papers, box 1, folder 1.

30. "Forming and Changing Attitudes of People."

31. "Univac Adapted to Readership Research."

32. "Psychology," June 1957, JMV Papers, box 1, folder 1.

33. Efron, "Brand New Brand Names," 29.

34. "Inside the Consumer," 92.

35. Radio script, Guthrier E. Janssen, "Why Did You Buy That?," NBC's *People*, broadcast 6 February 1954, JMV Papers, box 1, folder 1.

36. "Psychologist Finds Supermarkets Cast a Spell over Most Shoppers," *Louisville Courier-Journal*, 13 August 1954, JMV Papers, box 1, folder 1.

37. Cf. Vicary, "How Psychiatric Methods Can Be Applied to Market Research."

38. Packard, *The Hidden Persuaders*, 42.

39. "Sales through the Sub-Conscious."

40. "Visible Success Seen for those Unseen Ads."

41. Talese, "Most Hidden Hidden Persuasion," 22.

42. Mannes, "Ain't Nobody Here but Us Commercials," 35.

43. Brean, "'Hidden Sell' Technique is Almost Here," 107.

44. "Unseen Selling," *Postage Stamp*, February 1958, 6, JMV Papers, box 1, folder 21.

45. Brooks, "The Little Ad that Isn't There," 7.

46. *Final Report of the Commission to Study Subliminal Projection*, 3.

47. "Unseen TV Gets Exposure on Both Coasts," 99; "Whazzat?"; "New 'Invisible Commercial' Ad Agency Boon."

48. "New 'Invisible Commercial' Ad Agency Boon," 1.

49. Ibid.

50. "Whazzat?"

51. "'Invisible' Ads Tested."

52. Sconce, *Haunted Media*, 116.

53. Horowitz, *Vance Packard and American Social Criticism*, 105.

54. Ibid., 162.

55. Goodman, "Freud and the Hucksters."

56. Strong, "They're Selling your Unconscious."

57. "Inside the Consumer," 89.

58. Calkins, "The Ten Best Advertisements," 85.

59. "Psychology and the Ads."

60. Rolo, "Admen and the Id."

61. Ibid., 88.

62. "In 'Debate' with Packard, Weir Hits Book as 'Malicious.'"

63. "Marketing Men Debate Ways to Make Consumer Buy."

64. Ibid., 36. Decades later Weir was still on the offensive, publishing a denunciation of the furore about subliminal advertising: Weir, "Another Look at Subliminal 'Facts.'"

65. Roper, "How Powerful are the Persuaders?"

66. "'Hidden Persuaders' Hits Britain."

67. Van Den Haag, "Madison Avenue Witchcraft."

68. Spectorsky, "The MR Boys Are Out to Make you Buy and Buy and Buy."

69. Ibid.

70. Seldes, "What Makes the Consumer Tick?"; Horowitz, *Vance Packard*, 133.

71. By 1975 *The Hidden Persuaders* had over three million copies in print. Horowitz, *Vance Packard*, 133. Horowitz also includes a selection of advertising references to Packard's books.

72. Coser, "Kitsch Sociology."

73. "Sales Held Key, Not Ad Billings."

74. Cone, "Advertising Is Not a Plot."

75. "Morse Defends Motivational Research."

76. Packard, *The Hidden Persuaders*, 8.

77. Ibid., 35.

78. Ibid., 42, 106.
79. Rolo, "Admen and the Id."
80. Packard, *The Hidden Persuaders*, 42.
81. Packard, "Resurvey of 'Hidden Persuaders,'" 19.
82. Halberstam, *The Fifties*, 597.
83. Miller, Introduction.
84. Bach and Klein, "The Effects of Prolonged Subliminal Exposures of Words," 397; Smith, Spence, and Klein, "Effects of Subliminally Exposed Words upon Conscious Impressions of a Face"; Smith, Spence, and Klein, "Subliminal Effects of Verbal Stimuli."
85. "Subliminal Techniques."
86. "Supersoft Sell," 68.
87. Packard, "The Growing Power of Admen."

Chapter 5: Crossing the Popular Threshold

1. *Final Report of the Commission to Study Subliminal Projection*, 3.
2. Virginia Irwin, "Tempest over Hidden Commercials," *St. Louis Post Dispatch*, 5 February 1958, James M. Vicary Papers, Archives and Special Collections, Thomas J. Dodd Research Center, University of Connecticut Libraries [hereafter JMV Papers], box 1, folder 1.
3. Mannes, "Ain't Nobody Here but Us Commercials," 35. Vicary filed the patent application for an "Apparatus for and Method of Transmitting Intelligence" on 4 September 1956, with the application number 607,955. "Assignment from James M. Vicary to Subliminal Projection Co. Inc.," 8 February 1957, JMV Papers, box 1, folder 6. The U.S. Patent and Trademark Office could not confirm the existence of this application because failed applications are secret and not accessible by the public, unless they are referred to in subsequent patents.
4. Mannes, "Ain't Nobody Here but Us Commercials," 36.
5. Ibid.
6. Ibid.
7. "'Persuaders' Get Deeply 'Hidden' Tool."
8. "Devilish?," 100.
9. "New 'Invisible Commercial' Ad Agency Boon," 1.
10. "The 'Invisible' Invader."
11. "If Subliminal Ad's Hypnotic, It Won't Sell."
12. "'Ghost' Ads Overrated"; Wilcott, "Letter: Invisible Words, Invisible Evidence," also reflected this skepticism.
13. "Is Subliminal New?"
14. Ibid.
15. Woolf, "Subliminal Perception Is Nothing New."
16. "Invisible Ads Are Quick as a Flash, but Not Too Quick for FCC's X-Ray Eye"; "FCC Peers into Subliminal Picture on TV."

17. Schultz, "Letter: Don't Look Now, but It's Only a 'Tachistoscope.'" A version also appeared as Schultz, "Letter: Half Hour Commercials, Subliminal Programs?"

18. "Letter: Subliminal Perception."

19. "The Subliminal Fight Gets Hotter."

20. "K&E's Cox Hits Subliminal Ads."

21. Ibid.

22. "The Subliminal Fight Gets Hotter"; "Viewers Would Resist 'Manipulation.'"

23. DuShane, "Editorial: The Invisible Work, or No Thresholds Barred."

24. "Ads You'll Never See," 31.

25. Ibid.

26. "Diddling the Subconscious," 207.

27. Quoted in Brooks, "The Little Ad That Isn't There," 7.

28. "The Invisible Monster," 1157.

29. "Devilish?," 98.

30. Silverman, "Vance Packard ('Hidden Persuaders') Raps 'Call me MR' Addle-dazzle."

31. "What Sways the Family Shopper."

32. "Devilish?," 100.

33. Ibid.

34. "New 'Invisible Commercial' Ad Agency Boon," 1.

35. "Subliminal Perception Discussed by Meighan at KNXT (TV) Seminar."

36. "Visible Success Seen for Those Unseen Ads."

37. "Subliminal Advertising, Banned by TV Chains, May Hit Movie Houses."

38. Talese, "Most Hidden Hidden Persuasion," 59.

39. "Ads You'll Never See," 31. Becker and Corrigan finally received "the first United States patent on subliminal perception" in 1962. Jones, "Projector Patented for Hidden Images."

40. "Subliminal Ads Wash No Brains, Declare Moore, Becker, Developers of Precon Device."

41. "Unseen TV Gets Exposure on Both Coasts," 98.

42. "SP, PS Continue to Hold Stage," 32.

43. Ibid.

44. Griswold, "TV's New Trick."

45. "Dennis Sells Horror Yarn," *Hollywood Reporter*, 5 November 1957, *My World Dies Screaming* clipping file, Margaret Herrick Library, Academy of Motion Picture Arts and Sciences.

46. "My World Dies Screaming," *Variety*, 22 October 1958, *My World Dies Screaming* clipping file, Margaret Herrick Library, Academy of Motion Picture Arts and Sciences.

47. Press book for *My World Dies Screaming*, 1958, 2.

48. Heffernan, *Ghouls, Gimmicks, and Gold*, 64–89.

49. Press book for *My World Dies Screaming*, 2.

50. "My World Dies Screaming," *Variety*, 22 October 1958, *My World Dies Screaming*

clipping file, Margaret Herrick Library, Academy of Motion Picture Arts and Sciences.

51. Ibid.

52. Canby, *"My World Dies Screaming," Motion Picture Herald*, 8 November 1958, *My World Dies Screaming* clipping file, Margaret Herrick Library, Academy of Motion Picture Arts and Sciences.

53. "Is 'Subliminal' Semi-Operative in Theaters with Special Coke Breaks?"

54. "New Subliminal Era Slips In While Audience Not Looking," 72; later this would be described by the Federal Communications Commission, *Information Bulletin on Subliminals*, as a television station flashing "If you have seen this message, write wtwo," every eleven seconds, every second day, for two weeks, with no significant result.

55. "Radio Station Testing 'Subliminal' Ads, but Listeners Can Still Hear 'Em."

56. "Wha'd He Say?"; "The Busy Air"; "wcco Probes Subconsciousness with Pioneer 'Phantom Spots.'"

57. "sp, ps Continue to Hold Stage," 31.

58. "Psychic Hucksterism Stirs Call for Inquiry"; "Invisible Ads Are Quick as a Flash, but Not Too Quick for fcc's X-Ray Eye."

59. "fcc Peers into Subliminal Picture on tv"; "The Phantom Plug."

60. "Solon vs. 'Subliminal.'"

61. "'Subliminal' May Take Long Count."

62. Quoted in "The Day the fcc Got Potted."

63. Quoted in ibid.

64. "Subliminal Scare Stirs Congressmen," 72.

65. Ibid., 73.

66. "fcc: 'Nothing to Worry About.'"

67. "Invisible Ads Are Quick as a Flash, but Not Too Quick for fcc's X-Ray Eye."

68. John Doerfer, letter to William Dawson, 27 November 1957, Proceedings and Debates of the 85th Congress, second session, 104, 1228–30, 28 January 1958; "fcc Peers into Subliminal Picture on tv."

69. "nartb Warns on sp, 'Horror'"; Godbout, "Video Group Bans 'Subliminal' Ads"; Brooks, "The Little Ad that Isn't There," 10.

70. Quoted in Godbout, "'Subliminal' Ads over Air Studied."

71. Ibid.

72. "sp, ps Continue to Hold Stage," 31; Adams, "3 Networks Ban Subliminal Ads."

73. "Nets Vow They'll Eschew Subliminal Ads"; "'Subliminal Not for Us' Sez nbc."

74. "Subliminal Advertising, Banned by tv Chains, May Hit Movie Houses."

75. "'Subliminal P,' Men in White Banned for tv," 25; Federal Communications Commission, *Information Bulletin on Subliminals*.

76. Bernstein, "tv's 'Hidden Persuaders,' sp, All but Buried as Selling Medium."

77. "Subliminal Advertising, Banned by tv Chains, May Hit Movie Houses."

78. Schutz, "Just Whom did Invisible Screen Advertising Sell?"

79. "Sees Further Tests of 'Subliminal' Needed"; Kalis, "The Phantom of the Soap Opera," 6; Cash, "Subliminal Advertising," 18–19.

80. "Real Advertising Men's Viewpoint."

81. "FCC Peek into Method Postponed until 1958"; "'Subliminal' Test Okayed by FCC"; "FCC to Get First-hand Look at Subliminal Ads before Ruling on TV Use."

82. Adams, "Subliminal Ads Shown in Capital."

83. Ibid.

84. Ibid.

85. Ibid.

86. "Subliminal Has a Test"; "Unseen TV Gets Exposure on Both Coasts," 99.

87. "Subliminal Ad Is Transmitted in Test but Scores No Popcorn Sales."

88. "Periscoping the World: Red Gambits."

89. "Unseen TV Gets Exposure on Both Coasts," 98.

90. Ibid., 99.

91. Federal Communications Commission, *Information Bulletin on Subliminals*.

92. "Subliminal Ads May Become Fact If FCC Delays."

93. "Editorial: The Ad that Isn't There."

94. "KTLA Will Test Subliminal Ads within 90 Days."

95. Godbout, "Subliminal Test Planned in West."

96. Godbout, "Subliminal Ads Blocked on Coast"; "Hollywood TV Station Cancels Plans to Use Subliminal Ads."

97. "Editorial: Subliminal Silver Lining."

98. "Non-Coffee-Using Housewife Made Fresh Coffee after Hint in Subliminal Radio Tests."

99. "Whispering Campaign."

100. "CBC, Canadian Admen Disapprove Subliminal Pitches."

101. "CBC Is First to Broadcast Subliminal Test."

102. "'Phone Now,' Said CBC Subliminally."

103. "Canadians Brood over Subject of Subliminal Pitch."

104. Ibid.

105. "'Phone Now,' Said CBC Subliminally"; "TV Message Fruitless."

106. "How's That Again?," 66.

Chapter 6: The Hidden and the Overload

1. Holmes, "The Philosophy of the Beat Generation," 36.

2. Pyles, "Subliminal Words are Never Finalized."

3. Brown, *Beat, Beat, Beat.*

4. "Quicker Than the Eye."

5. Brean, "'Hidden Sell' Technique Is Almost Here."

6. Talese, "Most Hidden Hidden Persuasion," 59.

7. "Gladys the Beautiful Receptionist."

8. Cartoon, *New Yorker*, 15 March 1958, 37.

9. "Sneaky Advertisements."

10. "New Little Clubs Light Up U.S. Night Life."

11. Brooks, "The Little Ad That Isn't There," 9.

12. Cole, "The Subliminal Pitch."

13. "Subliminal Ads Lose."

14. "Teenagers Prod Reps into Passing State Law vs. 'Subliminal' Films."

15. Act no. 1823, State of New York, 22 January 1958, appended to *Final Report of the Commission to Study Subliminal Projection*, xvi; "N.Y. Legislature Weighs Bill Banning Subliminal Movie Ads"; "N.Y. State Senate Okays Subliminal Ban."

16. "N.Y. State Senate Okays Subliminal Ban."

17. Bill H.R. 1998, 86th Congress, 1st session, 9 January 1959, appended to *Final Report of the Commission to Study Subliminal Projection*, xv; "Unfair to the Subconscious."

18. Federal Communications Commission, *Information Bulletin on Subliminals*.

19. Jones, "Projector Patented for Hidden Images"; "No Sly Suggestion"; Federal Communications Commission, *Information Bulletin on Subliminals*.

20. Other members included Wallace Wirths, Douglas Rutherfurd, Albert McCay, John L. Kelly, Barry Kamm, and Donal C. Fox. *Final Report of the Commission to Study Subliminal Projection*.

21. Ibid.

22. Ibid., 3.

23. Ibid., 4.

24. Ibid., 8.

25. Ibid., 11.

26. Ibid., iv–vii.

27. De Fleur and Petranoff, "A Televised Test of Subliminal Persuasion."

28. *Final Report of the Commission to Study Subliminal Projection*, viii–xii.

29. Ibid., 10.

30. Ibid., 11.

31. Ibid., 13.

32. Ibid., xvii.

33. "Subliminal Message Hits Home, Stanford Researchers Report."

34. "Editorial: Subliminal Silver Lining."

35. "Subliminal Test Makes 32 Thirsty."

36. "Subliminal Message Does have Effect, Psychologist Finds."

37. "Nucoa Uses New Subliminal Twist."

38. Bernstein, "TV's 'Hidden Persuaders.'"

39. "Subliminal Ads Don't 'Brainwash' Viewers, College Dean Says."

40. Quoted in "Teen Is Pushover for 'Persuaders,' Educators are Told."

41. Kidd, "Subliminal Stimuli a 'Monster'?"

42. "Subliminal Ads May be Usable: Britt."

43. "Britt Proposes More Scientific Subliminal Test."

44. Ibid.

45. Britt, *The Spenders*, 158.

46. "Unconscious Sell Theme Tops '58 Ad Conference."

47. W. B. Booth and A. B. Scott, "The Third Communication," *Advertising and the Subconscious*, ed. Wooding, 11.

48. Vance Packard, "The Hidden Why's of Our Behavior," *Advertising and the Subconscious*, ed. Edmund Wooding, 37–48.
49. "Dubious about 'Subliminal' Claims Made without Science Control."
50. Elton B. McNeil, "Subliminal Stimulation: Omen of Things to Come," *Advertising and the Subconscious*, ed. Edmund Wooding, 60–68.
51. Ibid., 67.
52. Wooding, ed., *Advertising and the Subconscious*, 84.
53. "British Ad Group Set Probe of Subliminal Ads."
54. Ibid.
55. "British TV Row Breaks over Alleged 'Subliminal' Message."
56. Institute of Practitioners in Advertising, Ad Hoc Committee, *Subliminal Communication*; "British Ad Group Set Probe of Subliminal Ads."
57. "Banned in Britain."
58. Committee on Motivation Research, *The Application of Subliminal Perception in Advertising*, 1.
59. Ibid., iii. The other committee members were Bayard Badenhausen (manager, psychological research, for Batten, Barton, Durstine and Osborn), Thomas E. Coffin (research director, National Broadcasting Company), Herbert Fisher (consumer research director, Chrysler), Alberta Gilinsky (account research supervisor, Kenyon and Eckardt), Carl R. Gisler (research director, *True, the Man's Magazine*), Joel W. Harnett (director of promotions, *Look*), Melvin S. Hattwick (advertising director, Continental Oil), Arthur Koponen (research psychologist, J. Walter Thompson), Gove P. Laybourn (research analyst, General Mills,), Jack N. Peterman (psychological research director, Buchen Company), Charles K. Ramond II (manager, advertising research, Du Pont), Stanley H. Seeman (Wildroot Company), Charles E. Swanson (research manager, *Saturday Evening Post*), Eugene Webb (research psychologist, *Chicago Tribune*), and Donald E. West (director of marketing research, *Redbook*). Ex-officio members representing the ARF were A. W. Lehman and D. B. Lucas.
60. Ibid., 6.
61. Spielvogel, "Advertising: Two Agencies Near a Merger."
62. McConnell, Cutler, and McNeil, "Subliminal Stimulation: An Overview."
63. Ibid., 229.
64. Ibid., 237.
65. "Psychologists Hit Use of Subliminal Methods in Ads as 'Unprofessional.'"
66. "Vicary 'Delighted' at Academic Criticism."
67. "Psychologists Hit Subliminal Ads as 'Chimera,' Laud Clarity, Repetition."
68. "ARF Checks Data on Subliminal Ads."
69. Lewis, "Admen Hop on Critic of Subliminal Ads."
70. "Subliminal TV Ad's Dimness May Impair Value."
71. Klass, "The Ghost of Subliminal Advertising."
72. "Proponent of SP Deprecates Effect," 47.
73. Ibid., 48.
74. "Ludgin Says Ad Excess Makes All Ads Subliminal."

75. Ludgin, "Advertising Must Be Unexpected and Believable to Break through Sub-liminal Barrier, Says Ludgin."
76. "Ad Agencies Hatch a Radio Dilemma on Triple Spotting."
77. Machlup, *The Production and Distribution of Knowledge in the United States.*
78. Meier, *A Communications Theory of Urban Growth,* 2.
79. Ibid., 132.
80. Rosenberg, "Early Modern Information Overload."
81. Simmel, "The Metropolis and Mental Life," 409.
82. Deutsch, "On Social Communication and the Metropolis," refers to Richard L. Meier, "Characteristics of the New Urbanization," multigraph essay, University of Chicago, 1953; Meier, "Communications and Social Change"; Fadiman, "The Decline of Attention."
83. Miller, "Information Input Overload and Psychopathology," 704.
84. Deutsch, "On Social Communication and the Metropolis," 103.
85. Leiber, "The Girl with the Hungry Eyes," 19–20.
86. Griffith, "Captive Audience."
87. Ibid., 76.
88. Ibid., 70.
89. Ibid., 78.
90. Ibid., 79.
91. Pohl and Kornbluth, *The Space Merchants.* It had first appeared in condensed, serial form as "Gravy Planet" in *Galaxy.*
92. Ibid., 116.
93. Ibid., 129.
94. Ibid., 5.
95. Ibid., 47.
96. Boorstin, *The Image, or What Happened to the American Dream.*
97. Wolfe, *Ask Any Girl.*
98. Schlesinger, "The Crisis of American Masculinity," 65.
99. Ibid.

Chapter 7: From Mass Brainwashing to Rapid Mass Learning

1. Haber, "Public Attitudes Regarding Subliminal Advertising."
2. "TV Message Fruitless."
3. Adams, "Subliminal Ads Shown in Capital."
4. "Psychic Hucksterism Stirs Call for Inquiry."
5. "Subliminal TV Cited as Danger to Youth."
6. Moore, "From Self-Delusion to Mass Delusion—and Back Again?"
7. For an interesting parsing of the legal implications of subliminal communication see Silvergate, "Subliminal Perception and the First Amendment."
8. "Ads You'll Never See," 31.
9. Cousins, "Editorial: Smudging the Subconscious."
10. "Editorial: The Ad That Isn't There."

11. Packard, *The Hidden Persuaders*, 266.
12. Benedict, "Mind Control, Ultimate Tyranny."
13. Ibid.
14. Streatfeild, *Brainwash*. For a detailed study of the culture of "brainwashing" in the 1950s see Carruthers, *Cold War Captives*.
15. Lerner, *Sykewar*. For a complete history of the rising influence of psychology on public policy in the United States after the Second World War see Herman, *The Romance of American Psychology*.
16. Sargant, *Battle for the Mind*; Hunter, *Brainwashing in Red China*; Hunter, *Brainwashing*; Lifton, *Thought Reform and the Psychology of Totalism*.
17. McHugh, "Pavlov, Brainwashing and Foreign Policy," 613–14.
18. Fraiberg, "The Science of Thought Control," 420.
19. Abel, "Schwable Tells of P.O.W. Ordeal," 5.
20. Wicklein, "Brainwash Peril Seen over Nation."
21. "Brainwashing," *Random House Dictionary of the English Language*, 2nd edn (New York: Random House, 1987).
22. "Brainwashing," *Merriam-Webster's Collegiate Dictionary*, 10th edn (Springfield, Mass.: Merriam-Webster, 1993).
23. Gill and Brenman, *Hypnosis and Related States*, 177.
24. Pritchard, "Mass Hypnosis," 110.
25. Ibid., 112.
26. "Aid to the Reds Laid to Korea Prisoners."
27. Hunter, *Brainwashing*, 286.
28. "Professor's Talk on Races Backed."
29. King, "'Certain' Classes Banned by Bishop."
30. "Students Charge 'Left-Wing' Bias."
31. Root, *Brainwashing in the High Schools*.
32. Becker, "Pastors Oppose Faubus on Vote."
33. Sitton, "Faubus in Clash with Clergymen"; "A Church Leader Answers Faubus."
34. "Editors Split on South."
35. Lewis, "Russell Assails 2 Key Rights Aims."
36. Walker, *The Cold War*, 115.
37. Ranzal, "'No Mercy' Urged on Riesel Jury."
38. "Romney Asserts He Underwent 'Brainwashing' on Vietnam Trip"; "Politics: Romney's Brainwash"; "Romney Chances Assayed by G.O.P."
39. Weaver, "Romney Renews Vietnam Charge."
40. Huxley, *Brave New World Revisited*.
41. "Huxley Fears New Persuasion Methods Could Subvert Democratic Procedures." This interview was part of the short-lived series "Survival and Freedom," co-produced by ABC and the Ford Foundation's Fund for the Republic.
42. See Clowse, *Brainpower for the Cold War*.
43. Whitfield, *The Culture of the Cold War*, 72.
44. O'Neill, *American High*, 270.
45. "Pic to 'Editorialize' on U.S. Missile Lag."

46. Packard, "The Mass Manipulation of Human Behavior," 342.

47. Packard, *The Waste Makers*.

48. Packard, "The Mass Manipulation of Human Behavior," 344.

49. Interestingly, in 1961 a CBS television news documentary, *The Twentieth Century: P.O.W., Part 1, Korea*, hosted by Walter Cronkite, described "give-up-itis" as the term that American POWs used for dying. This unapologetic documentary was part of an effort to rehabilitate the bravery and strength of United States soldiers, making the collaborators seem like weakened humans. *Part 2, The Road to Resistance*, was about a camp where soldiers were trained to withstand brainwashing.

50. Packard, "The Mass Manipulation of Human Behavior," 344.

51. Ibid.

52. Sparke, *As Long as It's Pink*.

53. O'Neill, *American High*, 290; Galbraith, *The Affluent Society*.

54. Bakal, "The Schools of Tomorrow," 9.

55. Clowse, *Brainpower for the Cold War*, 3.

56. Halberstam, *The Fifties*, 626.

57. Hoban and van Ormer, *Instructional Film Research*.

58. "Schools Are Held in Need of Funds for Machine Aids." For a discussion of the discourses and ideological implications of the postwar expansion of audiovisual instruction, see Acland, "Curtains, Carts and the Mobile Screen."

59. McLuhan, *Report on Project in Understanding New Media*.

60. Saettler, *A History of Instructional Technology*, 349.

61. Guedry, "New Educational Media."

62. Saettler, *A History of Instructional Technology*, 350.

63. Filep and Schramm, *A Study of the Impact of Research on Utilization of Media for Educational Purposes*, 1.

64. Carlson, *Guide to the National Defense Education Act of 1958*, 3; Clowse, *Brainpower for the Cold War*, 159.

65. Michael Molenda, "Association for Educational Communications and Technology In the 20th Century: A Brief History," http://www.aect.org/About/History, 28 June 2005.

66. National Education Association, *Schools for the Sixties*, 98.

67. McLuhan, *Understanding Media*.

68. McLuhan, *Report on Project in Understanding New Media*, 3.

69. Ibid., 14.

70. Cf. ibid., 55.

71. Ibid., x.

72. Ibid., 2.

73. McLuhan, *Understanding Media*, 20.

74. Ibid., 285, 294, 299.

75. Ibid., 231.

76. Interview with Barry Day, quoted in McLuhan, "A McLuhan Mosaic," 14.

77. McLuhan, *Understanding Media*, 292.

78. Marshall McLuhan, "Classroom without Walls," *Explorations in Communication*, ed. Carpenter and McLuhan, 1–3.

79. McLuhan, "Cybernetics and Human Culture."

80. "News Notes: Classroom and Campus."

81. Hunter, "Teaching Device Growing Rapidly."

82. "The Growing Variety of Teaching Machines."

83. Saettler, *A History of Instructional Technology*, 349–50.

84. "U.S. to Help Set Up a 'Clearinghouse' for Teaching Aids."

85. Hechinger, "On the Automated Classroom."

86. Harrison, "Teacher Machine to Be Ready in '61."

87. "Push-Button Brains"; "New Grolier Machine Said to Speed Learning"; "New Tutoring Machine."

88. "Corporations: The Teaching Machine," 91.

89. Fowler, "Wall St. Studies Teaching Devices."

90. Ibid.

91. "News Notes: Classroom and Campus."

92. "Tireless," 26.

93. Boehm, "Can People Be Taught like Pigeons?"

94. Clowse, *Brainpower for the Cold War*, 3.

95. For example, Finn, "Teaching Machines"; Weisenberg, "Automation in the Classroom."

96. "How Machines Do Teaching Job"; Boroff, "The Three R's and Pushbuttons"; "New Grolier Machine Said to Speed Learning"; "New Tutoring Machine"; "Ford Aide Supports Programmed Classes."

97. "Education News." Inventories, in an effort to be comprehensive, can result in institutional embarrassment. Such was the case of a catalogue of programmed instruction for teaching machines, released by the U.S. Office of Education and prepared by the Center for Programmed Instruction, which included "The Official Girlwatcher's Manual." Apologies and deletions followed. "Girlwatching Guide Loses Status on U.S. List of Teachers' Aids."

98. "News Notes: Classroom and Campus"; Hechinger, "Concepts behind 'Teaching Machine.'"

99. Weisenberg, "Automation in the Classroom," 456.

100. "News Notes: Classroom and Campus."

101. Saettler, *A History of Instructional Technology*, 349–50.

102. "U.S. to Help Set Up a 'Clearinghouse' for Teaching Aids."

103. Cf. "How Machines Do Teaching Job," 112, 114.

104. Saettler, *A History of Instructional Technology*, 354.

105. Filep and Schramm, *A Study of the Impact of Research on Utilization of Media for Educational Purposes*, 6.

106. "Teaching Machine."

107. Fowler, "Wall St. Studies Teaching Devices."

108. "1.5 Million Grant to Schools Offers Visual Training Aids."

109. Cray, "Electronic Training Devices on Display."

110. Cray, "The Knowledge Industry"; Smith, "Sylvania Enters Education Field"; Saettler, *A History of Instructional Technology*, 360.

111. "Sidelights: Companies Ring School Bell."

112. Bedingfield, "Time and G.E. Plan Educational Unit," 45.

113. Black, "Automation Still in Future."

114. F. Dean McClusky, Introduction, *A History of Instructional Technology*, by Saettler, 81.

115. Cray, "The Knowledge Industry."

116. Rutter, "Education in U.S. Big and Growing."

117. Cray, "The Knowledge Industry."

118. Rutter, "Education in U.S. Big and Growing," 1.

119. Hechinger, "U.S. Education Chief Criticizes the Large Number of Automated Aids as Wasteful."

120. Farber, "Need for Standards in Industry Seen."

121. Hechinger, "U.S. Education Chief Criticizes the Large Number of Automated Aids as Wasteful."

122. Hechinger, "On the Automated Classroom."

123. National Education Association, *Schools for the Sixties*, 134.

124. Ibid., 135.

125. Key, *Subliminal Seduction*, 67.

126. Filep and Schramm, *A Study of the Impact of Research on Utilization of Media for Educational Purposes*, 48.

127. Talese, "Most Hidden Hidden Persuasion," 59.

128. Rose, "Motivation Research and Subliminal Advertising," 282.

129. Ibid., 284.

Chapter 8: Textual Strategies for Media Saturation

1. Jancovich, *Rational Fears*.

2. Pratt, *Projecting Paranoia*, 8.

3. For more on the cycle of "brain" narratives after the Second World War see Sconce, "Brains from Space."

4. The following pages cross-referenced each character with Rovin, *The Encyclopedia of Super Villains*; *Who's Who: The Definitive Directory of the DC Universe*; Waid, ed., *Who's Who: Update '88*; Michigan State University, Comic Art Collection, http://www.lib.msu.edu/services/spec_coll/nye/comic; and Sanderson, *Ultimate X-Men*. Comic book titles and issue numbers indicate the first appearance of these characters.

5. For a detailed study of the comic book scandal through an intellectual biography of Fredric Wertham, see Beaty, *Fredric Wertham and the Critique of Mass Culture*.

6. Aarons, "The Communicators."

7. Ibid., 50.

8. Ibid., 52.

9. Ibid., 53.

10. Ibid., 68.

11. Ibid., 52.

12. Ibid., 54.

13. Nelson, "Eight o' Clock in the Morning."

14. Ballard, "The Subliminal Man."

15. Dick, *Time Out of Joint.*

16. Dick, *The Three Stigmata of Palmer Eldritch*, 37.

17. Ibid., 80.

18. Burroughs, *Naked Lunch*, 28.

19. Ibid., 163.

20. Ibid., 36.

21. For a complete history of Burroughs's relationship to Gysin and the Dream Machine see Geiger, *Nothing Is True, Everything Is Permitted*; and Kerekes, ed., "Flicker Machine Edition."

22. Burroughs, *The Ticket That Exploded*, 1–5.

23. Ibid., 65.

24. Ibid., 178–83.

25. Ibid., 162–70.

26. Ibid., 167.

27. In another instance of the trading back and forth across cultural hierarchies, *Marvel Team-Up* (no. 97, 1980), with the Hulk and Spider-Woman, includes an obvious and cheeky nod to William Burroughs, with our heroes chasing the fugitive Johnny Yen and the villain Dr. W. Lee Benway. Both names are versions of characters used by Burroughs; Johnny Yen appears in *The Soft Machine* (1961/1966); *Naked Lunch* includes Burroughs's alter-egos Bill Lee and the warped Dr. Benway. This comic villain Benway lives in the New Mexico desert building robots, using human brains, and selling organs on the black market, with his weapon of choice, a "pleasure ray." As he zaps the Hulk he cries, "I'll give you *pleasure* . . . beyond your *wildest* dreams!"

28. Lancaster, *Introducing Op Art*, 9.

29. "A Date with Death," *Motion Picture Herald*, 20 June 1959, *Date with Death* clipping file, Margaret Herrick Library, Academy of Motion Picture Arts and Sciences.

30. "The New Wave in Titillation."

31. Ibid., 75.

32. Ibid.

33. "Subliminal Cuts Show 'Hot Car' in New Toyota Push." This spot was made by Tilton Films of San Diego for the Clinton E. Frank Agency.

34. "New Trade Program."

35. Ibid.

36. Gunning, "An Aesthetic of Astonishment."

37. McLuhan and Fiore, *The Medium is the Massage.*

38. McLuhan and Fiore, *War and Peace in the Global Village.*

39. McLuhan, *Counterblast*.

40. McLuhan and Parker, *Through the Vanishing Point*; McLuhan, *Culture Is Our Business*.

41. McLuhan, *Counterblast*, 132.

Chapter 9: Critical Reasoning in a Cluttered Age

1. Letter, Vicary to Donald H. Wilson, Arthur D. Little, Inc., 25 June 1962, James M. Vicary Papers, Archives and Special Collections, Thomas J. Dodd Research Center, University of Connecticut (hereafter JMV Papers), box 1, folder 11, 1962.

2. Danzig, "Subliminal Advertising," 72.

3. Ibid., 72, 74.

4. Ibid.

5. "Mr. Vicary's 'High Jinks.'"

6. Weir, "Another Look at Subliminal 'Facts.'"

7. "Trademark Management Institute, A Prospectus," JMV Papers, box 1, folder 8, 1959.

8. Letter, "Subject: Trademark Taboo Language," 29 February 1960, JMV Papers, box 1, folder 8, 1959; "Trademark Taboo Language Service," February 1960, JMV Papers, box 1, folder 8, 1959. Incidentally, according to Vicary's newsletter the words are *hindbaer*, *fjaert*, and *kaelling*.

9. Letter, Vicary to Irving Fishman, Restricted Merchandise Division, Bureau of Customs, 4 May 1961, JMV Papers, box 1, folder 10, 1961.

10. Letter, Vicary to Donald H. Wilson, Arthur D. Little, Inc., 23 April 1962, JMV Papers, box 1, folder 11, 1962.

11. Letter, Vicary to Robert E. Patterson, director, Marketing Services Company, 4 May 1962, JMV Papers, box 1, folder 20, "Studies Assembled in California," 1949–65, 5.

12. McGraw-Hill Inc., form employment termination statement, 7 May 1965, JMV Papers, box 1, folder 13, 1964–65 + 1967.

13. "James M. Vicary, 62."

14. Jones, "Projector Patented for Hidden Images."

15. Ewen, "The Public Eye."

16. Kittler, *Discourse Networks*, 222.

17. Koestler, *The Ghost in the Machine*.

18. Mills, *The Sociological Imagination*.

19. Adorno, *The Stars Down to Earth*, 53.

20. Ibid., 119.

21. Ibid., 155.

22. Boorstin, *The Image*, 3.

23. Ibid, 5.

24. "The Information Explosion," IBM advertising supplement, *New York Times*, 30 April 1961, 5.

25. Ibid., 19.

26. Toffler, *Future Shock*.

27. Klapp, *Overload and Boredom*, 8.

28. Wurman, *Information Anxiety*, 35.

29. Gladwell, *The Tipping Point*, 99.

30. Gladwell, *Blink*, 264.

31. Adorno, *The Stars Down to Earth*, 61.

32. Ibid., 62.

33. Sales may not have been increased, but it was the source for the name of the influential alternative rock group Hüsker Dü.

34. Federal Communications Commission, "Public Notice: Broadcast of Information by Means of 'Subliminal Perception' Techniques," FCC 74–78, 08055, 24 January 1974.

35. "Canada Holds Hearings on TV Subliminal Ads."

36. U.S. House of Representatives, Committee on Science and Technology, Subcommittee on Transportation, Aviation and Materials, *Subliminal Communication Technology*, 98th Congress, 2nd Session, 6 August 1984 (Washington: U.S. Government Printing Office, 1984).

Bibliography

Aarons, Edward S. "The Communicators." *Magazine of Fantasy and Science Fiction* 14, no. 6 (June 1958), 50–68.

Abel, Elie. "Schwable Tells of P.O.W. Ordeal." *New York Times*, 12 March 1954, 1, 5.

"A Church Leader Answers Faubus." *New York Times*, 21 September 1958, 64.

Acland, Charles R. "Curtains, Carts and the Mobile Screen." *Screen* 50, no. 1 (spring 2009), 148–66.

"Ad Agencies Hatch a Radio Dilemma on Triple Spotting." *Variety*, 4 December 1957, 28.

Adams, Val. "Subliminal Ads Shown in Capital." *New York Times*, 14 January 1958, 66.

———. "3 Networks Ban Subliminal Ads." *New York Times*, 4 December 1957, 61.

Adams, Virginia. "'Mommy and I Are One': Beaming Messages to Inner Space." *Psychology Today*, May 1982, 24, 25, 27, 28, 30, 32, 34, 36.

Adorno, Theodor W. *The Stars Down to Earth*. New York: Routledge, 1994 [1952–53].

"Ads You'll Never See." *Business Week*, 21 September 1957, 30–31.

"Agency Investigates 'Rats' Ad." *New York Times*, 18 September 2000, § A, 16.

"Aid to the Reds Laid to Korea Prisoners." *New York Times*, 20 June 1956, 5.

Aiken, Catherine. *Exercises in Mind-Training*. New York: Harper and Brothers, 1899.

———. *Method of Mind-Training: Concentrated Methods in Attention and Memory*. New York: Harper and Brothers, 1896.

Alterman, Rolland A. "Tachistoscopic Teaching." *Educational Screen and AV Guide* 37 (June 1958), 282, 283, 293.

"A Psychologist's Denial of the Existence of the Subconscious Mind." *Current Literature* 47 (August 1909), 206–8.

"ARF Checks Data on Subliminal Ads; Verdict: 'Insufficient.'" *Advertising Age*, 15 September 1958, 50.

Arnoult, Malcolm D. "Accuracy of Shape Discrimination as a Function of the Range of Exposure Intervals." *United States Air Force Human Resources Research Center Research Bulletin* 51, no. 32 (1951), 1–12.

Bach, S., and G. S. Klein. "The Effects of Prolonged Subliminal Exposures of Words." *American Psychologist* 12 (1957), 397–98.

Bakal, Carl. "The Schools of Tomorrow." *Saturday Review*, 24 August 1957, 9, 10, 11, 35, 36, 37.

Baldwin, Robert. "Kinetic Art: On the Use of Subliminal Stimulation for Visual Perception." *Leonardo* 7, no. 1 (1974), 1–5.

———. "Review: N. F. Dixon's *Subliminal Perception* and Wilson Bryan Key's *Subliminal Seduction*." *Leonardo* 9, no. 4 (autumn 1976), 334.

Ballard, J. G. "The Subliminal Man." *The Best Short Stories of J. G. Ballard*, 204–24. New York: Washington Square, 1985 [1963].

"Banned in Britain." *Printers' Ink* 264, no. 6 (8 August 1958), 12.

Barnette, G. C. *Learning through Seeing*. Meadville, Penn.: Keystone View, 1949.

Barrows, Susanna. *Distorting Mirrors: Visions of the Crowd in Late Nineteenth-Century France*. New Haven: Yale University Press, 1981.

Barthes, Roland. *Mythologies*, trans. Annette Lavers. New York: Hill and Wang, 1972 [1957].

Bartos, Rena. "Ernest Dichter: Motive Interpreter." *Journal of Advertising Research* 26, no. 1 (February–March 1986), 15–20.

Beattie, Earle. "Prof. Key and His Sex Book." *Media Probe* 2, no. 2 (1975), 12–17.

Beatty, Sharon E., and Del I. Hawkins. "Subliminal Stimulation: Some New Data and Interpretation." *Journal of Advertising* 18, no. 3 (1989), 4–8.

Beaty, Bart. *Fredric Wertham and the Critique of Mass Culture*. Jackson: University of Mississippi Press, 2005.

Becker, Bill. "Pastors Oppose Faubus on Vote." *New York Times*, 22 September 1958, 22.

Bedingfield, Robert E. "Time and G.E. Plan Educational Unit." *New York Times*, 20 November 1965, 45, 55.

Benedict, John. "Mind Control, Ultimate Tyranny." *American Mercury*, April 1960, 16.

Benjamin, Walter. *Selected Writings*, vol. 2, *1927–1934*, ed. Michael W. Jennings, Howard Eiland, and Gary Smith. Cambridge: Belknap Press of Harvard University Press, 1999.

———. *Selected Writings*, vol. 3, *1935–1938*, ed. Howard Eiland and Michael W. Jennings. Cambridge: Belknap Press of Harvard University Press, 2002.

Benschop, Ruth. *Unassuming Instruments: Tracing the Tachistoscope in Experimental Psychology*. Groningen: ADNP, 2001.

———. "What Is a Tachistoscope? Historical Explorations of an Instrument." *Science in Context* 11, no. 1 (1998), 23–50.

Benson, Frances M. "We Improved Spelling with the Tachistoscope." *Educational Screen and AV Guide* 35 (November 1956), 408.

Bent, Silas. "Dethroning the Will." *New York Times Magazine*, 29 October 1922, § 4, 1, 14.

Bernstein, Jack. "TV's 'Hidden Persuaders,' SP, All but Buried as Selling Medium—On Other Ad Agency Fronts." *Variety*, 23 April 1958, 24.

Bevan, William. "Subliminal Stimulation: A Pervasive Problem for Psychology." *Psychological Bulletin* 61, no. 2 (February 1964), 81–99.

Black, Hillel. "Automation Still in Future." *New York Times*, 12 January 1968, 74.

Boehm, George A. W. "Can People Be Taught like Pigeons?" *Fortune*, October 1960, 176, 177, 178, 179, 259, 260, 265, 266.

Boorstin, Daniel J. *The Image, or What Happened to the American Dream*. New York: Atheneum, 1962.

Bordwell, David. *The Way Hollywood Tells It: Story and Style in Modern Movies*. Berkeley: University of California Press, 2006.

Boroff, David. "The Three R's and Pushbuttons." *New York Times*, 25 September 1960, § 6, 36, 66, 68, 70, 72.

Boyd, E. G. "Portable Tachistoscope Based on a Commercial Slide-Viewer." *Bulletin of the British Psychological Society* 25, no. 87 (April 1972), 113.

Brean, Herbert. "'Hidden Sell' Technique Is Almost Here." *Life*, 31 March 1958, 102, 103, 104, 107, 108, 110, 113, 114.

"British Ad Group Set Probe of Subliminal Ads." *Advertising Age*, 13 January 1958, 71.

"British TV Row Breaks over Alleged 'Subliminal' Message." *Advertising Age*, 3 November 1958, 107.

Britt, Steuart Henderson. *The Spenders*. New York: McGraw-Hill, 1960.

"Britt Proposes More Scientific Subliminal Test." *Advertising Age*, 31 March 1958, 3, 30.

Brooks, John. "The Little Ad That Isn't There: A Look at Subliminal Advertising." *Consumer Reports*, January 1958, 7–10.

Brown, James I. "Vocabulary via Tachistoscope." *Educational Screen* 30 (September 1951), 274, 287.

Brown, James I., and Eugene S. Wright. *Manual of Instructions for Use with the Minnesota Efficient Reading Series: Timing Group*. Meadville, Penn.: Keystone View, 1955.

———. *Manual of Instructions for Use with the Minnesota Efficient Reading Series of Tachistoslides*. Meadville, Penn.: Keystone View, n.d. [ca. 1955].

Brown, William F. *Beat, Beat, Beat*. New York: Signet, 1959.

"Brr." *Time*, 30 December 1948, 82.

Bullock, August. *The Secret Sales Pitch*. San Jose: Norwich, 2004.

Burmeister, Lou E. *Foundations and Strategies for Teaching Children to Read*. Reading, Mass.: Addison-Wesley, 1983.

Burroughs, William S. *Naked Lunch*. New York: Grove, 1959.

———. *The Ticket That Exploded*. New York: Grove, 1962/1968.

Buxton, William J., and Charles R. Acland. "Interview with Dr. Frank N. Stanton: Radio Research Pioneer." *Journal of Radio Studies* 8, no. 1 (summer 2001), 191–229.

Caffyn, John. "Psychological Laboratory Techniques in Copy Research." *Journal of Advertising Research* 4, no. 4 (December 1964), 45–50.

Calkins, Earnest Elmo. "The Ten Best Advertisements." *Esquire*, April 1957, 83–86.

"Campaign Laugh Track." *New York Times*, 17 September 2000, 5.

"Canada Holds Hearings on TV Subliminal Ads." *Advertising Age*, 31 March 1975, 89.

"Canadians Brood over Subject of Subliminal Pitch." *Advertising Age*, 27 January 1958, 3, 34.

Cantril, Hadley, with Hazel Gaudet and Herta Herzog. *The Invasion from Mars: A Study in the Psychology of Panic*. Princeton: Princeton University Press, 1940.

Caplan, Eric. *Mind Games: American Culture and the Birth of Psychotherapy*. Berkeley: University of California Press, 1998.

Carlson, Theodora E. *Guide to the National Defense Education Act of 1958*. Washington: U.S. Department of Health, Education and Welfare, Office of Education, 1960.

Carpenter, Edmund, and Marshall McLuhan. *Explorations in Communication*. Boston: Beacon, 1960.

Carruthers, Susan L. *Cold War Captives: Imprisonment, Escape, and Brainwashing*. Berkeley: University of California Press, 2009.

Cash, H. C. "Subliminal Advertising: Our Analysis of Experiments Shows Inadequacies." *Advertising Age*, 23 May 1958, 14–19, 22.

Cattell, J. M. "The Inertia of the Eye and Brain." *Brain* 8 (October 1885), 295–312.

"CBC, Canadian Admen Disapprove Subliminal Pitches." *Advertising Age*, 2 December 1957, 1, 32.

"CBC Is First to Broadcast Subliminal Test." *Advertising Age*, 20 January 1958, 1.

Clowse, Barbara Barksdale. *Brainpower for the Cold War: The Sputnik Crisis and the National Defense Education Act of 1958*. Westport: Greenwood, 1981.

Cole, Jack. "The Subliminal Pitch." *Playboy*, September 1958, 59–61.

Committee on Motivation Research. *The Application of Subliminal Perception in Advertising*. New York: Advertising Research Foundation, 1958.

Condon, Richard. *The Manchurian Candidate*. New York: Quality Paperback, 1988 [1959].

Cone, Fairfax M. "Advertising Is Not a Plot: A Reply to Vance Packard." *Atlantic*, January 1958, 71–73.

Cook, Wesley W. M. *Practical Lessons in Hypnotism*. Chicago: Thompson and Thomas, 1900.

Cook, William A. "Lurking behind the Ice Cubes." *Journal of Advertising Research* 33, no. 2 (March–April 1993), 7–8

Cooper, John S. "Man, Dig These Crazy Tests! (to Evaluate Advertising Copy)." *Wall Street Journal*, 29 December 1952, 1, 9.

"Corporations: The Teaching Machine." *Time*, 7 November 1960, 91, 92, 94.

Coser, Lewis. "Kitsch Sociology." *Partisan Review*, summer 1959, 480–83.

Cousins, Norman. "Editorial: Smudging the Subconscious." *Saturday Review*, 5 October 1957, 20.

Crabtree, Adam. "'Automatism' and the Emergence of Dynamic Psychiatry." *Journal of the History of the Behavioral Sciences* 39, no. 1 (winter 2003), 51–70.

Crary, Jonathan. *Suspensions of Perception: Attention, Spectacle and Modern Culture*. Cambridge: MIT Press, 2001.

Cray, Douglas W. "Electronic Training Devices on Display." *New York Times*, 10 August 1966, 53, 59.

———. "The Knowledge Industry: Ideas and Profits." *New York Times*, 11 July 1965, § F, 1, 12.

Cunningham, Stuart. *Framing Culture: Criticism and Policy in Australia.* Sydney: Allen and Unwin, 1992.

Currell, Sue. "Streamlining the Eye: Speed Reading and the Revolution of Words, 1870–1940." *Residual Media*, ed. Charles R. Acland, 344–60. Minneapolis: University of Minnesota Press, 2007.

Danzig, Fred. "Subliminal Advertising: Today It's Just History Flashback for Researcher Vicary." *Advertising Age*, 17 September 1962, 72, 74.

Darnton, Robert. *Mesmerism and the End of the Enlightenment in France.* Cambridge: Harvard University Press, 1968.

Dearborn, W. F. "The Tachistoscope in Diagnostic Reading." *Psychological Monographs* 47, no. 212 (1936), 1–19.

"Deeper . . . Deeper . . . Dee. . . ." *Time*, 20 March 1950, 77–78.

De Fleur, Melvin L., and Robert M. Petranoff. "A Televised Test of Subliminal Persuasion." *Public Opinion Quarterly* 23, no. 2 (summer 1959), 168–80.

de la Peña, Carolyn Thomas. *The Body Electric: How Strange Machines Built the Modern American.* New York: New York University Press, 2003.

Dench, Ernest A. "Strange Effect of Photoplays on Spectators." *Illustrated World* 27 (June 1917), 788.

Deutsch, J. A. "The Reflecting Shutter Principle and Mechanical Tachistoscopes." *Quarterly Journal of Experimental Psychology* 12 (1960), 54–56.

Deutsch, Karl W. "On Social Communication and the Metropolis." *Daedalus* 90 (1961), 99–110.

"Devilish?" *Newsweek*, 14 October 1957, 98, 100.

Dick, Philip K. *The Three Stigmata of Palmer Eldritch.* New York: Vintage, 1991 [1965].

———. *Time Out of Joint.* New York: Vintage, 2002 [1959].

"Diddling the Subconscious." *Nation*, 5 October 1957, 206–7.

Dixon, Norman. *Preconscious Processing.* New York: John Wiley and Sons, 1981.

———. *Subliminal Perception: The Nature of a Controversy.* New York: McGraw-Hill, 1971.

Dodge, Raymond. "An Experimental Study of Visual Fixation." *Psychology Monograph* 8, no. 4 (1907), 1–95.

———. "An Improved Exposure Apparatus." *Psychological Bulletin* 4, no. 1 (January 1907), 10–13.

"Dr. Münsterberg on the Emotional Desiccation of the American People." *Current Literature* 45 (September 1908), 330–33.

"Dr. Murphy Tells of Telepathy Data." *New York Times*, 30 March 1924, 3.

"Dubious about 'Subliminal' Claims Made without Science Control." *Variety*, 7 May 1958, 2, 23.

Dumler, Marvin J. "A Study of Factors Related to Gains in the Reading Rate of College Students Trained with the Tachistoscope and Accelerator." *Journal of Educational Research* 52 (1958), 27–30.

During, Simon. *Modern Enchantments: The Cultural Power of Secular Magic.* Cambridge: Harvard University Press, 2002.

DuShane, Graham. "Editorial: The Invisible Work, or No Thresholds Barred." *Science*. 11 October 1957, 681.

"Editorial: Subliminal Silver Lining." *Wall Street Journal*, 14 March 1958, 8.

"Editorial: The Ad That Isn't There." *New York Times*, 23 January 1958, 26.

"Editors Split on South." *New York Times*, 10 October 1956, 28.

"Education News." *New York Times*, 30 August 1959, § 4, 11.

Edwards, A. E. "Subliminal Tachistoscopic Perception as a Function of Threshold Method." *Journal of Psychology* 50 (1960), 139–44.

Efron, Edith. "Brand New Brand Names." *New York Times Magazine*, 7 July 1957, 29–30.

Ellenberger, Henri. *The Discovery of the Unconscious*. New York: Basic Books, 1970.

Esper, E. A. "The Bradyscope: An Apparatus for the Automatic Presentation of Visual Stimuli at a Constant Slow Rate." *Journal of Experimental Psychology* 9 (1926), 56–59.

Evans, J. E. "A Tachistoscope for Exposing Large Areas." *American Journal of Psychology* 43 (1931), 285–86.

Ewen, Stuart. *All Consuming Images*. Cambridge: MIT Press, 1984.

———. "The Public Eye: On Desublimated Advertising." *Art Forum*, January 1991, 27.

Fadiman, Clifton. "The Decline of Attention." *Saturday Review Cavalcade*, 32–44. New York: Saturday Review Associates, 1950.

Farber, M. A. "Need for Standards in Industry Seen." *New York Times*, 10 August 1966, 53, 59.

"Fast Looks." *Time*, 24 September 1945, 76.

"Fast Reading vs. Fast Thinking." *Fortune*, May 1953, 47.

"FCC: 'Nothing to Worry About.'" *Variety*, 4 December 1957, 43.

"FCC Peek into Method Postponed until 1958." *Advertising Age*, 2 December 1957, 8.

"FCC Peers into Subliminal Picture on TV." *Advertising Age*, 2 December 1957, 1, 81.

"FCC to Get First-hand Look at Subliminal Ads before Ruling on TV Use." *Wall Street Journal*, 3 January 1958, 16.

Fearing, Kenneth. *Clark Gifford's Body*. New York: Random House, 1942.

Federal Communications Commission. *Information Bulletin on Subliminals*. Washington: U.S. Government Printing Office, 1977.

Fernald, L. Dodge, and Peter S. Fernald. *Introduction to Psychology*, 5th edn. Dubuque: Wm. C. Brown, 1985.

Filep, Robert, and Wilbur Schramm. *A Study of the Impact of Research on Utilization of Media for Educational Purposes*. Washington: U.S. Department of Health, Education and Welfare, Office of Education, 1970.

Final Report of the Commission to Study Subliminal Projection. State of New Jersey, Assembly Concurrent Resolution no. 33 (1958), May 1959.

Finn, James B. "Teaching Machines: Auto-Instructional Devices for the Teacher." *N.E.A. Journal*, November 1960, 41–44.

Fishman, Stephen M. "James and Lewes on Unconscious Judgment." *Journal of the History of the Behavioral Sciences* 4, no. 4 (October 1968), 335–48.

Flournoy, Théodore. *From India to the Planet Mars: A Study of a Case of Somnambu-lism with Glossolalia*, trans. Daniel B. Vermilye. New York: Harper and Brothers, 1900.

"Ford Aide Supports Programmed Classes." *New York Times*, 27 October 1961, 6.

"Forming and Changing Attitudes of People." *Public Relations Journal*, January 1955, 20–21.

Forrest, Derek. *Hypnotism: A History*. New York: Penguin, 1999.

Fowler, Elizabeth M. "Wall St. Studies Teaching Devices." *New York Times*, 14 May 1961, § 3, 7.

Fraiberg, Selma. "The Science of Thought Control." *Commentary*, May 1962, 420–29.

Free, E. E. "Radio's Aid Is Invoked to Explore Telepathy." *New York Times*, 30 August 1925, § 8, 3.

Freud, Sigmund. "Group Psychology and the Analysis of the Ego." *Sigmund Freud*, vol. 12, *Civilization, Society and Religion*, 91–178. New York: Penguin, 1985 [1921].

Galbraith, John Kenneth. *The Affluent Society*. Boston: Houghton Mifflin, 1958.

Galton, Lawrence. "2,000 WPM — but Is It Reading?" *New York Times*, 27 August 1961, § 6, 60, 62, 64, 66.

Gary, Brett. *The Nervous Liberals: Propaganda Anxieties from World War I to the Cold War*. New York: Columbia University Press, 1999.

Geiger, John. *Nothing Is True, Everything Is Permitted*. New York: Disinformation Company, 2005.

General Manual of Instructions: The Keystone Tachistoscope, Advanced Teaching Tech-niques. Meadville, Penn.: Keystone View, 1954.

"'Ghost' Ads Overrated." *Science News Letter*, 26 October 1957, 260.

Gill, Merton M., and Margaret Brenman. *Hypnosis and Related States: Psychoanalytic Studies in Regression*. New York: International Universities, 1959.

"Girlwatching Guide Loses Status on U.S. List of Teachers' Aids." *New York Times*, 29 September 1963, 61.

Gladwell, Malcolm. *Blink: The Power of Thinking without Thinking*. New York: Back Bay / Little, Brown, 2007.

———. *The Tipping Point: How Little Things Can Make a Big Difference*. New York: Little, Brown, 2000.

"Gladys the Beautiful Receptionist." *Advertising Age*, 10 February 1958, 12.

Glander, Timothy. *Origins of Mass Communications Research during the American Cold War: Educational Effects and Contemporary Implications*. Mahwah, N.J.: Lawrence Erlbaum, 2000.

Godbout, Oscar. "Subliminal Ads Blocked on Coast." *New York Times*, 7 March 1958, 49.

———. "'Subliminal' Ads over Air Studied." *New York Times*, 13 November 1957, 70.

———. "Subliminal Test Planned in West." *New York Times*, 22 January 1958, 54.

———. "Video Group Bans 'Subliminal' Ads." *New York Times*, 14 November 1957, 67.

"Good and Bad Effects of Mental Suggestion in the Theater." *Current Literature* 47 (November 1909), 550–51.

Goodman, Ralph. "Freud and the Hucksters." *Nation*, 14 February 1953, 143–45.

Graham, Robert. "Adman's Nightmare: Is the Prune a Witch?" *Reporter*, 13 October 1953, 27–31.

Gramsci, Antonio. *Selections from the Prison Notebooks*, ed. and trans. Quintin Hoare and Geoffrey Nowell Smith. New York: International, 1971.

Gregory, Joshua C. "Telepathy, Radiation and the Unconscious." *Fortnightly*, February 1948, 121–27.

Grieveson, Lee. "Cinema Studies and the Conduct of Conduct." *Inventing Film Studies*, ed. Lee Grieveson and Haidee Wasson, 3–37. Durham: Duke University Press, 2008.

Griffith, Ann Warren. "Captive Audience." *Tomorrow, Inc.: SF Stories about Big Business*, ed. Martin Harry Greenberg and Joseph D. Olander, 67–79. New York: Taplinger, 1976 [1953].

Grindley, G. C. "A New Form of Tachistoscope." *British Journal of Psychology* 23 (1933), 405–7.

Griswold, Wesley S. "tv's New Trick: Hidden Commercials." *Popular Science*, April 1958, 95–97, 252.

Grund, E. "Das Lessen des Wortanfanges bei Volkschulkindern verschiedener Altersstufen." *Neue psychologische Studien* 6 (1930), 311–16.

Guedry, Perry. "New Educational Media: A Progress Report." *School Life* 44, no. 2 (October 1961), 27–29.

Gunning, Tom. "An Aesthetic of Astonishment: Early Film and the (In)Credulous Spectator." *Viewing Positions: Ways of Seeing Film*, ed. Linda Williams, 114–33. New Brunswick: Rutgers University Press, 1997 [1989].

Haber, Ralph Norman. "Public Attitudes Regarding Subliminal Advertising." *Public Opinion Quarterly* 23, no. 2 (summer 1959), 291–93.

Haberstroh, Jack. *Ice Cube Sex: The Truth about Subliminal Advertising*. Notre Dame: Cross Cultural, 1994.

Hackett, Alice Payne, and James Henry Burke. *80 Years of Best Sellers*. New York: R. R. Bowker, 1977.

Haineault, Doris-Louise, and Jean-Yves Roy. *Unconscious for Sale: Advertising Psychoanalysis and the Public*, trans. Kimball Lockhart with Barbara Kerslake. Minneapolis: University of Minnesota Press, 1993 [1984].

Halberstam, David. *The Fifties*. New York: Fawcett Columbine, 1993.

Hamilton, James. "Unearthing Broadcasting in the Anglophone World." *Residual Media*, ed. Charles R. Acland, 283–328. Minneapolis: University of Minnesota Press, 2007.

Hansen, Miriam Bratu. "The Mass Production of the Senses: Classical Cinema as Vernacular Modernism." *Reinventing Film Studies*, ed. Christine Gledhill and Linda Williams, 332–50. London: Arnold, 2000.

Harrison, Emma. "Teacher Machine to Be Ready in '61." *New York Times*, 6 September 1959, 61.

Harvey, Carr. "Space Illusions." *Psychological Bulletin* 9, no. 7 (July 1912), 257–60.

Hawkins, Del. "The Effects of Subliminal Stimulation on Drive Level and Brand Preference." *Journal of Marketing Research* 7, no. 3 (August 1970), 322–26.

Hechinger, Fred M. "Concepts behind 'Teaching Machine.'" *New York Times*, 23 January 1963, 6.

———. "On the Automated Classroom." *New York Times*, 19 June 1966, § 4, 8.

———. "U.S. Education Chief Criticizes the Large Number of Automated Aids as Wasteful." *New York Times*, 15 June 1966, 35.

Heffernan, Kevin. *Ghouls, Gimmicks, and Gold: Horror Films and the American Movie Business, 1953–1968*. Durham: Duke University Press, 2004.

Heinlein, Robert A. *Stranger in a Strange Land*. New York: Ace, 1987 [1961].

Herman, Ellen. *The Romance of American Psychology: Political Culture in the Age of Experts*. Berkeley: University of California Press, 1995.

"'Hidden Persuaders' Hits Britain; Some Find It 'Hilarious'; Few Are Persuaded." *Advertising Age*, 13 January 1958, 44–45.

Hilliard, Robert L., and Michael Keith. *The Broadcast Century and Beyond: A Biography of American Broadcasting*, 3rd edn. Boston: Focal, 2001.

Hische, W. "Identifikation und Psychotechnik." *Psychotechnisches Zeitschrift* 5 (1930), 95–97.

Hoban, Charles, and Edward B. van Ormer. *Instructional Film Research, 1918–1950: Rapid Mass Learning*. New York: Arno, 1970 [1950].

"Hollywood TV Station Cancels Plans to Use Subliminal Ads." *Wall Street Journal*, 14 March 1958, 8.

Holmes, John Clellon. "The Philosophy of the Beat Generation." *Esquire*, February 1958, 35–38.

Horowitz, Daniel. *Vance Packard and American Social Criticism*. Chapel Hill: University of North Carolina Press, 1994.

"How Machines Do Teaching Job." *Business Week*, 17 September 1960, 111–14.

"How's That Again?" *Newsweek*, 3 February 1958, 65–66.

Hunter, Edward. *Brainwashing*. New York: Farrar, Straus and Cudahy, 1956.

———. *Brainwashing in Red China*. New York: Vanguard, 1951.

Hunter, Marjorie. "Teaching Device Growing Rapidly." *New York Times*, 18 January 1962, 15.

Hurt, Mary Jane. "Perception Training for Telephone Information Operators." *American Journal of Optometry* 32 (1955), 546–52.

Huxley, Aldous. *Brave New World Revisited*. New York: Harper and Row, 1958.

"Huxley Fears New Persuasion Methods Could Subvert Democratic Procedures." *New York Times*, 19 May 1958, 45.

"Hypnotism by Radio Is Latest Claim." *New York Times*, 15 July 1923, 19.

"Hypnotized Girls Sleep Months." *New York Times*, 14 October 1925, 10.

"Hypnotized Policeman Kills Three at a Séance." *New York Times*, 28 December 1923, 1.

"If Subliminal Ad's Hypnotic, It Won't Sell; If It Sells, It's Unethical, Say Doctors." *Advertising Age*, 23 September 1957, 2.

Illingworth, Frank. "The Future of Hypnotism." *Contemporary Review*, October 1946, 228–31.

"Images Reproduced in Brain as in Television Receiver." *Science News Letter*, 17 May 1941, 317–18.

"In 'Debate' with Packard, Weir Hits Book as 'Malicious.'" *Advertising Age*, 28 October 1957, 82–83.

"Inside the Consumer: The New Debate: Does He Know His Own Mind?" *Newsweek*, 10 October 1955, 89–93.

Institute of Practitioners in Advertising, Ad Hoc Committee. *Subliminal Communication*. London: Institute of Practitioners in Advertising, 1958.

"Invisible Ads Are Quick as a Flash, but Not Too Quick for FCC's X-Ray Eye." *Business Week*, 16 November 1957, 125.

"'Invisible' Ads Tested: New Process for TV and Movie Commercials Stepped Up Product Sales in First Test." *Printers' Ink* 260, no. 12 (20 September 1957), 44.

"Is Subliminal New?" *Printers' Ink* 261, no. 2 (11 October 1957), 58.

"Is 'Subliminal' Semi-operative in Theaters with Special Coke Breaks?" *Variety*, 18 December 1957, 1.

James, William. *The Essential Writings*, ed. Bruce W. Wilshire. Albany: SUNY Press, 1984.

"James M. Vicary, 62." *Salem Evening News*, 9 November 1977, 2.

Jamieson, Kathleen Hall. *Dirty Politics: Deception, Distraction, and Democracy*. Oxford: Oxford University Press, 1992.

Jancovich, Mark. *Rational Fears: American Horror in the 1950s*. Manchester: University of Manchester Press, 1996.

Janet, Pierre. "Report on Some Phenomena of Somnambulism," trans. Bert S. Kopell. *Journal of the History of the Behavioral Sciences* 4, no. 2 (April 1968 [1885]), 124–31.

———. "Second Observation of Sleep Provoked from a Distance and the Mental Suggestions during Somnambulistic Sleep." *Journal of the History of the Behavioral Sciences*, 4, no. 3 (July 1968 [1886]), 258–67.

Jenkins, John G. "A Simple Tachistoscope of Many Uses." *American Journal of Psychology* 45 (1933), 150.

Jones, Stacy V. "Projector Patented for Hidden Images." *New York Times*, 3 November 1962, 29, 36.

"K&E's Cox Hits Subliminal Ads." *Advertising Age*, 30 September 1957, 127.

Kalis, William H. "The Phantom of the Soap Opera." *Public Relations Journal*, March 1958, 6–8.

Kellner, Douglas. *Media Culture: Cultural Studies, Identity and Politics between the Modern and the Postmodern*. New York: Routledge, 1995.

Kerekes, David, ed. "Flicker Machine Edition." *Headpress* 25 (2003).

Key, Wilson Bryan, Jr. *The Age of Manipulation: The Con in Confidence, the Sin in Sincere*. New York: Henry Holt, 1989.

———. *The Clam-Plate Orgy: And Other Subliminals the Media Use to Manipulate Your Behavior*. New York: Prentice Hall, 1980.

———. "'Cloze Procedure': A Technique for Evaluating the Quality of Language Translation." *Journal of Communication* 9, no. 1 (1959), 14–18.

———. *Media Sexploitation*. New York: New American Library, 1977.

———. *Subliminal Ad-ventures in Erotic Art*. Boston: Branden, 1992.

———. *Subliminal Seduction: Ad Media's Manipulation of a Not So Innocent America*. Englewood Cliffs: Signet, 1973.

———. "Watch the Background, Not the Figure." *Antigonish Review* 74–75 (1988), 188–96.

Keyes, Daniel. *Flowers for Algernon*. New York: Harcourt, Brace and World, 1966.

Kidd, R. M. "Subliminal Stimuli a 'Monster'? Don't Worry—Mass Public's Individual Differences Blunt Its Power, Says Agency Man." *Advertising Age*, 11 August 1958, 56–57.

King, Seth S. "'Certain' Classes Banned by Bishop." *New York Times*, 3 September 1956, 11.

Kittler, Friedrich A. *Discourse Networks, 1800/1900*, trans. Michael Metteer with Chris Cullens. Stanford: Stanford University Press, 1990 [1985].

———. *Gramophone, Film, Typewriter*, trans. Geoffrey Winthrop-Young and Michael Wutz. Stanford: Stanford University Press, 1999 [1986].

Klapp, Orrin E. *Overload and Boredom: Essays on the Quality of Life in the Information Society*. New York: Greenwood, 1986.

Klass, Bertrand. "The Ghost of Subliminal Advertising." *Journal of Marketing* 23, no. 4 (October 1958), 146–50.

Knowles, J. T. "Wireless Telegraphy and 'Brain-Waves.'" *Nineteenth Century* 45 (May 1899), 857–64.

Koestler, Arthur. *The Ghost in the Machine*. New York: Macmillan, 1967.

Koontz, Dean. *Night Chills*. New York: Berkley, 1983 [1976].

Kopell, Bert S. "Pierre Janet's Description of Hypnotic Sleep Provoked from a Distance." *Journal of the History of the Behavioral Sciences* 4, no. 2 (April 1968), 119–31.

Krajick, Kevin. "Sound Too Good to Be True? Behind the Boom in Subliminal Tapes." *Newsweek*, 30 July 1990, 60–61.

"KTLA Will Test Subliminal Ads within 90 Days." *Advertising Age*, 27 January 1958, 107.

Lancaster, John. *Introducing Op Art*. New York: Watson-Guptill, 1973.

Larsen, John M., Jr. "Obituary: Samuel Renshaw (1892–1981)." *American Psychologist* 38, no. 2 (February 1983), 226.

Lazarsfeld, Paul F., and Robert K. Merton. "Mass Communication, Popular Taste and Organized Social Action." *Mass Communication*, ed. Wilbur Schramm, 492–578. Urbana: University of Illinois Press, 1960.

"Learn While You Sleep." *Time*, 2 February 1948, 35.

Le Bon, Gustave. *The Crowd: A Study of the Popular Mind*. Dunwoody, Ga.: Berg, 1895.

Lederman, Susan J., and Bill Nichols. "Flicker and Motion in Film." *Ideology and the Image: Social Representation in the Cinema and Other Media*, by Bill Nichols, 293–301. Bloomington: Indiana University Press, 1981.

Leiber, Fritz, Jr. "The Girl with the Hungry Eyes." *The Girl with the Hungry Eyes and Other Stories*, 3–20. New York: Avon, 1949.

Lerner, Daniel. *Sykewar: Psychological Warfare against Germany, D-Day to VE-Day.* New York: G. W. Stewart, 1949.

"Letter: Subliminal Perception." *Broadcasting/Telecasting* 53, no. 4 (30 September 1957), 18.

Lewis, Anthony. "Russell Assails 2 Key Rights Aims." *New York Times*, 2 March 1964, 12.

Lewis, Herschell G. "Admen Hop on Critic of Subliminal Ads; Flay 'Witch Burning,' Urge Further Study." *Advertising Age*, 11 August 1958, 56.

Lifton, Robert Jay. *Thought Reform and the Psychology of Totalism: A Study of "Brainwashing" in China.* New York: W. W. Norton, 1961.

Lloyd, James Hendrie. "Mental Contagion and Popular Crazes." *Scribner's* 69 (February 1921), 201–6.

Lobel, Michael. *Image Duplicator.* New Haven: Yale University Press, 2002.

———. "Technology Envisioned: Lichtenstein's Monocularity." *Oxford Art Journal* 24, no. 1 (2001), 131–54.

Longgood, William. "Shop Spy Tells Why of Baking: Expert Says Using Cake Mix Is like Having a Baby." *New York World-Telegram*, 25 April 1955, 17.

Lucas, Darrell Blaine. "The Optimum Length of Advertising Headline." *Journal of Applied Psychology* 18 (1934), 665–74.

Lucas, Darrell Blaine, and Steuart Henderson Britt. *Advertising Psychology and Research: An Introductory Book.* New York: McGraw-Hill, 1950.

Luce, Arnold E. "Flashfilm: Minnesota's Contribution to Better Driver Education." *Educational Screen and AV Guide* 37 (February 1958), 70, 71, 75.

Ludgin, Earle. "Advertising Must Be Unexpected and Believable to Break through Subliminal Barrier, Says Ludgin." *Advertising Age*, 19 January 1959, 81, 82, 84.

"Ludgin Says Ad Excess Makes All Ads Subliminal." *Advertising Age*, 17 February 1958, 2, 98.

Machaver, W. V., and W. A. Borrie. "A Reading Improvement Program for Industry." *Personnel* 28 (1951), 123–30.

Machlup, Fritz. *The Production and Distribution of Knowledge in the United States.* Princeton: Princeton University Press, 1962.

Mackinney, Arthur C. "A Validation of Tachistoscopic Training for Clerical Workers." *Personnel Psychology* 11 (1958), 13–23.

Mannes, Marya. "Ain't Nobody Here but Us Commercials." *Reporter*, 17 October 1957, 35–37.

"Marketing Men Debate Ways to Make Consumer Buy." *New York Times*, 18 October 1957, 33, 36.

"Marketing Men Hear about 'Mind Probing'; Projective Methods, Other Psychological Techniques Discussed." *Advertising Age*, 5 January 1953, 1, 48.

Marvel, John A. "Acquisition and Retention of Reading Performance on Two Response Dimensions as Related to 'Set' and Tachistoscopic Training." *Journal of Educational Research* 52 (1959), 232–37.

"Mass Observation: An American Researcher Peddles an English Technique for Use in the U.S." *Tide*, 1 July 1945.

Masson, Thomas L. "Read with Speed." *New York Times*, 18 February 1923, §§ 4, 5, 13.

Mathis, William, and Donald R. Senter. "Quantification of Contributions Made by Various Reading Instrument Combinations to the Reading Process." *Research and Information Report*, no. 7. New York: Educational Developmental Laboratories, 1973.

"Max Reinhardt Hypnotizing the World." *Current Literature* 52 (March 1912), 337–38.

McClelland, J. S. *The Crowd and the Mob: From Plato to Canetti*. Boston: Unwin Hyman, 1989.

McConnell, James V., Richard L. Cutler, and Elton B. McNeil. "Subliminal Stimulation: An Overview." *American Psychologist* 13, no. 5 (May 1958), 229–42.

McHugh, L. C. "Pavlov, Brainwashing and Foreign Policy." *America*, 10 September 1960, 612–14.

McLuhan, Marshall. *Counterblast*, designed by Harley Parker. Toronto: McClelland and Stewart, 1969.

———. *Culture Is Our Business*. New York: McGraw-Hill, 1970.

———. "Cybernetics and Human Culture." *Understanding Me: Lectures and Interviews*, ed. Stephanie McLuhan and David Staines, 44–55. Cambridge: MIT Press, 2003 [1961].

———. *Letters of Marshall McLuhan*, ed. Matie Molinaro, Corinne McLuhan, and William Toye. Toronto: Oxford University Press, 1987.

———. "A McLuhan Mosaic." *Antigonish Review* 74–75 (1988), 11–14.

———. *The Mechanical Bride: The Folklore of Industrial Man*. New York: Vanguard, 1951.

———. *Report on Project in Understanding New Media*. Washington: National Association of Educational Broadcasters / Office of Education, U.S. Department of Health, Education and Welfare, 1960.

———. *Understanding Media: The Extensions of Man*. New York: McGraw-Hill, 1964.

McLuhan, Marshall, and Quentin Fiore. *The Medium Is the Massage: An Inventory of Effects*. New York: Bantam, 1967.

———. *War and Peace in the Global Village*. New York: Bantam, 1968.

McLuhan, Marshall, and Harley Parker. *Through the Vanishing Point: Space in Poetry and Painting*. New York: Harper and Row, 1968.

McRobbie, Angela. *Postmodernism and Popular Culture*. New York: Routledge, 1994.

Meier, Richard L. "Communications and Social Change." *Behavioral Science* 1, no. 1 (1956), 43–58.

———. *A Communications Theory of Urban Growth*. Cambridge: Joint Center for Urban Studies of MIT and Harvard University, 1962.

Melcer, F. H., and B. G. Brown. "Tachistoscopic Training in the First Grade." *Optometric Weekly* 36 (1945), 1217–19.

Messaris, Paul. *Visual Persuasion: The Role of Images in Advertising*. Thousand Oaks: Sage, 1997.

Miller, James G. "Information Input Overload and Psychopathology." *American Journal of Psychiatry* 116 (February 1960), 695–704.

Miller, Mark Crispin. "Hollywood the Ad." *Atlantic Monthly*, April 1990, 41–54.

———. Introduction, *The Hidden Persuaders*, by Vance Packard, 9–27. Brooklyn: IG, 2007.

Mills, C. Wright. *The Sociological Imagination*. Oxford: Oxford University Press, 1959.

"Misuse of Hypnotism in Securing Confessions of Crime." *Current Literature* 42 (February 1907), 221–22.

Moore, Harriett B. "From Self-Delusion to Mass Delusion—and Back Again? Is Subliminal Perception Real?" *Art Direction*, May 1958, 38.

Moore, Timothy E. "Subliminal Advertising: What You See Is What You Get." *Journal of Marketing* 46 (spring 1982), 38–47.

"Morse Defends Motivational Research." *Broadcasting/Telecasting* 53, no. 4 (30 September 1957), 44.

"Mr. Vicary's 'High Jinks.'" *Advertising Age*, 24 September 1962, 16.

Münsterberg, Hugo. *Hugo Münsterberg on Film: The Photoplay: A Psychological Study and Other Writings*, ed. Allan Langdale. New York: Routledge, 2002 [1916].

———. "Hypnotism and Crime." *McClure's* 30 (January 1908), 317–22.

———. "The Prevention of Crime." *McClure's* 30 (April 1908), 750–56.

———. "Prohibition and Social Psychology." *McClure's* 31 (August 1908), 438–44.

———. "Psychology and the Market." *McClure's* 34 (November 1909), 87–93.

———. *Psychotherapy*. New York: Moffat and Yard, 1909.

Nadis, Fred. *Wonder Shows: Performing Science, Magic, and Religion in America*. New Brunswick: Rutgers University Press, 2005.

"NARTB Warns on SP, 'Horror.'" *Broadcasting* 53, no. 21 (18 November 1957), 68.

National Education Association. *Schools for the Sixties: A Report of the Project on Instruction*. New York: McGraw-Hill, 1963.

"Navy Novices Learn Radio While Asleep through Telephones Strapped to Ears." *New York Times*, 25 June 1923, 15.

Nelson, Ray Faraday. "Eight o' Clock in the Morning." *Reel Future*, ed. Forrest J. Ackerman and Jean Stine, 372–77. New York: Barnes and Noble, 1994 [1963].

Netschajeff, A. "Zur Frage über die qualitative Wahrnehmungsform." *Psychologische Studien*, 1929, 114–18.

"Nets Vow They'll Eschew Subliminal Ads." *Advertising Age*, 9 December 1957, 8.

"New Grolier Machine Said to Speed Learning." *New York Times*, 6 November 1960, § 3, 7.

Newhall, Sidney M. "Projection Tachistoscopy." *American Journal of Psychology* 48 (1936), 501–4.

"New 'Invisible Commercial' Ad Agency Boon." *Billboard*, 16 September 1957, 1, 13.

"New Little Clubs Light Up U.S. Night Life." *Life*, 3 February 1958, 95, 99, 100.

"News Notes: Classroom and Campus." *New York Times*, 4 December 1960, § 4, 7.

Newson, John L. "A Projection Tachistoscope." *Quarterly Journal of Experimental Psychology* 6 (1954), 93–94.

"Newspapers' Sensations and Suggestion." *Independent*, 21 February 1907, 449–51.

"New Subliminal Era Slips In While Audience Not Looking." *Broadcasting* 53, no. 22 (25 November 1957), 72, 74.

"New Trade Program." *New York Times*, 31 March 1958, 45.

"New Tutoring Machine." *New York Times*, 15 November 1960, 62.

Nixon, H. K. "A Study of Perception of Advertisements." *Journal of Applied Psychology* 11 (1927), 135–42.

"Non-Coffee-Using Housewife Made Fresh Coffee after Hint in Subliminal Radio Tests." *Advertising Age*, 3 February 1958, 3, 58.

"No Penalty for Stations That Showed 'Rats' Ad." *New York Times*, 10 March 2001, § A, 10.

"No Sly Suggestion." *Newsweek*, 2 February 1959, 19–20.

"Nucoa Uses New Subliminal Twist: It's 'Contrapuntal.'" *Advertising Age*, 24 March 1958, 2, 42.

"N.Y. Legislature Weighs Bill Banning Subliminal Movie Ads." *Advertising Age*, 3 February 1958, 3.

"N.Y. State Senate Okays Subliminal Ban." *Advertising Age*, 24 March 1958, 42.

"165 Girls Faint at Football Game; Mass Hysteria Grips 'Pep Squad.'" *New York Times*, 14 September 1952, 1.

O'Neill, William L. *American High: The Years of Confidence, 1945–1960*. New York: Free Press, 1986.

"1.5 Million Grant to Schools Offers Visual Training Aids." *New York Times*, 14 August 1963, 31.

Packard, Vance. "The Growing Power of Admen." *Atlantic*, September 1957, 55–59.

———. *The Hidden Persuaders*. New York: David McKay, 1957.

———. "The Mass Manipulation of Human Behavior." *America*, 14 December 1957, 342–44.

———. "Resurvey of 'Hidden Persuaders.'" *New York Times Magazine*, 11 May 1958, 10, 19, 20.

———. *The Waste Makers*. New York: David McKay, 1960.

Pearson, Norman. "Sub-human Consciousness." *Nineteenth Century* 80 (September 1916), 576–85.

"Performances to Be Discouraged." *New York Times*, 28 June 1909, 6.

"Periscoping the World: Red Gambits." *Newsweek*, 20 January 1958, 14.

"'Persuaders' Get Deeply 'Hidden' Tool: Subliminal Projection." *Advertising Age*, 16 September 1957, 127.

Peters, John Durham. *Speaking into the Air: A History of the Idea of Communication*. Chicago: University of Chicago Press, 1999.

"'Phone Now,' Said CBC Subliminally—but Nobody Did." *Advertising Age*, 10 February 1958, 8.

"Pic to 'Editorialize' on U.S. Missile Lag." *Variety*, 4 December 1957, 1.

Pohl, Frederik, and C. M. Kornbluth. *The Space Merchants*. New York: Del Rey, 1979 [1953].

"Politics: Romney's Brainwash." *New York Times*, 10 September 1967, § 4, 2.

Pooler, James S. "Ex–Office Boy Borrows from Psychiatry to Add New Touch to Poll-Taking." *Detroit Free Press*, 30 May 1948, § B, 2.

Pratt, Ray. *Projecting Paranoia: Conspiratorial Visions in American Film*. Lawrence: University Press of Kansas, 2001.

Price, Wesley. "New Ways to Learn Faster." *Science Digest*, March 1944, 12–16.

Pringle, Katherine, and Henry F. Pringle. "Time Yourself Reading This." *Nation's Business*, March 1953, 86–89.

Pritchard, Alfred W. "Mass Hypnosis: Soviet Secret Weapon." *American Mercury*, February 1959, 108–12.

"Professor's Talk on Races Backed." *New York Times*, 30 May 1955, 15.

"Proponent of SP Deprecates Effect." *Broadcasting* 54, no. 12 (24 March 1958), 47–48.

"Propose to Send Thought across the Atlantic Ocean." *New York Times*, 28 March 1924, 19.

"Psychic Hucksterism Stirs Call for Inquiry." *New York Times*, 6 October 1957, 38.

"Psychologists Hit Subliminal Ads as 'Chimera,' Laud Clarity, Repetition." *Advertising Age*, 8 September 1958, 1, 116.

"Psychologists Hit Use of Subliminal Methods in Ads as 'Unprofessional.'" *Advertising Age*, 16 June 1958, 85.

"Psychology and the Ads." *Time*, 13 May 1957, 51, 52, 54.

"Push-Button Brains." *Newsweek*, 26 October 1959, 95.

Pyles, Thomas. "Subliminal Words Are Never Finalized." *New York Times Magazine*, 15 June 1958, 16, 55, 57, 58.

"Quicker Than the Eye." *New Republic*, 27 January 1958, 5–6.

"Radio Station Testing 'Subliminal' Ads, but Listeners Can Still Hear 'Em." *Advertising Age*, 16 December 1957, 2, 93.

"'Radio Telepathy.'" *New York Times*, 21 November 1943, § 4, 13.

"Radio to Be Tried as Anaesthetizer." *New York Times*, 14 July 1923, 11.

Ranzal, Edward. "'No Mercy' Urged on Riesel Jury." *New York Times*, 6 December 1956, 42.

"Real Advertising Men's Viewpoint." *Advertising Age*, 16 December 1957, 12.

"Recognizing Planes." *New York Times*, 21 November 1943, § 4, 13.

Rees, W. J. "On the Terms 'Subliminal Perception' and 'Subception.'" *British Journal of Psychology* 624 (November 1971), 501–4.

Reeves, Bryon, and Clifford Nass. *The Media Equation: How People Treat Computers, Television, and New Media like Real People and Places*. Cambridge: Cambridge University Press, 1996.

Reichert, Tom. *The Erotic History of Advertising*. Amherst: Prometheus, 2003.

Renshaw, Samuel. *How to Use the Renshaw Tachistoscopic Trainer*. Chicago: Stereo Optical, 1950.

———. "The Visual Perception and Reproduction of Forms by Tachistoscopic Methods." *Journal of Psychology* 20 (1945), 217–32.

Renshaw, Samuel, and I. L. Hampton. "A Combined Chronoscope and Interval Timer." *American Journal of Psychology* 43 (1931), 637–38.

Renshaw, Samuel, Vernon L. Miller, and Dorothy P. Marquis. *Children's Sleep*. New York: Macmillan, 1933.

Robbins, Tom. *Still Life with Woodpecker: A Sort of Love Story*. New York: Bantam, 1980.

Rogers, Martha, and Christine A. Seiler. "The Answer Is No: A National Survey of Advertising Industry Practitioners and Their Clients about Whether They Use Subliminal Advertising." *Journal of Advertising Research* 34, no. 2 (March–April 1994), 36–45.

Rogers, Stuart. "How a Publicity Blitz Created the Myth of Subliminal Advertising." *Public Relations Quarterly* 37 (winter 1992–93), 12–17.

————. "People Love to Be Fooled." *Public Relations Quarterly* 37 (winter 1992–93), 16.

Rolo, Charles J. "Admen and the Id." *Atlantic*, June 1957, 87–88.

"Romney Asserts He Underwent 'Brainwashing' on Vietnam Trip." *New York Times*, 5 September 1967, 28.

"Romney Chances Assayed by G.O.P." *New York Times*, 17 September 1967, 47.

Root, E. Merrill. *Brainwashing in the High Schools.* New York: Devin-Adair, 1958.

Roper, Elmo. "How Powerful Are the Persuaders?" *Saturday Review*, 5 October 1957, 19.

Rose, Alvin W. "Motivation Research and Subliminal Advertising." *Journal of Social Research* 25, no. 3 (fall 1958), 271–84.

Rosenberg, Daniel. "Early Modern Information Overload." *Journal of the History of Ideas* 64, no. 1 (2003), 1–9.

Roszak, Theodore. *Flicker.* New York: Summit, 1991.

Rovin, Jeff. *The Encyclopedia of Super Villains.* New York: Facts on File, 1987.

Rutter, Richard. "Education in U.S. Big and Growing." *New York Times*, 5 September 1965, § F, 1, 10.

Saettler, Paul. *A History of Instructional Technology.* New York: McGraw-Hill, 1968.

"Sales Held Key, Not Ad Billings." *New York Times*, 12 June 1957, 57.

"Sales through the Sub-Conscious, 'Invisible' Advertisements." *Sunday Times* (London), 10 June 1956, 1.

Samuel, Lawrence R. *Freud on Madison Avenue: Motivation Research and Subliminal Advertising in America.* Philadelphia: University of Pennsylvania Press, 2010.

Sanderson, Peter. *Ultimate X-Men.* New York: Dorling Kindersley, 2000.

Sargant, William. *Battle for the Mind: A Physiology of Conversion and Brain-Washing.* London: Pan, 1957.

Sarris, Viktor, and Michael Wertheimer. "Max Wertheimer's Research on Aphasia and Brain Disorders: A Brief Account." *Gestalt Theory* 23, no. 4 (2001), 267–77.

Schaffer, Amy, and John D. Gould. "Eye Movement Patterns as a Function of Previous Tachistoscopic Practice." *Perceptual and Motor Skills* 19, no. 3 (1964), 701–2.

Schlesinger, Arthur, Jr. "The Crisis of American Masculinity." *Esquire* 50, no. 5 (November 1958), 63–66.

Schlosberg, Harold. "A Projection Tachistoscope." *American Journal of Psychology* 43 (1931), 499–501.

Schneck, Jerome M. "A Reevaluation of Freud's Abandonment of Hypnosis." *Journal of the History of the Behavioral Sciences* 1, no. 2 (April 1965), 191–95.

"Schools Are Held in Need of Funds for Machine Aids." *New York Times*, 2 October 1962, 33.

Schultz, Robert. "Letter: Don't Look Now, but It's Only a 'Tachistoscope.'" *Variety*, 9 October 1957, 24, 46.

———. "Letter: Half Hour Commercials, Subliminal Programs?" *Advertising Age*, 28 October 1957, 103.

Schutz, George. "Just Whom Did Invisible Screen Advertising Sell?" *Motion Picture Daily*, 16 December 1957, 1, 4.

Sconce, Jeffrey. "Brains from Space: Mapping the Mind in 50s Science and Cinema." *Science as Culture* 5, no. 2 (1995), 277–302.

———. *Haunted Media: Electronic Presence from Telegraphy to Television*. Durham: Duke University Press, 2000.

"Sees Further Tests of 'Subliminal' Needed." *Motion Picture Daily*, 17 December 1957, 1, 9.

Seldes, Gilbert. "What Makes the Consumer Tick?" *Saturday Review*, 1 June 1957, 29–30.

Seltzer, Mark. *Bodies and Machines*. New York: Routledge, 1992.

"Sidelights: Companies Ring School Bell." *New York Times*, 2 June 1966, 62.

Silvergate, Scot. "Subliminal Perception and the First Amendment: Yelling Fire in a Crowded Mind?" *University of Miami Law Review* 44 (1990), 1243–81.

Silverman, Syd. "Vance Packard ('Hidden Persuaders') Raps 'Call me MR' Addle-dazzle." *Variety*, 13 November 1957, 34.

Simley, O. A. "The Relation of Subliminal to Supraliminal Learning." *Archives of Psychology* 146 (January 1933), 5–40.

Simmel, Georg. "The Metropolis and Mental Life." *The Sociology of Georg Simmel*, ed. Kurt Wolff, 409–24. New York: Free Press, 1950 [1903].

Sitton, Claude. "Faubus in Clash with Clergymen." *New York Times*, 17 September 1958, 1, 25.

Smith, G. J. W., D. P. Spence, and G. S. Klein. "Effects of Subliminally Exposed Words upon Conscious Impressions of a Face." *American Psychologist* 12 (1957), 394.

———. "Subliminal Effects of Verbal Stimuli." *Journal of Abnormal Social Psychology* 59 (1959), 167–76.

Smith, Henry P., and Theodore R. Tate. "Improvements in Reading Rate and Comprehension of Subjects Training with the Tachistoscope." *Journal of Educational Psychology* 44 (1953), 176–84.

Smith, Seymour. "Total Measurements, Evaluating All Promotional Factors in a Campaign." *Proceedings, 11th Annual Conference, Advertising Research Foundation*, 5 October 1965, 76–80.

Smith, William D. "Sylvania Enters Education Field." *New York Times*, 21 March 1966, 49.

"Sneaky Advertisements." *Mad Magazine*, May 1958, 18–19.

Snyder, Alan. "The Flashreader in the Reading Laboratory." *The English Journal* 41 (May 1952), 269.

"Solon vs. 'Subliminal.'" *Variety*, 13 November 1957, 34.

Sparke, Penny. *As Long as It's Pink: The Sexual Politics of Taste*. New York: Harper Collins, 1995.

Spectorsky, A. C. "The MR Boys Are Out to Make you Buy and Buy and Buy." *New York Times*, 28 April 1957, § 8, 3.

Spielvogel, Carl. "Advertising: Two Agencies Near a Merger." *New York Times*, 8 September 1958, 40.

"SP, PS Continue to Hold Stage: NARTB, Networks Meet Secretly." *Broadcasting* 53, no. 23 (2 December 1957), 31–32.

Stam, Robert, Robert Burgoyne, and Sandy Flitterman-Lewis. *New Vocabularies in Film Semiotics: Structuralism, Post-Structuralism and Beyond*. New York: Routledge, 1992.

Stein, W. "Tachistoskopische Untersuchungen über das Lesen mit sukzessiver Darbietung." *Archiv für die gesamte Psychologie* 64 (1928), 301–46.

Streatfeild, Dominic. *Brainwash: The Secret History of Mind Control*. New York: Thomas Dunne / St. Martin's, 2007.

Strong, Lydia. "They're Selling your Unconscious." *Saturday Review*, 13 November 1954, 11–12, 60–63.

"Students Charge 'Left-Wing' Bias." *New York Times*, 3 March 1957, 83.

"Subliminal Ad Is Transmitted in Test but Scores No Popcorn Sales." *Advertising Age*, 20 January 1958, 2, 94.

"Subliminal Ads Don't 'Brainwash' Viewers, College Dean Says." *Advertising Age*, 12 May 1958, 52.

"Subliminal Ads Lose." *New York Times*, 13 March 1958, 20.

"Subliminal Ads May Become Fact If FCC Delays: Rep. Dawson." *Advertising Age*, 10 February 1958, 43.

"Subliminal Ads May Be Usable: Britt." *Advertising Age*, 3 February 1958, 58.

"Subliminal Ads Wash No Brains, Declare Moore, Becker, Developers of Precon Device." *Advertising Age*, 2 December 1957, 81.

"Subliminal Advertising, Banned by TV Chains, May Hit Movie Houses." *Wall Street Journal*, 5 December 1957, 19.

"Subliminal Cuts Show 'Hot Car' in New Toyota Push." *Advertising Age*, 19 September 1966, 3, 126.

"Subliminal Has a Test; Can't See If It Works." *Printers' Ink* 262, no. 3 (17 January 1958), 4–5.

"'Subliminal' May Take Long Count; Held 'Frightening.'" *Variety*, 27 November 1957, 1, 87.

"Subliminal Message Does Have Effect, Psychologist Finds." *Advertising Age*, 4 July 1960, 24.

"Subliminal Message Hits Home, Stanford Researchers Report." *Advertising Age*, 5 May 1958, 72.

"'Subliminal Not for Us' Sez NBC." *Variety*, 4 December 1957, 43.

"Subliminal Perception Discussed by Meighan at KNXT (TV) Seminar." *Broadcasting* 53, no. 18 (28 October 1957), 48.

"'Subliminal P,' Men in White Banned for TV." *Variety*, 25 June 1958, 25, 50.

"Subliminal Scare Stirs Congressmen." *Broadcasting* 53, no. 20 (11 November 1957), 72–73.

"Subliminal Techniques." *Science News Letter*, 11 June 1960, 372.

"Subliminal Test Makes 32 Thirsty; Seven 'Felt Sexy.'" *Advertising Age*, 24 February 1958, 3.

"'Subliminal' Test Okayed by FCC." *Variety*, 11 December 1957, 46.

"Subliminal TV Ad's Dimness May Impair Value: Psychologist." *Advertising Age*, 3 February 1958, 73.

"Subliminal TV Cited as Danger to Youth." *New York Times*, 29 January 1958, 24.

"Supersoft Sell." *Time*, 9 September 1957, 67–68.

Sutherland, Max. *Advertising and the Mind of the Consumer: What Works, What Doesn't, and Why*. St. Leonards, N.S.W.: Allen and Unwin, 1993.

Suzuki, Koji. *Ring*, trans. Robert B. Rohmer and Glynne Walley. New York: Harper Collins, 2005 [1991].

Swanson, D. E. "Common Elements in Silent and Oral Reading." *Psychological Monographs* 48 (1937), 36–60.

Talese, Gay. "Most Hidden Hidden Persuasion." *New York Times Magazine*, 12 January 1958, 22, 59, 60.

Tankard, James W., Jr. "Whose Seduction? Review of *Subliminal Seduction*." *Journal of Communication* 25, no. 2 (1975), 221–22.

Taylor, David. "A Study of the Tachistoscope." *British Journal of Marketing* 4 (spring 1970), 22–28.

Taylor, E. A. *Controlled Reading*. Chicago: University of Chicago Press, 1937.

"Teaching Machine." *New York Times*, 20 April 1961, 48.

"Teenagers Prod Reps into Passing State Law vs. 'Subliminal' Films." *Variety*, 19 March 1958, 19.

"Teen Is Pushover for 'Persuaders,' Educators Are Told." *Advertising Age*, 12 May 1958, 2.

"Telepathy Put to Real Tests." *New York Times*, 29 March 1924, 14.

"That Old Black Magic." *Time*, 19 September 1949, 57.

"The Busy Air." *Time*, 9 December 1957, 79.

"The Day the FCC Got Potted." *Variety*, 4 December 1957, 28.

"The Growing Variety of Teaching Machines." *New York Times*, 11 November 1962, 9.

"The 'Invisible' Invader." *Newsweek*, 23 September 1957, 70.

"The Invisible Monster." *Christian Century*, 2 October 1957, 1157.

"The New Charm of Black: Subliminal." *Vogue*, November 1957, 131.

"The New Wave in Titillation." *Gent*, October 1962, 75–77.

"The Phantom Plug." *Newsweek*, 18 November 1957, 46.

"The Subliminal Fight Gets Hotter." *Printers' Ink* 261, no. 1 (4 October 1957), 17.

Thomasson, Martin. "Machines at the Scene: The Cutting-Up and Redistribution of the Sensorium in Nietzsche, Wundt and Münsterberg." *Site Magazine* 3–4 (2002), 17–19.

"Thought and Electricity." *New York Times*, 6 March 1924, 16.

"Thought Is Not like Radio." *New York Times*, 29 March 1924, 14.

"Thought Waves by Radio Tested in Chicago; Persons Far Away Say They Got Them." *New York Times*, 4 March 1924, 1.

Thurstone, Louis Len. *Primary Mental Abilities*. Chicago: University of Chicago Press, 1938.

Tinker, M. A. "A Flexible Apparatus for Recording Reading Reactions." *Journal of Experimental Psychology* 15 (1932), 777–78.

"Tireless." *New Yorker*, 13 February 1960, 25–26.

Toffler, Alvin. *Future Shock*. New York: Random House, 1970.

"Topics of the Times." *New York Times*, 26 June 1923, 18.

Tracy, Michael. "Must Be Unseen to Be Believed: The Tachistoscope." *The People's Almanac*, ed. David Wallechinsky and Irving Wallace. Garden City: Doubleday, 1975.

"TV Message Fruitless." *New York Times*, 8 February 1958, 35.

Tweedy, Frank. "The Subliminal Brute." *The Discarded Confidante and Other Stories*, 195–206. New York: Neale, 1918.

Twitchell, James B. *Adcult USA: The Triumph of Advertising in American Culture*. New York: Columbia University Press, 1996.

"Unconscious Sell Theme Tops '58 Ad Conference." *Advertising Age*, 21 April 1958, 1, 142.

"Unfair to the Subconscious." *Economist*, 31 January 1959, 416.

"Univac Adapted to Readership Research." *Printers' Ink*, 28 September 1956, 74.

"Unseen TV Gets Exposure on Both Coasts." *Broadcasting* 54, no. 3 (20 January 1958), 98–99.

"U.S. to Help Set Up a 'Clearinghouse' for Teaching Aids." *New York Times*, 9 November 1966, 78.

Valsiner, Jaan, and René van der Veer. *The Social Mind: Construction of an Idea*. Cambridge: Cambridge University Press, 2000.

Van Den Haag, Ernest. "Madison Avenue Witchcraft." *Commonweal*, 29 November 1957, 230–32.

Vicary, James M. *Annotated Bibliography of Word Association References Important to Marketing Researchers*. New York: J. M. Vicary, n.d. [ca. 1954].

———. "Free Association Tests Can Help Advertisers." *Printers' Ink*, 3 September 1948, 44–50.

———. "*Gestalt* Theory and Paired Comparisons." *Public Opinion Quarterly* 14 (spring 1950), 139–41.

———. "How Psychiatric Methods Can Be Applied to Market Research." *Printers' Ink*, May 1951, 39–40.

———. "Labor, Management and Food." *Harvard Business Review* 26, no. 3 (May 1948), 305–12.

———. "Seasonal Psychology." *Journal of Marketing* 20, no. 4 (1956), 394–97.

———. "What's in a Name Change." *American Business*, January 1957, 14, 15, 24.

———. "Word Association and Opinion Research: 'Advertising': An Illustrative Example." *Public Opinion Quarterly* 12 (spring 1948), 81–98.

"Vicary 'Delighted' at Academic Criticism." *Advertising Age*, 16 June 1958, 85.

"Viewers Would Resist 'Manipulation': Shepard." *Advertising Age*, 30 September 1957, 127.

"Visible Success Seen for Those Unseen Ads." *Broadcasting/Telecasting* 53, no. 4 (30 September 1957), 44.

Waid, Mark, ed. *Who's Who: Update '88*, vols. 1–4. New York: DC Comics, 1988.

Walker, Martin. *The Cold War: A History*. New York: Henry Holt, 1993.

Watson, R. I., Sr. *The Great Psychologists*, 4th edn. New York: Lippincott, 1978.

"WCCO Probes Subconsciousness with Pioneer 'Phantom Spots.'" *Variety*, 27 November 1957, 38.

Weaver, Warren, Jr., "Romney Renews Vietnam Charge." *New York Times*, 10 September 1967, 1, 36.

Weber, C. O. "The Use of Tachistoscopic Exercises in the Improvement of Reading Speed." *Psychological Bulletin* 34 (1937), 533–34.

Weir, Walter. "Another Look at Subliminal 'Facts.'" *Advertising Age*, 15 October 1984, 46.

Weisenberg, Charles M. "Automation in the Classroom: Teaching Machines." *Commonweal*, 27 January 1961, 454–56.

Wertham, Fredric. *Seduction of the Innocent*. Port Washington, N.Y.: Kennikat, 1954.

"Wha'd He Say?" *Broadcasting* 53, no. 21 (18 November 1957), 5.

"What Hypnotism Is and Is Not: Predictions about It That Have Not Been Realized." *New York Times*, 21 November 1909, § 2, 2.

"What Sways the Family Shopper." *Business Week*, 30 November 1957, 46, 47, 48, 50.

"Whazzat?" *Broadcasting/Telecasting* 53, no. 12 (16 September 1957), 29.

Whipple, Guy Montrose. "The Effect of Practice upon the Range of Visual Attention and of Visual Apprehension." *Journal of Educational Psychology* 1, no. 5 (May 1910), 249–62.

"Whispering Campaign." *Time*, 24 February 1958, 60.

Whitfield, Stephen J. *The Culture of the Cold War*. Baltimore: Johns Hopkins University Press, 1991.

Who's Who: The Definitive Directory of the DC Universe, vols. 2–26. New York: DC Comics, 1985–87.

Wicklein, John. "Brainwash Peril Seen over Nation." *New York Times*, 28 November 1958, 35.

Wilcott, R. C. "Letter: Invisible Words, Invisible Evidence." *Science*, 6 December 1957, 1202.

Williams, Raymond. *The Long Revolution*. London: Chatto and Windus, 1961.

———. *Marxism and Literature*. Oxford: Oxford University Press, 1977.

Williamson, Judith. *Decoding Advertisements: Ideology and Meaning in Advertising*. New York: Marion Boyars, 1978.

Wilson, D. K. *The Manual-Verbal Response Tachistoscope: Distracting Device for Intelligibility Testing: Technology Report SDC104-2-20*. Port Washington, N.Y.: U.S. Navy Special Devices Center, 1950.

Winick, Darvin. "An Investigation of the Group Tachistoscopic Method of Evaluating Magazine Advertisements." *Dissertation Abstracts* 15 (1955), 2291.

Winter, Alison. *Mesmerized: Powers of Mind in Victorian Britain*. Chicago: University of Chicago Press, 1998.

Wolfe, Winifred. *Ask Any Girl*. New York: Bantam, 1958.

Wolfle, Daele L. "The Improved Form of the Gulliksen Tachistoscope." *Journal of General Psychology* 8 (1933), 479–84.

Wooding, Edmund, ed. *Advertising and the Subconscious: Advertising Conference Contributed Papers, April 17, 1958*. Ann Arbor: Bureau of Business Research, School of Business Administration, University of Michigan, 1959.

Woodworth, Robert S. *Experimental Psychology*. New York: Henry Holt, 1938.

Woolf, James D. "Subliminal Perception Is Nothing New." *Advertising Age*, 28 October 1957, 96.

Wurman, Richard Saul. *Information Anxiety: What to Do When Information Doesn't Tell You What You Need to Know*. New York: Bantam, 1990.

Youngblood, Gene. *Expanded Cinema*. New York: E. P. Dutton, 1970.

"Youth Confesses Strangling Boy, 4; Tied Up Victim to Emulate Action He Saw in Movie, He Tells Bronx Police." *New York Times*, 10 November 1944, 21.

Zanot, Eric J., J. David Pincus, and E. Joseph Lamp. "Public Perceptions of Subliminal Advertising." *Journal of Advertising* 12, no. 1 (1983), 39–45.

Index

Page numbers in *italics* refer to illustrations.

Aarons, Edward S., 201–3
ABC: Huxley on *Mike Wallace Interview*, 174; presidential election of 2008 and, 16; subliminal advertising and, 127
À Bout de souffle (Godard), 216
Adorno, Theodor, 3, 205, 230–31, 236–37
Advertisers and Agencies, 104
advertising: consciousness and, 152–53, 220–21; ethics and, 105, 106–7, 190; in fiction, 162–63; formatting of, 156–57; images vs. rhetoric in, 231; information overload and, 159–61; McLuhan and, 38, 39; media clutter and, 156; men in, 162–63; mental calluses and, 148; MR and, 107–8, 133–34; overload of, 148, 150; psychoanalysis and, 105, 106, 116; saturation point of, 156; shock-edits in, 21; speed and, 79–80; subliminal perception and, 154; on sub-threshold level, 152; tachistoscopes and, 79–80, 84; television, 220–21; unconscious and, 17, 106, 115, 116. *See also* subliminal advertising
Advertising Age: Ludgin on advertisement clutter, 156; Packard and, 107; paradox of invisible spot and, 137–38; Stanford University experiments and, 149; on subliminal advertising, 114, 128; Vicary and, 99–100, 154, 227–28
"Advertising and the Subconscious" (University of Michigan Advertising Conference), 150–52, 154
Advertising Executives Club of Chicago, 156
Advertising Federation of America, 108
advertising industry: effectiveness vs. ethics in, 164; ethics in, 133; fear of backlash in, 149; reputation of, 132, 152–53; subliminal advertising and, 16–17; subliminal thesis and, 132
Advertising Research Foundation (ARF), 116, 152–53
Advisory Committee on New Educational Media, 180
Ad World, 217
AFA Motivational Research committee, 155
Affluent Society, The (Galbraith), 176
Again? (Russell), 139
Agel, Jerome, 224
Agency (Kaczender), 23
Age of Manipulation, The (Key), 40
Aiken, Catherine, 76
Aladdin (Clements, Musker), 21
Albicocco, Jean-Gabriel, 214
alcohol, 54, 130
All Consuming Images (Ewen), 17
Allen, Steve, 141–43
All-Flash, 199
All Star Comics, 198

American Broadcasting–Paramount Theaters, 127
American Education Publication, 187
American Management Association, 187
American Marketing Association (AMA), 99–100, 118, 150
American Mercury, 168, 172
American Optical Company, 78
American Psychological Association, 154
American Psychologist, 153–54
Archeology of Knowledge, The (Foucault), 39
Arendt, Hannah, 170
Arnheim, Rudolf, 36
Arnold, Jack, 163
Ashcroft, John, 14
Ask Any Girl (Walters, Wolfe), 162–63
Association for Educational Communications and Technology, 181
Atlantic, 106, 108
attention: decline of, 158; modernity and, 70–71; overload and, 158; tachistoscope and orientation of, 88–89
audiovisual education, 75, 176–81, 183–84, 185
authoritarian irrationality, 230
Automatisme psychologique, L' (Janet), 48
AutoTutor, 187
AWARE, Inc., 172–73
awareness: media consumption and, 155–56; subliminality and threshold of, 18; unawareness vs., 19. *See also* consciousness

Baldwin, Robert, 41
Ballard, J. G., 205–6
Barnum, P. T., 95
barrage montages, 218, 221, 224
Barrows, Susanna, 51
Barthes, Roland, 151
Barthol, Richard, 109
Basic Systems, 187
Batman comics, 198–99
Battle for the Mind (Sargant), 107, 174
BBC: *Science Review*, 152; subliminal perception test, 103, 104
Beat, Beat, Beat (Brown), 135
Beatles, 22–23, 36, 221
Beaty, Bart, 263 n. 5
"Beautiful Dreamers," 24
Becker, Hal C., 118, *119*, 213, 237
Bedazzled (Donen), 26
behaviorism, 75, 169, 230

Belson, Jordan, 210–11
Benedict, John, 168
Benjamin, Walter, 68, 86
Benschop, Ruth, 66, 67, 74
Benton and Bowles, 95–96
Berelson, Bernard, 100
Bergman, Ingmar, 216
Bergson, Henri, 45
Bernheim, Hippolyte, 49–50
Bettelheim, Bruno, 170
Bevan, William, 20
Billboard, 104
Binet, Alfred, 44
Black, Hillel, 187
Black Magic (Ratoff), 6–12
"Black Magic on Mars," 7–12
Blair, George, 120
Blast (Lewis), 225
Blink (Gladwell), 235
Blood Feast (Lewis), 154
Blood of the Man Devil (*Date with Death*; Daniels), 120, 122, 148, 211–13
Body Snatchers, The (Finney), 194, 205
body snatching, 194–96
Boisrond, Michel, 214
Boone, Pat, 144
Boorstin, Daniel, 162, 231
Booth, W. B., 150–51
Bordwell, David, 25
Bourdieu, Pierre, 33
Boy Commandos, 199
bradyscope, 74
Braid, James, 48
Brain-Stealers, The (Leinster), 194, 196–97, 205
brainwashing: civil rights and, 172, 173; in comic books, 198, 199, 201; communism and, 171; consumer society and, 171; defined, 169–70, 171; democracy and, 174; in fiction, 23–24, 66, 168; in films, 169; forced actions and, 150; governments and, 173; hypnosis and, 171–72; Korean War and, 168, 170–71, 172, 176; modernity and, 170; MR and, 107; propaganda and, 169–70; reeducation and, 170; of students, 172–73; subliminal advertising and, 113, 131; subliminal communication and, 168–69; on television, 169
"Brainwashing of John Hayes, The" (Horner), 169
Bras, René, 111, *112*

Brave New World (Huxley), 58
Brave New World Revisited (Huxley), 174
Breedlove, Lee, 217
Breer, Robert, 218
Brenman, Margaret, 171–72
Breuer, Josef, 44
British Institute of Practitioners in Advertising, 152
Britt, Steuart, 96–97, 150
Broadcasting/Telecasting, 104, 114
Brown, B. G., 79
Brown, William F., 135
Brunvand, Jan David, 94
Brussels world exposition (1958), 210–11
Bureau of Applied Social Research, 97, 153
Burgoyne, Robert, 25
Burroughs, William S.: *Naked Lunch*, 208–9; *Ticket That Exploded*, 209–10
Bush, George W., 14, 15–16, 26, 237
Business Week, 115, 116
Butter-Nut Coffee, 143–44, *145*, 146, 163

Cabinet of Dr. Caligari, The (Wiene), 55
Cahn, Edward L., 193
Calderón, Felipe, 16
Canada Post, 217
Canadian Advertising Advisory Board, 237
Canadian Broadcasting Corporation (CBC), 130–31, 155
Canadian Radio and Television-Telecommunications Council, 237
Canby, Vincent, 122
Cantril, Hadley, 1–5
capitalism: consumer society and, 162, 175; fascism and, 231; Packard and, 107; in *Space Merchants*, 161; in *They Live*, 205
Caplan, Eric, 44
"Captive Audience" (Griffith), 159–60, 161, 201
Carnahan, Mel, 14
Carpenter, John, 205
Carroll, Mark K., 172
Carus, Carl Gustave, 44
Castellanos, Alex, 15
Castle, Max, 24
Cattell, James M., 66–67, 74–75
CBS: subliminal advertising and, 127; *The Twentieth Century*, 260 n. 49
Central Intelligence Agency (CIA), 169
cerebrograph, 58
Charcot, Jean-Martin, 44, 49–50

Chase, Stuart, 105
Chevrolet, 144, 146, 217
CHiPs, 24
Choking Doberman, The (Brunvand), 94
Christian Century, 115
chronoscope, 51, 87
CIA (Central Intelligence Agency), 169
cinema. *See* motion pictures
Citizen Kane (film), 11
Civilization and Its Discontents (Freud), 40
Clam-Plate Orgy, The (Key), 40
Clark Gifford's Body (Fearing), 6
Clements, Ron, 21
Clockwork Orange, A (Kubrick), 65
Close-up (CBC), 130–31
Clowse, Barbara Barksdale, 176
clutter: advertising, 21, 156, 160, 171; googlization and, 235; graphic, 97, 218, *225*; informational, 156, 236; McLuhan and, 38; media clutter, 156, 158, 210, 233–34, 236; media installations and, 210; sensory, 236; stickiness and, 235; textual, 161; typographical, *233*
Cold War, 168, 169, 191, 197, 200, 236
Cole, Jack, 139–40, *141*
Come Dance with Me (Boisrond), 214
comic books, 7–12, 197–201
command metaphors, 28–29
commonsense, 33–34, 42, 55
Commonweal, 107
communication, 157
Communications Act of 1934, 126
communication studies, 27
"Communicators, The" (Aarons), 201–3
communism, 107, 128, 147, 168, 169, 171, 172–73, 195
computers, 22, 28, 30, 67, 70, 88, 100, *101*, 184, 186, 190, 198, 231, 232–34, 237, 238
Condon, Richard, 65
conformity, 107, 163, 171, 194, 206, 230, 236
Conrad, Tony, 218, 224
consciousness: advertising and, 152–53, 220–21; corporations and, 207–8; false, 42, 174, 229–30; James and, 46; learning and, 87; media, 205, 207; ordinary or supraliminal, 45; perceptual limits of, 207; practical, 34, 42, 63, 229–30; stream of, 72; sub-human, 45; subliminal, 45; subliminal flashes and, 216; subliminality and threshold of, 18; subliminal patterning of, 181–82. *See also* awareness

conspiracy theory, 22–23, 196, 230
Consumer Reports, 139, *140*
consumer society: body snatching films and, 195; brainwashing and, 171; capitalism in, 162, 175; Packard on, 175–76; resistance to, 229; in science fiction, 205–6; subliminal communication and, 166; subliminal thesis and, 161–62
control: bio-, 168; at distance, 48–49; intelligence agencies and, 169; mass populations and, 36–37; satirical images of subliminal advertising and, 140–41; sensation and perception limits and, 19; social, 166, 204, 236; tachistoscope and, 89; telepathic, 48–49; over thought-transmission, 196–97. *See also* mind control
Controlled Reading (Taylor), 78
Conway, Jack, 105
Cook, Peter, 26
Corman, Roger: *The Trip*, 218, 220–21, *222–23*; *War of the Satellites*, 175
Corrigan, Robert C., 118, *119*, 128, 143, 148, 213
Coué, Emile, 45, 59
Council of Chief State School Officers, 185
Counterblast (McLuhan, Parker), 225, 226
Counterpoint (WNEW), 116
Cousins, Norman, 167
Cox, Edwin, 114
Crary, Jonathan, 70–71, 73, 74, 75, 89
Crichton, Michael, 23
Crowd, The (Le Bon), 5, 50–52, 106
crowds: hypnosis and, 48, 54, 106, 170; images and, 50–51; influence and, 50–51; as irrational and antidemocratic, 5–6; loss of self and, 170; malleability of, 64; manipulation and control of, 36–37; mass observation techniques and, 97; mind manipulation and, 174; suggestion and, 50–51, 61; unconsciousness and, 50–51
Cukor, George, 105
Culp, Robert, 24
cultural logistics, 68
cultural studies: anti-disciplinarity of, 33; multiperspectival, 25; resistance and, 33; subliminal influences and, 18
cultural work, 28
culture: of abundance, 207; acoustic, 224; industrially produced, 63–64; linear vs. nonlinear, 224–26; literate vs. post-literate, 224–26; media and, 181–82; terminology and, 134

Culture Is Our Business (McLuhan), 225–26
Cunningham, Stuart, 241 n. 43
Cutler, Richard I., 151
cut-ups, 209–10
cyberspace, 59

Daily Herald, 152
Daniels, Harold: *Date with Death*, 120, 122, 148, 211–13; *My World Dies Screaming*, 120–24
Daniels, Harry Walter, 154
Danzig, Fred, 227
Darnton, Robert, 243 n. 22
Date with Death (*Blood of the Man Devil*; Daniels), 120, 122, 148, 211–13
Daumier, Honoré, 49
Davis, Geena, 16
Dawson, William A., 125, 128–29
Decatur study, 100
Decoding Advertising (Williamson), 35
De Fleur, Melvin L., 148
De la Peña, 244 n. 63
democracy: advertising and, 156; critical abilities and, 3; mass populations and, 5; political campaigning and, 116; social order and, 64; subliminal advertising and, 115, 132; subliminal communication and, 166–67, 174; subliminality and, 95, 191; totalitarianism and, 170
Dennis, Robert C., 120
Department of Audio-Visual Instruction (DAVI), 181
Department of Visual Instruction, 181
"Descent into the Maelstrom" (Poe), 38–39, 210, 238
Desmond, Thomas C., 146
Detective Comics, 199
"Dethroning the Will," 45
Deutsch, Karl, 158
Devil Doll (Shonteff), 243 n. 28
Dewey, John, 184
Dichter, Ernest, 98, 105, 107, 108, 110, 115–16
Dick, Philip K., 207–8
Disturbing Behavior, 65
Dixon, Norman, 20, 36; *Subliminal Perception*, 41, 152
DJ Spooky, 210
Dodge, Raymond, 69
Doerfer, John C., 125, 126
Donen, Stanley, 26

Doors of Perception, The (Huxley), 174
Dorothy and Dick (WOR program), 100
Doubleday, 187
Double Exposure, 24
Dracula (Stoker), 50
Dream Machine, 209, 218
du Deffand, Madame, 42
Dumas, Alexandre, *père*, 6
du Maurier, George, 50, 55, 61
Dun and Bradstreet, 227, 229
Duncan, Leslie B., 60
Dunninger, Joseph, 60–61
During, Simon, 4–5

Eames, Charles, 211
Eames, Ray, 211
Eddy, Mary Baker, 57
Educational Development Laboratories
    (EDL), 78, 80–81, 82, 83, 84
Educational Media Index (McGraw-Hill), 185
Educational Screen, 80
educational technology, 75–76, 87, 177–81,
    183–84, 185–91
Edward, William, 120
Edwards, William S., 211–13
Efron, Edith, 101
"Eight O'Clock in the Morning" (Nelson),
    203–5
Eisenhower, Dwight, 125, 180
Eisenstein, Sergei, 214
Elfont, Harry, 23
Ellenberger, Henri, 44–45, 48
Engler, Henry J., 150
epiperceptualism, 20
ESP (Precon), 118
Espinas, Alfred, 51
Esquire, 106
ethics: advertising and, 105, 106–7, 133, 190;
    effectiveness vs., 164; Fort Lee Theater test
    and, 92; mesmeric control and, 129–30;
    MR and, 116, 131; presidential campaigns
    and, 16; privacy and, 167–68; subliminal
    advertising and, 113, 115, 125; unconscious
    and, 166; Vicary and, 113
Ewen, Stuart, 229; *All Consuming Images*, 17
Ewing, Frank, 127–28
Experimental Films, 118
Expo '67 (Montreal), 211

Face in the Crowd, A (Kazan), 91
Fadiman, Clifton, 158

Family Circle, 99
Family Guy, The, 24
Fantastic Four Annual, The, 200
fascism, 91, 95, 170, 195, 214, 231
Faubus, Orval E., 173
Fearing, Kenneth, 6
Federal Communications Commission
    (FCC): demonstration for, 143, 167; Hüsker
    Dü and, 237; political advertising and, 16;
    subliminal advertising and, 125, 126, 127,
    128–29, 168, 237
Federal Trade Commission, 126
fiction. *See* popular culture
Fight Club (Fincher), 21, 23
Filep, Robert, 186, 189–90
Fille aux yeux d'or, La (Albicocco), 214
films. *See* motion pictures
Fincher, David, 21
Finn, James D., 177, 184
Finney, Jack, 194, 205
Fiore, Quentin, 224
Fist Fight (Breer), 218
Flash, 199
flashcards, 76
flash-edits, 213–14, 216–18, 220–21
flashing images, 21, 109, 214, 216–21, 236
Flashmeter, 81–82
Fletcher, Scott, 180
Flicker (Roszak), 24
Flicker, The (Conrad), 218, 224
Flicker Film, The (McLaren), 218
flickers, 208–11, 218, 238
Flitterman-Lewis, Sandy, 25
Flournoy, Théodore, 4
Flowers for Algernon, 65
Fonda, Peter, 220, 222–23
For Love or Money (Gordon), 163
Forrest, Richard E., 117–18
Fort Lee Theater, 91–95, 104, 108, 127, 151,
    227–28
Fortune: on information explosion, 232–33;
    on programmed instruction, 184–85; on
    reading speed, 82
Foucault, Michel, 33; *The Archeology of
    Knowledge*, 39
Fowler, Elizabeth, 184
fragmentation, 68, 70, 71, 72, 74, 89, 236
Fraiberg, Selma, 170
Frankenheimer, John, 172, 243 n. 28
Freberg, Stan, 143–44, 145
Freud, Sigmund, 43; *Civilization and Its*

Freud, Sigmund (*continued*)
  Discontents, 40; influence of, 44–45; *The Interpretation of Dreams*, 44; Janet and, 47; McLuhan and, 39–40; new psychology and, 45; on relationships as love, 48; in Russell's skit, 139; unconscious and, 44
"Freud and the Hucksters" *(Nation)*, 105
Freudianism, 43–44, 45, 105
From India to the Planet Mars (Flournoy), 4

Galbraith, John Kenneth, 176
Galton, Lawrence, 84
Gardener, Burleigh, 99–100
Gaudet, Hazel, 1, 2–3
Gaynor, Mitzi, 163
gender: mass cultural forms and, 163, 164; roles, 139, 140, 217
General Electric, 187
General Learning Corporation, 184
Gent (magazine), 213–14, *215*
Ghost Hour (NBC), 60
Ghost in the Machine, The (Koestler), 230
Gill, Merton M., 171–72
"Girl with the Hungry Eyes, The" (Leiber), 159
Gladwell, Malcolm, 30, 235–36
Glickman, Dan, 237
globalization, 232
Godard, Jean-Luc, 216
Goldiamond, Israel, 148–49
Goldstein, Michael, 109
Gordon, Michael, 163
Gore, Al, 14–16, 26, 237
government: brainwashing and, 173; educational technology and, 185–86; subliminal advertising and, 146–49; subliminal communication and, 125–26
Gramsci, Antonio, 31, 33–34
graphic revolution, 231
Green Lantern, 199
Gregory, Joshua, 56
Grey Ghost, The, 128
Grieveson, Lee, 244 n. 54
Griffith, Ann Warren, 159–60, 161, 201
Grolier, Inc., 184
Grover's Mill, N.J., 94
"Growing Power of Admen, The" (Packard), 110
Grund, E., 77
Guild, Nancy, 7, 9
Gulliksen tachistoscope, 69

Gunning, Tom, 224
Gysin, Brion, 208–9

Haberstroh, Jack, 35–36
Haineault, Doris-Louise, 35
Halberstam, David, 108, 176
Hall, Stuart, 33
Hampton, I. L., 69
Hansen, Miriam, 63
happenings, 210, 218
"happy or angry" test, 109–10, 113, 153
Harcourt, Brace and World, 187
Hard Days' Night, A (Lester), 221
Hartmann, Eduard von, 44, 45
Harvey, Carr, 72
Hawthorne Effect, 131
Head (Rafelson), 221, 226
Heffernan, Kevin, 120
Heinlein, Robert A., 194, 195, 205
Helms, Jesse, 15
Herzog, Herta, 153; *The Invasion from Mars*, 1, 2–3
Hidden Persuaders, The (Packard), 35, 105–9, 111, 116, 134, 138, 167, 175, 228
"Hidden Why's of Our Behavior" (Packard), 151
Hische, W., 76
Hitchcock, Alfred: *Psycho*, 214; *Rebecca*, 122
Hitler, Adolf, 9, 61, 172
Hoban, Charles, 177
Holden, William, 92
Hollister, Bessie, 52
Hollywood Production Code, 214, 216
Holmes, John Clellon, 133
Hopper, Dennis, 220
Horner, Harry, 169
Horowitz, Daniel, 105
Howco International, 120
Howe, Harold, II, 183, 186, 188
Hucksters, The (Conway), 105
Hughes, Mildred Barry, 147, 148
Hullabaloo (Morgan), 6
Hunter, Edward, 168, 169, 172
Hurlburt, Glen, 150
Hüsker Dü, 237
Huxley, Aldous, 106, 115, 191; *Brave New World*, 58; *Brave New World Revisited*, 174; *The Doors of Perception*, 174
hypnopaedia, 58
hypnosis, hypnotism: audience and, 120; brainwashing and, 171–72; crime and, 52,

53, 54–55; crowds and, 48, 54, 106, 170; in fiction, 208; Freud and, 44; Hitler and, 61; influence and, 59–60; James and, 46; Janet and, 47; Key and, 36–37; liminal states and, 59; long-distance, 60; media and, 37; men mesmerizing women in, 140; mesmerism, 47–48, 54–55, 59, 203; modernity and, 50, 61; Münsterberg and, 52–53; *My World Dies Screaming* and, 122, 124; Nancy school and, 49–50; in popular culture, 54, 206–7; race and, 61; rise and expansion of, 51–52; shopping and, 101–2; somnambulism, 48, 49, 57, 86, 106, 162, 204; stage, 59; subliminal advertising and, 131; subliminality and, 45; telepathy and, 53; television, 61; unconscious and, 19; uses of, 53

Hypnotic Eye, The (Blair), 120
"Hypnotist, The" (Daumier), *49*
Hypno-Vision, 117
hysteria, 44

I Am Legend (Matheson), 194, 205
IBM: on communication problems, 231–32; Science Research Associates and, 187
Illingworth, Frank, 61
Image, The (Boorstin), 162, 231
Incredible Shrinking Man, The (Arnold), 163
Independent, 55
influence: crowds and, 50–51; from distance, 55–56, 60; ethics of, 59–60; hypnotism and, 59–60; modernity and, 55–56; psychological warfare and, 169; remote, 48–49; sensation and perception limits and, 19. *See also* media influence
information: anxiety and, 234–35; explosion of, 231–33; saturation and, 164, 189, 235; simultaneous, 224; understanding vs., 235
information age, 42, 68, 231, 233, 234, 236
Information Anxiety (Wurman), 234–35
information overload, 88; advertising and, 159–61; advertising saturation and, 156; irrationality and, 234; McLuhan and, 182, 183, 226; pattern recognition and, 226; social change and, 162, 232–33; subliminal thesis and, 235
informed consent, 92
Innis, Harold, 39
installations, art, 210, 211
Institute for Motivational Research, 98, 114

instructional technology, 75–76, 87, 177–81, 183–84, 185–91
Internet, 13, 16, 31, 39, 57, 234
Interpretation of Dreams, The (Freud), 44
Invasion from Mars, The (Cantril, Gaudet, Herzog), 1, 2–3, 5, 153
Invasion of the Body Snatchers (Siegel), 194–95
Invisible Invaders (Cahn), 193
"Invisible Monster, The" *(Christian Century)*, 115
It Should Happen to You (Cukor), 105
Ivens, Richard, 52

Jacobs, Henry, 210–11
James, William, 45, 46, 52, 72; *Varieties of Religious Experience*, 26
James M. Vicary Company, 96
Jamieson, Kathleen Hall, 15
Jancovich, Mark, 194
Janet, Pierre: *L'Automatisme psychologique*, 48; double self and, 46–47; Freud and, 47; hypnotism and, 44, 48–49, 60; Léonie B. and, 47, 48, 51, 106; somnambulism and, 57; subconscious and, 45; on synthesis, 72; telepathy and, 48
Javal, Émile, 76
Johnson, Lyndon B., 176
Johnson, Nunnally, 105
Jones, Ernest, 47
Jones, Merle S., 127
Jones, T. C., 221
Josie and the Pussycats (Elfont, Kaplan), 23
Journal of Advertising Research, 17–18
Journal of Communication, 40–41
Jung, Carl, 36, 45, 47, 99
Justice League of America, 199

Kaczender, George, 23
Kaplan, Deborah, 23
Kazan, Elia, 91
Kellner, Douglas, 25
Kennedy, John F., 82, 176
Kenyon and Eckhardt, 114
Keppel, Francis, 183–84
Kern, Stephen, 89
Key, Wilson Bryan, 39, 94, 189; *The Age of Manipulation*, 40; *The Clam-Plate Orgy*, 40; *Media Sexploitation*, 40; *Subliminal Ad-ventures in Erotic Art*, 36–37; *Subliminal Seduction*, 35–38, 40–41, 238

Keystone View Company, 81–82, 83, 84, 85
Kidd, R. M., 150
Killing Us Softly (Lazarus, Wunderlich), 35
Kittler, Friedrich, 70, 72, 73–74, 76, 87, 230
Klapp, Orrin, 35, 234
Klass, Bertrand, 155
Klein, George, 147; "happy or angry" test
    and, 109–10, 113, 153; Vicary and, 113
KLTI (radio station), 125
KNKT (television station), 117
Knotts, Don, 142, 163
knowledge industry, 157, 231
Koch, Howard, 1
Koestler, Arthur, 230
KOL (radio station), 130
Koontz, Dean, 27; Night Chills, 23–24
Korean War, 168, 170–71, 172, 176
Kornbluth, C. M., 160–61, 201
KTLA (television station), 129
Kubelka, Peter, 218
Kuleshov effect, 110
Kunstler, William, 116

Lancaster, John, 211
"Last Night" (Strokes), 21
La Tourette, Gilles de, 44
Laven, Arnold, 169
Lazarsfeld, Paul, 2, 27, 60, 97, 98, 100
Lazarus, Margaret, 35
learning: consciousness and, 87; mind con-
    trol vs., 174; rapid mass, 177, 183, 190–91;
    sleep-, 58; speed of, 74–75, 78–79, 185;
    tachistoscopes and, 85, 86
learning machines, 65–66
Le Bon, Gustave, 55, 60, 61, 63, 170; The
    Crowd, 5, 50–52, 106
Leiber, Fritz, Jr., 159
Leibniz, Gottfried Wilhelm von, 44, 86
Leinster, Murray, 194, 196–97, 205
Leo Diamond Orchestra, 139
Lerner, Daniel, 27; Sykewar, 169
Lerner, Murray, 111, 113
Lester, Richard, 221
Letterman, David, 15, 16
Lewis, E. O., 70
Lewis, Herschel Gordon, 154
Lewis, Wyndham, 225
Lichtenstein, Roy, 247–48 n. 60
Life, 136
Lifton, Robert Jay, 169
liminal zones, 59, 63, 68

Lipsett, Arthur, 218, 224, 226
Little Mermaid, The (Clements, Musker), 21
Litton Industries, 187
Livingston, J. Sterling, 188
Lloyd, James Hendrie, 61
Lobel, Michael, 247–48 n. 60
Lodge, Henry Cabot, 173
Lodge, Oliver, 57
Logan, Joshua, 91, 92
Looker (Crichton), 23
López Obrador, Andrés Manuel, 16
Los Angeles Advertising Club, 128–29
Lost, Lonely and Vicious (Myers), 120
LSD, 220
Ludgin, Earle, 156
Lumet, Sidney, 214, 216, 217

Machlup, Fritz, 157
Mad, 138
Mail Early for Christmas (McLaren), 217
Majors, Lee, 23
Malden, Karl, 169
Manchurian Candidate, The (Condon), 65, 172
Manchurian Candidate, The (Frankenheimer),
    172, 243 n. 28
Man in the Grey Flannel Suit, The (Johnson),
    105
Mannes, Marya, 111, 113
Marconi, Guglielmo, 57, 58
Marcuse, Herbert, 36, 194
Mark II Auto-tutor, 184
Martineau, Pierre, 139
Marvel Team-Up, 263 n. 27
"Mass Manipulation of Human Behavior,
    The" (Packard), 175–76
Matheson, Richard, 194, 205
Matrix, The (Wachowski, Wachowski), 206
Max Headroom, 24
May, Shirley, 6
Mayo, Elton, 131
McCain, John, 16
McCarthy, Joseph, 125
McClellan, John L., 172
McClusky, Dean, 187–88
McGraw-Hill, 185, 229
McLaren, Norman: The Flicker Film, 218;
    Mail Early for Christmas, 217
McLuhan, Marshall: advertising and, 38,
    39; Counterblast, 225, 226; Culture Is Our
    Business, 225–26; design collaborations
    of, 233; Freud and, 39–40; on information

overload, 226; joke, 241–42 n. 61; Key and, 36, 37–40; *The Mechanical Bride*, 37–38, 224–25; *The Medium Is the Massage*, 224–25; on modern media chaos, 210; popular media and, 38–39, 210; *Report on Project in Understanding New Media*, 180, 181–82; on shift to acoustic culture, 224; subliminality and, 191; subliminal thesis and, 37–38; technology and, 189; on television, 224; textual chaos and, 38–39; *Through the Vanishing Point*, 225–26; *Understanding Media*, 181, 182–83; *War and Peace in the Global Village*, 225

McNeil, Elton B., 151–52

McRobbie, Angela, 29

Mechanical Bride, The (McLuhan), 37–38, 224–25

media: abundance of images in, 207; chaos in, 210; choices in, 30–31; clutter in, 156, 158, 210, 233–34, 236; communism and, 172; consciousness of, 205; crime and, 61–62, 63; critical discourses of, 31; culture and, 181–82; electronic presence of, 55–56; entrancing, 55; fear of, 191; hypnosis and, 37; individual identity and, 171–72; innovations in, 58–59; literacy and, 27, 205; low- vs. high-definition, 182; new, 180, 181–82, 236; popular language of, 63; propaganda and, 84, 86; research in, 1–2; saturation of, 162, 231, 234; student knowledge of, 32; subliminal patterning of consciousness by, 181–82; suggestion and, 54–55; technology in, 31; thinking and, 18; visual, 210. *See also* popular culture

Media Equation, The (Reeves, Nass), 17

media influence, 54; communication studies and, 27; in fiction, 203; Fort Lee Theater test and, 91–92; massive- vs. limited-effects models of, 27–28; Mercury Theater broadcast and, 1, 6; mind-writing and, 87–88; studies of, 35

Media Sexploitation (Key), 40

media studies, 30, 32; Key and, 40; subliminality and, 18, 27

Medium Is the Massage, The (McLuhan, Fiore), 224–25

Meier, Richard, 157

Meighan, Howard S., 117

Melcer, F. H., 79

Mémoire de la découverte du magnétisme animal (Mesmer), 47

Memories of a Physician (Dumas), 6

Mercury Theater, 1, 2, 6, 11, 12, 204

Merton, Robert, 27, 60

Mesmer, Anton, 47

mesmerism, 47–48; Reinhardt and, 54–55; in science fiction, 203; vaudeville, 59. *See also* hypnosis, hypnotism; somnambulism

Messaris, Paul, 17

Methodist Temperance Board, 129–30

Metronoscope, 78

"Metropolis and Mental Life" (Simmel), 157–58

Miller, James G., 158

Miller, Mark Crispin, 25, 108–9

Mills, C. Wright, 230

mind control: in comic books, 197–98, 200, 201; in fiction and film, 23–24, 194–96; learning vs., 174; modernity and, 174; social inversion and, 140; subliminal advertising and, 128, 131; subliminal communication and, 201

Min-Max teaching machine, 184

Minnesota Mining and Manufacturing (3M), 187

Mitchum, Robert, 23

modernity: attention and, 70; brainwashing and, 170; cultural overload and, 157–58; excessive sensory stimuli and, 158; fragmentation and, 71–72; hypnosis and, 50, 61; individual identity and, 174; influence from distance and, 55–56; mind control and, 174; motion pictures and, 68; speed and, 86, 89; tachistoscope and, 88; transience and, 156

Mohr, Gerald, 120, 122, *123*, 211

Monitors, The (Shea), 218, *219*, 224

Monkees, 221, 226

Moore, Dudley, 26

Moore, H. Brown, 118

Moore, Harriett, 166

moral panics, 29

Morgan, Frank, 6

Morrison Planetarium, 210–11

Morse, Julia, 108

Moss, Charles, 127

Motion Picture Association of America, 237

Motion Picture Daily, 127

Motion Picture Herald, 211

motion pictures, 211–16; body snatching in, 194–96; brainwashing in, 169; children's sleep and, 78; effects of, 55; expanded

motion pictures (*continued*)
cinema, 221; exploration of sensory and, 221, 224; flow of images in, 224; mind control in, 194–96; modernity and, 68; reading and, 77; shock-edits in, 21, 218–21; subliminality in, 21, 23, 24, 25, 26; tachistoscopes and, 73, 74
motion picture theaters: exhibition novelties at, 117, 120; in Fort Lee, 91–95, 104, 108, 127, 151, 227–28; subliminal advertising in, 92–93, 95, 104, 113, 124–25; Subliminal Projection and, 117, 118; subliminal techniques in, 146; television vs., 117
motivational research (MR): advertising and, 107–8, 133–34; brainwashing and, 107; ethics of, 116, 131; in fiction, 160–61, 162–63; mainstreaming of, 116; Packard and, 105, 110, 116; publications on, 105–6, 107; Russell's skit on, 139; subliminal advertising and, 131, 149; Subliminal Projection vs., 118; subliminal techniques and, 116; Vicary and, 98–99, 101
Motivation in Advertising (Martineau), 139
MSNBC, 16
multimedia art events, 210–11
multiple personalities, 46–47
Münsterberg, Hugo, 44, 53–54, 55; *Psychology and Industrial Efficiency*, 45; "Psychology and the Market," 52
Murphy, Gardner, 60
music, back-masking in, 23, 26
Musker, John, 21
Muybridge, Eadweard, 74
Myers, Frank, 120
Myers, Frederic W. H., 45, 46, 47, 57
Mystery in Space, 199
Mythologies (Barthes), 151
My World Dies Screaming (*Terror in the Haunted House*; Daniels), 120–24, 148, 211

Nader, Ralph, 14
Nadis, Fred, 243 n. 22
Naked Lunch (Burroughs), 208–9
Nancy School, 49–50, 51, 52
Nass, Clifford, 17
Nation, 105, 115
National Association of Broadcasters, 154
National Association of Educational Broadcasters, 180
National Association of Food Chains, 101

National Association of Radio and Television Broadcasters (NARTB), 126–27, 128–29
National Conference of Christians and Jews, 171
National Defense Education Act, 180–81, 183, 185, 186, 190
National Education Association (NEA), 176, 181, 183, 188–89
NBC, 101; *Steve Allen Show*, 141–43; subliminal advertising and, 127
Nealon, Kevin, 24–25, 27
Nelson, Ray Faraday, 203–5
New Educational Media Program, 180, 185
Newhall, Sidney, 70
New Republic, 135–36
News Focus, 187
Newsweek: on MR, 101, 105–6; 3M's joint venture with, 187
New York Daily Graphic, 58
New Yorker, 138, 149
New York Times: on educational technology, 188; Gardner's telepathy test and, 60; *Hidden Persuaders* and, 107; IBM advertising supplement on "information explosion," 231–32; on reading speed, 82; on the subconscious as watchword, 58; on subliminal advertising, 129; on subliminal communication as invasion of privacy, 167; on Subliminal Projection test, 128
New York Times Magazine, 45, 136–37, 138
Next Voice You Hear, The (film), 6
Nietzsche, Friedrich, 44
Night Chills (Koontz), 23–24
1984 (Orwell), 38, 103, 168, 171, 206
Novak, Kim, 92

Obama, Barack, 16
O'Donnell, Cathy, 124
O'Neill, William, 175, 176
Op Art, 211
Ophthalmograph, 78
Orwell, George, 38, 103, 115, 168, 171, 206
overload: advertising, 148, 150; attention, 158; in communication systems, 157; of cultural material, 157–58; language of, 158; sensory, 210. *See also* information overload; saturation

Packard, Vance, 41, 103, 115, 161; advertising industry and, 146; Benedict on, 168;

Boorstin on, 231; "The Growing Power of Admen," 110; *The Hidden Persuaders*, 35, 105–9, 111, 116, 134, 138, 167, 175, 228; "Hidden Why's of Our Behavior," 151; Kunstler's interview with, 116; "The Mass Manipulation of Human Behavior," 175–76; Russell's MR skit and, 139; subliminal communication and, 108–9; *The Waste Makers*, 175

pandemic psychosis, 61

Parallax View, The (Pakula), 65

paranoia: Cold War, 168, 236; communist, 128, 169; in postwar popular literature, 196, 197; subliminal communication and, 93, 236; visionary, 196, 197

Parker, Harley, 225

Pawnbroker, The (Lumet), 214, 216, 217

Pearson, Norman, 45

Penfield, Wilder, 36

People's Almanac, 69

perception: control and limits of, 19; distance from sensation of, 18; influence and limits of, 19; psychology and, 71; reading and, 77; tachistoscope and, 87, 89; unconscious, 20; variable threshold of, 19

Percepto, 117

Perceptoscope, 80

Perceptual Development Laboratories, 80

Persona (Bergman), 216

Peterman, Jack N., 155

Peters, John Durham, 48, 55, 57, 58

phantom spots, 125, 130

"Philosophy of the Beat Generation, The" (Holmes), 133

Philosophy of the Unconscious (Hartmann), 44

Picnic (Logan), 91, 92

Piper, Rowdy Roddy, 205

Pirie, Gordon, 103

Pitt, Brad, 21, 23

Playboy, 139–40, *141*

Poe, Edgar Allan, 38–39, 210, 238

Pohl, Frederik, 160–61, 201

Pop Art, 211

popular culture: advertising in, 162–63; body snatching in, 194–96; brainwashing in, 168; consumerism in, 205–6; hypnosis in, 54, 206–7, 208; media control in, 203–5; media influence in, 203; mesmerism in, 203; mind control in, 194–96; MR

in, 162–63; subliminal advertising in, 202, 205–6; subliminality and, 23–24, 27–28, 201; understandings of, 32–33

Popular Science, 120

Potter, Charles, 125–26, 128, 143

Pratt, Ray, 196

Precon Process and Equipment Co.: demonstrations by, 128, 237; KTLA and, 129; New Jersey Commission and, 147, 148; origins of, 118–20; patents of, 190, 229; products of, 229; Psychorama and, 211, 213

Prentice Hall, 187

presidential elections, 13–16

Pressey, Sidney L., 184

Price, George, *140*

Princeton Radio Research Project (PRRP), 2, 3, 153

Pritchard, Alfred, 172

Production and Distribution of Knowledge in the United States (Machlup), 157

programmed instruction, 184, 189–90

Programmed Instruction, 185

projective techniques, 99, 100

propaganda, 84, 86, 169–70

pseudo-events, 162

Psyche (Carus), 44

psychedelia, 210, 218, 221

psychiatry, dynamic, 45

Psycho (Hitchcock), 214

psychoanalysis: advertising and, 105, 116; marketing and, 106; mass, 105, 106, 107; neologisms and, 134; psychoanalytic concepts vs., 43

psychology: crime and, 53–54; everyday uses of, 51; experimental, 71–72, 75, 87; Gestalt, 72, 99; neologisms and, 134; new, 45, 46; perception and, 71; perceptual threshold and, 19; subliminality and, 18, 19, 20, 26; tachistoscope and, 67–68, 70

Psychology and Industrial Efficiency (Münsterberg), 45

"Psychology and the Market" (Münsterberg), 52

Psychology of Vision, Demonstrations in Psychological Optics (Renshaw), 78

Psychorama, 118, 120–24, 211–13, 214

Puppet Masters, The (Heinlein), 194, 195, 205

Purdue Research Foundation, 150

Puységur, Marquis de, 47–48

Pyles, Thomas, 134

Question of Science, A (BBC), 103
Quo Vadis, 55

Rack, The (Laven), 169
radio communication, 57, 58, 60–61
Radler, H., 150
Rafelson, Bob, 221, 226
Random House, 187
Rantell, Peter, 113–14
Rappoport, Maurice, 114
Rateometer, 84
Rather, Dan, 14
Ratoff, Gregory, 7–12
RCA, 187
Reader's Digest, 187
reading: comprehension, 79; hyper-, 68;
    instructional technology and, 77, 81;
    machine-assisted, 65, 75–76; motion pic-
    tures and, 77; nonsequential, 226; pacers
    and, 81, 84; on page vs. screen, 68, 88;
    perception and, 77; silent, 75; tachisto-
    scopes and, 67, 73–74, 76–79, 81–82, 86,
    88, 114, 190
Rebecca (Hitchcock), 122
Rees, W. J., 20
Reeves, Bryon, 17
Reichert, Tom, 17
Reinhardt, Max, 54–55
Renshaw, Samuel, 69, 78–79, 84, 177, 181
Renshaw Recognition System, 79
Report on Project in Understanding New Media
    (McLuhan), 180, 181–82
"Responsive Eye, The" (Museum of Modern
    Art exhibition), 211
Rheem Manufacturing, 184, 187
Riesman, David, 181
Riley, Bridget, 211
Ritchie, Billy, 55
Ritter, Lloyd, 113
Robbins, Tom, 24
"Rock Devil Rock" (CHiPs episode), 24
Rockefeller Foundation, 2
Rodgers, Stuart, 98
Rogers, Stuart, 93–94
Romney, George, 173
Romney, Mitt, 173
Roosevelt, Theodore, 82
Root, E. Merrill, 173
Roper, Elmer, 107
Rose, Alvin, 191
Rose, Carl, 136–37, 138

Rose, Marvin, 127
Roszak, Theodore, 24
Roy, Jean-Yves, 35
Rubinek, Saul, 23
Russell, Anna, 139
Russell, Richard, Jr., 173

Saettler, Paul, 180, 185, 187–88
Sahl, Mort, 139
Salpêtrière Hospital, 44, 49–50
Samuel, Lawrence R., 250 n. 21
Sargant, William, 169; Battle for the Mind,
    107, 174
Sarnoff, Robert, 127
saturation: of advertisements, 148, 156,
    160, 161; of communication, 157, 158; of
    images, 29, 162, 231; of information, 164,
    189, 235; of media, 162, 231, 234; sensory,
    148. See also overload
Saturday Night Live, 24–25
Schiller, Herbert, 35
Schlesinger, Arthur, Jr., 163
Schlosberg, Harold, 70
Schopenhauer, Arthur, 45; The World as Will
    and Representation, 44
Schramm, Wilbur, 185, 186, 189–90
Schultz, Robert, 114
Schumann's tachistoscope, 69
Schwable, Frank H., 170–71
Schwechater (Kubelka), 218
Science, 115
Science and Health (Eddy), 57
Science Digest, 79
science fiction. See popular culture
Science News Letter, 113
Science Research Associates, 187
Sconce, Jeffrey, 5–6, 55–56, 57, 103, 240
    n. 19
Scott, A. B., 151
Second World War: instructional technology
    and, 177, 188; Nazi atrocities during, 170
Secrets of the Reef (Lerner, Ritter, Young),
    111, 113
Seduction of the Innocent (Wertham), 62
Seldes, Gilbert, 181
self-help industry, 23, 86
Seltzer, Mark, 68
Senate Permanent Investigating Subcommit-
    tee on Brainwashing in Korea, 172
Serenity (Whedon), 23
Se7en, 21

sexuality: in flash-edits, 213–14; Key and, 40, 41; McLuhan and, 40; in satirical images of subliminal advertising, 140; subliminality and, 20–21, 23; subliminal suggestion and, 17
Shadowscope, 84
Shannon and Weaver model of communication, 157
Sharps Toffee, 152
Shea, Jack, 218, 219, 224
Shepard, Albert, 114
Sherman, Hoyt, 247–48 n. 60
Sherover, Max, 58
shock-edits, 21
Shonteff, Lindsay, 243 n. 28
Shore, Dinah, 144
Siegel, Don, 194–95
Sighele, Scipio, 51
signs: in fiction, 205, 206; information threshold and, 158–59; meanings of, 238; speed and, 89, 224; subliminality and, 25; tachistoscope and, 230
Simley, O. A., 87
Simmel, Georg, 157–58
Simpsons, The, 21, 24
Skinner, B. F., 184; Walden Two, 174
Smith, Henry, 79
Smith, Seymour, 80
Smithsonian Institution, 184
social change: information overload and, 162, 232–33; speed of, 164; subliminal communication and, 166; subliminal thesis and, 162; textual assertions and, 230; as total upheaval, 196
social control: resistance to, 204; subliminal communication and, 166; unconscious and, 236
social engineering, 106, 189
social order: democracy and, 64; in science fiction, 194, 201; subliminal messsages and, 201–2; unconscious and, 39
Society for Psychical Research, 46
Society for Visual Education (sve), 80, 81
Society of Motion Picture and Television Engineers, 188
Soft Machine, The, 263 n. 27
somnambulism, 48, 49, 57, 86, 106, 162, 204
sound splicing, 209
Soviet Union: brainwashing in, 168–69; satellites and, 168, 176; show trials in,

168–69; Sputnik launched by, 39, 175, 176, 180, 185, 186, 197; subliminal audio device in, 128
Space Merchants, The (Pohl, Kornbluth), 160–61, 201
Sparke, Penny, 176
Spectorsky, A. C., 107
speed: advertising and, 79–80; of appearance and disappearance of images and text, 68, 88; of flashing images, 21, 109, 214, 216–21, 236; iconography of, 207, 224; of information, 81; of learning, 74–75, 78–79, 185; of mass learning, 177, 183, 190–91; McLuhan and, 38, 39, 224; of modernity, 61; modernity and, 86, 89; of perceptual and thinking functions, 74–75; of reading, 58, 65, 75–79, 82, 84, 85, 86, 190; of scientific discovery, 3; of screen sequencing, 74; of seeing, 210; of social change, 164; subliminality and, 86–87; tachistoscope and, 68, 88, 89
Speed-I-O-Scope, 80, 81
Spence, Donald, 147
Sputnik, 39, 175, 176, 180, 185, 186, 197
Stam, Robert, 25
Stanford University, 149
Stanton, Frank, 2
Star Trek, 57
Stein, W., 77
Stereo-Optical Tachitron, 79
Steve Allen Show, 141–43
Stevens, Andrew, 23
Stevenson, Robert Louis, 46
stickiness factor, 30, 235
Still Life with Woodpecker, 24
Stoker, Bram, 50
Strange Case of Dr. Jekyll and Mr. Hyde, The (Stevenson), 46
Stranger in a Strange Land, 65
Strange Tales, 200
Streatfeild, Dominic, 168–69
Strobonic Psycho-injection, 113–14
stroboscope, 72, 78–79, 206, 220
Strokes (band), 21
Strong, Lynda, 105
Studio (Scottish organization), 113–14
subception, 20, 108
subconscious: Janet and, 45; liminal perception and, 155; Münsterberg and, 52; in My World Dies Screaming, 122; unconscious vs., 155

subliminal, as term, 27, 92, 134, 141–42
"Subliminal" (Freberg), 143–44, *145*
Subliminal Ad-ventures in Erotic Art (Key), 36–37
subliminal advertising: bans on, 125, 127, 146–47, 152, 154, 237; brainwashing and, 113, 131; clutter and, 21; consumer resistance and, 229; control and comparison testing of, 150; as cultural norm, 148; Dichter on, 115–16; effectiveness of, 17, 128, 131–32, 147, 149, 150, 152, 153; ethics of, 113, 115, 125; FCC and, 127–28; in fiction, 202, 205–6; in films, 23; flashes in, 216–17; Fort Lee Theater test and, 91, 92; governments and, 146–49; growth of interest in, 103–4; hypnosis and, 131; McLuhan on, 182–83; mind control and, 128, 131; in movie theaters, 92–93, 95, 104, 113, 124–25; MR and, 131, 149; NARTB and, 126–27; as overload, 148; as persuasion without rhetoric, 167; Precon demonstrations of, 128–29; in presidential elections, 14; privacy and, 149; public knowledge of, 16–17; public reaction to, 149; radio and television tests of, 124–25; sexuality and, 17; sneakiness of, 152; spoofs of, 143–46; target marketing and, 137; television and, 24–25, 114; un-Americanness of, 127–28; unconscious and, 36, 37; Vicary and, 92, 113, 128, 229. *See also* Precon Process and Equipment Co.
"Subliminal Brute, The" (Tweedy), 46
subliminal communication, 21; action against will and, 129–30; behavior and, 148; brainwashing and, 168–69; conspiratorially minded, 22–23; democracy and, 166–67, 174, 191; of erotic images, 213–14; ethics of, 125–26, 167–68; FCC and, 125, 126; government and, 125–26; intellectual property and, 167; Key as victim of, 40; mind control and, 201; in *My World Dies Screaming*, 120–22; Packard and, 108–9; in presidential elections, 13–16; privacy and, 167–68; as proxy for social concerns, 132; sexuality and, 17; social order and, 201–2; understandings of, 165; websites and, 238
Subliminal Dynamics/Brain Management, 86
subliminality: adhesiveness of, 29–30; controversies in, 26–27; definitions of, 18, 26; flash-edits and, 217–18; folkloric status of,

27, 229; individual identity and, 163; influence of, 19; information society and, 234; media clutter and, 156; perception and, 20; perception and sensation distance and, 18; psychology and, 18, 19, 20, 26; public understanding of, 16–18; religion and, 26; sexual magnetism and, 20–21; shock-edits and, 21; speed and, 86–87; students and, 18; tachistoscope and, 87–88; unconscious and, 18, 19, 26; varied uses of, 25
"Subliminal Man, The" (Ballard), 205–6
Subliminal Perception (Dixon), 41, 152
"Subliminal Pitch, The" (Cole), 139–40, *141*
Subliminal Projection Company, 111–13, 116–17, 127–28, 130–31, 148, 190, 227
Subliminal Seduction (Key), 35–38, 40–41, 238
Subliminal Seduction (Stevens), 23
Subliminal Sounds (Leo Diamond Orchestra), 139
"Subliminal Stimulation: Omen of Things to Come" (McNeil), 151–52
subliminal thesis: advertising industry and, 132; appearance of, 30, 42; codes of conduct and, 166; commonsense and, 42; consumer environment and, 161–62; ethics and, 166; expansion of, 114–15; as form of semi-erudition, 237; information overload and, 235; media clutter and, 158; media culture vigilance and, 238; range of terms describing, 166; reflexivity of, 27; representation and, 41–42; satirical play on, 134–46; social change and, 162; trivialized critiques of image culture and, 237–38; unconscious and, 41, 236
sub-threshold, 103, 108, 110, 152, 226
suggestion, suggestibility: auto-, 59; in literature, 206–7; media and, 54–55; of populations, 61
Sunday Times, 103, 110
superheroes, 197–98, 200, 206
Superman #62, 7–12
"Survey of the Industry, A" (NEA), 183
Sutherland, Max, 17
sykewar, 27
Sykewar (Lerner), 169
Sylvania, 187
synthesis, sensory, 68, 72–73, 88

tachistoscopes, 19; advertising and, 79–80, 84; Catell's, 66–67; chronoscope and, 51;

in classroom, 76, 80; control and, 89; differences among, 69; "fall," 66–67; fragmentation vs. assemblage and, 72; for
group use, 80–81; "happy or angry" subliminal flashes and, 109–10; history of,
88; immobility of subject and, 70–71; for
individual use, 81; instructional technology
and, 75–76, 87; invention of, 69; learning
and, 85, 86; liminal zones of consciousness and, 68–69; malleability of, 68;
modernity and, 88; motion pictures and,
73, 74; movie projector and, 87; Navy pilots
and, 78–79, 177; orientation of attention
and, 88–89; perception and, 89; perceptual fragmentation vs. synthesis and, 68;
psychology and, 67–68, 70; Psychorama
vs., 118, 120; range of perception and, 87;
rapid appearance and disappearance of
images and text and, 68, 88; reading and,
67, 73–74, 76–78, 79, 81–82, 88; reading
on page vs. screen and, 68, 88; recognition
of signs and, 230; response times and, 75;
somnambulism and, 86; speed and, 68,
88, 89; speed of screen sequencing and,
73; speed reading and, 82, 84, 86, 114, 190;
subliminality and, 87–88; synthesis and,
72–73, 88; as typewriters, 87; uses of, 66,
67, 69–70, 72–73, 80–81, 88, 89; Vicary
and, 114
Tach-X Tachistoscope, 80–81
Taine, Hippolyte, 51
Talese, Gay, 136–37
Tales of Suspense, 200
Tankard, James, Jr., 40–41
Tarde, Gabriel, 51
Tashlin, Frank, 105, 163
Tate, Theodore, 79
Taylor, Carl C., 78
Taylor, Earl, 78
Taylor, James Y., 78
Taylor, Stanford, 84
Taylor family, 80
Taylorist instruction, 89
teaching machines, 177, 183, 184–85, 189–90
Teaching Machines, Inc., 184
technology: concern about new, 3–4; connec-
tions among people and minds and, 57–58;
hazards of, 58; individual identity and, 174;
instructional, 75–76, 87, 177–81, 183–84,
185–91; monopolies of knowledge and, 39;
terminology of, 57

telekinesis, 55, 198
telepathy: on *Ghost Hour*, 60; hypnosis and,
53; Janet and, 48–49; origin of term, 55, 57;
radio and, 60–61; study of, 48
telephone, 58, 59
teleplasm, 55
telesthesia, 55
television: advertising and, 117, 220–21;
brainwashing on, 169; educational, 189;
flash-edits and, 216–17; hypnotism and,
61; McLuhan and, 224; political campaigning on, 116; subliminal advertising and,
114, 137, 146, 148–49; subliminality in programs on, 21, 24–25; Subliminal Projection and, 117
Television Wales and West, 152
Terror in the Haunted House (*My World Dies
Screaming*; Daniels), 120–24, 148, 211
Thayer, Francis C., 111, *112*
They Live (Carpenter), 205
"They're Selling Your Unconscious"
(Strong), 105
They're Talking about Us! (National Associa-
tion of Food Chains), 101
third communication, 151
Thompson, J. Walter, 117
Three Stigmata of Palmer Eldritch (Dick), 208
Through the Vanishing Point (McLuhan),
225–26
Ticket That Exploded (Burroughs), 209–10
Time, 58; General Electric's joint venture
with, 187; on Klein's study, 109; on MR,
106; Renshaw's innovation in speed-
learning and, 79
Time Limit (Malden), 169
Time Out of Joint (Dick), 207–8
Timex, 143
Time-X, 80
Tipping Point, The (Gladwell), 235
Toffler, Alvin, 234
totalitarianism, 103, 170, 191, 194, 196,
203–5, 206, 234
Toynbee, Arnold, 231
Trademark Management Institute (TMI),
228–29
Tragedy of Waste, The (Chase), 105
Trilby (du Maurier), 50, 55, 61
Trip, The (Corman), 218, 220–21, *222–23*
Tweedy, Frank, 46
Twentieth Century, The (CBS), 260 n. 49
Twitchell, James, 17, 95

Two Thousand Maniacs! (Lewis), 154
Tyranny over the Mind, 174

unconscious: advertising and, 17, 106, 115, 116; communication and, 58; consumer activity and, 102; crowds and, 50–51; Freud and, 44; growing understanding of, 166; history of concept of, 44; hypnosis and, 19; James and, 46; MR and, 98; philosophy and, 45; subconscious vs., 155; subliminal advertising and, 36, 37; subliminality and, 18, 19, 26; subliminal thesis and, 41, 236; tachistoscopes and, 86; terminology for, 45–46; word association and, 99
Unconscious for Sale (Haineault, Roy), 35
Understanding Media (McLuhan), 181, 182–83
U.S. Air Force, 79, 155, 184–85
U.S. Industries, Inc., 184, 187
U.S. Navy, 58, 78–79, 84, 177
University of Michigan Advertising Conference, 150–52, 154
University of Nancy, 49–50, 51, 52

Valentine, C. W., 70
van Ormer, Edward B., 177
Varieties of Religious Experience (James), 26
Varley, A. N. C., 152
Verbinski, Gore, 23
vernacular cultural and media critique, 33, 42
Very Nice, Very Nice (Lipsett), 218, 224, 226
Vicary, James McDonald, 93, 100, 101, 129; Advertising Age interview with, 227–28; American Psychologist on claims of, 153–54; BBC test and, 104; on brand names, 233; CBC test and, 130–31, 155; control and comparison tests and, 150; Dichter and, 115–16; at Dun and Bradstreet, 227; ethical advertising and, 190; ethics and, 113; as exemplar of "adman," 162; Fort Lee Theater test and, 92, 102–3, 104, 110, 127, 151; "happy or angry" experiment and, 113; Hidden Persuaders and, 107, 115, 228; influence of, 202; Key and, 36; later employment of, 229; in marketing research, 95–98, 99–102; as Mr. Subliminal, 227; motivational research and, 98–99, 101; New Jersey commission and, 148; press conference of 1957 and, 111–13, 175, 191; secretiveness about procedures of, 127; shakiness of claims by, 127; subliminal advertising and,

113, 229; Subliminal Projections Company and, 111–13, 118; subliminal technology ban and, 127; tachistoscope and, 69, 190; test for FCC and congressmen and, 128, 143; TMI and, 228–29; women shoppers and, 100, 101–2, 108; on word association analysis, 99
Violent Summer (Zurlini), 214
Virilio, Paul, 89
visual art, 211
visual education, 75, 176
Visual Impact Laboratory, 154
Visual Psychology (Renshaw), 78
visual trauma, 224
Vogue, 20–21, 22
Volkmann, A. W., 66
Vortex, 210–11

WAAF (radio station), 125
Wachowski, Andy, 206
Wachowski, Lana, 206
Walden Two (Skinner), 174
Walker, Martin, 173
Wall Street Journal, 100, 149
Walters, Charles, 163
War and Peace in the Global Village (McLuhan), 225
War of the Satellites (Corman), 175
"War of the Worlds" (radio broadcast), 1–2, 5–6, 11, 12, 94, 104, 204
War of the Worlds, The (Wells), 1, 94, 104
Waste Makers, The (Packard), 175
Watson, Thomas, Jr., 231–32
WCCO-AM, 125
Weir, Walter, 107
Welch, Richard, 86
Welles, Orson: in Black Magic, 6–7, 11; "Black Magic on Mars" and, 7–12; in Citizen Kane, 11; in Superman #62, 7–12; in War of the Worlds, 1, 2, 12, 94, 104, 204
Wells, H. G., 1
Wertham, Fredric, 62
Wertheimer, Max, 72
Western Radio and Television Conference (San Francisco), 149–50
Westmoreland, William, 173
Whedon, Joss, 23
Whipple's tachistoscope, 69
Whitfield, Stephen J., 175
Who Framed Roger Rabbit (Zemeckis), 21
"Why Did You Buy That?" (NBC), 101

Why Johnny Can't Read, 176
Whyte, William, Jr., 168
Wiene, Robert, 55
Wilhelm, Ross, 155–56
Williams, D. Carleton, 39
Williams, R. J., 108
Williams, Raymond, 33, 34, 64, 233
Williamson, Judith, 35
Will Success Spoil Rock Hunter? (Tashlin),
  105, 163
Winter, Alison, 243 n. 22
wireless, 57
Wittgenstein, Ludwig, 67
wjaz (radio station), 60
wnew (radio station), 116
Wolfe, Winifred, 163
Wonder Woman, 199
Wood, Evelyn, 82, 84
wor (radio station), 100
word association, 96–97, 99
"Word Association and Opinion Research"
  (Vicary), 99
word cloud, 233

"Work of Art in the Age of Its Technological
  Reproducibility, The" (Benjamin), 68
World as Will and Representation, The
  (Schopenhauer), 44
World's Finest Comics, 198
Wright, Frank Lloyd, 150
Wright, James C., Jr., 146–47
wtop (television station), 128
wtwo-tv, 125
Wunderlich, Renner, 35
Wundt, Wilhelm, 66, 72
Wurman, Richard Saul, 234–35

Xerox Corporation, 187

Young, Robert M., 113
Youngblood, Gene, 221

Zemeckis, Robert, 21
Zuckerman, Marvin, 150
Zurlini, Valorio, 214
Zworykin, Vladimir, 147

Charles R. Acland is Professor and Concordia University Research Chair in Communication Studies. He is the author of *Screen Traffic: Movies, Multiplexes, and Global Culture* (Duke University Press, 2003) and editor of *Residual Media* (University of Minnesota Press, 2007).

Library of Congress Cataloging-in-Publication Data
Acland, Charles R., 1963–
Swift viewing : the popular life of subliminal influence /
Charles R. Acland.
p. cm.
Includes bibliographical references and index.
ISBN 978-0-8223-4924-2 (cloth : alk. paper)
ISBN 978-0-8223-4919-8 (pbk. : alk. paper)
1. Subliminal advertising — United States — History. 2. Advertising —
Moral and ethical aspects — United States. 3. Mass media — United
States — History. I. Title.
HF5827.9.A25 2012
659.101′9 — dc23   2011027424